AMAZON BASICS

BREAD MACHINE

COOKBOOK FOR

BEGINNERS

1000-DAY NEWEST AND EASY HOMEMADE RECIPES WITH DETAILED MAKING STEPS

RUSSELL VANCE

CONTENTS

INTRODUCTION 8

How Does the Amazon Basics Bread Maker work? 8

The Advantages of the Amazon Basics Bread Maker 8

Tips on Using Your Amazon Basics Bread Maker 9

The Amazon Basics Bread Machine Cleaning Steps 11

BREAKFAST BREAD RECIPES 13

Parmesan Nut Bread 13

Granola Bread 13

Cheddar Bacon Bread 14

Monterey Jack Loaf 14

Dried Apricot Whole Wheat Bread 15

Feta And Spinach Bread 16

Cheddar Olive Bread 16

Cinnamon Swirl Bread 17

Ricotta And Fresh Chive Bread 18

Egg Bread 18

Beer Bread With Cheddar 19

Dutch Sugar Loaf 19

Pain Aux Trois Parfums 20

Crescia Al Formaggio 21

Buttermilk Cheese Bread 21

Spicy Pear Bread 22

Chocolate Cherry Bread 23

Chocolate Challah 24

Greek Currant Bread 25

FRUIT BREAD RECIPES 27

Super Spice Bread 27

Cinnamon Figs Bread 27

Pineapple Carrot Bread 28

Toasted Coconut Bread 28

Applesauce Bread 29

Cranberry Walnut Wheat Bread 30

Cherry–wheat Berry Bread 30

Cocoa Date Bread 31

Raisin Bread 32

Prune Bread 32

Orange Bread 33

Cinnamon Apple Bread 33

Spice Peach Bread 34

Succulent Cranberry Cinnamon Bread 35

Honey Banana Bread 35

Banana Split Loaf 36

Strawberry Oat Bread 36

Cranberry Orange Pecan Bread 37

Black Olive Bread 37

Tomato Bread 38

Raisin Candied Fruit Bread 38

Cappuccino Orange Bread 39

Cranberry Honey Bread 39

Dried Cranberry Tea Bread 40

Wild Rice Cranberry Delight 41

HERB AND SPICE BREAD RECIPES 42

Basil Cheese Bread 42

Energizing Anise Lemon Bread 42

Whole Wheat Basil Bread 43

Parsley Garlic Bread 43

Lemon Flavored Poppy Loaf 44

Awesome Rosemary Bread 45

Crunchy Wheat Herbed Bread 45

Inspiring Cinnamon Bread 46

Anise Honey Bread 46

Apple Pie Bread 47

Lovely Aromatic Lavender Bread 47

Herb Garlic Cream Cheese Bread 48

Ricotta & Chive Loaf 48

Herb Bread 49

Cheesy Basil Bread 50
Delicious Honey Lavender Bread 50
Cardamom Honey Bread 51
Buttermilk Bread With Lavender 51
Romano Oregano Bread..52
Cinnamon-flavored Raisin Bread............................52

Fresh Herb Bread 53
Cinnamon Pull-apart Bread....................................53
Cardamom Tea Bread...54
Spice Pumpkin Bread 55
Sour Cream Semolina Bread With Herb Swirl 56

NUT AND SEED BREAD RECIPES 58

Mesmerizing Walnut Bread....................................58
Orange Almond Bread..58
Orange Walnut Candied Loaf 59
Olive Oil–pine Nut Bread 59
Brazilian Nuts & Nutmeg Loaf................................60
Herb Light Rye Bread...61
California Nut Bread...62
Fig And Walnut Bread..62
Polish Poppy Seed Bread..62
Corn, Poppy Seeds & Sour Cream Bread.....................63
Almond Milk Bread..63
Potato Bread With Caraway Seeds 64
Basic Pecan Bread 65

Pistachio Horseradish Apple Bread.........................65
Brown Sugar Date Nut Swirl Bread 66
Mix Seed Raisin Bread 67
Pistachio Cherry Bread 67
Toasted Walnut Bread..68
Pecan Raisin Bread 69
Orange-cumin Bread 70
Bourbon Nut Bread 70
Caramel Apple Pecan Loaf......................................71
Delicious Flax Honey Bread 72
Sunflower Oatmeal Bread.......................................72
Zuni Indian Bread 73

VEGETABLE BREAD RECIPES 74

Carrot Bread With Crystallized Ginger.....................74
Spicy Hot Red Pepper Bread 74
Pumpkin Coconut Almond Bread 75
Pain D'ail 76
Caraway Potato Bread..76
Basil Tomato Bread..77
Fresh Herb Stuffing Bread With Fennel Seed And
Pepper 77
Zucchini Bread..78
Green Onion Bread..79
Sweet Potato Bread 79
Chicken Stuffing Bread...80
Potato Honey Bread...81

Sauerkraut Rye Bread 81
Onion Chive Bread...82
Italian Onion Bread...82
Honey Potato Flakes Bread 83
Cornbread 83
Cheesy Broccoli & Cauliflower Bread......................84
Prosciutto Stuffing Bread..85
Cornmeal Stuffing Bread..85
Beetroot Bread 86
Carrot Bread 86
Zucchini Spice Bread..87
Hot Paprika Onion Bread 88
Zucchini Lemon Bread...88

CAKE RECIPES/QUICK BREAD/SWEET ROLLS.. 90

Cocoa Banana Bread 90
Sweet Flaxseed Bread 90
Sweet Almond Anise Bread 91
Buttermilk Pecan Bread 91
Milk Sweet Bread 92
Honey Bread..92
Cinnamon Pecan Coffee Cake.................................93

Cinnamon Rum Bread..94
Cinnabun Coffee Cake 94
King Cake 95
Honey Pound Cake...97
Multi-grain Honey Bread..97
Sweet Vanilla Bread...98
Rainbow Swirl Cake...98

Chocolate Marble Cake 99
Pumpkin Spice Cake 100
Carrot Cake Bread 100
Hazelnut Honey Bread..................................101
Apple Raisin Nut Cake 102
Chocolate Chip Bread...................................103

White And Dark Chocolate Tea Cake...................... 103
Lemon Cake 104
Choco Banana Oatmeal Bread 105
Sweet Pineapple Bread...................................... 105
Sweet Sour Maple Bread 106

HOLIDAY BREAD RECIPES 107

Holiday Eggnog Bread....................................107
Christmas Eggnog Bread 107
Welsh Bara Brith...108
Beer Pizza Dough..109
Orange Gingerbread With Orange Whipped Cream.109
Amaretto Bread 110
Milk Honey Sourdough Bread...........................111
Anise Christmas Bread....................................112
Holiday Chocolate Bread 112
Hungarian Spring Bread 113
Dry Fruit Cinnamon Bread...............................114
Classic Sourdough Bread..................................115
Basil Pizza Dough 116

Easter Bread... 116
Grandma's Favorite Gingerbread 117
Portuguese Sweet Bread..................................... 117
Challah Bread 118
Easter Rye Bread With Fruit 119
Holiday Raisin Bread With Candied Peels 120
Champagne-soaked Baba 121
Coffee Caraway Seed Bread 122
St. Patrick's Rum Bread..................................... 122
Cinnamon Beer Bread 123
White Chocolate Cranberry Party Loaf 123
Portuguese Holiday Bread 124

SOURDOUGH BREAD RECIPES 125

Classic Sourdough Rye....................................125
Sourdough Carrot Poppy Seed Bread 125
Sourdough Raisin Bread...................................126
Orange Sourdough Bread With Cranberries, Pecans,
And Golden Raisins 127
Sourdough Bread With Fresh Pears And Walnuts.....127
Sourdough Banana Nut Bread 128
Sourdough Pesto Bread....................................129

Sourdough Cottage Cheese Bread With Fresh Herbs 130
White Sourdough Bread...................................... 130
Sourdough Tomato Bread With Feta....................... 131
Sourdough Cornmeal Bread 131
Sourdough Sunflower Seed Honey Bread 132
Sourdough Buckwheat Bread 133
Sourdough Whole Wheat Bread 133

GLUTEN-FREE RECIPES 135

Gluten-free Cinnamon Raisin Bread 135
Mix Seed Bread 135
Gluten-free Pull-apart Rolls..............................136
Gluten-free Oat & Honey Bread 137
Cheese Potato Bread 137
Italian Herb Bread...138
Instant Cocoa Bread.......................................139
Pecan Cranberry Bread....................................140
Grain-free Chia Bread 140
Gluten-free Sourdough Bread 141
Garlic Parsley Bread 142
Walnut Banana Bread 143

Pecan Apple Spice Bread.................................... 144
Classic White Bread 144
Sorghum Bread Recipe 145
Easy Gluten-free, Dairy-free Bread........................ 146
Gluten-free Pumpkin Pie Bread............................ 146
Gluten-free Simple Sandwich Bread 147
Gluten-free Brown Bread 148
Basic Honey Bread... 149
Gluten-free Whole Grain Bread 149
Gluten-free Crusty Boule Bread............................ 150
Gluten-free Pizza Crust...................................... 151
Gluten-free Potato Bread 152

Onion Buttermilk Bread 152

EVERYDAY/WHITE/BASIC BREAD RECIPES..154

Peasant Bread 154
Slider Buns 154
Prosciutto Parmesan Breadsticks..155
Everything Bagel Loaf 156
Milk Bread 156
Pizza Dough 157
Brioche 157
French Bread 158
Rye Bread 158
French Sandwich Pain Au Lait 159
Cracked Wheat Bread 159
Sour Cream Bread 160
Sampler Oatmeal Loaf 161
House Bread 161
Onion Loaf 162
Maple Buttermilk Bread 162
Coconut Milk White Bread 163
Sampler Country White Loaf 163
Wine And Cheese Bread 164
Basic White Bread 165
Classic White Sandwich Bread..165
Sampler Honey Whole Wheat Loaf..166
Cheesy Sausage Loaf..166
Garlic Basil Knots 167
Potato Bread 168

SPECIALITY FLOUR BREAD RECIPES..169

Gluten-free Buttermilk White Bread..169
Chickpea Flour Bread 169
Brown Rice Flour Bread..170
Gluten-free Ricotta Potato Bread 171
Buckwheat-millet Bread..171
Cornmeal And Hominy Bread..172
Chestnut Flour Bread..173
Quinoa Bread 173
Gluten-free Mock Light Rye 174
Teff Honey Bread..175
Polenta-sunflower-millet Bread 175
Polenta-chestnut Bread..176
Cornmeal Honey Bread 177
Gluten-free Almond And Dried Fruit Holiday Bread177
Wild Rice Bread 178
Low-gluten White Spelt Bread 179
Barley Bread 180
Cornell Bread 180
Orange-buckwheat Bread 181
Gluten-free Chickpea-, Rice-, And Tapioca-flour
Bread 182

MULTIGRAIN BREAD RECIPES 184

Bran Packed Healthy Bread 184
Classic Whole Wheat Bread 184
Light Whole Wheat Bread 185
Old-fashioned Sesame-wheat Bread 185
Oat Quinoa Bread 186
Three-seed Whole Wheat Bread 186
Sennebec Hill Bread..187
Basic Seed Bread 188
Honey Wheat Berry Bread..188
Basic Bulgur Bread 189
Classic Corn Bread..190
Dakota Bread..190
White Whole Wheat Bread 191
Buttermilk Whole Wheat Bread 192
Oat Bran Nutmeg Bread..192
Awesome Golden Corn Bread..193
Nine-grain Honey Bread 193
Tecate Ranch Whole Wheat Bread 194
Whole-grain Daily Bread 195
Multigrain Honey Bread..195
Seven Grain Bread 196
Simple Dark Rye Loaf..196
Graham Indian Bread 197
Irish Potato Brown Bread 198
Scandinavian Light Rye 198

INTERNATIONAL BREAD RECIPES..200

British Hot Cross Buns 200
Italian Panettone 201
Greek Easter Bread 201
Russian Rye Bread 202
Russian Black Bread 203
Fiji Sweet Potato Bread 204
Za'atar Bread 204

Portuguese Corn Bread 205
Hawaiian Bread 205
Mexican Sweet Bread 206
Amish Wheat Bread 206
Challah 207
Bread Of The Dead (pan De Muertos) 207
Italian Bread 208

COUNTRY BREAD RECIPES 210

Pain De Paris 210
Pane Italiano 211
Pain De Maison Sur Poolish\ 211
Chuck Williams's Country French 212

Pain Ordinaire Au Beurre 212
Semolina Country Bread 213
Pane Toscana 214
Olive Oil Bread 214

RECIPE INDEX 216

INTRODUCTION

How Does the Amazon Basics Bread Maker work?

The making of bread in a bread maker is essentially the same across all models. According to the recipe, the basic ingredients of flour, water, and yeast, plus other ingredients, are added to the bread pan in the machine in a specific order and varying quantities.

In some machines, you can choose a loaf size, crust colour – and press start. The machine then springs into action, kneading, resting, rising, and baking.

The Advantages of the Amazon Basics Bread Maker

1.   Healthier and more flavorful bread – Unlike store-bought bread which is full of synthetic additives, homemade bread requires only natural ingredients. Aside from flour, yeast and water, you can also add special ingredients like seeds or nuts to make it even healthier. Due to the fact that you use fresh ingredients, homemade bread is also more flavorful, and you can personalize recipes according to your individual taste.

2.   Stress-free baking – The traditional way of baking bread requires a lot of hard work. Not only does the preparation of the bread take a lot of time and effort, but this is also a rather messy process. Let's face it, you can't really knead dough, without getting flour all over yourself and the entire kitchen. And if that is not enough, you also have to clean a lot of dishes afterwards. However, with a bread maker, all you have to do is throw in the ingredients, and clean the pan after the bread is done.

3.   Special recipes – Modern bread machines come with a lot of special settings that allow you to prepare many bread specialties. Such a machine can be particularly useful for people who are intolerant or allergic to certain ingredients, like gluten. Most bread machines also come with a recipe book, featuring dozens of recipes specifically designed for baking with this machine. With a few recipe adaptations, these machines can also be used for recipes other than bread, such as jam, fruit butter, tomato sauce, casseroles, scrambled eggs and even cakes.

4.   Modern features – A state of the art bread machine will come with a lot of sophisticated features meant to make your life easier. To see some of the features of the best bread machines, read

some reviews on Bread Machine Mom. From intuitive buttons, to easy-to-read displays, and even delay timers, these units are designed to make the baking process as effortless as possible. The delay timer is one of the best features, as it gives you the freedom to program the machine to start baking at a certain time, so that you can enjoy warm bread in the morning or when you come home from work. The seed and nut dispenser is also a great feature, as it automatically adds special ingredients at the right time during the kneading process. You can't add special ingredients along with the basic ingredients, because seeds, nuts and dry fruits will make it harder for the dough to mix properly.

5.   Savings – While supermarket bread is not extremely expensive, homemade bread is way cheaper, and owning a bread machine can save you a lot of money in the long run.

Tips on Using Your Amazon Basics Bread Maker

1. Aside from investing in quality ingredients and taking good care of her bread machine, a beginner should also follow these tips to get the most out of the appliance:

Begin with simple recipes. Never start with a complicated one; you'll just frustrate and disappoint yourself. You can begin with pizza dough because the recipe is almost idiot-proof. You can also make a simple loaf of white bread using white flour first. You may substitute the white flour with whole grain flours after being successful with white flour.

2. Open the lid if necessary. A lot of beginners are afraid of opening the lid because they think it'll ruin the entire process. Actually, taking a peek after 5 to 10 minutes into the process is a sight to behold! Opening the lid makes it easier for you to identify if there's something wrong with the blade or the machine, therefore allowing you to save the recipe at once. It's necessary to check the moisture of your dough as well and you can only do that if you open the lid. If the dough seems to be too moist, add a tablespoon of flour at a time until the dough ball becomes a little sticky. The dough should come in contact with the pan's wall and then draw away. What if the dough is too dry? Then add a tablespoon of water at a time until it becomes tacky. Don't worry much about the dough, remember there's this thing called beginner's luck. If you follow the procedure and the measurements of the recipe properly, then you don't have to get worked up.

3. Be very careful with your substitute ingredients. Beginners should always follow the list of ingredients in a recipe as much as possible. Doing so will increase their chances of being successful. If

you want to replace some ingredients, you ought to be cautious. For instance, if you're going to use whole wheat flour rather than white flour or use all-purpose flour instead of bread flour, you should know that the ratio isn't always 1:1. That means you should first study how they absorb moisture and the amount of gluten they contain before you consider substitutions. Also, be careful about the yeast because not all of them are similar. Other recipes might advise you to dissolve regular yeast first before adding it to the pan with other ingredients. At the end of the day, I recommend you to follow the ingredients exactly as they're listed first—it's the safest way for any beginner.

4. Mind the room temperature. Where is your bread machine situated? Is the spot cool or warm? If it's in a room that's too cool, you will have a problem with your dough rising to double in the time assigned by the Dough Cycle of your machine. It's best to move the appliance to a warmer area in the house. Sure, the bread machine has its own heating element, but the room temperature can still affect how fast or slow the dough will rise.

5. Maximize the dough cycle, I beg you. When I say maximize, I mean use it as often as possible, especially when mixing ingredients. This will allow your oven to rest and save energy for the bigger tasks. Doing this will also let you have more control and shaping choices—even a better crust!

The Amazon Basics Bread Machine Cleaning Steps

1. Remove crumbs and flour

First, unplug the unit from the power source and allow it to cool. It's better to be safe than to regret later. Use the butter basting brush or small paintbrush to sweep the crumbs out of the machine.

Because your bread maker contains heating elements, it may continue to bake these "bread bits" with every new loaf. If you don't remove the crumbs, they may compromise the performance of the appliance.

You may also experience burned smell every time you bake. Another way of removing the burned scraps is to use a non-abrasive cleaning cloth or a paper towel. Be gentle as you do the cleaning.

Never pour water in the appliance. If there's some dough, allow it to dry. This will make the job easier without the additional mess. Another cautionary measure is that you should avoid getting the gears of your bread machine wet.

They operate the kneading plate, so they should not get into contact with milk or water. If there are some spills inside the machine, use a microfiber cloth. The longer the bits of dough and flour sit inside the machine, the harder it gets to remove them.

2. Clean the heating elements

When you leave your heating elements dirty, you pose a risk of fire. And because they are fragile, you should avoid using water. This area requires gentle cleaning.

If you notice there's some dough in this area, use a microfiber cloth or a sponge to clean the entire length.

Do not use detergents, bleach, and other harsh chemicals. As you do the cleaning, avoid bending the heating elements in your bread maker.

3. Clean the bread pan

This is where you bake the dough. Just use a warm soapy cloth to wipe inside the pan and rinse. Make sure it dries completely. While most pans come with non-stick coating, you may get occasional sticking. If the bread pan is dishwasher safe, you can fill it with soapy water to remove the stickiness. Do not let the water sit for more than 30 minutes. Be sure to confirm the instruction manual.

It's worth mentioning that most pans are not dishwasher safe because the underside requires lubrication. Any dough on the pan should be removed with a silicone/plastic spatula.

Never use a metal spatula as it may damage the non-stick surface leading to rust. Furthermore, avoid using abrasives as they can erode the finish. When you scratch the pan, it will start to deteriorate. If it flakes off, you may have to replace it.

4. Clean the kneading blade

The kneading blade is what kneads the dough. If your bread is not rising, the problem could be the blade. That being said, you should clean this part after baking.

Since most blades are removable, you should clean by hand. If the blade gets stuck on the machine, add hot water to the pan and then try to remove it after 30 minutes.

Soaking the blade in soapy water will make the job easier. You can also remove the bits of bread that get stuck using a cleaning brush.

If the hole on the kneading blade gets clogged, you can use a toothpick to remove the bits of dough. Be careful to avoid crumbing the blades. After cleaning, make sure you dry the blade.

5. Clean the top and sides of the bread maker

While the color of the bread maker may change with time, it doesn't affect the performance of the machine. Use a damp cloth to wipe the outside parts.

You can also use an old toothbrush to clean the air vents and crumbs that may be sticking on the outer surface of the machine.

Don't immerse the body in water or splash any liquid as it may cause an electric shock. Instead, use mild spray solution or abrasive liquid cleanser to avoid the build-up of stains.

Chemical cleaners can destroy the heating elements of the machine.

6. Assemble the parts

Once you've washed all the removable parts, you should return them to the machine. Make sure they are dry to avoid rust. Also, you should never use chemical dust-coat, steel wool pads, paint thinner, or Benzene.

This will extend the life of the machine. Close the lid and avoid placing anything on top.

BREAKFAST BREAD RECIPES

Parmesan Nut Bread

Ingredients:

- 8 slices (1 pound)
- 2/3 cup water
- 1 tablespoon olive oil
- 2 cups bread flour
- 3/8 cup grated Parmesan cheese
- 2/3 tablespoon gluten
- Pinch of sugar
- 3/8 teaspoon salt
- 1 1/4 teaspoons SAF yeast or 1/2 tablespoon bread machine yeast
- 1/4 cup pine nuts, coarsely chopped
- 1/3 cup walnuts, coarsely chopped
- 12 slices (1 ½ pounds)
- 1 cup water
- 11/2 tablespoons olive oil
- 3 cups bread flour
- 2/3 cup grated Parmesan cheese
- 1 tablespoon gluten
- Pinch of sugar
- 1/2 teaspoon salt
- 2 teaspoons SAF yeast or 21/2 teaspoon bread machine yeast
- 1/3 cup pine nuts, coarsely chopped
- 1/2 cup walnuts, coarsely chopped
- 16 slices (2 pounds)
- 11/3 cups water
- 2 tablespoons olive oil
- 4 cups bread flour
- 3/4 cup grated Parmesan cheese
- 1 tablespoon plus 1 teaspoon gluten
- Pinch of sugar
- 3/4 teaspoon salt
- 21/2 teaspoons SAF yeast or 1 tablespoon bread machine yeast
- 1/2 cup pine nuts, coarsely chopped
- 2/3 cup walnuts, coarsely chopped

Directions:

1. Choose the size of loaf you would like to make and measure your ingredients.
2. Add the ingredients to the bread pan in the order listed above (except the nuts).
3. Place the pan in the bread machine and close the lid.
4. Turn on the bread maker. Select the Basic setting, then the loaf size, and finally the crust color. Start the cycle. (This recipe is not suitable for use with the Delay Timer.)
5. When the machine beeps, or between Knead 1 and Knead 2, add the nuts.
6. When the cycle is finished and the bread is baked, carefully remove the pan from the machine. Use a potholder as the handle will be very hot. Let rest for a few minutes.
7. Remove the bread from the pan and allow to cool on a wire rack for at least 10 minutes before slicing.

Granola Bread

Ingredients:

- 8 slices (1 pound)
- 3/4 cup buttermilk
- 1 1/2 tablespoons vegetable oil
- 1 1/2 tablespoons honey
- 1 3/8 cups bread flour
- 1/2 cup whole wheat flour
- 2/3 cup granola
- 1/2 tablespoon plus 1/2 teaspoon gluten
- 1 teaspoon salt
- 3/4 teaspoon ground cinnamon
- 1 1/4 teaspoons SAF yeast or 1/2 tablespoon bread machine yeast
- 12 slices (1 ½ pounds)
- 11/8 cups buttermilk
- 2 tablespoons vegetable oil
- 2 tablespoons honey
- 21/8 cups bread flour
- 3/4 cup whole wheat flour
- 11/4 cups granola
- 1 tablespoon gluten
- 11/2 teaspoons salt

- 1 teaspoon ground cinnamon
- 2 teaspoons SAF yeast or 21/2 teaspoons bread machine yeast
- 16 slices (2 pounds)
- 11/2 cups buttermilk
- 3 tablespoons vegetable oil
- 3 tablespoons honey
- 23/4 cups bread flour
- 1 cup whole wheat flour
- 11/3 cups granola
- 1 tablespoon plus 1 teaspoon gluten
- 2 teaspoons salt
- 11/2 teaspoons ground cinnamon
- 21/2 teaspoons SAF yeast or 1 tablespoon bread machine yeast

Directions:

1. Choose the size of loaf you would like to make and measure your ingredients.
2. Add the ingredients to the bread pan in the order listed above.
3. Place the pan in the bread machine and close the lid.
4. Turn on the bread maker. Select the White/Basic setting, then the loaf size, and finally the crust color. Start the cycle.
5. When the cycle is finished and the bread is baked, carefully remove the pan from the machine. Use a potholder as the handle will be very hot. Let rest for a few minutes.
6. Remove the bread from the pan and allow to cool on a wire rack for at least 10 minutes before slicing.

Cheddar Bacon Bread

Ingredients:
- 8 slices (1 pound)
- 1/3 cup lukewarm milk
- 1 teaspoon unsalted butter, melted
- 1 tablespoon honey
- 1 teaspoon table salt
- 1/3 cup green chilies, chopped
- 1/3 cup grated Cheddar cheese
- 1/3 cup cooked bacon, chopped
- 2 cups white bread flour
- 1 1/4 teaspoons bread machine yeast

- 12 slices (1 ½ pounds)
- ½ cup lukewarm milk
- 1½ teaspoons unsalted butter, melted
- 1½ tablespoons honey
- 1½ teaspoons table salt
- ½ cup green chilies, chopped
- ½ cup grated Cheddar cheese
- ½ cup cooked bacon, chopped
- 3 cups white bread flour
- 2 teaspoons bread machine yeast
- 16 slices (2 pounds)
- ⅔ cup lukewarm milk
- 2 teaspoons unsalted butter, melted
- 2 tablespoons honey
- 2 teaspoons table salt
- ⅔ cup green chilies, chopped
- ⅔ cup grated Cheddar cheese
- ⅔ cup cooked bacon, chopped
- 4 cups white bread flour
- 2½ teaspoons bread machine yeast

Directions:

1. Choose the size of loaf you would like to make and measure your ingredients.
2. Add the ingredients to the bread pan in the order listed above.
3. Place the pan in the bread machine and close the lid.
4. Turn on the bread maker. Select the White/Basic setting, then the loaf size, and finally the crust color. Start the cycle.
5. When the cycle is finished and the bread is baked, carefully remove the pan from the machine. Use a potholder as the handle will be very hot. Let rest for a few minutes.
6. Remove the bread from the pan and allow to cool on a wire rack for at least 10 minutes before slicing.

Monterey Jack Loaf

Ingredients:
- 8 slices (1 pound)
- 1 cup warm water
- 1 teaspoon salt
- 2 tablespoons white sugar
- ½ cup Monterey Jack cheese, shredded

- 6 tablespoons fresh jalapeno pepper, chopped
- 3 cups bread flour
- ½ teaspoon active dry yeast
- 12 slices (1 ½ pounds)
- 1 1/2 cups warm water
- 1 1/2teaspoons salt
- 3 tablespoons white sugar
- 3/4 cup Monterey Jack cheese, shredded
- 9 tablespoons fresh jalapeno pepper, chopped
- 4 1/2 cups bread flour
- 3/4 teaspoon active dry yeast
- 16 slices (2 pounds)
- 2 cups warm water
- 2 teaspoons salt
- 4 tablespoons white sugar
- 1 cup Monterey Jack cheese, shredded
- 12 tablespoons fresh jalapeno pepper, chopped
- 6 cups bread flour
- 1 teaspoon active dry yeast

Directions:

1. Choose the size of loaf you would like to make and measure your ingredients.

2. Add the ingredients to the bread pan in the order listed above.

3. Place the pan in the bread machine and close the lid.

4. Turn on the bread maker. Select the White/Basic setting, then the loaf size, and finally the crust color. Start the cycle.

5. When the cycle is finished and the bread is baked, carefully remove the pan from the machine. Use a potholder as the handle will be very hot. Let rest for a few minutes.

6. Remove the bread from the pan and allow to cool on a wire rack for at least 10 minutes before slicing.

Dried Apricot Whole Wheat Bread

Ingredients:

- 8 slices (1 pound)
- 1/2 cup apple or pear juice
- 3 1/2 tablespoons water
- 1 1/4 tablespoons honey
- 1 1/4 tablespoons nut or vegetable oil
- 1 1/6 cups bread flour
- 1/2 cup whole wheat flour
- 1/3 cup rolled oats
- 1/2 tablespoon plus 1/2 teaspoon gluten
- 3/4 teaspoons salt
- 1 1/4 teaspoons SAF yeast or 1/2 tablespoon bread machine yeast
- 1/3 cup finely chopped dried apricots
- 12 slices (1 ½ pounds)
- 3/4 cup apple or pear juice
- 6 tablespoons water
- 2 tablespoons honey
- 2 tablespoons nut or vegetable oil
- 11/2 cups bread flour
- 1 cup whole wheat flour
- 1/2 cup rolled oats
- 1 tablespoon gluten
- 11/4 teaspoons salt
- 2 teaspoons SAF yeast or 21/2 teaspoons bread machine yeast
- 1/2 cup finely chopped dried apricots
- 16 slices (2 pounds)
- 1 cup apple or pear juice
- 7 tablespoons water
- 21/2 tablespoons honey
- 21/2 tablespoons nut or vegetable oil
- 21/3 cups bread flour
- 1 cup whole wheat flour
- 2/3 cup rolled oats
- 1 tablespoon plus 1 teaspoon gluten
- 11/2 teaspoons salt
- 21/2 teaspoons SAF yeast or 1 tablespoon bread machine yeast
- 2/3 cup finely chopped dried apricots

Directions:

1. Choose the size of loaf you would like to make and measure your ingredients.

2. Add the ingredients to the bread pan in the order listed above (except the apricots).

3. Place the pan in the bread machine and close the lid.

4. Turn on the bread maker. Select the Whole Wheat/Fruit and Nut setting, then the loaf size, and finally the crust color. Start the cycle. (This recipe is not suitable for use with the Delay Timer)

5. When the machine beeps, or between Knead 1 and Knead 2, add the apricots.

6. When the cycle is finished and the bread is baked, carefully remove the pan from the machine. Use a potholder as the handle will be very hot. Let rest for a few minutes.

7. Remove the bread from the pan and allow to cool on a wire rack for at least 10 minutes before slicing.

Feta And Spinach Bread

Ingredients:

- 8 slices (1 pound)
- 3/16 cup water
- 1/2 cup frozen chopped spinach (defrosted and squeezed dry)
- 1 1/2 tablespoons olive oil
- 2 cups bread flour
- 2 1/2ounces crumbled feta cheese
- 3/4 tablespoon sugar
- 1/2 teaspoon salt
- 1 1/8 teaspoons SAF yeast or 1 3/8 teaspoons bread machine yeast
- 12 slices (1 ½ pounds)
- 7/8 cup water
- 3/4 cup frozen chopped spinach (defrosted and squeezed dry)
- 2 tablespoons olive oil
- 3 cups bread flour
- 4 ounces crumbled feta cheese
- 1 tablespoon sugar
- 1/2 teaspoon salt
- 13/4 teaspoons SAF yeast or 21/4 teaspoons bread machine yeast
- 16 slices (2 pounds)
- 11/8 cups water
- 1 cup frozen chopped spinach (defrosted and squeezed dry)
- 3 tablespoons olive oil
- 4 cups bread flour
- 5 ounces crumbled feta cheese
- 11/2 tablespoons sugar
- 1 teaspoon salt

- 21/4 teaspoons SAF yeast or 23/4 teaspoons bread machine yeast

Directions:

1. Choose the size of loaf you would like to make and measure your ingredients.

2. Add the ingredients to the bread pan in the order listed above.

3. Place the pan in the bread machine and close the lid.

4. Turn on the bread maker. Select the White/Basic setting, then the loaf size, and finally the crust color. Start the cycle.

5. When the cycle is finished and the bread is baked, carefully remove the pan from the machine. Use a potholder as the handle will be very hot. Let rest for a few minutes.

6. Remove the bread from the pan and allow to cool on a wire rack for at least 10 minutes before slicing.

Cheddar Olive Bread

Ingredients:

- 8 slices (1 pound)
- 1 cup water at room temperature
- 4 teaspoons sugar
- ¾ teaspoon salt
- 1¼ cups shredded sharp cheddar cheese
- 3 cups bread flour
- 2 teaspoons active dry yeast
- ¾ cup pimiento olives, drained and sliced
- 12 slices (1 ½ pounds)
- 1 1/2 cups water at room temperature
- 6 teaspoons sugar
- 1 1/8 teaspoons salt
- 1 7/8 cups shredded sharp cheddar cheese
- 4 1/2 cups bread flour
- 3 teaspoons active dry yeast
- 1 1 /8 cups pimiento olives, drained and sliced
- 16 slices (2 pounds)
- 2 cups water at room temperature
- 8 teaspoons sugar
- 1 1/2 teaspoons salt
- 2 1/2 cups shredded sharp cheddar cheese
- 6 cups bread flour
- 4 teaspoons active dry yeast

- 1 1/2 cups pimiento olives, drained and sliced

Directions:

1. Choose the size of loaf you would like to make and measure your ingredients.

2. Add the ingredients to the bread pan in the order listed above (except olives).

3. Place the pan in the bread machine and close the lid.

4. Turn on the bread maker. Select the White/Basic setting, then the loaf size, and finally the crust color. Start the cycle.

5. Once the machine beeps, add olives.

6. When the cycle is finished and the bread is baked, carefully remove the pan from the machine. Use a potholder as the handle will be very hot. Let rest for a few minutes.

7. Remove the bread from the pan and allow to cool on a wire rack for at least 10 minutes before slicing.

Cinnamon Swirl Bread

Ingredients:

- 8 slices (1 pound)
- For the dough:
- 2/3 cup water
- 1 1/2 tablespoons unsalted butter, cut into pieces
- 1/6 cup sugar
- 2 cups bread flour
- 1/8 cup dry buttermilk powder
- 1/2 tablespoon plus 1/2 teaspoon gluten
- 3/4 teaspoon salt
- 1 1/4 teaspoons SAF yeast or 1/2 tablespoon bread machine yeast
- For the cinnamon swirl:
- 2 tablespoons unsalted butter, melted, for brushing
- 1/3 cup light brown sugar
- 1 tablespoon ground cinnamon
- 12 slices (1 ½ pounds)
- For the dough:
- 1 cup water
- 2 tablespoons unsalted butter, cut into pieces
- 1/4 cup sugar
- 3 cups bread flour
- 1/3 cup dry buttermilk powder
- 1 tablespoon gluten

- 11/4 teaspoons salt
- 2 teaspoons SAF yeast or 21/2 teaspoons bread machine yeast
- For the cinnamon swirl:
- 2 tablespoons unsalted butter, melted, for brushing
- 1/3 cup light brown sugar
- 1 tablespoon ground cinnamon
- 16 slices (2 pounds)
- For the dough:
- 11/3 cups water
- 3 tablespoons unsalted butter, cut into pieces
- 1/3 cup sugar
- 4 cups bread flour
- 1/4 cup dry buttermilk powder
- 1 tablespoon plus 1 teaspoon gluten
- 11/2 teaspoons salt
- 21/2 teaspoons SAF yeast or 1 tablespoon bread machine yeast
- For the cinnamon swirl:
- 2 tablespoons unsalted butter, melted, for brushing
- 1/3 cup light brown sugar
- 1 tablespoon ground cinnamon

Directions:

1. Choose the size of loaf you would like to make and measure your ingredients.

2. Add the ingredients to the bread pan in the order listed above.

3. Place the pan in the bread machine and close the lid.

4. Turn on the bread maker. Select the Basic setting, then the loaf size, and finally the crust on medium. Start the cycle.

5. After Rise 2 ends on the Basic cycle, or when the display shows Shape in the Variety cycle, press Pause, remove the pan, and close the lid. Immediately turn the dough out onto a lightly floured work surface; pat into an 8-by-12-inch fat rectangle. Brush with the melted butter. Sprinkle with the sugar and cinnamon, leaving a 1-inch space all the way around the edge. Starting at a short edge, roll the dough up jelly-roll fashion. Tuck the ends under and pinch the bottom seam. Coat the bottom of the dough with cooking spray, remove the kneading blade, and place the dough back in the pan; press Start to continue to rise and bake as programmed.

6. When the cycle is finished and the bread is baked, carefully remove the pan from the machine. Use a potholder as the handle will be very hot. Let rest for a few minutes.

7. Remove the bread from the pan and allow to cool on a wire rack for at least 10 minutes before slicing.

Ricotta And Fresh Chive Bread

Ingredients:

- 8 slices (1 pound)
- 2/3 cup water
- 1/4 cup whole or part-skim ricotta cheese
- 2 cups bread flour
- 3/4 tablespoon light brown sugar
- 2/3 tablespoon gluten
- 1 teaspoon salt
- 3/8 cup chopped fresh chives
- Dash of ground black pepper
- 1/2 tablespoon SAF yeast or 1/2 tablespoon plus 1/4 teaspoon bread machine yeast
- 12 slices (1 ½ pounds)
- 1 cup water
- 1/3 cup whole or part-skim ricotta cheese
- 3 cups bread flour
- 1 tablespoon light brown sugar
- 1 tablespoon gluten
- 11/2 teaspoons salt
- 1/2 cup chopped fresh chives
- Dash of ground black pepper
- 21/2 teaspoons SAF yeast or 1 tablespoon bread machine yeast
- 16 slices (2 pounds)
- 11/3 cups water
- 1/2 cup whole or part-skim ricotta cheese
- 4 cups bread flour
- 11/2 tablespoons light brown sugar
- 1 tablespoon plus 1 teaspoon gluten
- 2 teaspoons salt
- 3/4 cup chopped fresh chives
- Dash of ground black pepper
- 1 tablespoon SAF yeast or 1 tablespoon plus 1/2 teaspoon bread machine yeast

Directions:

1. Choose the size of loaf you would like to make and measure your ingredients.

2. Add the ingredients to the bread pan in the order listed above.

3. Place the pan in the bread machine and close the lid.

4. Turn on the bread maker. Select the Basic setting, then the loaf size, and finally the crust color. Start the cycle.

5. When the cycle is finished and the bread is baked, carefully remove the pan from the machine. Use a potholder as the handle will be very hot. Let rest for a few minutes.

6. Remove the bread from the pan and allow to cool on a wire rack for at least 10 minutes before slicing.

Egg Bread

Ingredients:

- 8 slices (1 pound)
- 2/3 cup water
- 1/2 large egg
- 2 cups bread flour
- 3/4 tablespoon sugar
- 1/2 tablespoon plus 1/2 teaspoon gluten
- 3/4 teaspoon salt
- 1 1/4 teaspoons SAF yeast or 1/2 tablespoon bread machine yeast
- 12 slices (1 ½ pounds)
- 1 cup water
- 1 large egg
- 3 cups bread flour
- 1 tablespoon sugar
- 1 tablespoon gluten
- 11/4 teaspoons salt
- 2 teaspoons SAF yeast or 21/2 teaspoons bread machine yeast
- 16 slices (2 pounds)
- 11/3 cups water
- 1 large egg
- 4 cups bread flour
- 11/2 tablespoons sugar
- 1 tablespoon plus 1 teaspoon gluten
- 11/2 teaspoons salt

- 21/2 teaspoons SAF yeast or 1 tablespoon bread machine yeast

Directions:

1. Choose the size of loaf you would like to make and measure your ingredients.
2. Pour the boiling water over the cracked rye in a bowl. Add the brown sugar, butter, and salt. Let stand 1 hour on the counter to soften.
3. Add the ingredients to the bread pan in the order listed above. Adding the grain and its soaking liquid as the liquid ingredients.
4. Place the pan in the bread machine and close the lid.
5. Turn on the bread maker. Select the Basic/French setting, then the loaf size, and finally the crust color. Start the cycle.
6. When the cycle is finished and the bread is baked, carefully remove the pan from the machine. Use a potholder as the handle will be very hot. Let rest for a few minutes.
7. Remove the bread from the pan and allow to cool on a wire rack for at least 10 minutes before slicing.

Beer Bread With Cheddar

Ingredients:

- 8 slices (1 pound)
- 2/3 cup (5 1/2 ounces) beer
- 2 1/4 cups bread flour
- 5/8 cup shredded Colby or mild cheddar cheese (2 1/2 ounces)
- 1/6 cup sugar
- 5/8 teaspoon salt
- 1 1/8 teaspoons SAF yeast or 1 3/8 teaspoons bread machine yeast
- 12 slices (1 ½ pounds)
- 1 cup (8 ounces) beer
- 31/2 cups bread flour
- 3/4 cup shredded Colby or mild cheddar cheese (3 ounces)
- 1/4 cup sugar
- 3/4 teaspoon salt
- 13/4 teaspoons SAF yeast or 21/4 teapoons bread machine yeast
- 16 slices (2 pounds)

- 11/3 cups (11 ounces) beer
- 41/2 cups bread flour
- 11/4 cups shredded Colby or mild cheddar cheese (5 ounces)
- 1/3 cup sugar
- 11/4 teaspoons salt
- 21/4 teaspoons SAF yeast or 23/4 teaspoons bread machine yeast

Directions:

1. Choose the size of loaf you would like to make and measure your ingredients.
2. Open the container of beer and let stand at room temperature for a few hours to go flat.
3. Add the ingredients to the bread pan in the order listed above.
4. Place the pan in the bread machine and close the lid.
5. Turn on the bread maker. Select the Basic setting, then the loaf size, and finally the crust color. Start the cycle.
6. When the cycle is finished and the bread is baked, carefully remove the pan from the machine. Use a potholder as the handle will be very hot. Let rest for a few minutes.
7. Remove the bread from the pan and allow to cool on a wire rack for at least 10 minutes before slicing.

Dutch Sugar Loaf

Ingredients:

- 8 slices (1 pound)
- 3/8 cup sugar cubes
- 1 teaspoon ground cinnamon
- Small pinch of ground cloves
- 2/3 cup fat-free milk
- 1 tablespoon unsalted butter or margarine, cut into pieces
- 2 cups bread flour
- 1/2 tablespoon plus 1/2 teaspoon gluten
- 7/8 teaspoon salt
- 1 1/4 teaspoons SAF yeast or 1/2 tablespoon bread machine yeast
- 12 slices (1 ½ pounds)
- 2/3 cup sugar cubes
- 11/2 teaspoons ground cinnamon

- Small pinch of ground cloves
- 11/8 cups fat-free milk
- 1 tablespoon unsalted butter or margarine, cut into pieces
- 3 cups bread flour
- 1 tablespoon gluten
- 11/4 teaspoons salt
- 2 teaspoons SAF yeast or 21/2 teaspoons bread machine yeast
- 16 slices (2 pounds)
- 3/4 cup sugar cubes
- 2 teaspoons ground cinnamon
- Small pinch of ground cloves
- 11/3 cups fat-free milk
- 2 tablespoons unsalted butter or margarine, cut into pieces
- 4 cups bread flour
- 1 tablespoon plus 1 teaspoon gluten
- 13/4 teaspoons salt
- 21/2 teaspoons SAF yeast or 1 tablespoon bread machine yeast

Directions:

1. Choose the size of loaf you would like to make and measure your ingredients.
2. Add the ingredients to the bread pan in the order listed above(except the spice-coated sugar cubes).
3. Place the pan in the bread machine and close the lid.
4. Turn on the bread maker. Select the Sweet Bread setting, then the loaf size, and finally the crust color. Start the cycle. Five minutes into the kneading segment, press Pause and sprinkle in half of the sugar cube mixture. Press Start to resume the cycle. Three minutes later, press Pause and add the rest of the sugar cube mixture. Press Start to resume the cycle.
5. When the cycle is finished and the bread is baked, carefully remove the pan from the machine. Use a potholder as the handle will be very hot. Let rest for a few minutes.
6. Remove the bread from the pan and allow to cool on a wire rack for at least 10 minutes before slicing.

Pain Aux Trois Parfums

Ingredients:

- 8 slices (1 pound)
- 3/8 cup milk
- 1/4 cup water
- 1/2 large egg plus 1/2 egg yolk
- 2 tablespoons pistachio oil or melted unsalted butter
- 5/8 teaspoon mint extract
- 1 3/4 cups bread flour
- 1/6 cup sugar
- 2 tablespoons unsweetened Dutch-process cocoa powder
- 2/3 tablespoon gluten
- 3/4 teaspoon salt
- 1 1/4 teaspoons SAF yeast or 1/2 tablespoon bread machine yeast
- 1/3 cup bittersweet chocolate chips
- 1/4 cup chopped pistachios
- 12 slices (1½ pounds)
- 1/2 cup milk
- 1/2 cup water
- 1 large egg plus 1 egg yolk
- 3 tablespoons pistachio oil or melted unsalted butter
- 1 teaspoon mint extract
- 22/3 cups bread flour
- 1/4 cup sugar
- 3 tablespoons unsweetened Dutch-process cocoa powder
- 1 tablespoon plus 1 teaspoon gluten
- 1 teaspoon salt
- 2 teaspoons SAF yeast or 21/2 teaspoons bread machine yeast
- 1/2 cup bittersweet chocolate chips
- 1/3 cup chopped pistachios
- 16 slices (2 pounds)
- 3/4 cup milk
- 1/2 cup water
- 1 large egg plus 1 egg yolk
- 4 tablespoons pistachio oil or melted unsalted butter
- 11/4 teaspoons mint extract
- 31/2 cups bread flour
- 1/3 cup sugar
- 4 tablespoons unsweetened Dutch-process cocoa powder
- 1 tablespoon plus 2 teaspoons gluten
- 11/2 teaspoons salt

- 21/2 teaspoons SAF yeast or 1 tablespoon bread machine yeast
- 2/3 cup bittersweet chocolate chips
- 1/2 cup chopped pistachios

Directions:

1. Choose the size of loaf you would like to make and measure your ingredients.
2. Add the ingredients to the bread pan in the order listed above (except the chocolate chips and pistachios).
3. Place the pan in the bread machine and close the lid.
4. Turn on the bread maker. Select the Sweet Bread setting, then the loaf size, and finally the crust color. Start the cycle. (This recipe is not suitable for use with the Delay Timer.)
5. When the machine beeps, or between Knead 1 and Knead 2, add the chocolate chips and pistachios.
6. When the cycle is finished and the bread is baked, carefully remove the pan from the machine. Use a potholder as the handle will be very hot. Let rest for a few minutes.
7. Remove the bread from the pan and allow to cool on a wire rack for at least 10 minutes before slicing.

Crescia Al Formaggio

Ingredients:

- 8 slices (1 pound)
- 1/3 cup plus 2/3 tablespoon water
- 2 large eggs
- 2 tablespoons olive oil
- 2 1/6 cups bread flour
- 1/2 cup grated Asiago or Locatelli cheese
- 1 tablespoon nonfat dry milk
- 2/3 tablespoon sugar
- 1 1/3 teaspoons gluten
- 3/4 teaspoon salt
- 1 1/3 teaspoons SAF yeast or 1 2/3 teaspoons bread machine yeast
- 12 slices (1 ½ pounds)
- 1/2 cup plus 1 tablespoon water
- 3 large eggs
- 3 tablespoons olive oil
- 31/4 cups bread flour
- 3/4 cup grated Asiago or Locatelli cheese

- 11/2 tablespoons nonfat dry milk
- 1 tablespoon sugar
- 2 teaspoons gluten
- 1/2 teaspoon salt
- 2 teaspoons SAF yeast or 21/2 teaspoons bread machine yeast
- 16 slices (2 pounds)
- 2/3 cup plus 1 1 /3 tablespoons water
- 4 large eggs
- 4 tablespoons olive oil
- 4 1/3 cups bread flour
- 1 cup grated Asiago or Locatelli cheese
- 2 tablespoons nonfat dry milk
- 1 1/3 tablespoons sugar
- 2 2/3 teaspoons gluten
- 1 1/2 teaspoons salt
- 2 2/3 teaspoons SAF yeast or 3 1/3 teaspoons bread machine yeast

Directions:

1. Choose the size of loaf you would like to make and measure your ingredients.
2. Add the ingredients to the bread pan in the order listed above.
3. Place the pan in the bread machine and close the lid.
4. Turn on the bread maker. Select the Basic setting, then the loaf size, and finally the crust color. Start the cycle.
5. When the cycle is finished and the bread is baked, carefully remove the pan from the machine. Use a potholder as the handle will be very hot. Let rest for a few minutes.
6. Remove the bread from the pan and allow to cool on a wire rack for at least 10 minutes before slicing.

Buttermilk Cheese Bread

Ingredients:

- 8 slices (1 pound)
- 5/8 cup buttermilk
- 1/3 cup water
- 2 1/4 cups bread flour
- 5/8 cup shredded Swiss cheese (2 1/2 ounces)
- 1 tablespoon sugar
- 3/4 teaspoon baking powder

- 1 teaspoon salt
- 1 1/4 teaspoons SAF yeast or 1/2 tablespoon bread machine yeast
- 12 slices (1 ½ pounds)
- 1 cup buttermilk
- 1/2 cup water
- 31/2 cups bread flour
- 1 cup shredded Swiss cheese (4 ounces)
- 11/2 tablespoons sugar
- 11/4 teaspoons baking powder
- 11/2 teaspoons salt
- 2 teaspoons SAF yeast or 21/2 teaspoons bread machine yeast
- 16 slices (2 pounds)
- 1 1/4 cups buttermilk
- 2/3 cup water
- 4 1/2 cups bread flour
- 1 1/4 cups shredded Swiss cheese (5 ounces)
- 2 tablespoons sugar
- 1 1/2 teaspoons baking powder
- 2 teaspoons salt
- 2 1/2 teaspoons SAF yeast or 1 tablespoon bread machine yeast

Directions:

1. Choose the size of loaf you would like to make and measure your ingredients.
2. Add the ingredients to the bread pan in the order listed above.
3. Place the pan in the bread machine and close the lid.
4. Turn on the bread maker. Select the Basic setting, then the loaf size, and finally the crust color. Start the cycle.
5. When the cycle is finished and the bread is baked, carefully remove the pan from the machine. Use a potholder as the handle will be very hot. Let rest for a few minutes.
6. Remove the bread from the pan and allow to cool on a wire rack for at least 10 minutes before slicing.

Spicy Pear Bread

Ingredients:
- 8 slices (1 pound)
- For the dough:
- 1/4 cup plus 1 tablespoon milk
- 1/4 cup water
- 1 large egg
- 3 tablespoons unsalted butter, partially melted
- 21/2 cups unbleached all-purpose flour
- 1/4 cup sugar
- 1 teaspoon salt
- 2 teaspoons SAF yeast or 21/2 teaspoons bread machine yeast
- For the fruit filling:
- 3/4 cup dry red wine
- 1/4 cup kirsch
- 1/4 cup sugar
- Grated zest of 1 lemon
- 1/2 teaspoon ground cinnamon
- 1/4 teaspoon fresh-ground nutmeg
- 8 ounces dried pears, chopped (2 cups)
- 6 ounces dried figs, stemmed and chopped (11/2 cups)
- 4 ounces pitted prunes (1 heaping cup)
- 1/4 cup raisins
- 1 egg yolk beaten with 1 tablespoon milk, for glaze
- 12 slices (1 ½ pounds)
- For the dough:
- 3/8 cup plus 1 1/2 tablespoons milk
- 3/8 cup water
- 1 1/2 large eggs
- 4 1/2 tablespoons unsalted butter, partially melted
- 3 3/4 cups unbleached all-purpose flour
- 3/8 cup sugar
- 1 1/2 teaspoons salt
- 3 teaspoons SAF yeast or 3 3/4 teaspoons bread machine yeast
- For the fruit filling:
- 1 1/8 cups dry red wine
- 3/8 cup kirsch
- 3/8 cup sugar
- Grated zest of 1 1/2 lemons
- 3/4 teaspoon ground cinnamon
- 3/8 teaspoon fresh-ground nutmeg
- 12 ounces dried pears, chopped (3 cups)
- 9 ounces dried figs, stemmed and chopped (2 1/4 cups)
- 6 ounces pitted prunes (1 1/2 heaping cups)

- 3/8 cup raisins
- 1 1/2 egg yolks beaten with 1 1/2 tablespoons milk, for glaze
- 16 slices (2 pounds)
- For the dough:
- 1/2 cup plus 2 tablespoons milk
- 1/2 cup water
- 2 large eggs
- 6 tablespoons unsalted butter, partially melted
- 5 cups unbleached all-purpose flour
- 1/2 cup sugar
- 2 teaspoons salt
- 4 teaspoons SAF yeast or 5 teaspoons bread machine yeast
- For the fruit filling:
- 1 1/2 cups dry red wine
- 1/2 cup kirsch
- 1/2 cup sugar
- Grated zest of 2 lemons
- 1 teaspoon ground cinnamon
- 1/2 teaspoon fresh-ground nutmeg
- 16 ounces dried pears, chopped (4 cups)
- 12 ounces dried figs, stemmed and chopped (3 cups)
- 8 ounces pitted prunes (2 heaping cups)
- 1/2 cup raisins
- 2 egg yolks beaten with 2 tablespoons milk, for glaze

Directions:

1. Choose the size of loaf you would like to make and measure your ingredients.

2. Add the ingredients to the bread pan in the order listed above.

3. Place the pan in the bread machine and close the lid.

4. While the dough is rising, make the filling. Combine the wine, kirsch, sugar, zest, and spices in a small saucepan and bring to a boil. Lower heat and add the dried fruit. Simmer, uncovered, for 10 minutes. Remove from the heat, cover, and let stand until room temperature and all of the liquid is absorbed, about 1 hour. Place in a food processor and pulse to make a thick jam that is not totally smooth.

5. Turn on the bread maker. Select the Dough setting, then the loaf size, and finally the crust color. Start the cycle.

6. When the cycle is finished and the bread is baked, carefully remove the pan from the machine. Use a potholder as the handle will be very hot. Let rest for a few minutes.

7. Remove the bread from the pan and allow to cool on a wire rack for at least 10 minutes before slicing.

8. 2 While the dough is rising, make the filling. Combine the wine, kirsch, sugar, zest, and spices in a small saucepan and bring to a boil. Lower heat and add the dried fruit. Simmer, uncovered, for 10 minutes. Remove from the heat, cover, and let stand until room temperature and all of the liquid is absorbed, about 1 hour. Place in a food processor and pulse to make a thick jam that is not totally smooth.

9. 3 Line a baking sheet with parchment paper. To assemble the loaf, when the machine beeps at the end of the cycle, press Stop and unplug the machine. Turn the dough out onto a lightly floured work surface. With a rolling pin, roll out into a 12-by-16-inch rectangle. With a metal spatula, spread the filling evenly over the dough, leaving 1/2-inch borders on three sides and a 1-inch border on one long side. Beginning at the long edge with the 1/2-inch border, roll up jelly-roll fashion to make a log. Moisten the 1-inch border with some water and seal. Pinch the bottom seam, leaving the ends open. Press to even the ends. Using the tines of a fork, prick the dough all over. Brush with the egg glaze. Let rest at room temperature, covered loosely with a clean tea towel, until doubled in bulk, about 45 minutes.

10. 4 Twenty minutes before baking, preheat the oven to 350°F.

11. 5 Brush the roll once more with the egg glaze. Bake for 30 to 40 minutes, until golden brown and firm to the touch. Let cool on the baking sheet.

Chocolate Cherry Bread

Ingredients:
- 8 slices (1 pound)
- 2/3 cup milk
- 1/2 large egg
- 3/8 teaspoon vanilla extract
- 3/8 teaspoon almond extract
- 2 tablespoons unsalted butter, cut into pieces

- 1 7/8 cups bread flour
- 1/4 cup unsweetened Dutch-process cocoa powder
- 1/6 cup light brown sugar
- 2/3 tablespoon gluten
- 3/4 teaspoon salt
- 1 1/4 teaspoons SAF yeast or 1/2 tablespoon bread machine yeast
- 7/16 cup snipped glacéed tart dried cherries
- 12 slices (1½ pounds)
- 1 cup milk
- 1 large egg
- 1/2 teaspoon vanilla extract
- 1/2 teaspoon almond extract
- 3 tablespoons unsalted butter, cut into pieces
- 27/8 cups bread flour
- 1/3 cup unsweetened Dutch-process cocoa powder
- 1/4 cup light brown sugar
- 1 tablespoon gluten
- 11/4 teaspoons salt
- 2 teaspoons SAF yeast or 21/2 teaspoons bread machine yeast
- 3/4 cup snipped glacéed tart dried cherries
- 16 slices (2 pounds)
- 11/3 cups milk
- 1 large egg
- 3/4 teaspoon vanilla extract
- 3/4 teaspoon almond extract
- 4 tablespoons unsalted butter, cut into pieces
- 33/4 cups bread flour
- 1/2 cup unsweetened Dutch-process cocoa powder
- 1/3 cup light brown sugar
- 1 tablespoon plus 1 teaspoon gluten
- 11/2 teaspoons salt
- 21/2 teaspoons SAF yeast or 1 tablespoon bread machine yeast
- 7/8 cup snipped glacéed tart dried cherries

Directions:

1. Choose the size of loaf you would like to make and measure your ingredients.

2. Add the ingredients to the bread pan in the order listed above (except the cherries).

3. Place the pan in the bread machine and close the lid.

4. Turn on the bread maker. Select the Basic/Sweet Bread setting, then the loaf size, and finally the crust color. Start the cycle. (This recipe is not suitable for use with the Delay Timer.)

5. When the machine beeps, or between Knead 1 and Knead 2, add the cherries.

6. When the cycle is finished and the bread is baked, carefully remove the pan from the machine. Use a potholder as the handle will be very hot. Let rest for a few minutes.

7. Remove the bread from the pan and allow to cool on a wire rack for at least 10 minutes before slicing.

Chocolate Challah

Ingredients:
- 8 slices (1 pound)
- 5/8 cup water
- 1 large egg
- 1 1/2 tablespoons vegetable oil
- 1/2 tablespoon vanilla extract
- 2 cups bread flour
- 1/3 cup sugar
- 1/6 cup unsweetened Dutch-process cocoa powder
- 2/3 tablespoon gluten
- 1 teaspoon salt
- 1 teaspoon SAF yeast or 1 1/4 teaspoons bread machine yeast
- 1/3 cup semisweet chocolate chips
- 12 slices (1½ pounds)
- 1 cup water
- 1 large egg plus 1 egg yolk
- 2 tablespoons vegetable oil
- 2 teaspoons vanilla extract
- 3 cups bread flour
- 1/2 cup sugar
- 1/4 cup unsweetened Dutch-process cocoa powder
- 1 tablespoon gluten
- 11/2 teaspoons salt
- 13/4 teaspoons SAF yeast or 21/4 teaspoons bread machine yeast
- 1/2 cup semisweet chocolate chips
- 16 slices (2 pounds)
- 11/4 cups water

- 2 large eggs
- 3 tablespoons vegetable oil
- 1 tablespoon vanilla extract
- 4 cups bread flour
- 2/3 cup sugar
- 1/3 cup unsweetened Dutch-process cocoa powder
- 1 tablespoon plus 1 teaspoon gluten
- 2 teaspoons salt
- 2 teaspoons SAF yeast or 21/2 teaspoons bread machine yeast
- 2/3 cup semisweet chocolate chips

Directions:

1. Choose the size of loaf you would like to make and measure your ingredients.

2. Add the ingredients to the bread pan in the order listed above (except the chocolate chips).

3. Place the pan in the bread machine and close the lid.

4. Turn on the bread maker. Select the Basic/Sweet Bread setting, then the loaf size, and finally the crust color. Start the cycle.

5. At the beep, add the chocolate chips.

6. When the cycle is finished and the bread is baked, carefully remove the pan from the machine. Use a potholder as the handle will be very hot. Let rest for a few minutes.

7. Remove the bread from the pan and allow to cool on a wire rack for at least 10 minutes before slicing.

Greek Currant Bread

Ingredients:

- 8 slices (1 pound)
- 2/3 cup currants
- 1/8 cup orange juice
- One 1-inch piece cinnamon stick
- 1 whole cloves
- Pinch of ground mastika or allspice
- 9/16 cup plus 1/2 tablespoon evaporated milk
- 1 teaspoon orange-flower water
- 1/8 cup honey
- 2 cups bread flour
- 1/2 tablespoon plus
- 1/2 teaspoon gluten
- 1 teaspoon salt
- 1 1/4 teaspoons SAF yeast or 1/2 tablespoon bread machine yeast
- 12 slices (1 ½ pounds)
- 11/4 cups currants
- 3 tablespoons orange juice
- One 2-inch piece cinnamon stick
- 2 whole cloves
- Pinch of ground mastika or allspice
- 1 cup evaporated milk
- 11/2 teaspoons orange-flower water
- 3 tablespoons honey
- 3 cups bread flour
- 1 tablespoon gluten
- 11/2 teaspoons salt
- 2 teaspoons SAF yeast or 21/2 teaspoons bread machine yeast
- 16 slices (2 pounds)
- 11/3 cups currants
- 1/4 cup orange juice
- One 2-inch piece cinnamon stick
- 2 whole cloves
- Pinch of ground mastika or allspice
- 11/8 cups plus 1 tablespoon evaporated milk
- 2 teaspoons orange-flower water
- 1/4 cup honey
- 4 cups bread flour
- 1 tablespoon plus
- 1 teaspoon gluten
- 2 teaspoons salt
- 21/2 teaspoons SAF yeast or 1 tablespoon bread machine yeast

Directions:

1. Choose the size of loaf you would like to make and measure your ingredients.

2. Place the currants in a small bowl. Add the orange juice, cinnamon stick, cloves, and mastika or allspice. Toss to combine. Cover and let stand at room temperature for 1 hour. The currants will be soft and plump. Remove and discard the cinnamon stick and cloves.

3. Drain and reserve any extra orange juice from the currants. Add to the juice enough water to equal 2

tablespoons if you are making the 11/2-pound loaf or 3 tablespoons if you are making the 2-pound loaf.

4. Add the ingredients to the bread pan in the order listed above (except the currants). Add the juice and water mixture with the liquid ingredients.

5. Place the pan in the bread machine and close the lid.

6. Turn on the bread maker. Select the Sweet Bread or Fruit and Nut setting, then the loaf size, and finally the crust color. Start the cycle. (This recipe is not suitable for use with the Delay Timer.)

7. When the machine beeps, or between Knead 1 and Knead 2, add the currants.

8. When the cycle is finished and the bread is baked, carefully remove the pan from the machine. Use a potholder as the handle will be very hot. Let rest for a few minutes.

9. Remove the bread from the pan and allow to cool on a wire rack for at least 10 minutes before slicing.

FRUIT BREAD RECIPES

Super Spice Bread

Ingredients:

- 8 slices (1 pound)
- 2/3 cup lukewarm milk
- 1 egg, at room temperature
- 1 tablespoon unsalted butter, melted
- 1 1/3 tablespoons honey
- 2/3 teaspoon table salt
- 2 cups white bread flour
- 2/3 teaspoon ground cinnamon
- 1/3 teaspoon ground cardamom
- 1/3 teaspoon ground nutmeg
- 1 1/8 teaspoons bread machine yeast
- 12 slices (1 ½ pounds)
- 1 cup lukewarm milk
- 2 eggs, at room temperature
- 1½ tablespoons unsalted butter, melted
- 2 tablespoons honey
- 1 teaspoon table salt
- 3 cups white bread flour
- 1 teaspoon ground cinnamon
- ½ teaspoon ground cardamom
- ½ teaspoon ground nutmeg
- 2 teaspoons bread machine yeast
- 16 slices (2 pounds)
- 1⅓ cups lukewarm milk
- 2 eggs, at room temperature
- 2 tablespoons unsalted butter, melted
- 2⅔ tablespoons honey
- 1⅓ teaspoons table salt
- 4 cups white bread flour
- 1⅓ teaspoons ground cinnamon
- ⅔ teaspoon ground cardamom
- ⅔ teaspoon ground nutmeg
- 2¼ teaspoons bread machine yeast

Directions:

1. Choose the size of loaf you would like to make and measure your ingredients.
2. Add the ingredients to the bread pan in the order listed above.
3. Place the pan in the bread machine and close the lid.
4. Turn on the bread maker. Select the White/Basic setting, then the loaf size, and finally the crust color. Start the cycle.
5. When the cycle is finished and the bread is baked, carefully remove the pan from the machine. Use a potholder as the handle will be very hot. Let rest for a few minutes.
6. Remove the bread from the pan and allow to cool on a wire rack for at least 10 minutes before slicing.

Cinnamon Figs Bread

Ingredients:

- 8 slices (1 pound)
- 3/4 cup lukewarm water
- 1 1/2 tablespoons unsalted butter, melted
- 1/8 cup sugar
- 1/2 teaspoon table salt
- 1/4 teaspoon cinnamon, ground
- 1/2 teaspoon orange zest
- Pinch ground nutmeg
- 1 1/4 cups whole-wheat flour
- 3/4 cup white bread flour
- 1 teaspoon bread machine yeast
- 5/8 cup chopped fresh plums or sliced figs
- 12 slices (1 ½ pounds)
- 1⅛ cups lukewarm water
- 2¼ tablespoons unsalted butter, melted
- 3 tablespoons sugar
- ¾ teaspoon table salt
- ⅓ teaspoon cinnamon, ground
- ¾ teaspoon orange zest
- Pinch ground nutmeg
- 1⅞ cups whole-wheat flour
- 1⅛ cups white bread flour
- 1½ teaspoons bread machine yeast
- 1 cup chopped plums or sliced figs
- 16 slices (2 pounds)
- 1½ cups lukewarm water
- 3 tablespoons unsalted butter, melted
- ¼ cup sugar

- 1 teaspoon table salt
- ½ teaspoon cinnamon, ground
- 1 teaspoon orange zest
- Pinch ground nutmeg
- 2½ cups whole-wheat flour
- 1½ cups white bread flour
- 2 teaspoons bread machine yeast
- 1¼ cups chopped fresh plums or sliced figs

Directions:

1. Choose the size of loaf you would like to make and measure your ingredients.

2. Add all of the ingredients except for the plums to the bread pan in the order listed above.

3. Place the pan in the bread machine and close the lid.

4. Turn on the bread maker. Select the White/Basic or Fruit/Nut (if your machine has this setting) setting, then the loaf size, and finally the crust color. Start the cycle.

5. When the machine signals to add ingredients, add the plums. (Some machines have a fruit/nut hopper where you can add the plums when you start the machine. The machine will automatically add them to the dough during the baking process.)

6. When the cycle is finished and the bread is baked, carefully remove the pan from the machine. Use a potholder as the handle will be very hot. Let rest for a few minutes.

7. Remove the bread from the pan and allow to cool on a wire rack for at least 10 minutes before slicing.

Pineapple Carrot Bread

Servings: 12
Cooking Time: 3 Hours

Ingredients:

- 1 (8-ounce) can crushed pineapple, with juice
- 1/2 cup carrots, shredded
- 2 eggs
- 2 tablespoons butter
- 4 cups bread flour
- 3 tablespoons sugar
- 1 teaspoon salt
- 3/4 teaspoon ground ginger
- 1 1/4 teaspoons active dry yeast

Directions:

1. Add all of the ingredients (except yeast) to the bread maker pan in the order listed above.

2. Make a well in the center of the dry ingredients and add the yeast.

3. Select the Basic bread cycle and press Start.

4. Transfer baked loaf to a cooling rack for 15 minutes before slicing to serve.

Nutrition:

- al Info Calories: 203, Sodium: 222 mg, Dietary Fiber: 1.6 g, Fat: 3.1 g, Carbs: 38 g, Protein: 5.6 g.

Toasted Coconut Bread

Ingredients:

- 8 slices (1 pound)
- 11/4 cups (about 21/2 ounces) shredded unsweetened coconut
- 11/8 cups half-and-half (regular or fat-free)
- 2 large eggs
- 1/4 cup canola oil
- 2 teaspoons coconut extract
- 1 teaspoon vanilla extract
- 3/4 cup sugar
- 2 cups unbleached all-purpose flour
- 1 tablespoon baking powder
- 1/2 teaspoon salt
- 12 slices (1 ½ pounds)
- 1 7/8 cups (about 21/2 ounces) shredded unsweetened coconut
- 1 11/16 cups half-and-half (regular or fat-free)
- 3 large eggs
- 3/8 cup canola oil
- 3 teaspoons coconut extract
- 1 1/2 teaspoons vanilla extract
- 1 1/8 cups sugar
- 3 cups unbleached all-purpose flour
- 1 1/2 tablespoons baking powder
- 3/4 teaspoon salt
- 16 slices (2 pounds)
- 2 1/2 cups (about 21/2 ounces) shredded unsweetened coconut
- 2 1/4 cups half-and-half (regular or fat-free)
- 4 large eggs
- 1/2 cup canola oil

- 4 teaspoons coconut extract
- 2 teaspoons vanilla extract
- 1 1/2 cups sugar
- 4 cups unbleached all-purpose flour
- 2 tablespoons baking powder
- 1 teaspoon salt

Directions:

1. Choose the size of loaf you would like to make and measure your ingredients.

2. Preheat the oven to 350°F.

3. Sprinkle the coconut on an ungreased baking sheet and toast in the oven until lightly browned, about 3 minutes. Transfer immediately to a small bowl and let cool to room temperature.

4. Add the ingredients to the bread pan in the order listed above. Adding the coconut with the dry ingredients.

5. Place the pan in the bread machine and close the lid.

6. Turn on the bread maker. Select the Quick Bread/Cake setting, then the loaf size, and finally the crust color. Start the cycle.

7. When the cycle is finished and the bread is baked, carefully remove the pan from the machine. Use a potholder as the handle will be very hot. Let rest for a few minutes.

8. Remove the bread from the pan and allow to cool on a wire rack for at least 10 minutes before slicing.

Applesauce Bread

Ingredients:

- 8 slices (1 pound)
- 1/4 cup apple juice
- 3/8 cup unsweetened applesauce
- 1/2 large egg
- 1 1/2 tablespoons unsalted butter, cut into pieces
- 2 cups bread flour
- 1/8 cup light brown sugar, optional
- 1/2 tablespoon plus 1/2 teaspoon gluten
- 1 teaspoon salt
- 5/8 teaspoon ground cinnamon or apple pie spice
- 1/4 teaspoon baking soda
- 1 1/8 teaspoons SAF yeast or 1 3/8 teaspoons bread machine yeast

- 12 slices (1 ½ pounds)
- 1/4 cup apple juice
- 1/2 cup unsweetened applesauce
- 1 large egg
- 2 tablespoons unsalted butter, cut into pieces
- 3 cups bread flour
- 3 tablespoons light brown sugar, optional
- 1 tablespoon gluten
- 11/2 teaspoons salt
- 1 teaspoon ground cinnamon or apple pie spice
- 1/3 teaspoon baking soda
- 2 teaspoons SAF yeast or 21/2 teaspoons bread machine yeast
- 16 slices (2 pounds)
- 1/2 cup apple juice
- 3/4 cup unsweetened applesauce
- 1 large egg
- 3 tablespoons unsalted butter, cut into pieces
- 4 cups bread flour
- 1/4 cup light brown sugar, optional
- 1 tablespoon plus 1 teaspoon gluten
- 2 teaspoons salt
- 11/4 teaspoons ground cinnamon or apple pie spice
- 1/2 teaspoon baking soda
- 21/4 teaspoons SAF yeast or 23/4 teaspoons bread machine yeast

Directions:

1. Choose the size of loaf you would like to make and measure your ingredients.

2. Add the ingredients to the bread pan in the order listed above.

3. Place the pan in the bread machine and close the lid.

4. Turn on the bread maker. Select the Basic/Sweet Bread setting, then the loaf size, and finally the crust color. Start the cycle.

5. When the cycle is finished and the bread is baked, carefully remove the pan from the machine. Use a potholder as the handle will be very hot. Let rest for a few minutes.

6. Remove the bread from the pan and allow to cool on a wire rack for at least 10 minutes before slicing.

Cranberry Walnut Wheat Bread

Ingredients:

- 8 slices (1 pound)
- 1 cup warm water
- 1 tablespoon molasses
- 2 tablespoons butter
- 1 teaspoon salt
- 2 cups 100% whole wheat flour
- 1 cup unbleached flour
- 2 tablespoons dry milk
- 1 cup cranberries
- 1 cup walnuts, chopped
- 2 teaspoons active dry yeast
- 12 slices (1 ½ pounds)
- 1 1/2 cups warm water
- 1 1/2 tablespoons molasses
- 3 tablespoons butter
- 1 1/2 teaspoons salt
- 3 cups 100% whole wheat flour
- 1 1/2 cups unbleached flour
- 3 tablespoons dry milk
- 1 1/2 cup cranberries
- 1 1/2 cups walnuts, chopped
- 3 teaspoons active dry yeast
- 16 slices (2 pounds)
- 2 cups warm water
- 2 tablespoons molasses
- 4 tablespoons butter
- 2 teaspoons salt
- 4 cups 100% whole wheat flour
- 2 cups unbleached flour
- 4 tablespoons dry milk
- 2 cups cranberries
- 2 cups walnuts, chopped
- 4 teaspoons active dry yeast

Directions:

1. Choose the size of loaf you would like to make and measure your ingredients.

2. Add the ingredients to the bread pan in the order listed above (except the yeast, walnuts and cranberries).

3. Place the pan in the bread machine and close the lid.

4. Turn on the bread maker. Select the Wheat Bread setting, then the loaf size, and finally the crust color. Start the cycle.

5. Add cranberries and walnuts after first kneading cycle is finished.

6. When the cycle is finished and the bread is baked, carefully remove the pan from the machine. Use a potholder as the handle will be very hot. Let rest for a few minutes.

7. Remove the bread from the pan and allow to cool on a wire rack for at least 10 minutes before slicing.

Cherry–wheat Berry Bread

Ingredients:

- 8 slices (1 pound)
- 1/4 cup wheat berries
- 1/2 cup water
- 5/8 cup water
- 1/2 large egg white
- 1 1/2 tablespoons canola oil
- 1/6 cup honey
- 2 cups bread flour
- 1/2 tablespoon gluten
- 1 teaspoon salt
- 1/2 tablespoon SAF yeast or 1/2 tablespoon plus 1/4 teaspoon bread machine yeast
- 1/3 cup tart dried cherries tossed with 1/2 tablespoon flour
- 12 slices (1 ½ pounds)
- 1/3 cup wheat berries
- 1 cup water
- 1 cup water
- 1 large egg white
- 2 tablespoons canola oil
- 1/4 cup honey
- 3 cups bread flour
- 2 teaspoons gluten
- 11/2 teaspoons salt
- 21/2 teaspoons SAF yeast or 1 tablespoon bread machine yeast
- 1/2 cup tart dried cherries tossed with 1 tablespoon flour
- 16 slices (2 pounds)

- 1/2 cup wheat berries
- 1 cup water
- 11/4 cups water
- 1 large egg white
- 3 tablespoons canola oil
- 1/3 cup honey
- 4 cups bread flour
- 1 tablespoon gluten
- 2 teaspoons salt
- 1 tablespoon SAF yeast or 1 tablespoon plus 1/2 teaspoon bread machine yeast
- 2/3 cup tart dried cherries tossed with 1 tablespoon flour

Directions:

1. Choose the size of loaf you would like to make and measure your ingredients.
2. Combine the wheat berries and the 1 cup of water in a saucepan. Bring to a boil. Reduce the heat, partially cover, and simmer for about 45 minutes, until chewy and tender. Drain off the excess water.
3. Add the ingredients to the bread pan in the order listed above (except the wheat berries and the cherries).
4. Place the pan in the bread machine and close the lid.
5. Turn on the bread maker. Select the Basic setting, then the loaf size, and finally the crust color. Start the cycle. (This recipe is not suitable for use with the Delay Timer.)
6. When the machine beeps, or at the pause between Knead 1 and 2, add the wheat berries and the cherries.
7. When the cycle is finished and the bread is baked, carefully remove the pan from the machine. Use a potholder as the handle will be very hot. Let rest for a few minutes.
8. Remove the bread from the pan and allow to cool on a wire rack for at least 10 minutes before slicing.

Cocoa Date Bread

Ingredients:
- 8 slices (1 pound)
- 1/2 cup lukewarm water
- 1/4 cup lukewarm milk
- 1 tablespoon unsalted butter, melted
- 1 1/2 tablespoons honey
- 1 1/2 tablespoons molasses
- 1/2 tablespoon sugar
- 1 1/2 tablespoons skim milk powder
- 1/2 teaspoon table salt
- 1 cup white bread flour
- 1 1/4 cups whole-wheat flour
- 1/2 tablespoon cocoa powder, unsweetened
- 3/4 teaspoon bread machine yeast
- 1/2 cup dates, chopped
- 12 slices (1 ½ pounds)
- ¾ cup lukewarm water
- ½ cup lukewarm milk
- 2 tablespoons unsalted butter, melted
- ¼ cup honey
- 3 tablespoons molasses
- 1 tablespoon sugar
- 2 tablespoons skim milk powder
- 1 teaspoon table salt
- 1¼ cups white bread flour
- 2¼ cups whole-wheat flour
- 1 tablespoon cocoa powder, unsweetened
- 1½ teaspoons bread machine yeast
- ¾ cup dates, chopped
- 16 slices (2 pounds)
- 1 cup lukewarm water
- ½ cup lukewarm milk
- 2 tablespoons unsalted butter, melted
- 5 tablespoons honey
- 3 tablespoons molasses
- 1 tablespoon sugar
- 3 tablespoons skim milk powder
- 1 teaspoon table salt
- 2 cups white bread flour
- 2½ cups whole-wheat flour
- 1 tablespoon cocoa powder, unsweetened
- 1½ teaspoons bread machine yeast
- 1 cup dates, chopped

Directions:

1. Choose the size of loaf you would like to make and measure your ingredients.
2. Add all of the ingredients except for the dates to the bread pan in the order listed above.
3. Place the pan in the bread machine and close the lid.

4. Turn on the bread maker. Select the White/Basic or Fruit/Nut (if your machine has this setting) setting, then the loaf size, and finally the crust color. Start the cycle.

5. When the machine signals to add ingredients, add the dates. (Some machines have a fruit/nut hopper where you can add the dates when you start the machine. The machine will automatically add them to the dough during the baking process.)

6. When the cycle is finished and the bread is baked, carefully remove the pan from the machine. Use a potholder as the handle will be very hot. Let rest for a few minutes.

7. Remove the bread from the pan and allow to cool on a wire rack for at least 10 minutes before slicing.

Raisin Bread

Servings: 12
Cooking Time: 3 Hours

Ingredients:
- 1 cup warm water
- 3 tablespoons vegetable oil
- 3 cups flour
- 1 teaspoon cinnamon
- 1/8 teaspoon nutmeg
- 1/3 cup sugar
- 1 1/2 teaspoons salt
- 1 packet instant dry yeast
- 3/4 cup raisins

Directions:
1. Add the water and oil to the bread maker.
2. Add flour and sprinkle with cinnamon and nutmeg.
3. On top of the flour, add sugar to one corner of the bread maker, salt in the other corner and yeast in another corner, so the yeast is not touching sugar and salt.
4. Set to Basic bread cycle, medium crust color, and press Start.
5. Add the raisins when the dough cycle is finished.
6. When the baking cycle is finished, transfer to a cooling rack for 15 minutes before slicing.

Nutrition:
- al Info Calories: 193, Sodium: 1068 mg, Dietary Fiber: 1.3 g, Fat: 3.8 g, Carbs: 36.8 g, Protein: 3.5 g.

Prune Bread

Ingredients:
- 8 slices (1 pound)
- 3/4 cups water
- 2 tablespoons unsalted butter, cut into pieces
- 1 3/8 cups bread flour
- 5/8 cups whole wheat flour
- 1 1/2 tablespoons light brown sugar
- 1/2 tablespoon plus 1/2 teaspoon gluten
- 7/8 teaspoons salt
- 5/8 teaspoons ground cinnamon
- 1/6 teaspoon fresh-ground nutmeg
- 1 1/4 teaspoons SAF yeast or 1/2 tablespoon bread machine yeast
- 6 pitted prunes (about 2 ounces), chopped
- 12 slices (1 ½ pounds)
- 11/8 cups water
- 3 tablespoons unsalted butter, cut into pieces
- 21/4 cups bread flour
- 3/4 cup whole wheat flour
- 2 tablespoons light brown sugar
- 1 tablespoon gluten
- 11/4 teaspoons salt
- 1 teaspoon ground cinnamon
- 1/4 teaspoon fresh-ground nutmeg
- 2 teaspoons SAF yeast or 21/2 teaspoons bread machine yeast
- 9 pitted prunes (about 3 ounces), chopped
- 16 slices (2 pounds)
- 11/2 cups water
- 4 tablespoons unsalted butter, cut into pieces
- 23/4 cups bread flour
- 11/4 cups whole wheat flour
- 3 tablespoons light brown sugar
- 1 tablespoon plus 1 teaspoon gluten
- 13/4 teaspoons salt
- 11/4 teaspoons ground cinnamon
- 1/3 teaspoon fresh-ground nutmeg
- 21/2 teaspoons SAF yeast or 1 tablespoon bread machine yeast
- 12 pitted prunes (about 4 ounces), chopped

Directions:

1. Choose the size of loaf you would like to make and measure your ingredients.

2. Add the ingredients to the bread pan in the order listed above (except the prunes).

3. Place the pan in the bread machine and close the lid.

4. Turn on the bread maker. Select the Basic/Fruit and Nut setting, then the loaf size, and finally the crust color. Start the cycle. (This recipe is not suitable for use with the Delay Timer.)

5. When the machine beeps, or between Knead 1 and Knead 2, add the prunes. If you like big chunks of prunes, press Pause at the beginning of Rise 1, remove the dough, pat it into a rectangle, and sprinkle with the prunes. Roll up the dough and gently knead it a few times to distribute the prunes. Return the dough ball to the machine and press Start to resume the rising.

6. When the cycle is finished and the bread is baked, carefully remove the pan from the machine. Use a potholder as the handle will be very hot. Let rest for a few minutes.

7. Remove the bread from the pan and allow to cool on a wire rack for at least 10 minutes before slicing.

Orange Bread

Ingredients:
- 8 slices (1 pound)
- 5/8 cup lukewarm milk
- 1/8 cup orange juice
- 1/8 cup sugar
- 3/4 tablespoon unsalted butter, melted
- 5/8 teaspoon table salt
- 2 cups white bread flour
- Zest of 1/2 orange
- 7/8 teaspoon bread machine yeast
- 12 slices (1 ½ pounds)
- 1 cup lukewarm milk
- 3 tablespoons orange juice
- 3 tablespoons sugar
- 1 tablespoon unsalted butter, melted
- 1 teaspoon table salt
- 3 cups white bread flour
- Zest of 1 orange
- 1¼ teaspoons bread machine yeast

- 16 slices (2 pounds)
- 1¼ cups lukewarm milk
- ¼ cup orange juice
- ¼ cup sugar
- 1½ tablespoons unsalted butter, melted
- 1¼ teaspoons table salt
- 4 cups white bread flour
- Zest of 1 orange
- 1¾ teaspoons bread machine yeast

Directions:
1. Choose the size of loaf you would like to make and measure your ingredients.

2. Add the ingredients to the bread pan in the order listed above.

3. Place the pan in the bread machine and close the lid.

4. Turn on the bread maker. Select the White/Basic setting, then the loaf size, and finally the crust color. Start the cycle.

5. When the cycle is finished and the bread is baked, carefully remove the pan from the machine. Use a potholder as the handle will be very hot. Let rest for a few minutes.

6. Remove the bread from the pan and allow to cool on a wire rack for at least 10 minutes before slicing.

Cinnamon Apple Bread

Ingredients:
- 8 slices (1 pound)
- 2/3 cup lukewarm milk
- 1 2/3 tablespoons butter, melted
- 1 1/3 tablespoons sugar
- 1 teaspoon table salt
- 2/3 teaspoon cinnamon, ground
- A pinch ground cloves
- 2 cups white bread flour
- 1 1/8 teaspoons bread machine yeast
- 2/3 cup peeled apple, finely diced
- 12 slices (1 ½ pounds)
- 1 cup lukewarm milk
- 2½ tablespoons butter, melted
- 2 tablespoons sugar
- 1½ teaspoons table salt
- 1 teaspoon cinnamon, ground

- A pinch ground cloves
- 3 cups white bread flour
- 2¼ teaspoons bread machine yeast
- 1 cup peeled apple, finely diced
- 16 slices (2 pounds)
- 1⅓ cups lukewarm milk
- 3⅓ tablespoons butter, melted
- 2⅔ tablespoons sugar
- 2 teaspoons table salt
- 1⅓ teaspoons cinnamon, ground
- A pinch ground cloves
- 4 cups white bread flour
- 2¼ teaspoons bread machine yeast
- 1⅓ cups peeled apple, finely diced

Directions:

1. Choose the size of loaf you would like to make and measure your ingredients.

2. Add the ingredients to the bread pan in the order listed above (except for the apples).

3. Place the pan in the bread machine and close the lid.

4. Turn on the bread maker. Select the Basic/Fruit and Nut setting, then the loaf size, and finally the crust color. Start the cycle.

5. When the machine signals to add ingredients, add the apples.

6. When the cycle is finished and the bread is baked, carefully remove the pan from the machine. Use a potholder as the handle will be very hot. Let rest for a few minutes.

7. Remove the bread from the pan and allow to cool on a wire rack for at least 10 minutes before slicing.

Spice Peach Bread

Ingredients:
- 8 slices (1 pound)
- 1/4 cup lukewarm heavy whipping cream
- 1/2 egg, beaten
- 3/4 tablespoon unsalted butter, melted
- 1 1/2 tablespoons sugar
- 3/4 teaspoon table salt
- 1/8 teaspoon nutmeg, ground
- 1/4 teaspoon cinnamon, ground
- 1 3/4 cups white bread flour
- 1/4 cup whole-wheat flour
- 3/4 teaspoon bread machine yeast
- 1/2 cup canned peaches, drained and chopped
- 12 slices (1 ½ pounds)
- ⅓ cup lukewarm heavy whipping cream
- 1 egg, beaten
- 1 tablespoon unsalted butter, melted
- 2¼ tablespoons sugar
- 1⅛ teaspoons table salt
- ⅛ teaspoon nutmeg, ground
- ⅓ teaspoon cinnamon, ground
- 2⅔ cups white bread flour
- ⅓ cup whole-wheat flour
- 1⅛ teaspoons bread machine yeast
- ¾ cup canned peaches, drained and chopped
- 16 slices (2 pounds)
- ½ cup lukewarm heavy whipping cream
- 1 egg, beaten
- 1½ tablespoons unsalted butter, melted
- 3 tablespoons sugar
- 1½ teaspoons table salt
- ¼ teaspoon nutmeg, ground
- ½ teaspoon cinnamon, ground
- 3½ cups white bread flour
- ½ cup whole-wheat flour
- 1½ teaspoons bread machine yeast
- 1 cup canned peaches, drained and chopped

Directions:

1. Choose the size of loaf you would like to make and measure your ingredients.

2. Add all of the ingredients except for the peach to the bread pan in the order listed above.

3. Place the pan in the bread machine and close the lid.

4. Turn on the bread maker. Select the White/Basic or Fruit/Nut (if your machine has this setting) setting, then the loaf size, and finally the crust color. Start the machine.

5. When the machine signals to add ingredients, add the peaches. (Some machines have a fruit/nut hopper where you can add the peaches when you start the machine. The machine will automatically add them to the dough during the baking process.)

6. When the cycle is finished and the bread is baked, carefully remove the pan from the machine. Use a potholder as the handle will be very hot. Let rest for a few minutes.

7. Remove the bread from the pan and allow to cool on a wire rack for at least 10 minutes before slicing.

Succulent Cranberry Cinnamon Bread

Ingredients:
* 8 slices (1 pound)
* 1¼ cup water
* 2 tablespoons soft butter
* 2½ tablespoons sugar
* 3½ cups bread flour
* 2¼ teaspoons dry yeast
* 1 cup dried cranberries
* 1½ teaspoons cinnamon
* 12 slices (1 ½ pounds)
* 1 7/8 cups water
* 3 tablespoons soft butter
* 3 3/4 tablespoons sugar
* 5 1/4 cups bread flour
* 3 3/8 teaspoons dry yeast
* 1 1/2 cups dried cranberries
* 2 1/4 teaspoons cinnamon
* 16 slices (2 pounds)
* 2 1/2 cups water
* 4 tablespoons soft butter
* 5 tablespoons sugar
* 7 cups bread flour
* 4 1/2 teaspoons dry yeast
* 2 cups dried cranberries
* 3 teaspoons cinnamon

Directions:
1. Choose the size of loaf you would like to make and measure your ingredients.
2. Add the ingredients to the bread pan in the order listed above (except cranberries).
3. Place the pan in the bread machine and close the lid.
4. Turn on the bread maker. Select the White/Basic setting, then the loaf size, and finally the crust color. Start the cycle.

Honey Banana Bread

Ingredients:
* 8 slices (1 pound)
* 1/3 cup lukewarm milk
* 2/3 cup banana, mashed
* 1/2 egg, beaten
* 1 tablespoon unsalted butter, melted
* 1/8 cup honey
* 2/3 teaspoon pure vanilla extract
* 1/3 teaspoon table salt
* 2/3 cup whole-wheat flour
* 5/6 cup white bread flour
* 1 teaspoon bread machine yeast
* 12 slices (1 ½ pounds)
* ½ cup lukewarm milk
* 1 cup banana, mashed
* 1 egg, beaten
* 1½ tablespoons unsalted butter, melted
* 3 tablespoons honey
* 1 teaspoon pure vanilla extract
* ½ teaspoon table salt
* 1 cup whole-wheat flour
* 1¼ cups white bread flour
* 1½ teaspoons bread machine yeast
* 16 slices (2 pounds)
* ⅔ cup lukewarm milk
* 1⅓ cups banana, mashed
* 1 egg, beaten
* 2 tablespoons unsalted butter, melted
* ¼ cup honey
* 1⅓ teaspoons pure vanilla extract
* ⅔ teaspoon table salt
* 1⅓ cups whole-wheat flour
* 1⅔ cups white bread flour
* 2 teaspoons bread machine yeast

Directions:

1. Choose the size of loaf you would like to make and measure your ingredients.

2. Add the ingredients to the bread pan in the order listed above.

3. Place the pan in the bread machine and close the lid.

4. Turn on the bread maker. Select the Sweet setting, then the loaf size, and finally the crust color. Start the cycle.

5. When the cycle is finished and the bread is baked, carefully remove the pan from the machine. Use a potholder as the handle will be very hot. Let rest for a few minutes.

6. Remove the bread from the pan and allow to cool on a wire rack for at least 10 minutes before slicing.

Banana Split Loaf

Servings: 12
Cooking Time: 1 Hour

Ingredients:
- 2 eggs
- 1/3 cup butter, melted
- 2 tablespoons whole milk
- 2 overripe bananas, mashed
- 2 cups all-purpose flour
- 2/3 cups sugar
- 1 1/4 teaspoons baking powder
- 1/2 teaspoon baking soda
- 1/2 teaspoon salt
- 1 cup chopped walnuts
- 1/2 cup chocolate chips

Directions:
1. Pour eggs, butter, milk and bananas into the bread maker pan and set aside.

2. Stir together all dry ingredients in a large mixing bowl.

3. Add dry ingredients to bread maker pan.

4. Set to Basic setting, medium crust color, and press Start.

5. Remove bread and place on a cooling rack before serving.

Nutrition:
- al Info Calories: 260, Sodium: 203 mg, Dietary Fiber: 1.6 g, Fat: 11.3 g, Carbs: 35.9 g, Protein: 5.2 g.

Strawberry Oat Bread

Ingredients:
- 8 slices (1 pound)
- 3/4 cup lukewarm milk
- 1/8 cup unsalted butter, melted
- 1/8 cup sugar
- 1 teaspoon table salt
- 3/4 cup quick oats
- 1 1/2 cups white bread flour
- 1 teaspoon bread machine yeast
- 1/2 cup strawberries, sliced
- 12 slices (1 ½ pounds)
- 1⅛ cups lukewarm milk
- 3 tablespoons unsalted butter, melted
- 3 tablespoons sugar
- 1½ teaspoons table salt
- 1 cup quick oats
- 2¼ cups white bread flour
- 1½ teaspoons bread machine yeast
- ¾ cup strawberries, sliced
- 16 slices (2 pounds)
- 1½ cups lukewarm milk
- ¼ cup unsalted butter, melted
- ¼ cup sugar
- 2 teaspoons table salt
- 1½ cups quick oats
- 3 cups white bread flour
- 2 teaspoons bread machine yeast
- 1 cup strawberries, sliced

Directions:
1. Choose the size of loaf you would like to make and measure your ingredients.

2. Add all of the ingredients except for the strawberries to the bread pan in the order listed above.

3. Place the pan in the bread machine and close the lid.

4. Turn on the bread maker. Select the White/Basic or Fruit/Nut (if your machine has this setting) setting, then the loaf size, and finally the crust color. Start the cycle.

5. When the machine signals to add ingredients, add the strawberries. (Some machines have a fruit/nut hopper where you can add the strawberries when you start the machine. The machine will automatically add them to the dough during the baking process.)

6. When the cycle is finished and the bread is baked, carefully remove the pan from the machine. Use a potholder as the handle will be very hot. Let rest for a few minutes.

7. Remove the bread from the pan and allow to cool on a wire rack for at least 10 minutes before slicing.

Cranberry Orange Pecan Bread

Servings: 16

Cooking Time: 2 Hours 50 Minutes

Ingredients:
* 1 cup water
* 1/4 cup orange juice
* 2 teaspoons salt
* 1/3 cup sugar
* 2 1/2 tablespoons nonfat dry milk
* 2 1/2 tablespoons butter, cubed
* 4 cups bread flour
* 2 1/2 teaspoons orange zest
* 2 1/2 teaspoons bread machine yeast
* 1/2 cup dried cranberries
* 1/2 cup pecans, chopped

Directions:
1. Set aside cranberries and pecans, then place all other ingredients in the bread maker pan in order listed.
2. Choose Sweet cycle, light crust and press Start.
3. Add cranberries and pecans at the end of the kneading cycle.
4. Transfer to a plate and let cool 10 minutes before slicing with a bread knife.

Nutrition:
* al Info Calories: 247 Sodium: 311 Dietary Fiber: 2.6 g, Fat: 11.5 g, Carbs: 31.5 g, Protein: 5.4 g.

Black Olive Bread

Ingredients:
* 8 slices (1 pound)
* 2/3 cup fat-free milk
* 1/6 cup olive oil
* 3/4 tablespoon honey
* 1 5/8 cups bread flour
* 3/8 cup rye flour
* 1/2 tablespoon plus 1 teaspoons gluten
* 3/8 teaspoon salt
* 1 1/4 teaspoons SAF yeast or 1/2 tablespoon bread machine yeast
* 5/8 full cup pitted black olive pieces
* 12 slices (1 ½ pounds)
* 11/8 cups fat-free milk
* 1/4 cup olive oil
* 1 tablespoon honey
* 21/2 cups bread flour
* 1/2 cup rye flour
* 1 tablespoon plus 1 teaspoon gluten
* 1/2 teaspoon salt
* 21/4 teaspoons SAF yeast or 23/4 teaspoons bread machine yeast
* 1 full cup pitted black olive pieces
* 16 slices (2 pounds)
* 11/3 cups fat-free milk
* 1/3 cup olive oil
* 11/2 tablespoons honey
* 31/4 cups bread flour
* 3/4 cup rye flour
* 1 tablespoon plus 2 teaspoons gluten
* 3/4 teaspoon salt
* 21/2 teaspoons SAF yeast or 1 tablespoon bread machine yeast
* 11/4 full cups pitted black olive pieces

Directions:
1. Choose the size of loaf you would like to make and measure your ingredients.
2. Add the ingredients to the bread pan in the order listed above (except the olives).
3. Place the pan in the bread machine and close the lid.
4. Turn on the bread maker. Select the French setting, then the loaf size, and finally the crust color. Start the cycle. (This recipe is not suitable for use with the Delay Timer.)
5. Halfway through Knead 2, open the machine and add the olives. If you like big chunks of olives, press Pause at the beginning of Rise 1 instead, remove the dough, pat it into a rectangle, and sprinkle with the olives. Roll up the dough and gently knead a few times to distribute the olives. Return the dough ball to the machine and press Start to resume the rising.

6. When the cycle is finished and the bread is baked, carefully remove the pan from the machine. Use a potholder as the handle will be very hot. Let rest for a few minutes.

7. Remove the bread from the pan and allow to cool on a wire rack for at least 10 minutes before slicing.

Tomato Bread

Ingredients:

- 8 slices (1 pound)
- 3/4 cup water
- 1/8 cup tomato paste
- 1/4 cup chopped oil-packed sun-dried tomatoes, with their oil
- 1 5/6 cups bread flour
- 1/3 cup whole wheat flour
- 1 tablespoon gluten
- 1 teaspoon salt
- 1 1/8 teaspoons SAF yeast or 1 3/8 teaspoons bread machine yeast
- 12 slices (1 ½ pounds)
- 11/4 cups water
- 3 tablespoons tomato paste
- 1/3 cup chopped oil-packed sun-dried tomatoes, with their oil
- 23/4 cups bread flour
- 1/2 cup whole wheat flour
- 11/2 tablespoons gluten
- 11/2 teaspoons salt
- 2 teaspoons SAF yeast or 21/2 teaspoons bread machine yeast
- 16 slices (2 pounds)
- 11/2 cups water
- 1/4 cup tomato paste
- 1/2 cup chopped oil-packed sun-dried tomatoes, with their oil
- 32/3 cups bread flour
- 2/3 cup whole wheat flour
- 2 tablespoons gluten
- 2 teaspoons salt
- 21/4 teaspoons SAF yeast or 23/4 teaspoons bread machine yeast

Directions:

1. Choose the size of loaf you would like to make and measure your ingredients.

2. Add the ingredients to the bread pan in the order listed above.

3. Place the pan in the bread machine and close the lid.

4. Turn on the bread maker. Select the Basic setting, then the loaf size, and finally the crust color. Start the cycle.

5. When the cycle is finished and the bread is baked, carefully remove the pan from the machine. Use a potholder as the handle will be very hot. Let rest for a few minutes.

6. Remove the bread from the pan and allow to cool on a wire rack for at least 10 minutes before slicing.

Raisin Candied Fruit Bread

Ingredients:

- 8 slices (1 pound)
- 1/2 egg, beaten
- 3/4 cup + 1/2 tablespoon lukewarm water
- 1/3 teaspoon ground cardamom
- 5/8 teaspoon table salt
- 1 tablespoon sugar
- 1/6 cup butter, melted
- 2 cups bread flour
- 5/8 teaspoon bread machine yeast
- 1/4 cup raisins
- 1/4 cup mixed candied fruit
- 12 slices (1 ½ pounds)
- 1 egg, beaten
- 1⅛ cup lukewarm water
- ½ teaspoon ground cardamom
- 1 teaspoon table salt
- 1½ tablespoons sugar
- ¼ cup butter, melted
- 3 cups bread flour
- 1 teaspoon bread machine yeast
- ⅓ cup raisins
- ⅓ cup mixed candied fruit
- 16 slices (2 pounds)
- 1 egg, beaten
- 1½ cups + 1 tablespoon lukewarm water
- ⅔ teaspoon ground cardamom

- 1¼ teaspoons table salt
- 2 tablespoons sugar
- ⅓ cup butter, melted
- 4 cups bread flour
- 1¼ teaspoons bread machine yeast
- ½ cup raisins
- ½ cup mixed candied fruit

Directions:

1. Choose the size of loaf you would like to make and measure your ingredients.

2. Add all of the ingredients except for the candied fruits and raisins to the bread pan in the order listed above.

3. Place the pan in the bread machine and close the lid.

4. Turn on the bread maker. Select the White/Basic or Fruit/Nut (if your machine has this setting) setting, then the loaf size, and finally the crust color. Start the cycle.

5. When the machine signals to add ingredients, add the candied fruits and raisins. (Some machines have a fruit/nut hopper where you can add the fruits and raisins when you start the machine. The machine will automatically add them to the dough during the baking process.)

6. When the cycle is finished and the bread is baked, carefully remove the pan from the machine. Use a potholder as the handle will be very hot. Let rest for a few minutes.

7. Remove the bread from the pan and allow to cool on a wire rack for at least 10 minutes before slicing.

Cappuccino Orange Bread

Ingredients:
- 8 slices (1 pound)
- 1 cup water
- 1 tablespoon instant coffee granules
- 2 tablespoons butter, soften
- 1 teaspoon orange peel, grated
- 3 cups bread flour
- 2 tablespoons dry milk
- ¼ cup sugar
- 1¼ teaspoons salt
- 2¼ teaspoons bread machine yeast
- 12 slices (1 ½ pounds)

- 1 1/2 cups water
- 1 1/2 tablespoons instant coffee granules
- 3 tablespoons butter, soften
- 1 1/2 teaspoons orange peel, grated
- 4 1/2 cups bread flour
- 3 tablespoons dry milk
- 3/8 cup sugar
- 1 7/8 teaspoons salt
- 3 3/8 teaspoons bread machine yeast
- 16 slices (2 pounds)
- 2 cups water
- 2 tablespoons instant coffee granules
- 4 tablespoons butter, soften
- 2 teaspoons orange peel, grated
- 6 cups bread flour
- 4 tablespoons dry milk
- 1/2 cup sugar
- 2 1/2 teaspoons salt
- 4 1/2 teaspoons bread machine yeast

Directions:

1. Choose the size of loaf you would like to make and measure your ingredients.

2. Add the ingredients to the bread pan in the order listed above.

3. Place the pan in the bread machine and close the lid.

4. Turn on the bread maker. Select the White/Basic setting, then the loaf size, and finally the crust color. Start the cycle.

5. When the cycle is finished and the bread is baked, carefully remove the pan from the machine. Use a potholder as the handle will be very hot. Let rest for a few minutes.

6. Remove the bread from the pan and allow to cool on a wire rack for at least 10 minutes before slicing.

Cranberry Honey Bread

Ingredients:
- 8 slices (1 pound)
- 5/8 cup + 1/2 tablespoon lukewarm water
- 1/8 cup unsalted butter, melted
- 1 1/2 tablespoons honey or molasses
- 2 cups white bread flour
- 1/4 cup cornmeal

- 1 teaspoon table salt
- 1 1/4 teaspoons bread machine yeast
- 3/8 cup cranberries, dried
- 12 slices (1 ½ pounds)
- 1 cup + 1 tablespoon lukewarm water
- 2 tablespoons unsalted butter, melted
- 3 tablespoons honey or molasses
- 3 cups white bread flour
- ⅓ cup cornmeal
- 1½ teaspoons table salt
- 2 teaspoons bread machine yeast
- ½ cup cranberries, dried
- 16 slices (2 pounds)
- 1¼ cups + 1 tablespoon lukewarm water
- ¼ cup unsalted butter, melted
- 3 tablespoons honey or molasses
- 4 cups white bread flour
- ½ cup cornmeal
- 2 teaspoons table salt
- 2½ teaspoons bread machine yeast
- ¾ cup cranberries, dried

Directions:

1. Choose the size of loaf you would like to make and measure your ingredients.

2. Add all of the ingredients except for the dried cranberries to the bread pan in the order listed above.

3. Place the pan in the bread machine and close the lid.

4. Turn on the bread maker. Select the White/Basic or Fruit/Nut (if your machine has this setting) setting, then the loaf size, and finally the crust color. Start the cycle.

5. When the machine signals to add ingredients, add the dried cranberries. (Some machines have a fruit/nut hopper where you can add the dried cranberries when you start the machine. The machine will automatically add them to the dough during the baking process.)

6. When the cycle is finished and the bread is baked, carefully remove the pan from the machine. Use a potholder as the handle will be very hot. Let rest for a few minutes.

7. Remove the bread from the pan and allow to cool on a wire rack for at least 10 minutes before slicing.

Dried Cranberry Tea Bread

Ingredients:

- 8 slices (1 pound)
- 11/2 cups dried cranberries
- Boiling water
- 2 large eggs
- 2 teaspoons almond extract
- 1 teaspoon vanilla extract
- 1/4 cup canola or vegetable oil
- 3/4 cup frozen unsweetened apple juice concentrate, thawed
- 1 cup sugar
- 11/4 cups unbleached all-purpose flour
- 1 cup whole wheat pastry flour
- 1 tablespoon baking powder
- 1/2 teaspoon baking soda
- 1 teaspoon ground cinnamon
- 1/2 teaspoon fresh-ground nutmeg
- 1/2 teaspoon salt
- 12 slices (1 ½ pounds)
- 2 1/4 cups dried cranberries
- Boiling water
- 3 large eggs
- 3 teaspoons almond extract
- 1 1/2 teaspoons vanilla extract
- 3/8 cup canola or vegetable oil
- 1 1/8 cups frozen unsweetened apple juice concentrate, thawed
- 1 1/2 cups sugar
- 1 7/8 cups unbleached all-purpose flour
- 1 1/2 cups whole wheat pastry flour
- 1 1/2 tablespoons baking powder
- 3/4 teaspoon baking soda
- 1 1/2 teaspoons ground cinnamon
- 3/4 teaspoon fresh-ground nutmeg
- 3/4 teaspoon salt
- 16 slices (2 pounds)
- 3 cups dried cranberries
- Boiling water
- 4 large eggs
- 4 teaspoons almond extract
- 2 teaspoons vanilla extract
- 1/2 cup canola or vegetable oil
- 1 1/2 cups frozen unsweetened apple juice concentrate, thawed
- 2 cups sugar

- 2 1/2 cups unbleached all-purpose flour
- 2 cups whole wheat pastry flour
- 2 tablespoons baking powder
- 1 teaspoon baking soda
- 2 teaspoons ground cinnamon
- 1 teaspoon fresh-ground nutmeg
- 1 teaspoon salt

Directions:

1. Choose the size of loaf you would like to make and measure your ingredients.

2. Cover the cranberries with boiling water in a small bowl, and let stand for 20 minutes to soften. Drain and pat dry with paper towels. Set aside.

3. Add the ingredients to the bread pan in the order listed above. Adding the cranberries with the dry ingredients.

4. Place the pan in the bread machine and close the lid.

5. Turn on the bread maker. Select the Quick Bread/Cake setting, then the loaf size, and finally the crust color. Start the cycle.

6. When the cycle is finished and the bread is baked, carefully remove the pan from the machine. Use a potholder as the handle will be very hot. Let rest for a few minutes.

7. Remove the bread from the pan and allow to cool on a wire rack for at least 10 minutes before slicing.

Wild Rice Cranberry Delight

Ingredients:

- 8 slices (1 pound)
- 1¼ cups water
- ¼ cup skim milk powder
- 1¼ teaspoon salt
- 2 tablespoons liquid honey
- 1 tablespoon extra-virgin olive oil
- 3 cups all-purpose flour
- ¾ cup cooked wild rice
- ¼ cup pine nuts
- ¾ teaspoon celery seeds
- 1 teaspoon bread machine yeast
- 2/3 cup dried cranberries
- 1/8 teaspoon black pepper, ground

- 12 slices (1 ½ pounds)
- 1 7/8 cups water
- 3/8 cup skim milk powder
- 1 7/8 teaspoons salt
- 3 tablespoons liquid honey
- 1 1/2 tablespoons extra-virgin olive oil
- 4 1/2 cups all-purpose flour
- 1 1/8 cups cooked wild rice
- 3/8 cup pine nuts
- 1 1/8 teaspoons celery seeds
- 1 1/2 teaspoons bread machine yeast
- 1 cup dried cranberries
- 3/16 teaspoon black pepper, ground
- 16 slices (2 pounds)
- 2 1/2 cups water
- 1/2 cup skim milk powder
- 2 1/2 teaspoons salt
- 4 tablespoons liquid honey
- 2 tablespoon extra-virgin olive oil
- 6 cups all-purpose flour
- 1 1/2 cups cooked wild rice
- 1/2 cup pine nuts
- 1 1/2 teaspoons celery seeds
- 2 teaspoons bread machine yeast
- 1 1/3 cups dried cranberries
- 1/4 teaspoon black pepper, ground

Directions:

1. Choose the size of loaf you would like to make and measure your ingredients.

2. Add the ingredients to the bread pan in the order listed above (except cranberries).

3. Place the pan in the bread machine and close the lid.

4. Turn on the bread maker. Select the White/Basic setting, then the loaf size, and finally the crust color. Start the cycle.

5. Once the machine beeps, add cranberries.

6. When the cycle is finished and the bread is baked, carefully remove the pan from the machine. Use a potholder as the handle will be very hot. Let rest for a few minutes.

7. Remove the bread from the pan and allow to cool on a wire rack for at least 10 minutes before slicing.

HERB AND SPICE BREAD RECIPES

Basil Cheese Bread

Ingredients:

- 8 slices (1 pound)
- 2/3 cup lukewarm milk
- 2 teaspoons unsalted butter, melted
- 2 teaspoons sugar
- 5/8 teaspoon dried basil
- 1/2 teaspoon table salt
- 1/2 cup sharp Cheddar cheese, shredded
- 2 cups white bread flour
- 1 teaspoon bread machine yeast
- 12 slices (1 ½ pounds)
- 1 cup lukewarm milk
- 1 tablespoon unsalted butter, melted
- 1 tablespoon sugar
- 1 teaspoon dried basil
- ¾ teaspoon table salt
- ¾ cup sharp Cheddar cheese, shredded
- 3 cups white bread flour
- 1½ teaspoons bread machine yeast
- 16 slices (2 pounds)
- 1⅓ cups lukewarm milk
- 4 teaspoons unsalted butter, melted
- 4 teaspoons sugar
- 1¼ teaspoons dried basil
- 1 teaspoon table salt
- 1 cup sharp Cheddar cheese, shredded
- 4 cups white bread flour
- 2 teaspoons bread machine yeast

Directions:

1. Choose the size of loaf you would like to make and measure your ingredients.
2. Add the ingredients to the bread pan in the order listed above.
3. Place the pan in the bread machine and close the lid.
4. Turn on the bread maker. Select the White/Basic setting, then the loaf size, and finally the crust color. Start the cycle.
5. When the cycle is finished and the bread is baked, carefully remove the pan from the machine. Use a potholder as the handle will be very hot. Let rest for a few minutes.
6. Remove the bread from the pan and allow to cool on a wire rack for at least 10 minutes before slicing.

Energizing Anise Lemon Bread

Ingredients:

- 8 slices (1 pound)
- ⅔ cup water at 80 degrees F
- 1 whole egg, at room temperature
- 2⅔ tablespoons butter, melted and cooled
- 2⅔ tablespoons honey
- ⅓ teaspoon salt
- ⅔ teaspoon anise seed
- ⅔ teaspoon lemon zest
- 2 cups white bread flour
- 1⅓ teaspoons instant yeast
- 12 slices (1 ½ pounds)
- 1 cup water at 80 degrees F
- 1 1/2 whole eggs, at room temperature
- 4 tablespoons butter, melted and cooled
- 4 tablespoons honey
- 1/2 teaspoon salt
- 1 teaspoon anise seed
- 1 teaspoon lemon zest
- 3 cups white bread flour
- 2 teaspoons instant yeast
- 16 slices (2 pounds)
- 1 1/3 cups water at 80 degrees F
- 2 whole eggs, at room temperature
- 5 1/3 tablespoons butter, melted and cooled
- 5 1/3 tablespoons honey
- 2/3 teaspoon salt
- 1 1/3 teaspoons anise seed
- 1 1/3 teaspoons lemon zest
- 4 cups white bread flour
- 2/3 teaspoon instant yeast

Directions:

1. Choose the size of loaf you would like to make and measure your ingredients.

2. Add the ingredients to the bread pan in the order listed above.

3. Place the pan in the bread machine and close the lid.

4. Turn on the bread maker. Select the White/Basic setting, then the loaf size, and finally the crust color. Start the cycle.

5. When the cycle is finished and the bread is baked, carefully remove the pan from the machine. Use a potholder as the handle will be very hot. Let rest for a few minutes.

6. Remove the bread from the pan and allow to cool on a wire rack for at least 10 minutes before slicing.

Whole Wheat Basil Bread

Ingredients:

- 8 slices (1 pound)
- 1/2 cup buttermilk
- 1/4 cup water
- 1 1/2 tablespoons butter, cut into pieces
- 1 1/2 tablespoons honey
- 2 cups white whole wheat flour
- 1/6 cup chopped fresh basil
- 1/6 cup pine nuts, chopped
- 2/3 tablespoon gluten
- 1 teaspoon salt
- 1 1/4 teaspoons SAF yeast or 1/2 tablespoon bread machine yeast
- 12 slices (1½ pounds)
- 3/4 cup buttermilk
- 1/3 cup water
- 2 tablespoons butter, cut into pieces
- 2 tablespoons honey
- 3 cups white whole wheat flour
- 1/4 cup chopped fresh basil
- 1/4 cup pine nuts, chopped
- 1 tablespoon gluten
- 11/2 teaspoons salt
- 2 teaspoons SAF yeast or 21/2 teaspoons bread machine yeast
- 16 slices (2 pounds)
- 1 cup buttermilk
- 1/2 cup water
- 3 tablespoons butter, cut into pieces

- 3 tablespoons honey
- 4 cups white whole wheat flour
- 1/3 cup chopped fresh basil
- 1/3 cup pine nuts, chopped
- 1 tablespoon plus 1 teaspoon gluten
- 2 teaspoons salt
- 21/2 teaspoons SAF yeast or 1 tablespoon bread machine yeast

Directions:

1. Choose the size of loaf you would like to make and measure your ingredients.

2. Add the ingredients to the bread pan in the order listed above.

3. Place the pan in the bread machine and close the lid.

4. Turn on the bread maker. Select the Basic setting, then the loaf size, and finally the crust color. Start the cycle.

5. When the cycle is finished and the bread is baked, carefully remove the pan from the machine. Use a potholder as the handle will be very hot. Let rest for a few minutes.

6. Remove the bread from the pan and allow to cool on a wire rack for at least 10 minutes before slicing.

Parsley Garlic Bread

Ingredients:

- 8 slices (1 pound)
- 2/3 cup lukewarm milk
- 1 tablespoon unsalted butter, melted
- 2 teaspoons sugar
- 1 teaspoon table salt
- 1 1/3 teaspoons garlic powder
- 1 1/3 teaspoons fresh parsley, chopped
- 2 cups white bread flour
- 1 1/8 teaspoons bread machine yeast
- 12 slices (1 ½ pounds)
- 1 cup lukewarm milk
- 1½ tablespoons unsalted butter, melted
- 1 tablespoon sugar
- 1½ teaspoons table salt
- 2 teaspoons garlic powder
- 2 teaspoons fresh parsley, chopped
- 3 cups white bread flour

- 1¾ teaspoons bread machine yeast
- 16 slices (2 pounds)
- 1⅓ cups lukewarm milk
- 2 tablespoons unsalted butter, melted
- 4 teaspoons sugar
- 2 teaspoons table salt
- 2⅔ teaspoons garlic powder
- 2⅔ teaspoons fresh parsley, chopped
- 4 cups white bread flour
- 2¼ teaspoons bread machine yeast

Directions:

1. Choose the size of loaf you would like to make and measure your ingredients.

2. Add the ingredients to the bread pan in the order listed above.

3. Place the pan in the bread machine and close the lid.

4. Turn on the bread maker. Select the White/Basic setting, then the loaf size, and finally the crust color. Start the cycle.

5. When the cycle is finished and the bread is baked, carefully remove the pan from the machine. Use a potholder as the handle will be very hot. Let rest for a few minutes.

6. Remove the bread from the pan and allow to cool on a wire rack for at least 10 minutes before slicing.

Lemon Flavored Poppy Loaf

Ingredients:
- 8 slices (1 pound)
- 1 and 1/3 cups hot water
- 3 tablespoons powdered milk
- 2 tablespoons Crisco shortening
- 2 tablespoons sugar
- 1½ teaspoon salt
- 1 tablespoon lemon juice
- 4¼ cups bread flour
- ½ teaspoon nutmeg
- 2 teaspoons grated lemon rind
- 2 tablespoons poppy seeds
- 1¼ teaspoon bread machine yeast
- 2 teaspoons wheat gluten
- 12 slices (1 ½ pounds)
- 1 1/2 and 1/2 cups hot water

- 4 1/2 tablespoons powdered milk
- 3 tablespoons Crisco shortening
- 3 tablespoons sugar
- 2 1/4 teaspoons salt
- 1 1/2 tablespoons lemon juice
- 6 3/8 cups bread flour
- 3/4 teaspoon nutmeg
- 3 teaspoons grated lemon rind
- 3 tablespoons poppy seeds
- 1 7/8 teaspoons bread machine yeast
- 3 teaspoons wheat gluten
- 16 slices (2 pounds)
- 2 and 2/3 cups hot water
- 6 tablespoons powdered milk
- 4 tablespoons Crisco shortening
- 4 tablespoons sugar
- 3 teaspoons salt
- 2 tablespoons lemon juice
- 8 1/2 cups bread flour
- 1 teaspoon nutmeg
- 4 teaspoons grated lemon rind
- 4 tablespoons poppy seeds
- 8 1/2 teaspoons bread machine yeast
- 4 teaspoons wheat gluten

Directions:

1. Choose the size of loaf you would like to make and measure your ingredients.

2. Add the ingredients to the bread pan in the order listed above.

3. Place the pan in the bread machine and close the lid.

4. Turn on the bread maker. Select the White/Basic setting, then the loaf size, and finally the crust color. Start the cycle.

5. When the cycle is finished and the bread is baked, carefully remove the pan from the machine. Use a potholder as the handle will be very hot. Let rest for a few minutes.

6. Remove the bread from the pan and allow to cool on a wire rack for at least 10 minutes before slicing.

Awesome Rosemary Bread

Ingredients:
- 8 slices (1 pound)
- ¾ cup + 1 tablespoon water at 80 degrees F
- 1⅔ tablespoons melted butter, cooled
- 2 teaspoons sugar
- 1 teaspoon salt
- 1 tablespoon fresh rosemary, chopped
- 2 cups white bread flour
- 1⅓ teaspoons instant yeast
- 12 slices (1 ½ pounds)
- 1 1/8 cups + 1 1/2 tablespoons water at 80 degrees F
- 4 1/6 tablespoons melted butter, cooled
- 3 teaspoons sugar
- 1 1/2 teaspoons salt
- 1 1/2 tablespoons fresh rosemary, chopped
- 3 cups white bread flour
- 2 teaspoons instant yeast
- 16 slices (2 pounds)
- 1 1/2 cups + 2 tablespoons water at 80 degrees F
- 3 1/3 tablespoons melted butter, cooled
- 4 teaspoons sugar
- 2 teaspoons salt
- 2 tablespoons fresh rosemary, chopped
- 4 cups white bread flour
- 2 2/3 teaspoons instant yeast

Directions:

1. Choose the size of loaf you would like to make and measure your ingredients.

2. Add the ingredients to the bread pan in the order listed above.

3. Place the pan in the bread machine and close the lid.

4. Turn on the bread maker. Select the White/Basic setting, then the loaf size, and finally the crust color. Start the cycle.

5. When the cycle is finished and the bread is baked, carefully remove the pan from the machine. Use a potholder as the handle will be very hot. Let rest for a few minutes.

6. Remove the bread from the pan and allow to cool on a wire rack for at least 10 minutes before slicing.

Crunchy Wheat Herbed Bread

Ingredients:
- 8 slices (1 pound)
- 1¼ cups water
- 1½ cups bread flour
- 1½ cups whole wheat flour
- 2 tablespoons sugar
- 2 tablespoons dry milk
- 2 tablespoons butter
- 1½ teaspoons salt
- 1½ teaspoons dried basil leaves
- 1 teaspoon dried thyme leaves
- 2 teaspoons bread machine yeast
- ½ cup dry roasted sunflower seeds
- 12 slices (1 ½ pounds)
- 1 7/8 cups water
- 2 1/4 cups bread flour
- 2 1/4 cups whole wheat flour
- 3 tablespoons sugar
- 3 tablespoons dry milk
- 3 tablespoons butter
- 2 1/4 teaspoons salt
- 2 1/4 teaspoons dried basil leaves
- 1 1/2 teaspoons dried thyme leaves
- 3 teaspoons bread machine yeast
- 3/4 cup dry roasted sunflower seeds
- 16 slices (2 pounds)
- 2 1/2 cups water
- 3 cups bread flour
- 3 cups whole wheat flour
- 4 tablespoons sugar
- 4 tablespoons dry milk
- 4 tablespoons butter
- 3 teaspoons salt
- 3 teaspoons dried basil leaves
- 2 teaspoons dried thyme leaves
- 4 teaspoons bread machine yeast
- 1 cup dry roasted sunflower seeds

Directions:

1. Choose the size of loaf you would like to make and measure your ingredients.

2. Add the ingredients to the bread pan in the order listed above (except seeds).

3. Place the pan in the bread machine and close the lid.

4. Turn on the bread maker. Select the White/Basic setting, then the loaf size, and finally the crust color. Start the cycle.

5. Add seeds once the machine beeps.

6. When the cycle is finished and the bread is baked, carefully remove the pan from the machine. Use a potholder as the handle will be very hot. Let rest for a few minutes.

7. Remove the bread from the pan and allow to cool on a wire rack for at least 10 minutes before slicing.

Inspiring Cinnamon Bread

Ingredients:

- 8 slices (1 pound)
- ⅔ cup milk at 80 degrees F
- 1 whole egg, beaten
- 3 tablespoons melted butter, cooled
- ⅓ cup sugar
- ⅓ teaspoon salt
- 1 teaspoon ground cinnamon
- 2 cups white bread flour
- 1⅓ teaspoons active dry yeast
- 12 slices (1 ½ pounds)
- 1 cup milk at 80 degrees F
- 1 1/2 whole eggs, beaten
- 4 1/2 tablespoons melted butter, cooled
- 1/2 cup sugar
- 1/2 teaspoon salt
- 1 1/2 teaspoons ground cinnamon
- 3 cups white bread flour
- 2 teaspoons active dry yeast
- 16 slices (2 pounds)
- 1 1/3 cups milk at 80 degrees F
- 2 whole eggs, beaten
- 6 tablespoons melted butter, cooled
- 2/3 cup sugar
- 2/3 teaspoon salt
- 2 teaspoons ground cinnamon
- 4 cups white bread flour
- 2 2/3 teaspoons active dry yeast

Directions:

1. Choose the size of loaf you would like to make and measure your ingredients.

2. Add the ingredients to the bread pan in the order listed above.

3. Place the pan in the bread machine and close the lid.

4. Turn on the bread maker. Select the White/Basic setting, then the loaf size, and finally the crust color. Start the cycle.

5. When the cycle is finished and the bread is baked, carefully remove the pan from the machine. Use a potholder as the handle will be very hot. Let rest for a few minutes.

6. Remove the bread from the pan and allow to cool on a wire rack for at least 10 minutes before slicing.

Anise Honey Bread

Ingredients:

- 8 slices (1 pound)
- 1/2 cup + 1/2 tablespoon lukewarm water
- 1/2 egg, at room temperature
- 1/6 cup butter, melted and cooled
- 1/6 cup honey
- 1/3 teaspoon table salt
- 2 cups white bread flour
- 2/3 teaspoon anise seed
- 2/3 teaspoon lemon zest
- 1 1/4 teaspoons bread machine yeast
- 12 slices (1 ½ pounds)
- ¾ cup lukewarm water
- 1 egg, at room temperature
- ¼ cup butter, melted and cooled
- ¼ cup honey
- ½ teaspoon table salt
- 3 cups white bread flour
- 1 teaspoon anise seed
- 1 teaspoon lemon zest
- 2 teaspoons bread machine yeast
- 16 slices (2 pounds)
- 1 cup + 1 tablespoon lukewarm water
- 1 egg, at room temperature
- ⅓ cup butter, melted and cooled
- ⅓ cup honey
- ⅔ teaspoon table salt

- 4 cups white bread flour
- 1⅓ teaspoons anise seed
- 1⅓ teaspoons lemon zest
- 2½ teaspoons bread machine yeast

Directions:

1. Choose the size of loaf you would like to make and measure your ingredients.
2. Add the ingredients to the bread pan in the order listed above.
3. Place the pan in the bread machine and close the lid.
4. Turn on the bread maker. Select the White/Basic setting, then the loaf size, and finally the crust color. Start the cycle.
5. When the cycle is finished and the bread is baked, carefully remove the pan from the machine. Use a potholder as the handle will be very hot. Let rest for a few minutes.
6. Remove the bread from the pan and allow to cool on a wire rack for at least 10 minutes before slicing.

Apple Pie Bread

Ingredients:

- 8 slices (1 pound)
- 1½ teaspoons active dry yeast
- 1½ teaspoons ground cinnamon
- 3¼ cups bread flour
- 1½ teaspoons salt
- 3 tablespoons powdered buttermilk
- 1¼ cups apple pie filling
- 1½ tablespoons butter, soft
- ½ cup water
- 12 slices (1 ½ pounds)
- 2 1/4 teaspoons active dry yeast
- 2 1/4 teaspoons ground cinnamon
- 4 7/8 cups bread flour
- 2 1/4 teaspoons salt
- 4 1/2 tablespoons powdered buttermilk
- 1 7/8 cups apple pie filling
- 2 1/4 tablespoons butter, soft
- 3/4 cup water
- 16 slices (2 pounds)
- 3 teaspoons active dry yeast
- 3 teaspoons ground cinnamon

- 6 1/2 cups bread flour
- 3 teaspoons salt
- 6 tablespoons powdered buttermilk
- 2 1/2 cups apple pie filling
- 3 tablespoons butter, soft
- 1 cup water

Directions:

1. Choose the size of loaf you would like to make and measure your ingredients.
2. Add the ingredients to the bread pan in the order listed above.
3. Place the pan in the bread machine and close the lid.
4. Turn on the bread maker. Select the White/Basic setting, then the loaf size, and finally the crust color. Start the cycle.
5. When the cycle is finished and the bread is baked, carefully remove the pan from the machine. Use a potholder as the handle will be very hot. Let rest for a few minutes.
6. Remove the bread from the pan and allow to cool on a wire rack for at least 10 minutes before slicing.

Lovely Aromatic Lavender Bread

Ingredients:

- 8 slices (1 pound)
- ¾ cup milk at 80 degrees F
- 1 tablespoon melted butter, cooled
- 1 tablespoon sugar
- ¾ teaspoon salt
- 1 teaspoon fresh lavender flower, chopped
- ¼ teaspoon lemon zest
- ¼ teaspoon fresh thyme, chopped
- 2 cups white bread flour
- ¾ teaspoon instant yeast
- 12 slices (1 ½ pounds)
- 1 1/8 cups milk at 80 degrees F
- 1 1/2 tablespoons melted butter, cooled
- 1 1/2 tablespoons sugar
- 1 1/8 teaspoons salt
- 1 1/2 teaspoons fresh lavender flower, chopped
- 3/8 teaspoon lemon zest
- 3/8 teaspoon fresh thyme, chopped
- 3 cups white bread flour

- 1 1/8 teaspoons instant yeast
- 16 slices (2 pounds)
- 1 1/2 cups milk at 80 degrees F
- 2 tablespoons melted butter, cooled
- 2 tablespoons sugar
- 1 1/2 teaspoons salt
- 2 teaspoons fresh lavender flower, chopped
- 1/2 teaspoon lemon zest
- 1/2 teaspoon fresh thyme, chopped
- 4 cups white bread flour
- 1 1/2 teaspoons instant yeast

Directions:

1. Choose the size of loaf you would like to make and measure your ingredients.

2. Add the ingredients to the bread pan in the order listed above.

3. Place the pan in the bread machine and close the lid.

4. Turn on the bread maker. Select the White/Basic setting, then the loaf size, and finally the crust color. Start the cycle.

5. When the cycle is finished and the bread is baked, carefully remove the pan from the machine. Use a potholder as the handle will be very hot. Let rest for a few minutes.

6. Remove the bread from the pan and allow to cool on a wire rack for at least 10 minutes before slicing.

Herb Garlic Cream Cheese Bread

Ingredients:
- 8 slices (1 pound)
- 1/3 cup water, at room temperature
- 1/3 cup herb and garlic cream cheese mixture
- 1 whole egg
- 4 teaspoons melted butter, cooled
- 1 tablespoon sugar
- 2/3 teaspoon salt
- 2 cups white bread flour
- 1 teaspoon bread machine yeast
- 12 slices (1 ½ pounds)
- 1/2 cup water, at room temperature
- 1/2 cup herb and garlic cream cheese mixture
- 1 1/2 whole eggs
- 6 teaspoons melted butter, cooled

- 1 1/2 tablespoons sugar
- 1 teaspoon salt
- 3 cups white bread flour
- 1 1/2 teaspoons bread machine yeast
- 16 slices (2 pounds)
- 2/3 cup water, at room temperature
- 2/3 cup herb and garlic cream cheese mixture
- 2 whole eggs
- 8 teaspoons melted butter, cooled
- 2 tablespoons sugar
- 1 1/3 teaspoons salt
- 4 cups white bread flour
- 2 teaspoons bread machine yeast

Directions:

1. Choose the size of loaf you would like to make and measure your ingredients.

2. Add the ingredients to the bread pan in the order listed above.

3. Place the pan in the bread machine and close the lid.

4. Turn on the bread maker. Select the White/Basic setting, then the loaf size, and finally the crust color. Start the cycle.

5. When the cycle is finished and the bread is baked, carefully remove the pan from the machine. Use a potholder as the handle will be very hot. Let rest for a few minutes.

6. Remove the bread from the pan and allow to cool on a wire rack for at least 10 minutes before slicing.

Ricotta & Chive Loaf

Ingredients:
- 8 slices (1 pound)
- 1 cup lukewarm water
- 1/3 cup whole ricotta cheese
- 1½ teaspoons salt
- 1 tablespoon granulated sugar
- 3 cups bread flour
- ½ cup chopped chives
- 2½ teaspoons instant yeast
- 12 slices (1 ½ pounds)
- 1 1/2 cups lukewarm water
- 1/2 cup whole ricotta cheese
- 2 1/4 teaspoons salt

- 1 1/2 tablespoons granulated sugar
- 4 1/2 cups bread flour
- 3/4 cup chopped chives
- 3 3/4 teaspoons instant yeast
- 16 slices (2 pounds)
- 2 cups lukewarm water
- 2/3 cup whole ricotta cheese
- 3 teaspoons salt
- 2 tablespoons granulated sugar
- 6 cups bread flour
- 1 cup chopped chives
- 5 teaspoons instant yeast

Directions:

1. Choose the size of loaf you would like to make and measure your ingredients.

2. Add the ingredients to the bread pan in the order listed above (except dried fruits).

3. Place the pan in the bread machine and close the lid.

4. Turn on the bread maker. Select the White/Basic setting, then the loaf size, and finally the crust color. Start the cycle.

5. Once the machine beeps, add fruits.

6. When the cycle is finished and the bread is baked, carefully remove the pan from the machine. Use a potholder as the handle will be very hot. Let rest for a few minutes.

7. Remove the bread from the pan and allow to cool on a wire rack for at least 10 minutes before slicing.

Herb Bread

Ingredients:

- 8 slices (1 pounds)
- 3/4 cup water
- 1 tablespoon nut oil or olive oil
- 2 cups bread flour
- 3/4 tablespoon sugar
- 2/3 tablespoon gluten
- 1 teaspoon salt
- 5/8 teaspoon dried marjoram
- 5/8 teaspoon dried basil
- 5/8 teaspoon dried tarragon
- 1 1/8 teaspoons SAF yeast or 1 3/8 teaspoons bread machine yeast
- 12 slices (1 ½ pounds)
- 11/8 cups water
- 11/2 tablespoons nut oil or olive oil
- 3 cups bread flour
- 1 tablespoon sugar
- 1 tablespoon gluten
- 11/2 teaspoons salt
- 1 teaspoon dried marjoram
- 1 teaspoon dried basil
- 1 teaspoon dried tarragon
- 2 teaspoons SAF yeast or 21/2 teaspoons bread machine yeast
- 16 slices (2 pounds)
- 11/2 cups water
- 2 tablespoons nut oil or olive oil
- 4 cups bread flour
- 11/2 tablespoons sugar
- 1 tablespoon plus 1 teaspoon gluten
- 2 teaspoons salt
- 11/4 teaspoons dried marjoram
- 11/4 teaspoons dried basil
- 11/4 teaspoons dried tarragon
- 21/4 teaspoons SAF yeast or 23/4 teaspoons bread machine yeast

Directions:

1. Choose the size of loaf you would like to make and measure your ingredients.

2. Add the ingredients to the bread pan in the order listed above.

3. Place the pan in the bread machine and close the lid.

4. Turn on the bread maker. Select the Basic setting, then the loaf size, and finally the crust color. Start the cycle.

5. When the cycle is finished and the bread is baked, carefully remove the pan from the machine. Use a potholder as the handle will be very hot. Let rest for a few minutes.

6. Remove the bread from the pan and allow to cool on a wire rack for at least 10 minutes before slicing.

Cheesy Basil Bread

Ingredients:
- 8 slices (1 pound)
- 2/3 cup milk, at 80 degrees F
- 2 teaspoons melted butter, cooled
- 2 teaspoons sugar
- 2/3 teaspoon dried basil
- ½ cup (2 ounces) shredded sharp cheddar cheese
- ½ teaspoon salt
- 2 cups white bread flour
- 1 teaspoon active dry yeast
- 12 slices (1 ½ pounds)
- 1 cup milk, at 80 degrees F
- 3 teaspoons melted butter, cooled
- 3 teaspoons sugar
- 1 teaspoon dried basil
- 3/4 cup (3 ounces) shredded sharp cheddar cheese
- 3/4 teaspoon salt
- 3 cups white bread flour
- 1 1/2 teaspoons active dry yeast
- 16 slices (2 pounds)
- 1 1/3 cups milk, at 80 degrees F
- 4 teaspoons melted butter, cooled
- 4 teaspoons sugar
- 1 1/3 teaspoons dried basil
- 1 cup (4 ounces) shredded sharp cheddar cheese
- 1 teaspoon salt
- 4 cups white bread flour
- 2 teaspoons active dry yeast

Directions:
1. Choose the size of loaf you would like to make and measure your ingredients.
2. Add the ingredients to the bread pan in the order listed above.
3. Place the pan in the bread machine and close the lid.
4. Turn on the bread maker. Select the White/Basic setting, then the loaf size, and finally the crust color. Start the cycle.
5. When the cycle is finished and the bread is baked, carefully remove the pan from the machine. Use a potholder as the handle will be very hot. Let rest for a few minutes.
6. Remove the bread from the pan and allow to cool on a wire rack for at least 10 minutes before slicing.

Delicious Honey Lavender Bread

Ingredients:
- 8 slices (1 pound)
- 3/4 cup wheat flour
- 1 1/6 cups wholemeal flour
- 1/2 teaspoon fresh yeast
- 3/4 cup water
- 1/2 teaspoon lavender
- 3/4 tablespoon honey
- 1/2 teaspoon salt
- 12 slices (1 ½ pounds)
- 1 1/8 cups wheat flour
- 1 3/4 cups wholemeal flour
- 3/4 teaspoon fresh yeast
- 1 1/8 cups water
- 3/4 teaspoon lavender
- 1 1/8 tablespoons honey
- 3/4 teaspoon salt
- 16 slices (2 pounds)
- 1½ cups wheat flour
- 2⅓ cups wholemeal flour
- 1 teaspoon fresh yeast
- 1½ cups water
- 1 teaspoon lavender
- 1½ tablespoons honey
- 1 teaspoon salt

Directions:
1. Choose the size of loaf you would like to make and measure your ingredients.
2. Sift both types of flour in a bowl and mix.
3. Add the ingredients to the bread pan in the order listed above.
4. Place the pan in the bread machine and close the lid.
5. Turn on the bread maker. Select the White/Basic setting, then the loaf size, and finally the crust color. Start the cycle.
6. When the cycle is finished and the bread is baked, carefully remove the pan from the machine. Use a potholder as the handle will be very hot. Let rest for a few minutes.
7. Remove the bread from the pan and allow to cool on a wire rack for at least 10 minutes before slicing.

Cardamom Honey Bread

Ingredients:
- 8 slices (1 pound)
- 9/16 cup lukewarm milk
- 1/2 egg, at room temperature
- 1 teaspoon unsalted butter, melted
- 1/8 cup honey
- 2/3 teaspoon table salt
- 2 cups white bread flour
- 2/3 teaspoon ground cardamom
- 5/6 teaspoon bread machine yeast
- 12 slices (1 ½ pounds)
- ¾ cup lukewarm milk
- 1 egg, at room temperature
- 1½ teaspoons unsalted butter, melted
- 3 tablespoons honey
- 1 teaspoon table salt
- 3 cups white bread flour
- 1 teaspoon ground cardamom
- 1¼ teaspoons bread machine yeast
- 16 slices (2 pounds)
- 1⅛ cups lukewarm milk
- 1 egg, at room temperature
- 2 teaspoons unsalted butter, melted
- ¼ cup honey
- 1⅓ teaspoons table salt
- 4 cups white bread flour
- 1⅓ teaspoons ground cardamom
- 1⅔ teaspoons bread machine yeast

Directions:

1. Choose the size of loaf you would like to make and measure your ingredients.

2. Add the ingredients to the bread pan in the order listed above.

3. Place the pan in the bread machine and close the lid.

4. Turn on the bread maker. Select the White/Basic setting, then the loaf size, and finally the crust color. Start the cycle.

5. When the cycle is finished and the bread is baked, carefully remove the pan from the machine. Use a potholder as the handle will be very hot. Let rest for a few minutes.

6. Remove the bread from the pan and allow to cool on a wire rack for at least 10 minutes before slicing.

Buttermilk Bread With Lavender

Ingredients:
- 8 slices (1 pound)
- 1/4 cup water
- 7/16 cup buttermilk
- 1/8 cup olive oil
- 2 cups bread flour
- 1 1/2 tablespoons finely chopped fresh lavender leaves
- 5/8 teaspoon finely chopped fresh lavender flowers
- Grated zest of 1/2 small lemon
- 2/3 tablespoon gluten
- 1 teaspoon salt
- 1 1/8 teaspoons SAF yeast or 1 3/8 teaspoons bread machine yeast
- 12 slices (1½ pounds)
- 1/3 cup water
- 3/4 cup buttermilk
- 3 tablespoons olive oil
- 3 cups bread flour
- 2 tablespoons finely chopped fresh lavender leaves
- 1 teaspoon finely chopped fresh lavender flowers
- Grated zest of 1 small lemon
- 1 tablespoon gluten
- 11/2 teaspoons salt
- 2 teaspoons SAF yeast or 21/2 teaspoons bread machine yeast
- 16 slices (2 pounds)
- 1/2 cups water
- 7/8 cup buttermilk
- 1/4 cup olive oil
- 4 cups bread flour
- 3 tablespoons finely chopped fresh lavender leaves
- 11/4 teaspoons finely chopped fresh lavender flowers
- Grated zest of 1 small lemon
- 1 tablespoon plus 1 teaspoon gluten
- 2 teaspoons salt
- 21/4 teaspoons SAF yeast or 23/4 teaspoons bread machine yeast

Directions:

1. Choose the size of loaf you would like to make and measure your ingredients.
2. Add the ingredients to the bread pan in the order listed above.
3. Place the pan in the bread machine and close the lid.
4. Turn on the bread maker. Select the Basic setting, then the loaf size, and finally the crust color. Start the cycle.
5. When the cycle is finished and the bread is baked, carefully remove the pan from the machine. Use a potholder as the handle will be very hot. Let rest for a few minutes.
6. Remove the bread from the pan and allow to cool on a wire rack for at least 10 minutes before slicing.

Romano Oregano Bread

Ingredients:
- 8 slices (1 pound)
- 2/3 cup lukewarm water
- 1/8 cup sugar
- 1 tablespoon olive oil
- 2/3 teaspoon table salt
- 2/3 tablespoon dried leaf oregano
- 1/3 cup cheese (Romano or Parmesan), freshly grated
- 2 cups white bread flour
- 1 1/4–1 1/2 teaspoons bread machine yeast
- 12 slices (1 ½ pounds)
- 1 cup lukewarm water
- 3 tablespoons sugar
- 1½ tablespoons olive oil
- 1 teaspoon table salt
- 1 tablespoon dried leaf oregano
- ½ cup cheese (Romano or Parmesan), freshly grated
- 3 cups white bread flour
- 2 teaspoons bread machine yeast
- 16 slices (2 pounds)
- 1⅓ cups lukewarm water
- ¼ cup sugar
- 2 tablespoons olive oil
- 1⅓ teaspoons table salt
- 1⅓ tablespoons dried leaf oregano
- ⅔ cup cheese (Romano or Parmesan), freshly grated

- 4 cups white bread flour
- 2½–3 teaspoons bread machine yeast

Directions:
1. Choose the size of loaf you would like to make and measure your ingredients.
2. Add the ingredients to the bread pan in the order listed above.
3. Place the pan in the bread machine and close the lid.
4. Turn on the bread maker. Select the White/Basic setting, then the loaf size, and finally the crust color. Start the cycle.
5. When the cycle is finished and the bread is baked, carefully remove the pan from the machine. Use a potholder as the handle will be very hot. Let rest for a few minutes.
6. Remove the bread from the pan and allow to cool down on a wire rack for at least 10 minutes or more before slicing.

Cinnamon-flavored Raisin Bread

Ingredients:
- 8 slices (1 pound)
- ¾ cup milk at 80 degrees F
- 1 tablespoon melted butter, cooled
- 1 tablespoon sugar
- ¾ teaspoon salt
- ½ teaspoon ground cinnamon
- 2 cups white bread flour
- 1 teaspoon instant yeast
- ½ cup golden raisins
- 12 slices (1 ½ pounds)
- 1 1/8 cups milk at 80 degrees F
- 1 1/2 tablespoons melted butter, cooled
- 1 1/2 tablespoons sugar
- 1 1/8 teaspoons salt
- 3/4 teaspoon ground cinnamon
- 3 cups white bread flour
- 1 1/2 teaspoons instant yeast
- 3/4 cup golden raisins
- 16 slices (2 pounds)
- 1 1/2 cups milk at 80 degrees F
- 2 tablespoons melted butter, cooled
- 2 tablespoons sugar

- 1 1/2 teaspoons salt
- 1 teaspoon ground cinnamon
- 4 cups white bread flour
- 2 teaspoons instant yeast
- 1 cup golden raisins

Directions:

1. Choose the size of loaf you would like to make and measure your ingredients.
2. Add the ingredients to the bread pan in the order listed above (except raisins).
3. Place the pan in the bread machine and close the lid.
4. Turn on the bread maker. Select the Sweet Bread setting, then the loaf size, and finally the crust color. Start the cycle.
5. Add raisins at the raisin/nut signal (should be after 1 - 1½ hours).
6. When the cycle is finished and the bread is baked, carefully remove the pan from the machine. Use a potholder as the handle will be very hot. Let rest for a few minutes.
7. Remove the bread from the pan and allow to cool on a wire rack for at least 10 minutes before slicing.

Fresh Herb Bread

Ingredients:

- 8 slices (1 pound)
- 2/3 cup plus 1 1/3 tablespoons water (for 9 1/3-ounce mix) or 1 10/12 cups water (for 2/3-pound mix)
- One 9 1/3-ounce or 1-pound box white or whole wheat bread machine mix
- 1/3 cup chopped fresh herbs, any combination of parsley, chervil, basil, marjoram, sage, chives, mint, thyme, or lovage
- 1/6 cup chopped hazelnuts
- Grated zest of 2/3 lemon
- 1 1/3 teaspoons gluten
- 2/3 yeast packet (included in mix)
- 12 slices (1½ pounds)
- 1 cup plus 2 tablespoons water (for 14-ounce mix) or 11/4 cups water (for 1-pound mix)
- One 14-ounce or 1-pound box white or whole wheat bread machine mix

- 1/2 cup chopped fresh herbs, any combination of parsley, chervil, basil, marjoram, sage, chives, mint, thyme, or lovage
- 1/4 cup chopped hazelnuts
- Grated zest of 1 lemon
- 2 teaspoons gluten
- 1 yeast packet (included in mix)
- 16 slices (2 pounds)
- 1 1/3 cup plus 2 2/3 tablespoons water (for 18 2/3-ounce mix) or 3 4/6 cups water (for 1 1/3-pound mix)
- One 18 2/3-ounce or 2-pound box white or whole wheat bread machine mix
- 2/3 cup chopped fresh herbs, any combination of parsley, chervil, basil, marjoram, sage, chives, mint, thyme, or lovage
- 1/3 cup chopped hazelnuts
- Grated zest of 1 1/3 lemon
- 2 2/3 teaspoons gluten
- 1 1/3 yeast packet (included in mix)

Directions:

1. Choose the size of loaf you would like to make and measure your ingredients.
2. Add the ingredients to the bread pan in the order listed above.
3. Place the pan in the bread machine and close the lid.
4. Turn on the bread maker. Select the Basic setting, then the loaf size, and finally the crust color. Start the cycle.
5. When the cycle is finished and the bread is baked, carefully remove the pan from the machine. Use a potholder as the handle will be very hot. Let rest for a few minutes.
6. Remove the bread from the pan and allow to cool on a wire rack for at least 10 minutes before slicing.

Cinnamon Pull-apart Bread

Ingredients:

- 8 slices (1 pound)
- 1/2 cup whole milk
- 2 2/3 tablespoons unsalted butter
- 1/6 cup warm water
- 2/3 teaspoon pure vanilla extract
- 1 1/3 large eggs

- 2 cups all-purpose flour
- 1/6 cup sugar
- 1/3 teaspoon salt
- 1 1/2 teaspoons active dry yeast
- For the Filling:
- 2 2/3 tablespoons unsalted butter, melted until browned (will smell like warm caramel)
- 2/3 cup sugar
- 1 1/3 teaspoons ground cinnamon
- Pinch of ground nutmeg
- 12 slices (1 ½ pounds)
- 1/3 cup whole milk
- 4 tablespoons unsalted butter
- 1/4 cup warm water
- 1 teaspoon pure vanilla extract
- 2 large eggs
- 3 cups all-purpose flour
- 1/4 cup sugar
- 1/2 teaspoon salt
- 2 1/4 teaspoons active dry yeast
- For the Filling:
- 4 tablespoons unsalted butter, melted until browned (will smell like warm caramel)
- 1 cup sugar
- 2 teaspoons ground cinnamon
- Pinch of ground nutmeg
- 16 slices (2 pounds)
- 1 cup whole milk
- 5 1/3 tablespoons unsalted butter
- 1/3 cup warm water
- 1 1/3 teaspoons pure vanilla extract
- 2 2/3 large eggs
- 4 cups all-purpose flour
- 1/3 cup sugar
- 2/3 teaspoon salt
- 3 teaspoons active dry yeast
- For the Filling:
- 5 1/3 tablespoons unsalted butter, melted until browned (will smell like warm caramel)
- 1 1/3 cupd sugar
- 2 2/3 teaspoons ground cinnamon
- Pinch of ground nutmeg

Directions:

1. Choose the size of loaf you would like to make and measure your ingredients.
2. Add milk and butter to a saucepan and heat on medium-low until the butter melts; Add liquid to the bread pan.
3. Add the rest of the ingredients (except yeast) in the order listed.
4. Make a well in the center of the dry ingredients and add the yeast.
5. Place the pan in the bread machine and close the lid.
6. Turn on the bread maker. Select the Dough setting, then the loaf size, and finally the crust color. Start the cycle.
7. When the cycle is finished and the bread is baked, roll it out into a big sheet of dough, and brush the dough with the browned butter.
8. Combine sugar cinnamon and nutmeg in a mixing bowl and sprinkle over buttered dough.
9. Cut the dough into long thin strips and cut the strips into squares. Stack in threes, and place the dough squares next to one another in a greased bread pan.
10. Let rise in a warm place until doubled in size; cover with plastic wrap and refrigerate overnight to bake for breakfast.
11. Preheat an oven to 350°F.
12. Bake for 30 to 35 minutes, until the top is very golden brown.
13. When bread is done, transfer to a plate to cool and serve warm.

Cardamom Tea Bread

Ingredients:
- 8 slices (1 pound)
- 1/3 cup vegetable oil
- 3 large eggs
- 1/4 cup buttermilk
- 1 tablepoon vanilla extract
- 1 cup sour cream
- 3/4 cup sugar
- 21/4 cups unbleached all-purpose flour
- 2 teaspoons baking powder
- 1 teaspoon baking soda
- 21/2 teaspoons ground cardamom

- 1/2 teaspoon salt
- 12 slices (1 ½ pounds)
- 1/2 cup vegetable oil
- 4 1/2 large eggs
- 3/8 cup buttermilk
- 1 1/2 tablepoons vanilla extract
- 1 1/2 cups sour cream
- 1 1/8 cups sugar
- 3 3/8 cups unbleached all-purpose flour
- 3 teaspoons baking powder
- 1 1/2 teaspoons baking soda
- 3 3/4 teaspoons ground cardamom
- 3/4 teaspoon salt
- 16 slices (2 pounds)
- 2/3 cup vegetable oil
- 6 large eggs
- 1/2 cup buttermilk
- 2 tablepoons vanilla extract
- 2 cups sour cream
- 1 1/2 cups sugar
- 4 1/2 cups unbleached all-purpose flour
- 4 teaspoons baking powder
- 2 teaspoons baking soda
- 5 teaspoons ground cardamom
- 1 teaspoon salt

Directions:

1. Choose the size of loaf you would like to make and measure your ingredients.

2. Add the ingredients to the bread pan in the order listed above.

3. Place the pan in the bread machine and close the lid.

4. Turn on the bread maker. Select the Quick Bread/Cake setting, then the loaf size, and finally the crust color. Start the cycle.

5. When the cycle is finished and the bread is baked, carefully remove the pan from the machine. Use a potholder as the handle will be very hot. Let rest for a few minutes.

6. Remove the bread from the pan and allow to cool on a wire rack for at least 10 minutes before slicing.

Spice Pumpkin Bread

Ingredients:

- 8 slices (1 pound)
- Butter for grease
- 1½ cups pumpkin puree
- 3 whole eggs
- 1/3 cup butter, melted
- 1 cup sugar
- 3 cups all-purpose flour
- 1½ teaspoons baking powder
- ¾ teaspoon ground cinnamon
- ½ teaspoon baking soda
- ¼ teaspoon ground nutmeg
- ¼ teaspoon ground ginger
- ¼ teaspoon salt
- Pinch of ground cloves
- 12 slices (1 ½ pounds)
- Butter for grease
- 2 1/4 cups pumpkin puree
- 4 1/2 whole eggs
- 1/2 cup butter, melted
- 1 1/2 cups sugar
- 4 1/2 cups all-purpose flour
- 2 1/4 teaspoons baking powder
- 1 1/8 teaspoons ground cinnamon
- 3/4 teaspoon baking soda
- 3/8 teaspoon ground nutmeg
- 3/8 teaspoon ground ginger
- 3/8 teaspoon salt
- Pinch of ground cloves
- 16 slices (2 pounds)
- Butter for grease
- 3 cups pumpkin puree
- 6 whole eggs
- 2/3 cup butter, melted
- 2 cups sugar
- 6 cups all-purpose flour
- 3 teaspoons baking powder
- 1 1/2 teaspoons ground cinnamon
- 2 teaspoons baking soda
- 1/2 teaspoon ground nutmeg
- 1/2 teaspoon ground ginger
- 1/2 teaspoon salt
- Pinch of ground cloves

Directions:

1. Choose the size of loaf you would like to make and measure your ingredients.

2. Grease the bread pan with butter.

3. Add pumpkin, eggs, butter, and sugar to the bread pan.

4. Place the pan in the bread machine and close the lid.

5. Turn on the bread maker. Select the Quick/Rapid Bread setting, then the loaf size, and finally the crust color. Start the cycle.

6. Take a bowl, add flour, baking powder, cinnamon, baking soda, nutmeg, ginger, salt, cloves, and add the mixture to the machine once the machine beeps.

7. When the cycle is finished and the bread is baked, carefully remove the pan from the machine. Use a potholder as the handle will be very hot. Let rest for a few minutes.

8. Remove the bread from the pan and allow to cool on a wire rack for at least 10 minutes before slicing.

Sour Cream Semolina Bread With Herb Swirl

Ingredients:
- 8 slices (1 pound)
- For the dough:
- 1/2 cup water
- 3/4 tablespoon olive oil
- 1/3 cup sour cream
- 1 1/8 cups bread flour
- 5/8 cup semolina flour
- 1/2 tablespoon sugar
- 2/3 tablespoon gluten
- 7/8 teaspoon salt
- 1 1/4 teaspoons SAF yeast or 1/2 tablespoon bread machine yeast
- For the herb swirl:
- 1/6 cup chopped fresh flat-leaf parsley
- 1 1/2 to 2 tablespoons chopped fresh herbs, such as dill, basil, chervil, marjoram or tarragon
- 5/8 teaspoon dried herb mixture, such as Italian herbs
- 12 slices (1½ pounds)
- For the dough:
- 3/4 cup water

- 1 tablespoon olive oil
- 1/2 cup sour cream
- 11/2 cups bread flour
- 1 cup semolina flour
- 2 teaspoons sugar
- 1 tablespoon gluten
- 11/2 teaspoons salt
- 2 teaspoons SAF yeast or 21/2 teaspoons bread machine yeast
- For the herb swirl:
- 1/3 cup chopped fresh flat-leaf parsley
- 3 to 4 tablespoons chopped fresh herbs, such as dill, basil, chervil, marjoram or tarragon
- 11/4 teaspoons dried herb mixture, such as Italian herbs
- 16 slices (2 pounds)
- For the dough:
- 1 cup water
- 11/2 tablespoons olive oil
- 2/3 cup sour cream
- 21/4 cups bread flour
- 11/4 cups semolina flour
- 1 tablespoon sugar
- 1 tablespoon plus 1 teaspoon gluten
- 13/4 teaspoons salt
- 21/2 teaspoons SAF yeast or 1 tablespoon bread machine yeast
- For the herb swirl:
- 1/3 cup chopped fresh flat-leaf parsley
- 3 to 4 tablespoons chopped fresh herbs, such as dill, basil, chervil, marjoram or tarragon
- 11/4 teaspoons dried herb mixture, such as Italian herbs

Directions:
1. Choose the size of loaf you would like to make and measure your ingredients.

2. Add the ingredients to the bread pan in the order listed above.

3. Place the pan in the bread machine and close the lid.

4. Turn on the bread maker. Select the Basic setting, then the loaf size, and finally the crust color. Start the cycle.

5. To mix and bake the dough in the machine: After Rise 2 of the Basic cycle has ended, press Pause, or when the display shows Shape in the Variety cycle, remove the pan and close the lid. Immediately remove the dough and place it on a lightly floured work surface; pat into a 12-by-8-inch fat rectangle. Brush with 2 tablespoons olive oil. Sprinkle with the parsley and the rest of the herbs, leaving a 1-inch space all the way around. Starting at a short edge, roll up jelly-roll fashion. Tuck the ends under and pinch the bottom seam. Coat the bottom of the dough with cooking spray. Remove the kneading blade and place the dough back in the pan; press Start to continue to rise and bake as programmed.

6. When the cycle is finished and the bread is baked, carefully remove the pan from the machine. Use a potholder as the handle will be very hot. Let rest for a few minutes.

7. Remove the bread from the pan and allow to cool on a wire rack for at least 10 minutes before slicing.

NUT AND SEED BREAD RECIPES

Mesmerizing Walnut Bread

Ingredients:

- 8 slices (1 pound)
- 2 cups wheat flour
- 1/4 cup water
- 1/4 cup milk
- 1 whole egg, beaten
- 1/4 cup walnut
- 1/2 tablespoon vegetable oil
- 1/2 tablespoon sugar
- 1/2 teaspoon salt
- 1/2 teaspoon bread machine yeast
- 12 slices (1 ½ pounds)
- 3 cups wheat flour
- 3/8 cup water
- 3/8 cup milk
- 1 1/2 whole eggs, beaten
- 3/8 cup walnut
- 3/4 tablespoon vegetable oil
- 3/4 tablespoon sugar
- 3/4 teaspoon salt
- 3/4 teaspoon bread machine yeast
- 16 slices (2 pounds)
- 4 cups wheat flour
- ½ cup water
- ½ cup milk
- 2 whole eggs, beaten
- ½ cup walnut
- 1 tablespoon vegetable oil
- 1 tablespoon sugar
- 1 teaspoon salt
- 1 teaspoon bread machine yeast

Directions:

1. Choose the size of loaf you would like to make and measure your ingredients.
2. Add the ingredients to the bread pan in the order listed above (except the walnuts) .
3. Place the pan in the bread machine and close the lid.
4. Turn on the bread maker. Select the French Bread setting, then the loaf size, and finally the crust color. Start the cycle.
5. Slightly fry the walnuts in a dry frying pan until crispy; then let them cool.
6. Once the bread maker gives the signal, add the walnuts to the bread maker and mix with a spatula.
7. Let the remaining cycle complete.
8. When the cycle is finished and the bread is baked, carefully remove the pan from the machine. Use a potholder as the handle will be very hot. Let rest for a few minutes.
9. Remove the bread from the pan and allow to cool on a wire rack for at least 10 minutes before slicing.

Orange Almond Bread

Ingredients:

- 8 slices (1 pound)
- 2 cups all-purpose flour
- 3/8 cup sweet almonds, chopped
- 1 1/2 tablespoons brown sugar
- peels of 1 orange, grated
- 1/2 cup orange juice
- 1 tablespoon sweet almond oil
- 1/2 teaspoon salt
- powdered sugar for sprinkling
- 1 1/4 bread machine yeast
- 12 slices (1 ½ pounds)
- 3 cups all-purpose flour
- 9/10 cup sweet almonds, chopped
- 2 1/4 tablespoons brown sugar
- peels of 1 1/2 oranges, grated
- 3/4 cup orange juice
- 1 1/2 tablespoons sweet almond oil
- 3/4 teaspoon salt
- powdered sugar for sprinkling
- 1 7/8 bread machine yeast
- 16 slices (2 pounds)
- 4 cups all-purpose flour
- ¾ cup sweet almonds, chopped
- 3 tablespoons brown sugar

- peels of 2 oranges, grated
- 1 cup orange juice
- 2 tablespoons sweet almond oil
- 1 teaspoon salt
- powdered sugar for sprinkling
- 2½ bread machine yeast

Directions:

1. Choose the size of loaf you would like to make and measure your ingredients.

2. Add the ingredients to the bread pan in the order listed above (except the powdered sugar and ¼ cup of almonds).

3. Place the pan in the bread machine and close the lid.

4. Turn on the bread maker. Select the White/Basic setting, then the loaf size, and finally the crust color. Start the cycle.

5. When the cycle is finished and the bread is baked, carefully remove the pan from the machine. Use a potholder as the handle will be very hot. Let rest for a few minutes.

6. Moisten the surface with water and sprinkle with remaining almonds and powdered sugar.

7. Remove the bread from the pan and allow to cool on a wire rack for at least 10 minutes before slicing.

Orange Walnut Candied Loaf

Ingredients:

- 8 slices (1 pound)
- 1/3 cup warm whey
- 2/3 tablespoon bread machine yeast
- 2 2/3 tablespoons sugar
- 1 1/3 orange juice
- 2 2/3 cups flour
- 2/3 teaspoon salt
- 1 tablespoons salt
- 2 teaspoons orange zest
- 4/9 teaspoon vanilla
- 2 tablespoons (walnut + almonds)
- 1/3 cup candied fruit
- 12 slices (1 ½ pounds)
- ½ cup warm whey
- 1 tablespoon bread machine yeast
- 4 tablespoons sugar

- 2 orange juice
- 4 cups flour
- 1 teaspoon salt
- 1½ tablespoons salt
- 3 teaspoons orange zest
- ⅓ teaspoon vanilla
- 3 tablespoons (walnut + almonds)
- ½ cup candied fruit
- 16 slices (2 pounds)
- 2/3 cup warm whey
- 1 1/3 tablespoons bread machine yeast
- 5 1/3 tablespoons sugar
- 2 2/3 orange juice
- 5 1/3 cups flour
- 1 1/3 teaspoons salt
- 2 tablespoons salt
- 4 teaspoons orange zest
- 8/9 teaspoon vanilla
- 4 tablespoons (walnut + almonds)
- 2/3 cup candied fruit

Directions:

1. Choose the size of loaf you would like to make and measure your ingredients.

2. Add the ingredients to the bread pan in the order listed above.

3. Place the pan in the bread machine and close the lid.

4. Turn on the bread maker. Select the White/Basic/Sweet Bread setting, then the loaf size, and finally the crust color. Start the cycle.

5. When the cycle is finished and the bread is baked, carefully remove the pan from the machine. Use a potholder as the handle will be very hot. Let rest for a few minutes.

6. Remove the bread from the pan and allow to cool on a wire rack for at least 10 minutes before slicing.

Olive Oil–pine Nut Bread

Ingredients:

- 8 slices (1 pound)
- 1/3 cup water
- 1/3 cup dry white wine
- 1/6 cup olive oil
- 1 1/3 cups bread flour

- 1/2 cup whole wheat flour
- 1/6 cup rye flour
- 2/3 tablespoon gluten
- 1/2 tablespoon plus 1 teaspoon sugar
- 1 teaspoon salt
- 1 1/4 teaspoons SAF yeast or 1/2 tablespoon bread machine yeast
- 1/4 cup pine nuts, coarsely chopped
- 12 slices (1 ½ pounds)
- 1/2 cup water
- 1/2 cup dry white wine
- 1/4 cup olive oil
- 2 cups bread flour
- 3/4 cup whole wheat flour
- 1/4 cup rye flour
- 1 tablespoon gluten
- 1 tablespoon sugar
- 11/2 teaspoons salt
- 2 teaspoons SAF yeast or 21/2 teaspoons bread machine yeast
- 1/3 cup pine nuts, coarsely chopped
- 16 slices (2 pounds)
- 2/3 cup water
- 2/3 cup dry white wine
- 1/3 cup olive oil
- 22/3 cups bread flour
- 1 cup whole wheat flour
- 1/3 cup rye flour
- 1 tablespoon plus 1 teaspoon gluten
- 1 tablespoon plus 2 teaspoons sugar
- 2 teaspoons salt
- 21/2 teaspoons SAF yeast or 1 tablespoon bread machine yeast
- 1/2 cup pine nuts, coarsely chopped

Directions:

1. Choose the size of loaf you would like to make and measure your ingredients.

2. Add the ingredients to the bread pan in the order listed above (except the pine nuts).

3. Place the pan in the bread machine and close the lid.

4. Turn on the bread maker. Select the Basic or French Bread setting, then the loaf size, and finally the crust color. Start the cycle. (This recipe is not suitable for use with the Delay Timer.)

5. Five minutes into Knead 2, sprinkle in the pine nuts.

6. When the cycle is finished and the bread is baked, carefully remove the pan from the machine. Use a potholder as the handle will be very hot. Let rest for a few minutes.

7. Remove the bread from the pan and allow to cool on a wire rack for at least 10 minutes before slicing.

Brazilian Nuts & Nutmeg Loaf

Ingredients:
- 8 slices (1 pound)
- 1¼ cups water
- 2 tablespoons olive oil
- 1 tablespoon honey
- 3 cups wholemeal bread flour
- 1½ teaspoons salt
- 1 teaspoon fresh grated nutmeg
- 1½ teaspoons active dried yeast
- ¾ cup brazil nuts, coarsely chopped
- 12 slices (1 ½ pounds)
- 1 7/8 cups water
- 3 tablespoons olive oil
- 1 1/2 tablespoons honey
- 4 1/2 cups wholemeal bread flour
- 2 1/4 teaspoons salt
- 1 1/2 teaspoons fresh grated nutmeg
- 2 1/4 teaspoons active dried yeast
- 1 1/8 cups brazil nuts, coarsely chopped
- 16 slices (2 pounds)
- 2 1/2 cups water
- 4 tablespoons olive oil
- 2 tablespoons honey
- 6 cups wholemeal bread flour
- 3 teaspoons salt
- 2 teaspoons fresh grated nutmeg
- 3 teaspoons active dried yeast
- 1 1/2 cups brazil nuts, coarsely chopped

Directions:

1. Choose the size of loaf you would like to make and measure your ingredients.

2.   Add the ingredients to the bread pan in the order listed above (except nuts).

3.   Place the pan in the bread machine and close the lid.

4.   Turn on the bread maker. Select the White/Basic setting, then the loaf size, and finally the crust color. Start the cycle.

5.   Add nuts once the machine beeps.

6.   When the cycle is finished and the bread is baked, carefully remove the pan from the machine. Use a potholder as the handle will be very hot. Let rest for a few minutes.

7.   Remove the bread from the pan and allow to cool on a wire rack for at least 10 minutes before slicing.

Herb Light Rye Bread

Ingredients:

*   8 slices (1 pound)
*   3/8 teaspoon dill seed
*   3/8 teaspoon poppy seeds
*   1/6 teaspoon celery seeds
*   9/16 cup plus 1/2 tablespoon water
*   1/2 large egg
*   1 tablespoon minced shallot
*   3/4 tablespoon molasses
*   1 1/2 cups bread flour
*   1/2 cup medium or dark rye flour
*   1/2 tablespoon plus 1 teaspoon gluten
*   2/3 teaspoon caraway seed
*   1 1/8 teaspoons salt
*   1 1/4 teaspoons SAF yeast or 1/2 tablespoon bread machine yeast
*   12 slices (1 ½ pounds)
*   1/2 teaspoon dill seed
*   1/2 teaspoon poppy seeds
*   1/4 teaspoon celery seeds
*   7/8 cup water
*   1 large egg
*   11/2 tablespoons minced shallot
*   1 tablespoon molasses
*   21/4 cups bread flour
*   3/4 cup medium or dark rye flour
*   1 tablespoon gluten
*   11/2 teaspoons caraway seed

*   13/4 teaspoons salt
*   2 teaspoons SAF yeast or 21/2 teaspoons bread machine yeast
*   16 slices (2 pounds)
*   3/4 teaspoon dill seed
*   3/4 teaspoon poppy seeds
*   1/3 teaspoon celery seeds
*   11/8 cups plus 1 tablespoon water
*   1 large egg
*   2 tablespoons minced shallot
*   11/2 tablespoons molasses
*   3 cups bread flour
*   1 cup medium or dark rye flour
*   1 tablespoon plus 1 teaspoon gluten
*   11/3 teaspoons caraway seed
*   21/4 teaspoons salt
*   21/2 teaspoons SAF yeast or 1 tablespoon bread machine yeast

Directions:

1.   Choose the size of loaf you would like to make and measure your ingredients.

2.   Using a mortar and pestle, combine the dill seeds, poppy seeds, and celery seeds and crush them together coarsely. Or place the seeds between 2 sheets of waxed paper and crush them with a rolling pin.

3.   Add the ingredients to the bread pan in the order listed above. Adding the crushed seeds with the dry ingredients.

4.   Place the pan in the bread machine and close the lid.

5.   Turn on the bread maker. Select the Basic setting, then the loaf size, and finally the crust color. Start the cycle.

6.   When the cycle is finished and the bread is baked, carefully remove the pan from the machine. Use a potholder as the handle will be very hot. Let rest for a few minutes.

7.   Remove the bread from the pan and allow to cool on a wire rack for at least 10 minutes before slicing.

California Nut Bread

Ingredients:

- 8 slices (1 pound)
- 1/2 cup (2 to 2 1/2 ounces) nutmeat pieces
- 5/6 cup buttermilk
- 1/4 cup nut oil
- 2 cups bread flour
- 3/4 tablespoon dark brown sugar
- 2/3 tablespoon gluten
- 1 teaspoon salt
- 1/2 tablespoon SAF yeast or 1/2 tablespoon plus 1/4 teaspoon bread machine yeast
- 12 slices (1 ½ pounds)
- 3/4 cup (3 to 4 ounces) nutmeat pieces
- 11/4 cups buttermilk
- 1/3 cup nut oil
- 3 cups bread flour
- 1 tablespoon dark brown sugar
- 1 tablespoon gluten
- 11/2 teaspoons salt
- 21/2 teaspoons SAF yeast or 1 tablespoon bread machine yeast
- 16 slices (2 pounds)
- 1 cup (4 to 5 ounces) nutmeat pieces
- 12/3 cups buttermilk
- 1/2 cup nut oil
- 4 cups bread flour
- 11/2 tablespoons dark brown sugar
- 1 tablespoon plus 1 teaspoon gluten
- 2 teaspoons salt
- 1 tablespoon SAF yeast or 1 tablespoon plus 1/2 teaspoon bread machine yeast

Directions:

1. Choose the size of loaf you would like to make and measure your ingredients.
2. Preheat the oven to 350°F.
3. Spread the nuts evenly on a baking sheet. Bake until lightly toasted, about 5 to 7 minutes. Remove from the oven and let cool.
4. Add the ingredients to the bread pan in the order listed above (except the nuts).
5. Place the pan in the bread machine and close the lid.
6. Turn on the bread maker. Select the Basic setting, then the loaf size, and finally the crust color. Start the cycle.
7. When the machine beeps or between Knead 1 and Knead 2, add the nuts.
8. When the cycle is finished and the bread is baked, carefully remove the pan from the machine. Use a potholder as the handle will be very hot. Let rest for a few minutes.
9. Remove the bread from the pan and allow to cool on a wire rack for at least 10 minutes before slicing.

Fig And Walnut Bread

Ingredients:

- 8 slices (1 pound)
- 12 slices (1 ½ pounds)
- 16 slices (2 pounds)
- 11/2-POUND LOAF
- 1 cup water (for 14-ounce mix) or 1 cup plus 2 tablespoons water (for 1-pound mix)
- One 14-ounce or 1-pound box white bread machine mix
- 2 teaspoons gluten
- 1 yeast packet (included in mix)
- 3/4 cup chopped dried figs
- 1/4 cup chopped walnuts

Directions:

1. Place the ingredients, except the figs and walnuts, in the pan according to the order in the manufacturer's instructions. Set the crust for dark and program for the Basic or Fruit and Nut cycle; press Start. When the machine beeps, or between Knead 1 and Knead 2, add the figs and walnuts.
2. When the baking cycle ends, immediately remove the bread from the pan and place it on a rack. Let cool to room temperature before slicing.

Polish Poppy Seed Bread

Ingredients:

- 8 slices (1 pound)
- 12 slices (1 ½ pounds)
- 16 slices (2 pounds)
- 11/2-POUND LOAF

- 1 cup (for 14-ounce mix) or 1 cup plus 2 tablespoons (for 1-pound mix) fat-free milk
- 1 egg yolk
- 1 teaspoon almond extract
- One 14-ounce or 1-pound box white bread machine mix
- 1/2 cup chopped slivered blanched almonds
- 1/3 cup currants
- 1 tablespoon poppy seeds
- 1 tablespoon light brown sugar
- 2 teaspoons gluten
- 1 yeast packet (included in mix)

Directions:

1. Place all the ingredients in the pan according to the order in the manufacturer's instructions. Set the crust for medium and program for the Basic cycle; press Start.

2. When the baking cycle ends, immediately remove the bread from the pan and place it on a rack. Let cool to room temperature before slicing.

Corn, Poppy Seeds & Sour Cream Bread

Ingredients:

- 8 slices (1 pound)
- 1 3/4 cups wheat flour
- 7/8 cup cornflour
- 2 1/2 ounces sour cream
- 1 tablespoon corn oil
- 1 teaspoon active dried yeast
- 1 teaspoon salt
- 8 1/8 ounces water
- poppy seeds for sprinkling
- 12 slices (1 ½ pounds)
- 2 5/8 cups wheat flour
- 1 5/16 cups cornflour
- 3 3/4 ounces sour cream
- 1 1/2 tablespoons corn oil
- 1 1/2 teaspoons active dried yeast
- 1 1/2 teaspoons salt
- 12 3/16 ounces water
- poppy seeds for sprinkling
- 16 slices (2 pounds)
- 3½ cups wheat flour

- 1¾ cups cornflour
- 5 ounces sour cream
- 2 tablespoons corn oil
- 2 teaspoons active dried yeast
- 2 teaspoons salt
- 16 ¼ ounces water
- poppy seeds for sprinkling

Directions:

1. Choose the size of loaf you would like to make and measure your ingredients.

2. Add the ingredients to the bread pan in the order listed above (except the poppy seeds).

3. Place the pan in the bread machine and close the lid.

4. Turn on the bread maker. Select the White/Basic setting, then the loaf size, and finally the crust color. Start the cycle.

5. When the cycle is finished and the bread is baked, carefully remove the pan from the machine. Use a potholder as the handle will be very hot. Let rest for a few minutes.

6. Moisten the surface with water and sprinkle with poppy seeds.

7. Remove the bread from the pan and allow to cool on a wire rack for at least 10 minutes before slicing.

Almond Milk Bread

Ingredients:

- 8 slices (1 pound)
- 1/2cup lukewarm milk
- 1 egg, at room temperature
- 11/3 tablespoons butter, melted and cooled
- 1/6 cup sugar
- 1/2 teaspoon table salt
- 1 1/6 teaspoons lemon zest
- 2 cups white bread flour
- 11/8 teaspoons bread machine yeast
- 1/4 cup slivered almonds, chopped
- 1/4 cup golden raisins, chopped
- 12 slices (1 ½ pounds)
- ¾ cup lukewarm milk
- 2 eggs, at room temperature
- 2 tablespoons butter, melted and cooled
- ¼ cup sugar

- 1 teaspoon table salt
- 2 teaspoons lemon zest
- 3 cups white bread flour
- 2 teaspoons bread machine yeast
- ⅓ cup slivered almonds, chopped
- ⅓ cup golden raisins, chopped
- 16 slices (2 pounds)
- 1 cup lukewarm milk
- 2 eggs, at room temperature
- 2⅔ tablespoons butter, melted and cooled
- ⅓ cup sugar
- 1 teaspoon table salt
- 2⅓ teaspoons lemon zest
- 4 cups white bread flour
- 2¼ teaspoons bread machine yeast
- ½ cup slivered almonds, chopped
- ½ cup golden raisins, chopped

Directions:

1. Choose the size of loaf you would like to make and measure your ingredients.

2. Add all of the ingredients except for the raisins and almonds to the bread pan in the order listed above.

3. Place the pan in the bread machine and close the lid.

4. Turn on the bread maker. Select the White/Basic or Fruit/Nut (if your machine has this setting) setting, then the loaf size, and finally the crust color. Start the cycle.

5. When the machine signals to add ingredients, add the raisins and almonds. (Some machines have a fruit/nut hopper where you can add the raisins and almonds when you start the machine. The machine will automatically add them to the dough during the baking process.)

6. When the cycle is finished and the bread is baked, carefully remove the pan from the machine. Use a potholder as the handle will be very hot. Let rest for a few minutes.

7. Remove the bread from the pan and allow to cool on a wire rack for at least 10 minutes before slicing.

Potato Bread With Caraway Seeds

Ingredients:

- 8 slices (1 pound)
- 5/6 cup warm water
- 1 1/2 tablespoons instant potato flakes
- 1 tablespoon butter or lard
- 1 3/4 cups bread flour
- 1/4 cup potato starch flour
- 1 tablespoon sugar
- 1/2 tablespoon gluten
- 1/2 tablespoon caraway seeds
- 1 teaspoon salt
- 1 teaspoon SAF yeast or 1 1/4 teaspoons bread machine yeast
- 12 slices (1 ½ pounds)
- 11/3 cups warm water
- 2 tablespoons instant potato flakes
- 11/2 tablespoons butter or lard
- 22/3 cups bread flour
- 1/3 cup potato starch flour
- 11/2 tablespoons sugar
- 2 teaspoons gluten
- 2 teaspoons caraway seeds
- 11/2 teaspoons salt
- 13/4 teaspoons SAF yeast or 21/4 teaspoons bread machine yeast
- 16 slices (2 pounds)
- 12/3 cups warm water
- 3 tablespoons instant potato flakes
- 2 tablespoons butter or lard
- 31/2 cups bread flour
- 1/2 cup potato starch flour
- 2 tablespoons sugar
- 1 tablespoon gluten
- 1 tablespoon caraway seeds
- 2 teaspoons salt
- 2 teaspoons SAF yeast or 21/2 teaspoons bread machine yeast

Directions:

1. Choose the size of loaf you would like to make and measure your ingredients.

2. Place the instant potato flakes in the water in a bowl. Let stand for 5 minutes. The flakes will expand and soften, and the water become cloudy.

3. Add the ingredients to the bread pan in the order listed above. Adding the potato water with the butter or lard as the liquid ingredients.

4. Place the pan in the bread machine and close the lid.

5. Turn on the bread maker. Select the Quick Yeast Bread/Rapid setting, then the loaf size, and finally the crust color. Start the cycle.

6. If the dough rises more than two-thirds of the way up the pan, gently deflate the dough a bit. This will keep the dough from hitting the window during baking.

7. When the cycle is finished and the bread is baked, carefully remove the pan from the machine. Use a potholder as the handle will be very hot. Let rest for a few minutes.

8. Remove the bread from the pan and allow to cool on a wire rack for at least 10 minutes before slicing.

Basic Pecan Bread

Ingredients:

- 8 slices (1 pound)
- 2/3 cups lukewarm milk
- 11/3 tablespoons unsalted butter, melted
- 1/2 egg, at room temperature
- 1 1/3 tablespoons sugar
- 2/3 teaspoons table salt
- 2 cups white bread flour
- 1 teaspoons bread machine yeast
- 2/3 cups chopped pecans, toasted
- 12 slices (1 ½ pounds)
- 1 cup lukewarm milk
- 2 tablespoons unsalted butter, melted
- 1 egg, at room temperature
- 2 tablespoons sugar
- 1 teaspoon table salt
- 3 cups white bread flour
- 1½ teaspoons bread machine yeast
- 1 cup chopped pecans, toasted
- 16 slices (2 pounds)
- 1⅓ cups lukewarm milk
- 2⅔ tablespoons unsalted butter, melted
- 1 egg, at room temperature
- 2⅔ tablespoons sugar
- 1⅓ teaspoons table salt
- 4 cups white bread flour
- 2 teaspoons bread machine yeast
- 1⅓ cups chopped pecans, toasted

Directions:

1. Choose the size of loaf you would like to make and measure your ingredients.

2. Add all of the ingredients except for the toasted pecans to the bread pan in the order listed above.

3. Place the pan in the bread machine and close the lid.

4. Turn on the bread maker. Select the White/Basic or Fruit/Nut (if your machine has this setting) setting, then the loaf size, and finally the crust color. Start the cycle.

5. When the machine signals to add ingredients, add the toasted pecans. (Some machines have a fruit/nut hopper where you can add the toasted pecans when you start the machine. The machine will automatically add them to the dough during the baking process.)

6. When the cycle is finished and the bread is baked, carefully remove the pan from the machine. Use a potholder as the handle will be very hot. Let rest for a few minutes.

7. Remove the bread from the pan and allow to cool on a wire rack for at least 10 minutes before slicing.

Pistachio Horseradish Apple Bread

Ingredients:

- 8 slices (1 pound)
- 1 1/2 cups wheat flour
- 1 whole egg, beaten
- 1 1/2 tablespoons horseradish, grated
- 1/4 cup apple puree
- 1/2 tablespoon sugar
- 2 tablespoons olive oil
- 1/4 cup pistachios, peeled and chopped
- 1/2 teaspoon instant yeast
- 1/2 cup + 1/2 tablespoon water
- 1/2 teaspoon salt
- 12 slices (1 ½ pounds)
- 2 1/4 cups wheat flour
- 1 1/2 whole eggs, beaten
- 2 1/4 tablespoons horseradish, grated
- 3/8 cup apple puree
- 3/4 tablespoon sugar
- 3 tablespoons olive oil
- 3/8 cup pistachios, peeled and chopped
- 3/4 teaspoon instant yeast

- 3/4 cup + 3/4 tablespoon water
- 3/4 teaspoon salt
- 16 slices (2 pounds)
- 3 cups wheat flour
- 2 whole eggs, beaten
- 3 tablespoons horseradish, grated
- ½ cup apple puree
- 1 tablespoon sugar
- 4 tablespoons olive oil
- ½ cup pistachios, peeled and chopped
- 1 teaspoon instant yeast
- 1 cup + 1 tablespoon water
- 1 teaspoon salt

Directions:

1. Choose the size of loaf you would like to make and measure your ingredients.

2. Add the ingredients to the bread pan in the order listed above.

3. Place the pan in the bread machine and close the lid.

4. Turn on the bread maker. Select the White/Basic setting, then the loaf size, and finally the crust color. Start the cycle.

5. When the cycle is finished and the bread is baked, carefully remove the pan from the machine. Use a potholder as the handle will be very hot. Let rest for a few minutes.

6. Remove the bread from the pan and allow to cool on a wire rack for at least 10 minutes before slicing.

Brown Sugar Date Nut Swirl Bread

Ingredients:

- 8 slices (1 pound)
- 1 cup milk
- 1 large egg
- 4 tablespoons butter
- 4 tablespoons sugar
- 1 teaspoon salt
- 4 cups flour
- 1 2/3 teaspoons yeast
- For the filling:
- 1/2 cup packed brown sugar
- 1 cup walnuts, chopped
- 1 cup medjool dates, pitted and chopped

- 2 teaspoons cinnamon
- 2 teaspoons clove spice
- 1 1/3 tablespoons butter
- Powdered sugar, sifted
- 12 slices (1 ½ pounds)
- 1 1/2 cups milk
- 1 1/2 large eggs
- 6 tablespoons butter
- 6 tablespoons sugar
- 1 1/2 teaspoons salt
- 6 cups flour
- 2 1/2 teaspoons yeast
- For the filling:
- 1/2 cup packed brown sugar
- 1 cup walnuts, chopped
- 1 cup medjool dates, pitted and chopped
- 2 teaspoons cinnamon
- 2 teaspoons clove spice
- 1 1/3 tablespoons butter
- Powdered sugar, sifted
- 16 slices (2 pounds)
- 2 cups milk
- 2 large eggs
- 8 tablespoons butter
- 8 tablespoons sugar
- 2 teaspoons salt
- 8 cups flour
- 3 1/3 teaspoons yeast
- For the filling:
- 1 cup packed brown sugar
- 2 cups walnuts, chopped
- 2 cups medjool dates, pitted and chopped
- 4 teaspoons cinnamon
- 4 teaspoons clove spice
- 2 2/3 tablespoons butter
- Powdered sugar, sifted

Directions:

1. Choose the size of loaf you would like to make and measure your ingredients.

2. Add the ingredients to the bread pan in the order listed above (except yeast).

3. Make a well in the center of the dry ingredients and add the yeast.

4.   Place the pan in the bread machine and close the lid.

5.   Turn on the bread maker. Select the Dough setting, then the loaf size, and finally the crust color. Start the cycle.

6.   When the cycle is finished and the bread is baked, carefully remove the pan from the machine. Use a potholder as the handle will be very hot. Let rest for a few minutes.

7.   Mix the brown sugar with walnuts, dates and spices; set aside.

8.   Roll the dough into a rectangle, on a lightly floured surface.

9.   Baste with a tablespoon of butter, add the filling.

10. Start from the short side and roll the dough to form a jelly roll shape.

11. Place the roll into a greased loaf pan and cover.

12. Let it rise in a warm place, until nearly doubled in size; about 30 minutes.

13. Bake at 350°F for approximately 30 minutes.

14. Cover with foil during the last 10 minutes of cooking.

15. Transfer to a cooling rack for 15 minutes; sprinkle with the powdered sugar and serve.

Mix Seed Raisin Bread

Ingredients:

- 8 slices (1 pound)
- 3/4 cup lukewarm milk
- 1 tablespoon unsalted butter, melted
- 1 tablespoon honey
- 1/2 teaspoon table salt
- 11/4 cups white bread flour
- 1/8 cup flaxseed
- 1/8 cup sesame seeds
- 3/4 cup whole-wheat flour
- 11/8 teaspoons bread machine yeast
- 1/4 cup raisins
- 12 slices (1 ½ pounds)
- 1⅛ cups lukewarm milk
- 1½ tablespoons unsalted butter, melted
- 1½ tablespoons honey
- ¾ teaspoon table salt
- 1¾ cups white bread flour
- 3 tablespoons flaxseed
- 3 tablespoons sesame seeds
- 1¼ cups whole-wheat flour
- 1¾ teaspoons bread machine yeast
- ⅓ cup raisins
- 16 slices (2 pounds)
- 1½ cups lukewarm milk
- 2 tablespoons unsalted butter, melted
- 2 tablespoons honey
- 1 teaspoon table salt
- 2½ cups white bread flour
- ¼ cup flaxseed
- ¼ cup sesame seeds
- 1½ cups whole-wheat flour
- 2¼ teaspoons bread machine yeast
- ½ cup raisins

Directions:

1.   Choose the size of loaf you would like to make and measure your ingredients.

2.   Add the ingredients to the bread pan in the order listed above.

3.   Place the pan in the bread machine and close the lid.

4.   Turn on the bread maker. Select the White/Basic setting, then the loaf size, and finally the crust color. Start the cycle.

5.   When the cycle is finished and the bread is baked, carefully remove the pan from the machine. Use a potholder as the handle will be very hot. Let rest for a few minutes.

6.   Remove the bread from the pan and allow to cool on a wire rack for at least 10 minutes before slicing.

Pistachio Cherry Bread

Ingredients:

- 8 slices (1 pound)
- 3/16 cup lukewarm water
- 1/2 egg, at room temperature
- 1/8 cup butter, softened
- 1/8 cup packed dark brown sugar
- 3/4 teaspoon table salt
- 1 7/8 cups white bread flour
- 1/4 teaspoon ground nutmeg
- Dash allspice

- 1 teaspoon bread machine yeast
- 1/2 cup dried cherries
- 1/4 cup unsalted pistachios, chopped
- 12 slices (1 ½ pounds)
- ¾ cup lukewarm water
- 1 egg, at room temperature
- 3 tablespoons butter, softened
- 3 tablespoons packed dark brown sugar
- 1⅛ teaspoons table salt
- 2¾ cups white bread flour
- ½ teaspoon ground nutmeg
- Dash allspice
- 1½ teaspoons bread machine yeast
- ¾ cup dried cherries
- ⅓ cup unsalted pistachios, chopped
- 16 slices (2 pounds)
- 1⅛ cups lukewarm water
- 1 egg, at room temperature
- ¼ cup butter, softened
- ¼ cup packed dark brown sugar
- 1½ teaspoons table salt
- 3¾ cups white bread flour
- ½ teaspoon ground nutmeg
- Dash allspice
- 2 teaspoons bread machine yeast
- 1 cup dried cherries
- ½ cup unsalted pistachios, chopped

Directions:

1. Choose the size of loaf you would like to make and measure your ingredients.

2. Add all of the ingredients except for the pistachios and cherries to the bread pan in the order listed above.

3. Place the pan in the bread machine and close the lid.

4. Turn on the bread maker. Select the White/Basic or Fruit/Nut (if your machine has this setting) setting, then the loaf size, and finally the crust color. Start the cycle.

5. When the machine signals to add ingredients, add the pistachios and cherries. (Some machines have a fruit/nut hopper where you can add the pistachios and cherries when you start the machine. The machine will automatically add them to the dough during the baking process.)

6. When the cycle is finished and the bread is baked, carefully remove the pan from the machine. Use a potholder as the handle will be very hot. Let rest for a few minutes.

7. Remove the bread from the pan and allow to cool on a wire rack for at least 10 minutes before slicing.

Toasted Walnut Bread

Ingredients:

- 8 slices (1 pound)
- 1/2 cup (2 to 2 1/2 ounces) walnut pieces
- 2/3 cup water
- 1 large egg white, lightly beaten
- 1 tablespoon butter, cut into pieces
- 2 cups bread flour
- 1 1/2 tablespoons sugar
- 1 1/2 tablespoons nonfat dry milk
- 2/3 tablespoon gluten
- 1/2 teaspoon salt
- 1 teaspoon SAF yeast or 1 1/4 teaspoons bread machine yeast
- 12 slices (1 ½ pounds)
- 3/4 cup (3 to 4 ounces) walnut pieces
- 1 cup water
- 2 large egg whites, lightly beaten
- 11/2 tablespoons butter, cut into pieces
- 3 cups bread flour
- 2 tablespoons sugar
- 2 tablespoons nonfat dry milk
- 1 tablespoon gluten
- 3/4 teaspoon salt
- 11/2 teaspoons SAF yeast or 2 teaspoons bread machine yeast
- 16 slices (2 pounds)
- 1 cup (4 to 5 ounces) walnut pieces
- 11/3 cups water
- 2 large egg whites, lightly beaten
- 2 tablespoons butter, cut into pieces
- 4 cups bread flour
- 3 tablespoons sugar
- 3 tablespoons nonfat dry milk
- 1 tablespoon plus 1 teaspoon gluten
- 1 teaspoon salt

- 2 teaspoons SAF yeast or 21/2 teaspoons bread machine yeast

Directions:

1. Choose the size of loaf you would like to make and measure your ingredients.

2. Preheat the oven to 350°F.

3. Spread the walnuts on a baking sheet and place in the center of the oven for 4 minutes to toast lightly. Set aside to cool.

4. Add the ingredients to the bread pan in the order listed above (except the walnuts).

5. Place the pan in the bread machine and close the lid.

6. Turn on the bread maker. Select the Basic/Fruit and Nut cycle setting, then the loaf size, and finally the crust color. Start the cycle. (This recipe is not suitable for use with the Delay Timer.)

7. When the cycle is finished and the bread is baked, carefully remove the pan from the machine. Use a potholder as the handle will be very hot. Let rest for a few minutes.

8. When the machine beeps, or between Knead 1 and Knead 2, add the walnuts.

9. Remove the bread from the pan and allow to cool on a wire rack for at least 10 minutes before slicing.

Pecan Raisin Bread

Ingredients:

- 8 slices (1 pound)
- 5/8 cup (about 3 ounces) pecan halves
- 3/4 cup water
- 3/4 tablespoon butter, cut into pieces
- 1 2/3 cups bread flour
- 1/3 cup dark rye flour
- 3/4 tablespoon dark brown sugar
- 1/2 tablespoon plus 1 teaspoons gluten
- 1 teaspoon salt
- 1 1/4 teaspoons SAF yeast or 1/2 tablespoon bread machine yeast
- 1/4 cup dark raisins
- 12 slices (1 ½ pounds)
- 1 cup (about 4 ounces) pecan halves
- 1 cup plus 2 tablespoons water
- 1 tablespoon butter, cut into pieces

- 21/2 cups bread flour
- 1/2 cup dark rye flour
- 1 tablespoon dark brown sugar
- 1 tablespoon plus 1 teaspoon gluten
- 11/2 teaspoons salt
- 21/4 teaspoons SAF yeast or 23/4 teaspoons bread machine yeast
- 1/3 cup dark raisins
- 16 slices (2 pounds)
- 11/4 cups (about 6 ounces) pecan halves
- 11/2 cups water
- 11/2 tablespoons butter, cut into pieces
- 31/3 cups bread flour
- 2/3 cup dark rye flour
- 11/2 tablespoons dark brown sugar
- 1 tablespoon plus 2 teaspoons gluten
- 2 teaspoons salt
- 21/2 teaspoons SAF yeast or 1 tablespoon bread machine yeast
- 1/2 cup dark raisins

Directions:

1. Choose the size of loaf you would like to make and measure your ingredients.

2. Preheat the oven to 350°F.

3. Spread the nuts on a baking sheet. Bake for 10 minutes, stirring twice. Cool on the baking sheet. Chop the nuts into large pieces and set aside.

4. Add the ingredients to the bread pan in the order listed above (except the nuts and the raisins).

5. Place the pan in the bread machine and close the lid.

6. Turn on the bread maker. Select the Basic/Fruit and Nut setting, then the loaf size, and finally the crust color. Start the cycle. (This recipe is not suitable for use with the Delay Timer.)

7. When the machine beeps, or between Knead 1 and Knead 2, add the nuts and the raisins.

8. When the cycle is finished and the bread is baked, carefully remove the pan from the machine. Use a potholder as the handle will be very hot. Let rest for a few minutes.

9. Remove the bread from the pan and allow to cool on a wire rack for at least 10 minutes before slicing.

Orange-cumin Bread

Ingredients:

- 8 slices (1 pound)
- 1/3 cup orange juice
- 1/2 cup fat-free milk
- 2 tablespoons butter, cut into pieces
- 1 3/4 cups bread flour
- 1/4 cup whole wheat flour
- 1/6 cup light brown sugar
- 2/3 tablespoon gluten
- 1 teaspoon cumin seed, crushed in a mortar and pestle
- 1 teaspoon salt
- 1 1/8 teaspoons SAF yeast or 1 3/8 teaspoons bread machine yeast
- 12 slices (1 ½ pounds)
- 1/2 cup orange juice
- 2/3 cup fat-free milk
- 3 tablespoons butter, cut into pieces
- 22/3 cups bread flour
- 1/3 cup whole wheat flour
- 1/4 cup light brown sugar
- 1 tablespoon gluten
- 11/2 teaspoons cumin seed, crushed in a mortar and pestle
- 11/2 teaspoons salt
- 2 teaspoons SAF yeast or 21/2 teaspoons bread machine yeast
- 16 slices (2 pounds)
- 2/3 cup orange juice
- 7/8 cup fat-free milk
- 4 tablespoons butter, cut into pieces
- 31/2 cups bread flour
- 1/2 cup whole wheat flour
- 1/3 cup light brown sugar
- 1 tablespoon plus 1 teaspoon gluten
- 2 teaspoons cumin seed, crushed in a mortar and pestle
- 2 teaspoons salt
- 21/4 teaspoons SAF yeast or 23/4 teaspoons bread machine yeast

Directions:

1. Choose the size of loaf you would like to make and measure your ingredients.
2. Add the ingredients to the bread pan in the order listed above.
3. Place the pan in the bread machine and close the lid.
4. Turn on the bread maker. Select the Basic setting, then the loaf size, and finally the crust color. Start the cycle.
5. When the cycle is finished and the bread is baked, carefully remove the pan from the machine. Use a potholder as the handle will be very hot. Let rest for a few minutes.
6. Remove the bread from the pan and allow to cool on a wire rack for at least 10 minutes before slicing.

Bourbon Nut Bread

Ingredients:

- 8 slices (1 pound)
- 1/4 cup nut oil or vegetable oil
- 2 large eggs
- 11/2 teaspoons almond extract
- 11/2 cups sour cream
- 1/2 cup bourbon
- 1 cup light brown sugar
- 21/4 cups unbleached all-purpose flour
- 21/2 teaspoons baking powder
- 1/2 teaspoon baking soda
- 1/2 teaspoon salt
- 11/2 teaspoons ground nutmeg
- 1 teaspoon instant espresso powder
- 11/4 cups (6 ounces) coarsely chopped pecans or walnuts
- 12 slices (1 ½ pounds)
- 3/8 cup nut oil or vegetable oil
- 3 large eggs
- 2 1/4 teaspoons almond extract
- 2 1/4 cups sour cream
- 3/4 cup bourbon
- 1 1/2 cups light brown sugar
- 3 3/8 cups unbleached all-purpose flour
- 3 3/4 teaspoons baking powder
- 3/4 teaspoon baking soda
- 3/4 teaspoon salt

- 2 1/4 teaspoons ground nutmeg
- 1 1/2 teaspoons instant espresso powder
- 1 7/8 cups (9 ounces) coarsely chopped pecans or walnuts
- 16 slices (2 pounds)
- 1/2 cup nut oil or vegetable oil
- 4 large eggs
- 3 teaspoons almond extract
- 3 cups sour cream
- 1 cup bourbon
- 2 cups light brown sugar
- 4 1/2 cups unbleached all-purpose flour
- 5 teaspoons baking powder
- 1 teaspoon baking soda
- 1 teaspoon salt
- 3 teaspoons ground nutmeg
- 2 teaspoons instant espresso powder
- 2 1/2 cups (3 ounces) coarsely chopped pecans or walnuts

Directions:

1. Choose the size of loaf you would like to make and measure your ingredients.
2. Add the ingredients to the bread pan in the order listed above.
3. Place the pan in the bread machine and close the lid.
4. Turn on the bread maker. Select the Quick Bread/Cake setting, then the loaf size, and finally the crust color. Start the cycle.
5. When the cycle is finished and the bread is baked, carefully remove the pan from the machine. Use a potholder as the handle will be very hot. Let rest for a few minutes.
6. Remove the bread from the pan and allow to cool on a wire rack for at least 10 minutes before slicing.

Caramel Apple Pecan Loaf

Ingredients:

- 8 slices (1 pound)
- 1 cup water
- 2 tablespoons butter
- 3 cups bread flour
- ¼ cup packed brown sugar
- ¾ teaspoon ground cinnamon
- 1 teaspoon salt
- 2 teaspoons quick yeast
- ½ cup apple, chopped
- ⅓ cup coarsely chopped pecans, toasted
- 12 slices (1 ½ pounds)
- 1 1/2 cups water
- 3 tablespoons butter
- 4 1/2 cups bread flour
- 3/8 cup packed brown sugar
- 1 1/8 teaspoons ground cinnamon
- 1 1/2 teaspoons salt
- 3 teaspoons quick yeast
- 3/4 cup apple, chopped
- 1/2 cup coarsely chopped pecans, toasted
- 16 slices (2 pounds)
- 2 cups water
- 4 tablespoons butter
- 6 cups bread flour
- 1/2 cup packed brown sugar
- 1 1/2 teaspoons ground cinnamon
- 2 teaspoons salt
- 4 teaspoons quick yeast
- 1 cup apple, chopped
- 2/3 cup coarsely chopped pecans, toasted

Directions:

1. Choose the size of loaf you would like to make and measure your ingredients.
2. Add the ingredients to the bread pan in the order listed above (except apples and pecans).
3. Place the pan in the bread machine and close the lid.
4. Turn on the bread maker. Select the White/Basic setting, then the loaf size, and finally the crust color. Start the cycle.
5. Once the bread maker beeps, add pecans and apples.
6. When the cycle is finished and the bread is baked, carefully remove the pan from the machine. Use a potholder as the handle will be very hot. Let rest for a few minutes.
7. Remove the bread from the pan and allow to cool on a wire rack for at least 10 minutes before slicing.

Delicious Flax Honey Bread

Ingredients:

- 8 slices (1 pound)
- ¾ cup milk, at room temperature
- 1 tablespoon melted butter
- 1 tablespoon honey
- ¾ teaspoon salt
- 2 tablespoons flaxseeds
- 2 cups white bread flour
- ¾ teaspoon bread machine yeast
- 12 slices (1 ½ pounds)
- 1 1/8cups milk, at room temperature
- 1 1/2 tablespoons melted butter
- 1 1/2 tablespoons honey
- 1 1/8 teaspoons salt
- 3 tablespoons flaxseeds
- 3 cups white bread flour
- 1 1/8 teaspoons bread machine yeast
- 16 slices (2 pounds)
- 1 1/2 cups milk, at room temperature
- 2 tablespoons melted butter
- 2 tablespoons honey
- 1 1/2 teaspoons salt
- 4 tablespoons flaxseeds
- 4 cups white bread flour
- 1 1/2 teaspoons bread machine yeast

Directions:

1. Choose the size of loaf you would like to make and measure your ingredients.

2. Add the ingredients to the bread pan in the order listed above.

3. Place the pan in the bread machine and close the lid.

4. Turn on the bread maker. Select the White/Basic setting, then the loaf size, and finally the crust color. Start the cycle.

5. When the cycle is finished and the bread is baked, carefully remove the pan from the machine. Use a potholder as the handle will be very hot. Let rest for a few minutes.

6. Remove the bread from the pan and allow to cool on a wire rack for at least 10 minutes before slicing.

Sunflower Oatmeal Bread

Ingredients:

- 8 slices (1 pound)
- 1/3 cup water
- 1/2 cup buttermilk
- 1/2 large egg
- 1 tablespoon butter, cut into pieces
- 1 1/2 tablespoons honey
- 3/4 tablespoon molasses
- 1 2/3 cups bread flour
- 1/3 cup rolled oats
- 1/3 cup whole wheat flour
- 1/3 cup raw sunflower seeds
- 2/3 tablespoon gluten
- 1 teaspoon salt
- 1 1/8 teaspoons SAF yeast or 1 3/8 teaspoons bread machine yeast
- 12 slices (1 ½ pounds)
- 1/2 cup water
- 5/8 cup buttermilk
- 1 large egg
- 11/2 tablespoons butter, cut into pieces
- 2 tablespoons honey
- 1 tablespoon molasses
- 21/2 cups bread flour
- 1/2 cup rolled oats
- 1/2 cup whole wheat flour
- 1/2 cup raw sunflower seeds
- 1 tablespoon gluten
- 11/2 teaspoons salt
- 2 teaspoons SAF yeast or 21/2 teaspoons bread machine yeast
- 16 slices (2 pounds)
- 2/3 cup water
- 7/8 cup buttermilk
- 1 large egg
- 2 tablespoons butter, cut into pieces
- 3 tablespoons honey
- 11/2 tablespoons molasses
- 31/3 cups bread flour
- 2/3 cup rolled oats
- 2/3 cup whole wheat flour
- 2/3 cup raw sunflower seeds

- 1 tablespoon plus 1 teaspoon gluten
- 2 teaspoons salt
- 21/4 teaspoons SAF yeast or 23/4 teaspoons bread machine yeast

Directions:

1. Choose the size of loaf you would like to make and measure your ingredients.

2. Add the ingredients to the bread pan in the order listed above.

3. Place the pan in the bread machine and close the lid.

4. Turn on the bread maker. Select the Basic setting, then the loaf size, and finally the crust color. Start the cycle.

5. When the cycle is finished and the bread is baked, carefully remove the pan from the machine. Use a potholder as the handle will be very hot. Let rest for a few minutes.

6. Remove the bread from the pan and allow to cool on a wire rack for at least 10 minutes before slicing.

Zuni Indian Bread

Ingredients:

- 8 slices (1 pound)
- 2/3 cup buttermilk
- 1/2 large egg
- 1 1/2 tablespoons sunflower seed oil
- 1 1/4 cups bread flour
- 1/2 cup whole wheat flour
- 1/4 cup cornmeal
- 1/3 cup raw sunflower seeds
- 1 1/2 tablespoons dark brown sugar
- 1 tablespoon gluten
- 1 teaspoon salt
- 1 1/4 teaspoons SAF yeast or 1/2 tablespoon bread machine yeast
- 12 slices (1 ½ pounds)
- 1 cup buttermilk
- 1 large egg
- 2 tablespoons sunflower seed oil
- 2 cups bread flour
- 2/3 cup whole wheat flour
- 1/3 cup cornmeal
- 1/2 cup raw sunflower seeds
- 2 tablespoons dark brown sugar
- 11/2 tablespoons gluten
- 11/2 teaspoons salt
- 21/4 teaspoons SAF yeast or 23/4 teaspoons bread machine yeast
- 16 slices (2 pounds)
- 11/3 cups buttermilk
- 1 large egg
- 3 tablespoons sunflower seed oil
- 21/2 cups bread flour
- 1 cup whole wheat flour
- 1/2 cup cornmeal
- 2/3 cup raw sunflower seeds
- 3 tablespoons dark brown sugar
- 2 tablespoons gluten
- 2 teaspoons salt
- 21/2 teaspoons SAF yeast or 1 tablespoon bread machine yeast

Directions:

1. Choose the size of loaf you would like to make and measure your ingredients.

2. Add the ingredients to the bread pan in the order listed above.

3. Place the pan in the bread machine and close the lid.

4. Turn on the bread maker. Select the Whole Wheat setting, then the loaf size, and finally the crust color. Start the cycle.

5. When the cycle is finished and the bread is baked, carefully remove the pan from the machine. Use a potholder as the handle will be very hot. Let rest for a few minutes.

6. Remove the bread from the pan and allow to cool on a wire rack for at least 10 minutes before slicing.

VEGETABLE BREAD RECIPES

Carrot Bread With Crystallized Ginger

Ingredients:

- 8 slices (1 pound)
- 1/8 cup fat-free milk
- One 3-ounce jar junior baby food strained carrots or 3/8 cup pureed carrots
- 1 large eggs
- 1 1/2 tablespoons unsalted butter, cut into pieces
- 2 cups bread flour
- 1/6 cup chopped crystallized ginger
- 1/2 tablespoon plus 1/2 teaspoon gluten
- 1 teaspoon salt
- 1 teaspoon SAF yeast or 1 1/4 teaspoons bread machine yeast
- 12 slices (1½ pounds)
- 3 tablespoons fat-free milk
- One 6-ounce jar junior baby food strained carrots or 3/4 cup pureed carrots
- 2 large eggs
- 2 tablespoons unsalted butter, cut into pieces
- 3 cups bread flour
- 1/4 cup chopped crystallized ginger
- 1 tablespoon gluten
- 11/2 teaspoons salt
- 13/4 teaspoons SAF yeast or 21/4 teaspoons bread machine yeast
- 16 slices (2 pounds)
- 1/4 cup fat-free milk
- One 6-ounce jar junior baby food strained carrots or 3/4 cup pureed carrots
- 2 large eggs
- 3 tablespoons unsalted butter, cut into pieces
- 4 cups bread flour
- 1/3 cup chopped crystallized ginger
- 1 tablespoon plus 1 teaspoon gluten
- 2 teaspoons salt
- 2 teaspoons SAF yeast or 21/2 teaspoons bread machine yeast

Directions:

1. Choose the size of loaf you would like to make and measure your ingredients.
2. Add the ingredients to the bread pan in the order listed above.
3. Place the pan in the bread machine and close the lid.
4. Turn on the bread maker. Select the Basic setting, then the loaf size, and finally the crust color. Start the cycle.
5. When the cycle is finished and the bread is baked, carefully remove the pan from the machine. Use a potholder as the handle will be very hot. Let rest for a few minutes.
6. Remove the bread from the pan and allow to cool on a wire rack for at least 10 minutes before slicing.

Spicy Hot Red Pepper Bread

Ingredients:

- 8 slices (1 pound)
- ¾ cup + 1 tablespoons milk at room temperature
- 2 and 2/3 tablespoons red pepper relish
- 4 teaspoons chopped roasted red pepper
- 2 tablespoons melted butter, cooled
- 2 tablespoons light brown sugar
- 2/3 teaspoon salt
- 2 cups white bread flour
- 1 teaspoon bread machine yeast
- 12 slices (1 ½ pounds)
- 1 1/8 cups + 1 1/2 tablespoons milk at room temperature
- 3 and 1 tablespoons red pepper relish
- 6 teaspoons chopped roasted red pepper
- 3 tablespoons melted butter, cooled
- 3 tablespoons light brown sugar
- 1 teaspoon salt
- 3 cups white bread flour
- 1 1/2 teaspoons bread machine yeast
- 16 slices (2 pounds)
- 1 1/2 cups + 2 tablespoons milk at room temperature
- 4 and 1 1/3 tablespoons red pepper relish
- 8 teaspoons chopped roasted red pepper
- 4 tablespoons melted butter, cooled

- 4 tablespoons light brown sugar
- 1 1/3 teaspoons salt
- 4 cups white bread flour
- 2 teaspoons bread machine yeast

Directions:

1. Choose the size of loaf you would like to make and measure your ingredients.

2. Add the ingredients to the bread pan in the order listed above.

3. Place the pan in the bread machine and close the lid.

4. Turn on the bread maker. Select the White/Basic setting, then the loaf size, and finally the crust color. Start the cycle.

5. When the cycle is finished and the bread is baked, carefully remove the pan from the machine. Use a potholder as the handle will be very hot. Let rest for a few minutes.

6. Remove the bread from the pan and allow to cool on a wire rack for at least 10 minutes before slicing.

Pumpkin Coconut Almond Bread

Ingredients:

- 8 slices (1 pound)
- 1/4 cup vegetable oil
- 2 large eggs
- 1 cups canned pumpkin puree
- 2/3 cup sugar
- 1 teaspoons baking powder
- 1/3 teaspoon baking soda
- 1/6 teaspoon salt
- 2/3 tablespoon allspice
- 2 cups all-purpose flour
- 1/3 cup coconut flakes, plus a small handful for the topping
- 1/2 cup slivered almonds, plus a tablespoonful for the topping
- Non-stick cooking spray
- 12 slices (1 ½ pounds)
- 1/3 cup vegetable oil
- 3 large eggs
- 1 1/2 cups canned pumpkin puree
- 1 cup sugar
- 1 1/2 teaspoons baking powder
- 1/2 teaspoon baking soda
- 1/4 teaspoon salt
- 1 tablespoon allspice
- 3 cups all-purpose flour
- 1/2 cup coconut flakes, plus a small handful for the topping
- 2/3 cup slivered almonds, plus a tablespoonful for the topping
- Non-stick cooking spray
- 16 slices (2 pounds)
- 1/2 cup vegetable oil
- 4 large eggs
- 2 cups canned pumpkin puree
- 1 1/3 cups sugar
- 1 teaspoon baking powder
- 2/3 teaspoon baking soda
- 1/3 teaspoon salt
- 1 1/3 tablespoons allspice
- 4 cups all-purpose flour
- 2/3 cup coconut flakes, plus a small handful for the topping
- 1 cup slivered almonds, plus a tablespoonful for the topping
- Non-stick cooking spray

Directions:

1. Choose the size of loaf you would like to make and measure your ingredients.

2. Spray bread maker pan with non-stick cooking spray.

3. Mix oil, eggs, and pumpkin in a large mixing bowl.

4. Mix remaining ingredients together in a separate mixing bowl.

5. Add wet ingredients to bread pan, and dry ingredients on top.

6. Place the pan in the bread machine and close the lid.

7. Turn on the bread maker. Select the Dough/Rapid setting, then the loaf size, and finally the crust color. Start the cycle.

8. Open lid and sprinkle top of bread with reserved coconut and almonds.

9. When the cycle is finished and the bread is baked, carefully remove the pan from the machine. Use a potholder as the handle will be very hot. Let rest for a few minutes.

10. Remove the bread from the pan and allow to cool on a wire rack for at least 10 minutes before slicing.

Pain D'ail

Ingredients:

- 8 slices (1 pound)
- 2 cloves garlic
- 1 1/2 tablespoons unsalted butter, softened
- 3/4 cup water
- 2 cups bread flour
- 1/2 tablespoon plus 1/2 teaspoon gluten
- 3/4 tablespoon sugar
- 7/8 teaspoon salt
- 1 1/4 teaspoons SAF yeast or 1/2 tablespoon bread machine yeast
- 12 slices (1½ pounds)
- 3 cloves garlic
- 2 tablespoons unsalted butter, softened
- 11/4 cups water
- 31/8 cups bread flour
- 1 tablespoon gluten
- 1 tablespoon sugar
- 11/2 teaspoons salt
- 2 teaspoons SAF yeast or 21/2 teaspoons bread machine yeast
- 16 slices (2 pounds)
- 4 cloves garlic
- 3 tablespoons unsalted butter, softened
- 11/2 cups water
- 4 cups bread flour
- 1 tablespoon plus 1 teaspoon gluten
- 11/2 tablespoons sugar
- 13/4 teaspoons salt
- 21/2 teaspoons SAF yeast or 1 tablespoon bread machine yeast

Directions:

1. Choose the size of loaf you would like to make and measure your ingredients.

2. Peel the garlic cloves and press into the butter. Mash together.

3. Add the ingredients to the bread pan in the order listed above.

4. Add the garlic butter with the liquid ingredients.

5. Place the pan in the bread machine and close the lid.

6. Turn on the bread maker. Select the French setting, then the loaf size, and finally the crust color. Start the cycle.

7. When the cycle is finished and the bread is baked, carefully remove the pan from the machine. Use a potholder as the handle will be very hot. Let rest for a few minutes.

8. Remove the bread from the pan and allow to cool on a wire rack for at least 10 minutes before slicing.

Caraway Potato Bread

Ingredients:

- 8 slices (1 pound)
- 1¼ cups water
- 2 tablespoons butter, at room temperature
- 3 cups bread flour
- 2 teaspoons caraway seeds
- ½ cup instant mashed potatoes
- 1 tablespoon white sugar
- 1½ teaspoon salt
- 2 teaspoons bread machine yeast
- 12 slices (1 ½ pounds)
- 1 7/8 cups water
- 3 tablespoons butter, at room temperature
- 4 1/2 cups bread flour
- 3 teaspoons caraway seeds
- 3/4 cup instant mashed potatoes
- 1 1/2 tablespoons white sugar
- 2 1/4 teaspoons salt
- 3 teaspoons bread machine yeast
- 16 slices (2 pounds)
- 2 1/2 cups water
- 4 tablespoons butter, at room temperature
- 6 cups bread flour
- 4 teaspoons caraway seeds
- 1 cup instant mashed potatoes
- 2 tablespoons white sugar
- 3 teaspoons salt
- 4 teaspoons bread machine yeast

Directions:

1. Choose the size of loaf you would like to make and measure your ingredients.

2. Add the ingredients to the bread pan in the order listed above.

3. Place the pan in the bread machine and close the lid.

4. Turn on the bread maker. Select the White/Basic setting, then the loaf size, and finally the crust color. Start the cycle.

5. When the cycle is finished and the bread is baked, carefully remove the pan from the machine. Use a potholder as the handle will be very hot. Let rest for a few minutes.

6. Remove the bread from the pan and allow to cool on a wire rack for at least 10 minutes before slicing.

Basil Tomato Bread

Ingredients:

- 8 slices (1 pound)
- 1/2 cup lukewarm tomato sauce
- 1/2 tablespoon olive oil
- 1/2 tablespoon sugar
- 1/2 teaspoon table salt
- 1 1/2 cups white bread flour
- 1/8 cup grated Parmesan cheese
- 1 tablespoon dried basil
- 1/2 tablespoon dried oregano
- 1 1/8 teaspoons bread machine yeast
- 12 slices (1 ½ pounds)
- ¾ cup lukewarm tomato sauce
- ¾ tablespoon olive oil
- ¾ tablespoon sugar
- ¾ teaspoon table salt
- 2¼ cups white bread flour
- 1½ tablespoons dried basil
- ¾ tablespoon dried oregano
- 3 tablespoons grated Parmesan cheese
- 2 teaspoons bread machine yeast
- 16 slices (2 pounds)
- 1 cup lukewarm tomato sauce
- 1 tablespoon olive oil
- 1 tablespoon sugar
- 1 teaspoon table salt
- 3 cups white bread flour
- ¼ cup grated Parmesan cheese
- 2 tablespoons dried basil

- 1 tablespoon dried oregano
- 2¼ teaspoons bread machine yeast

Directions:

1. Choose the size of loaf you would like to make and measure your ingredients.

2. Add the ingredients to the bread pan in the order listed above.

3. Place the pan in the bread machine and close the lid.

4. Turn on the bread maker. Select the White/Basic setting, then the loaf size, and finally the crust color. Start the cycle.

5. When the cycle is finished and the bread is baked, carefully remove the pan from the machine. Use a potholder as the handle will be very hot. Let rest for a few minutes.

6. Remove the bread from the pan and allow to cool on a wire rack for at least 10 minutes before slicing.

Fresh Herb Stuffing Bread With Fennel Seed And Pepper

Ingredients:

- 8 slices (1 pound)
- 3/4 cup water
- 1 1/2 tablespoons olive oil
- 1 1/2 cups bread flour
- 1/2 cup whole wheat flour
- 1/4 cup chopped fresh herbs
- 2 tablespoons chopped walnuts or pine nuts
- 1 tablespoon sugar
- 1 tablespoon dry buttermilk powder
- 1/2 tablespoon gluten
- 3/4 teaspoon salt
- 5/8 teaspoon fennel seed
- 3/8 teaspoon grated lemon zest
- 3/8 teaspoon ground black, white, or red peppercorns
- 1 1/8 teaspoons SAF yeast or 1 3/8 teaspoons bread machine yeast
- 12 slices (1½ pounds)
- 11/8 cups water
- 2 tablespoons olive oil
- 21/2 cups bread flour
- 1/2 cup whole wheat flour

- 1/3 cup chopped fresh herbs
- 3 tablespoons chopped walnuts or pine nuts
- 11/2 tablespoons sugar
- 11/2 tablespoons dry buttermilk powder
- 2 teaspoons gluten
- 11/4 teaspoons salt
- 1 teaspoon fennel seed
- 1/2 teaspoon grated lemon zest
- 1/2 teaspoon ground black, white, or red peppercorns
- 2 teaspoons SAF yeast or 21/2 teaspoons bread machine yeast
- 16 slices (2 pounds)
- 11/2 cups water
- 3 tablespoons olive oil
- 3 cups bread flour
- 1 cup whole wheat flour
- 1/2 cup chopped fresh herbs
- 4 tablespoons chopped walnuts or pine nuts
- 2 tablespoons sugar
- 2 tablespoons dry buttermilk powder
- 1 tablespoon gluten
- 11/2 teaspoons salt
- 11/4 teaspoons fennel seed
- 3/4 teaspoon grated lemon zest
- 3/4 teaspoon ground black, white, or red peppercorns
- 21/4 teaspoons SAF yeast or 23/4 teaspoons bread machine yeast

Directions:

1. Choose the size of loaf you would like to make and measure your ingredients.
2. Add the ingredients to the bread pan in the order listed above.
3. Place the pan in the bread machine and close the lid.
4. Turn on the bread maker. Select the Basic setting, then the loaf size, and finally the crust color. Start the cycle.
5. When the cycle is finished and the bread is baked, carefully remove the pan from the machine. Use a potholder as the handle will be very hot. Let rest for a few minutes.

6. Remove the bread from the pan and allow to cool on a wire rack for at least 10 minutes before slicing.

Zucchini Bread

Ingredients:

- 8 slices (1 pound)
- 2 large eggs
- 1/2 cup vegetable oil
- 11/2 teaspoons vanilla extract
- 1 cup sugar
- 11/4 cups lightly packed shredded zucchini (about 2 medium)
- 11/2 cups unbleached all-purpose flour
- 1 teaspoon baking soda
- 3/4 teaspoon baking powder
- 11/4 teaspoons ground cinnamon or apple pie spice
- 1/4 teaspoon salt
- 1/2 cup coarsely chopped walnuts
- 12 slices (1 ½ pounds)
- 3 large eggs
- 3/4 cup vegetable oil
- 2 1/4 teaspoons vanilla extract
- 1 1/2 cups sugar
- 1 7/8 cups lightly packed shredded zucchini (about 2 medium)
- 2 1/4 cups unbleached all-purpose flour
- 1 1/2 teaspoons baking soda
- 1 1/8 teaspoons baking powder
- 1 7/8 teaspoons ground cinnamon or apple pie spice
- 3/8 teaspoon salt
- 3/4 cup coarsely chopped walnuts
- 16 slices (2 pounds)
- 4 large eggs
- 1 cup vegetable oil
- 3 teaspoons vanilla extract
- 2 cups sugar
- 2 1/2 cups lightly packed shredded zucchini (about 2 medium)
- 3 cups unbleached all-purpose flour
- 2 teaspoons baking soda
- 1 1/2 teaspoons baking powder
- 2 1/2 teaspoons ground cinnamon or apple pie spice
- 1/2 teaspoon salt

- 1 cup coarsely chopped walnuts

Directions:

1. Choose the size of loaf you would like to make and measure your ingredients.
2. Add the ingredients to the bread pan in the order listed above.
3. Place the pan in the bread machine and close the lid.
4. Turn on the bread maker. Select the Quick Bread/Cake setting, then the loaf size, and finally the crust color. Start the cycle.
5. When the cycle is finished and the bread is baked, carefully remove the pan from the machine. Use a potholder as the handle will be very hot. Let rest for a few minutes.
6. Remove the bread from the pan and allow to cool on a wire rack for at least 10 minutes before slicing.

Green Onion Bread

Ingredients:
- 8 slices (1 pound)
- ½ cup green onion, sliced
- ½ teaspoon dried basil
- ½ teaspoon dried thyme
- ¼ teaspoon dried rosemary
- 2 tablespoons butter
- 1 cup milk
- 1 whole egg
- 2 tablespoons sugar
- ¾ teaspoons salt
- 3 cups bread flour
- 2 teaspoons active dry yeast
- 12 slices (1 ½ pounds)
- 3/4 cup green onion, sliced
- 3/4 teaspoon dried basil
- 3/4 teaspoon dried thyme
- 3/8 teaspoon dried rosemary
- 3 tablespoons butter
- 1 1/2 cups milk
- 1 1/2 whole eggs
- 3 tablespoons sugar
- 1 1/8 teaspoons salt
- 4 1/2 cups bread flour
- 3 teaspoons active dry yeast

- 16 slices (2 pounds)
- 1 cup green onion, sliced
- 1 teaspoon dried basil
- 1 teaspoon dried thyme
- 1/2 teaspoon dried rosemary
- 4 tablespoons butter
- 2 cups milk
- 2 whole eggs
- 4 tablespoons sugar
- 1 1/2 teaspoons salt
- 6 cups bread flour
- 4 teaspoons active dry yeast

Directions:

1. Choose the size of loaf you would like to make and measure your ingredients.
2. Add the ingredients to the bread pan in the order listed above.
3. Place the pan in the bread machine and close the lid.
4. Turn on the bread maker. Select the White/Basic setting, then the loaf size, and finally the crust color. Start the cycle.
5. When the cycle is finished and the bread is baked, carefully remove the pan from the machine. Use a potholder as the handle will be very hot. Let rest for a few minutes.
6. Remove the bread from the pan and allow to cool on a wire rack for at least 10 minutes before slicing.

Sweet Potato Bread

Ingredients:
- 8 slices (1 pound)
- 5/16 cup lukewarm water
- 1/2 cup plain sweet potatoes, peeled and mashed
- 1 tablespoon unsalted butter, melted
- 1/6 cup dark brown sugar
- 3/4 teaspoon table salt
- 2 cups bread flour
- 1/8 teaspoon ground nutmeg
- 1/8 teaspoon cinnamon
- 1/2 teaspoon vanilla extract
- 1 tablespoon dry milk powder
- 1 teaspoon bread machine yeast
- 12 slices (1 ½ pounds)

- ⅓ cup + 2 tablespoons lukewarm water
- ¾ cup plain sweet potatoes, peeled and mashed
- 1½ tablespoons unsalted butter, melted
- ¼ cup dark brown sugar
- 1 teaspoon table salt
- 3 cups bread flour
- ⅛ teaspoon ground nutmeg
- ⅛ teaspoon cinnamon
- ¾ teaspoon vanilla extract
- 1½ tablespoons dry milk powder
- 1½ teaspoons bread machine yeast
- 16 slices (2 pounds)
- ⅝ cup lukewarm water
- 1 cup plain sweet potatoes, peeled and mashed
- 2 tablespoons unsalted butter, melted
- ⅓ cup dark brown sugar
- 1½ teaspoons table salt
- 4 cups bread flour
- ¼ teaspoon ground nutmeg
- ¼ teaspoon cinnamon
- 1 teaspoon vanilla extract
- 2 tablespoons dry milk powder
- 2 teaspoons bread machine yeast

Directions:

1. Choose the size of loaf you would like to make and measure your ingredients.
2. Add the ingredients to the bread pan in the order listed above.
3. Place the pan in the bread machine and close the lid.
4. Turn on the bread maker. Select the White/Basic setting, then the loaf size, and finally the crust color. Start the cycle.
5. When the cycle is finished, and the bread is baked, carefully remove the pan from the machine. Use a potholder as the handle will be very hot. Let rest for a few minutes.
6. Remove the bread from the pan and allow to cool on a wire rack for at least 10 minutes before slicing.

Chicken Stuffing Bread

Ingredients:

- 8 slices (1 pound)
- 3/4 cup fat-free milk
- 1 1/2 tablespoons butter, cut into pieces
- 2 cups bread flour
- 3/4 tablespoon sugar
- 2/3 tablespoon gluten
- 1 1/2 tablespoons chopped fresh chives
- 3/4 tablespoon dried marjoram
- 3/4 teaspoon dried basil
- 3/4 teaspoon dried thyme
- 1 teaspoon salt
- 1 1/4 teaspoons SAF yeast or 1/2 tablespoon bread machine yeast
- 12 slices (1½ pounds)
- 11/8 cups fat-free milk
- 2 tablespoons butter, cut into pieces
- 3 cups bread flour
- 1 tablespoon sugar
- 1 tablespoon gluten
- 2 tablespoons chopped fresh chives
- 1 tablespoon dried marjoram
- 1 teaspoon dried basil
- 1 teaspoon dried thyme
- 11/2 teaspoons salt
- 2 teaspoons SAF yeast or 21/2 teaspoons bread machine yeast
- 16 slices (2 pounds)
- 11/2 cups fat-free milk
- 3 tablespoons butter, cut into pieces
- 4 cups bread flour
- 11/2 tablespoons sugar
- 1 tablespoon plus 1 teaspoon gluten
- 3 tablespoons chopped fresh chives
- 11/2 tablespoons dried marjoram
- 11/2 teaspoons dried basil
- 11/2 teaspoons dried thyme
- 2 teaspoons salt
- 21/2 teaspoons SAF yeast or 1 tablespoon bread machine yeast

Directions:

1. Choose the size of loaf you would like to make and measure your ingredients.
2. Add the ingredients to the bread pan in the order listed above.
3. Place the pan in the bread machine and close the lid.

4. Turn on the bread maker. Select the Basic setting, then the loaf size, and finally the crust color. Start the cycle.

5. When the cycle is finished and the bread is baked, carefully remove the pan from the machine. Use a potholder as the handle will be very hot. Let rest for a few minutes.

6. Remove the bread from the pan and allow to cool on a wire rack for at least 10 minutes before slicing.

Potato Honey Bread

Ingredients:

- 8 slices (1 pound)
- 1/2 cup lukewarm water
- 1/3 cup finely mashed potatoes, at room temperature
- 1/2 egg, at room temperature
- 1/4 cup unsalted butter, melted
- 1 1/3 tablespoons honey
- 2/3 teaspoon table salt
- 2 cups white bread flour
- 1 1/8 teaspoons bread machine yeast
- 12 slices (1 ½ pounds)
- ¾ cup lukewarm water
- ½ cup finely mashed potatoes, at room temperature
- 1 egg, at room temperature
- ¼ cup unsalted butter, melted
- 2 tablespoons honey
- 1 teaspoon table salt
- 3 cups white bread flour
- 2 teaspoons bread machine yeast
- 16 slices (2 pounds)
- 1 cup lukewarm water
- ⅔ cup finely mashed potatoes, at room temperature
- 1 egg, at room temperature
- ½ cup unsalted butter, melted
- 2⅔ tablespoons honey
- 1⅓ teaspoons table salt
- 4 cups white bread flour
- 2¼ teaspoons bread machine yeast

Directions:

1. Choose the size of loaf you would like to make and measure your ingredients.

2. Add the ingredients to the bread pan in the order listed above.

3. Place the pan in the bread machine and close the lid.

4. Turn on the bread maker. Select the White/Basic setting, then the loaf size, and finally the crust color. Start the cycle.

5. When the cycle is finished and the bread is baked, carefully remove the pan from the machine. Use a potholder as the handle will be very hot. Let rest for a few minutes.

6. Remove the bread from the pan and allow to cool on a wire rack for at least 10 minutes before slicing.

Sauerkraut Rye Bread

Ingredients:

- 8 slices (1 pound)
- 1 cup sauerkraut, rinsed and drained
- ¾ cup warm water
- 1½ tablespoons molasses
- 1½ tablespoons butter
- 1½ tablespoons brown sugar
- 1 teaspoon caraway seeds
- 1½ teaspoons salt
- 1 cup rye flour
- 2 cups bread flour
- 1½ teaspoons active dry yeast
- 12 slices (1 ½ pounds)
- 1 1/2 cups sauerkraut, rinsed and drained
- 1 1/8 cups warm water
- 2 1/4 tablespoons molasses
- 2 1/4 tablespoons butter
- 2 1/4 tablespoons brown sugar
- 1 1/2 teaspoons caraway seeds
- 2 1/4 teaspoons salt
- 1 1/2 cups rye flour
- 3 cups bread flour
- 2 1/4 teaspoons active dry yeast
- 16 slices (2 pounds)
- 2 cups sauerkraut, rinsed and drained
- 1 1/2 cups warm water
- 3 tablespoons molasses
- 3 tablespoons butter
- 3 tablespoons brown sugar

- 2 teaspoons caraway seeds
- 3 teaspoons salt
- 2 cups rye flour
- 4 cups bread flour
- 3 teaspoons active dry yeast

Directions:

1. Choose the size of loaf you would like to make and measure your ingredients.

2. Add the ingredients to the bread pan in the order listed above.

3. Place the pan in the bread machine and close the lid.

4. Turn on the bread maker. Select the White/Basic setting, then the loaf size, and finally the crust color. Start the cycle.

5. When the cycle is finished and the bread is baked, carefully remove the pan from the machine. Use a potholder as the handle will be very hot. Let rest for a few minutes.

6. Remove the bread from the pan and allow to cool on a wire rack for at least 10 minutes before slicing.

Onion Chive Bread

Ingredients:

- 8 slices (1 pound)
- 5/8 cup lukewarm water
- 1/8 cup unsalted butter, melted
- 1 tablespoon sugar
- 3/4 teaspoon table salt
- 2 1/8 cups white bread flour
- 1/8 cup dried minced onion
- 1 tablespoon fresh chives, chopped
- 1 1/8 teaspoons bread machine yeast
- 12 slices (1 ½ pounds)
- 1 cup lukewarm water
- 3 tablespoons unsalted butter, melted
- 1½ tablespoons sugar
- 1⅛ teaspoons table salt
- 3⅛ cups white bread flour
- 3 tablespoons dried minced onion
- 1½ tablespoons fresh chives, chopped
- 1⅔ teaspoons bread machine yeast
- 16 slices (2 pounds)
- 1¼ cups lukewarm water

- ¼ cup unsalted butter, melted
- 2 tablespoons sugar
- 1½ teaspoons table salt
- 4¼ cups white bread flour
- ¼ cup dried minced onion
- 2 tablespoons fresh chives, chopped
- 2¼ teaspoons bread machine yeast

Directions:

1. Choose the size of loaf you would like to make and measure your ingredients.

2. Add the ingredients to the bread pan in the order listed above.

3. Place the pan in the bread machine and close the lid.

4. Turn on the bread maker. Select the White/Basic setting, then the loaf size, and finally the crust color. Start the cycle.

5. When the cycle is finished and the bread is baked, carefully remove the pan from the machine. Use a potholder as the handle will be very hot. Let rest for a few minutes.

6. Remove the bread from the pan and allow to cool on a wire rack for at least 10 minutes before slicing.

Italian Onion Bread

Ingredients:

- 8 slices (1 pound)
- 1 cup warm milk, at room temperature
- 1 large whole egg
- 2 tablespoons butter, soft
- ¼ cup dried onion, minced
- 1½ teaspoons salt
- 2 tablespoons dried parsley flakes
- 1 teaspoon dried oregano
- 3½ cups bread flour
- 2 teaspoons dry yeast
- 12 slices (1 ½ pounds)
- 1 1/2 cups warm milk, at room temperature
- 1 1/2 large whole eggs
- 3 tablespoons butter, soft
- 3/8 cup dried onion, minced
- 2 1/4 teaspoons salt
- 3 tablespoons dried parsley flakes
- 1 1/2 teaspoons dried oregano

- 5 1/4 cups bread flour
- 3 teaspoons dry yeast
- 16 slices (2 pounds)
- 2 cups warm milk, at room temperature
- 2 large whole eggs
- 4 tablespoons butter, soft
- 1/2 cup dried onion, minced
- 3 teaspoons salt
- 4 tablespoons dried parsley flakes
- 2 teaspoons dried oregano
- 7 cups bread flour
- 4 teaspoons dry yeast

Directions:

1. Choose the size of loaf you would like to make and measure your ingredients.

2. Add the ingredients to the bread pan in the order listed above.

3. Place the pan in the bread machine and close the lid.

4. Turn on the bread maker. Select the White/Basic setting, then the loaf size, and finally the crust color. Start the cycle.

5. When the cycle is finished and the bread is baked, carefully remove the pan from the machine. Use a potholder as the handle will be very hot. Let rest for a few minutes.

6. Remove the bread from the pan and allow to cool on a wire rack for at least 10 minutes before slicing.

Honey Potato Flakes Bread

Ingredients:

- 8 slices (1 pound)
- 5/6 cup lukewarm milk
- 1 1/3 tablespoons unsalted butter, melted
- 2 teaspoons honey
- 1 teaspoon table salt
- 2 cups white bread flour
- 3/4 teaspoon dried thyme
- 1/3 cup instant potato flakes
- 1 1/4 teaspoons bread machine yeast
- 12 slices (1 ½ pounds)
- 1¼ cups lukewarm milk
- 2 tablespoons unsalted butter, melted
- 1 tablespoon honey

- 1½ teaspoons table salt
- 3 cups white bread flour
- 1 teaspoon dried thyme
- ½ cup instant potato flakes
- 2 teaspoons bread machine yeast
- 16 slices (2 pounds)
- 1⅔ cups lukewarm milk
- 2⅔ tablespoons unsalted butter, melted
- 4 teaspoons honey
- 2 teaspoons table salt
- 4 cups white bread flour
- 1½ teaspoons dried thyme
- ⅔ cup instant potato flakes
- 2½ teaspoons bread machine yeast

Directions:

1. Choose the size of loaf you would like to make and measure your ingredients

2. Add the ingredients to the bread pan in the order listed above.

3. Place the pan in the bread machine and close the lid.

4. Turn on the bread maker. Select the White/Basic setting, then the loaf size, and finally the crust color. Start the cycle.

5. When the cycle is finished and the bread is baked, carefully remove the pan from the machine. Use a potholder as the handle will be very hot. Let rest for a few minutes.

6. Remove the bread from the pan and allow to cool on a wire rack for at least 10 minutes before slicing.

Cornbread

Ingredients:

- 8 slices (1 pound)
- 1 large egg
- 11/4 cups buttermilk
- 6 tablespoons unsalted butter, melted
- 1/3 cup sugar
- 1 cup fine-grind yellow cornmeal, preferably stone-ground
- 1 cup unbleached all-purpose flour
- 2 tablespoons toasted wheat germ
- 1 teaspoon baking soda
- 1/2 teaspoon baking powder

- 1/2 teaspoon salt
- 12 slices (1 ½ pounds)
- 1 1/2 large eggs
- 1 7/8 cups buttermilk
- 9 tablespoons unsalted butter, melted
- 1/2 cup sugar
- 1 1/2 cup fine-grind yellow cornmeal, preferably stone-ground
- 1 1/2 cups unbleached all-purpose flour
- 3 tablespoons toasted wheat germ
- 1 1/2 teaspoons baking soda
- 3/4 teaspoon baking powder
- 3/4 teaspoon salt
- 16 slices (2 pounds)
- 2 large eggs
- 2 1/2 cups buttermilk
- 12 tablespoons unsalted butter, melted
- 2/3 cup sugar
- 2 cups fine-grind yellow cornmeal, preferably stone-ground
- 2 cups unbleached all-purpose flour
- 4 tablespoons toasted wheat germ
- 2 teaspoons baking soda
- 1 teaspoon baking powder
- 1 teaspoon salt

Directions:

1. Place the ingredients in the pan according to the order in the manufacturer's instructions. Set the crust for medium, if your machine offers crust control for this cycle, and program for the Quick Bread/Cake cycle; press Start. The batter will be thick. When the machine beeps at the end of the cycle, check the loaf for doneness. The cornbread is done when it shrinks slightly from the sides of the pan, the sides are dark brown, and the top is firm to a gentle pressure when touched with your finger. A toothpick or metal skewer will come out clean when inserted into the center of the bread.

2. When the bread is done baking, immediately remove the pan from the machine. Let the bread stand in the pan for 15 minutes before gently turning it out, right side up, to cool on a rack. Serve warm or at room temperature, the day it is baked, cut into thick slices.

Cheesy Broccoli & Cauliflower Bread

Ingredients:

- 8 slices (1 pound)
- ¼ cup water
- 4 tablespoons olive oil
- 1 egg white
- 1 teaspoon lemon juice
- 2/3 cup grated cheddar cheese
- 3 tablespoons green onion
- ½ cup broccoli, chopped
- ½ cup cauliflower, chopped
- ½ teaspoon lemon pepper seasoning
- 2 cups bread flour
- 1 teaspoon bread machine yeast
- 12 slices (1 ½ pounds)
- 3/8 cup water
- 6 tablespoons olive oil
- 1 1/2 egg whites
- 1 1/2 teaspoons lemon juice
- 1 cup grated cheddar cheese
- 4 1/2 tablespoons green onion
- 3/4 cup broccoli, chopped
- 3/4 cup cauliflower, chopped
- 3/4 teaspoon lemon pepper seasoning
- 3 cups bread flour
- 1 1/2 teaspoons bread machine yeast
- 16 slices (2 pounds)
- 1/2 cup water
- 8 tablespoons olive oil
- 2 egg whites
- 2 teaspoons lemon juice
- 1 1/3 cups grated cheddar cheese
- 6 tablespoons green onion
- 1 cup broccoli, chopped
- 1 cup cauliflower, chopped
- 1 teaspoon lemon pepper seasoning
- 4 cups bread flour
- 2 teaspoons bread machine yeast

Directions:

1. Choose the size of loaf you would like to make and measure your ingredients.

2. Add the ingredients to the bread pan in the order listed above.

3.   Place the pan in the bread machine and close the lid.

4.   Turn on the bread maker. Select the White/Basic setting, then the loaf size, and finally the crust color. Start the cycle.

5.   When the cycle is finished and the bread is baked, carefully remove the pan from the machine. Use a potholder as the handle will be very hot. Let rest for a few minutes.

6.   Remove the bread from the pan and allow to cool on a wire rack for at least 10 minutes before slicing.

Prosciutto Stuffing Bread

Ingredients:
- 8 slices (1 pound)
- 5/8 cup water
- 1/6 cup olive oil
- 2 cups bread flour
- 2 ounces prosciutto, coarsely chopped
- 1/2 tablespoon plus 1/2 teaspoon gluten
- 1/2 tablespoon plus 1/2 teaspoon sugar
- 5/8 teaspoon ground black pepper
- 3/8 teaspoon salt
- 1 teaspoon SAF yeast or 1 1/4 teaspoons bread machine yeast
- 12 slices (1½ pounds)
- 7/8 cup water
- 1/4 cup olive oil
- 3 cups bread flour
- 3 ounces prosciutto, coarsely chopped
- 1 tablespoon gluten
- 1 tablespoon sugar
- 1 teaspoon ground black pepper
- 1/2 teaspoon salt
- 11/2 teaspoons SAF yeast or 2 teaspoons bread machine yeast
- 16 slices (2 pounds)
- 11/4 cups water
- 1/3 cup olive oil
- 4 cups bread flour
- 4 ounces prosciutto, coarsely chopped
- 1 tablespoon plus 1 teaspoon gluten
- 1 tablespoon plus 1 teaspoon sugar
- 11/4 teaspoons ground black pepper

- 3/4 teaspoon salt
- 2 teaspoons SAF yeast or 21/2 teaspoons bread machine yeast

Directions:
1.   Choose the size of loaf you would like to make and measure your ingredients.

2.   Add the ingredients to the bread pan in the order listed above.

3.   Place the pan in the bread machine and close the lid.

4.   Turn on the bread maker. Select the Basic setting, then the loaf size, and finally the crust color. Start the cycle.

5.   When the cycle is finished and the bread is baked, carefully remove the pan from the machine. Use a potholder as the handle will be very hot. Let rest for a few minutes.

6.   Remove the bread from the pan and allow to cool on a wire rack for at least 10 minutes before slicing.

Cornmeal Stuffing Bread

Ingredients:
- 8 slices (1 pound)
- One 5 1/2-ounce can of corn with liquid
- 1/6 cup buttermilk
- 1 1/2 tablespoons canola or olive oil
- 1 1/2 tablespoons honey
- 1 3/8 cups bread flour
- 5/8 cup yellow cornmeal
- 1/6 cup minced fresh parsley
- 7/8 tablespoon poultry seasoning
- 3/8 teaspoon garlic powder
- 1/2 tablespoon plus 1 teaspoons gluten
- 3/4 teaspoon salt
- 1 1/4 teaspoons SAF yeast or 1/2 tablespoon bread machine yeast
- 12 slices (1½ pounds)
- One 11-ounce can of corn with liquid
- 1/4 cup buttermilk
- 2 tablespoons canola or olive oil
- 2 tablespoons honey
- 2 cups bread flour
- 1 cup yellow cornmeal
- 1/4 cup minced fresh parsley

- 11/2 tablespoons poultry seasoning
- 1/2 teaspoon garlic powder
- 1 tablespoon plus 1 teaspoon gluten
- 11/4 teaspoons salt
- 2 teaspoons SAF yeast or 21/2 teaspoons bread machine yeast
- 16 slices (2 pounds)
- One 11-ounce can of corn with liquid
- 1/3 cup buttermilk
- 3 tablespoons canola or olive oil
- 3 tablespoons honey
- 23/4 cups bread flour
- 11/4 cups yellow cornmeal
- 1/3 cup minced fresh parsley
- 13/4 tablespoons poultry seasoning
- 3/4 teaspoon garlic powder
- 1 tablespoon plus 2 teaspoons gluten
- 11/2 teaspoons salt
- 21/2 teaspoons SAF yeast or 1 tablespoon bread machine yeast

Directions:

1. Choose the size of loaf you would like to make and measure your ingredients.
2. Add the ingredients to the bread pan in the order listed above.
3. Place the pan in the bread machine and close the lid.
4. Turn on the bread maker. Select the Basic setting, then the loaf size, and finally the crust color. Start the cycle.
5. When the cycle is finished and the bread is baked, carefully remove the pan from the machine. Use a potholder as the handle will be very hot. Let rest for a few minutes.
6. Remove the bread from the pan and allow to cool on a wire rack for at least 10 minutes before slicing.

Beetroot Bread

Ingredients:

- 8 slices (1 pound)
- 1/2 cup lukewarm water
- 1/2 cup grated raw beetroot
- 1 tablespoon unsalted butter, melted
- 1 tablespoon sugar

- 1 teaspoon table salt
- 2 cups white bread flour
- 5/6 teaspoon bread machine yeast
- 12 slices (1 ½ pounds)
- ¾ cups lukewarm water
- ¾ cup grated raw beetroot
- 1½ tablespoons unsalted butter, melted
- 1½ tablespoons sugar
- 1¼ teaspoons table salt
- 3 cups white bread flour
- 1¼ teaspoons bread machine yeast
- 16 slices (2 pounds)
- 1 cup lukewarm water
- 1 cup grated raw beetroot
- 2 tablespoons unsalted butter, melted
- 2 tablespoons sugar
- 2 teaspoons table salt
- 4 cups white bread flour
- 1⅔ teaspoons bread machine yeast

Directions:

1. Choose the size of loaf you would like to make and measure your ingredients.
2. Add the ingredients to the bread pan in the order listed above.
3. Place the pan in the bread machine and close the lid.
4. Turn on the bread maker. Select the White/Basic setting, then the loaf size, and finally the crust color. Start the cycle.
5. When the cycle is finished and the bread is baked, carefully remove the pan from the machine. Use a potholder as the handle will be very hot. Let rest for a few minutes.
6. Remove the bread from the pan and allow to cool on a wire rack for at least 10 minutes before slicing.

Carrot Bread

Ingredients:

- 8 slices (1 pound)
- 2 2/3 large eggs
- 1/3 cup nut oil
- 1/3 cup vegetable or light olive oil
- 1 1/3 teaspoons vanilla extract
- 1 1/3 cups lightly packed shredded raw carrots

- 1 1/3 cups sugar
- 2 cups unbleached all-purpose flour
- 1 2/3 teaspoons baking powder
- 1 teaspoon baking soda
- 1 2/3 teaspoons ground cinnamon or apple pie spice
- 3/4 teaspoon salt
- 12 slices (1 ½ pounds)
- 4 large eggs
- 1/2 cup nut oil
- 1/2 cup vegetable or light olive oil
- 2 teaspoons vanilla extract
- 2 cups lightly packed shredded raw carrots
- 2 cups sugar
- 3 cups unbleached all-purpose flour
- 21/2 teaspoons baking powder
- 11/2 teaspoons baking soda
- 21/2 teaspoons ground cinnamon or apple pie spice
- 1 teaspoon salt
- 16 slices (2 pounds)
- 5 1/3 large eggs
- 2/3 cup nut oil
- 2/3 cup vegetable or light olive oil
- 2 2/3 teaspoons vanilla extract
- 2 2/3 cups lightly packed shredded raw carrots
- 2 2/3 cups sugar
- 4 cups unbleached all-purpose flour
- 3 1/3 teaspoons baking powder
- 2 teaspoons baking soda
- 3 1/3 teaspoons ground cinnamon or apple pie spice
- 1 1/2 teaspoons salt

Directions:

1. Choose the size of loaf you would like to make and measure your ingredients.

2. Add the ingredients to the bread pan in the order listed above.

3. Place the pan in the bread machine and close the lid.

4. Turn on the bread maker. Select the Quick Bread/Cake setting, then the loaf size, and finally the crust color. Start the cycle.

5. When the machine beeps at the end of the cycle, press Stop/Reset and program for the Bake Only cycle for an additional 10 to 15 minutes to finish baking.

6. When the cycle is finished and the bread is baked, carefully remove the pan from the machine. Use a potholder as the handle will be very hot. Let rest for a few minutes.

7. Remove the bread from the pan and allow to cool on a wire rack for at least 10 minutes.

8. Wrap tightly in plastic wrap and let sit at room temperature overnight, or up to 3 days before serving.

Zucchini Spice Bread

Ingredients:

- 8 slices (1 pound)
- 1 eggs, at room temperature
- 1/3 cup unsalted butter, melted
- 1/3 teaspoon table salt
- 1/2 cup shredded zucchini
- 1/3 cup light brown sugar
- 1 1/2 tablespoons sugar
- 1 cups all-purpose flour
- 1/3 teaspoon baking powder
- 1/3 teaspoon baking soda
- 1/6 teaspoon ground allspice
- 2/3 teaspoons ground cinnamon
- 1/3 cup chopped pecans
- 12 slices (1 ½ pounds)
- 2 eggs, at room temperature
- ½ cup unsalted butter, melted
- ½ teaspoon table salt
- ¾ cup shredded zucchini
- ½ cup light brown sugar
- 2 tablespoons sugar
- 1½ cups all-purpose flour
- ½ teaspoon baking powder
- ½ teaspoon baking soda
- ¼ teaspoon ground allspice
- 1 teaspoon ground cinnamon
- ½ cup chopped pecans
- 16 slices (2 pounds)
- 2 eggs, at room temperature
- ⅔ cup unsalted butter, melted
- ⅔ teaspoon table salt
- 1 cup shredded zucchini
- ⅔ cup light brown sugar

- 3 tablespoons sugar
- 2 cups all-purpose flour
- ⅔ teaspoon baking powder
- ⅔ teaspoon baking soda
- ⅓ teaspoon ground allspice
- 1⅓ teaspoons ground cinnamon
- ⅔ cup chopped pecans

Directions:

1. Choose the size of loaf you would like to make and measure your ingredients.
2. Add the ingredients to the bread pan in the order listed above.
3. Place the pan in the bread machine and close the lid.
4. Turn on the bread maker. Select the Quick/Rapid setting, then the loaf size, and finally the crust color. Start the cycle.
5. When the cycle is finished and the bread is baked, carefully remove the pan from the machine. Use a potholder as the handle will be very hot. Let rest for a few minutes.
6. Remove the bread from the pan and allow to cool down on a wire rack for at least 10 minutes or more before slicing.

Hot Paprika Onion Bread

Ingredients:
- 8 slices (1 pound)
- 1 cup water at room temperature
- 2 tablespoons butter, soft
- 1/3 cup onion, finely chopped
- 1½ teaspoon salt
- 1 teaspoon sugar
- 1 teaspoon paprika
- 3 cups bread flour
- 1 pack active dry yeast
- 12 slices (1 ½ pounds)
- 1 1/2 cups water at room temperature
- 3 tablespoons butter, soft
- 1/2 cup onion, finely chopped
- 2 1/4 teaspoons salt
- 1 1/2 teaspoons sugar
- 1 1/2 teaspoons paprika
- 4 1/2 cups bread flour

- 1 1/2 packs active dry yeast
- 16 slices (2 pounds)
- 2 cups water at room temperature
- 4 tablespoons butter, soft
- 2/3 cup onion, finely chopped
- 3 teaspoons salt
- 2 teaspoons sugar
- 2 teaspoons paprika
- 6 cups bread flour
- 2 packs active dry yeast

Directions:

1. Choose the size of loaf you would like to make and measure your ingredients.
2. Add the ingredients to the bread pan in the order listed above.
3. Place the pan in the bread machine and close the lid.
4. Turn on the bread maker. Select the White/Basic setting, then the loaf size, and finally the crust color. Start the cycle.
5. When the cycle is finished and the bread is baked, carefully remove the pan from the machine. Use a potholder as the handle will be very hot. Let rest for a few minutes.
6. Remove the bread from the pan and allow to cool on a wire rack for at least 10 minutes before slicing.

Zucchini Lemon Bread

Ingredients:
- 8 slices (1 pound)
- 1/3 cup lukewarm milk
- 1/2 cup finely shredded zucchini
- 1/6 teaspoon lemon juice, at room temperature
- 2 teaspoons olive oil
- 2 teaspoons sugar
- 2/3 teaspoon table salt
- 1/2 cup whole-wheat flour
- 1 cup white bread flour
- 1/2 cup quick oats
- 1 1/8 teaspoons bread machine yeast
- 12 slices (1 ½ pounds)
- ½ cup lukewarm milk
- ¾ cup finely shredded zucchini
- ¼ teaspoon lemon juice, at room temperature

- 1 tablespoon olive oil
- 1 tablespoon sugar
- 1 teaspoon table salt
- ¾ cup whole-wheat flour
- 1½ cups white bread flour
- ¾ cup quick oats
- 2¼ teaspoons bread machine yeast
- 16 slices (2 pounds)
- ⅔ cup lukewarm milk
- 1 cup finely shredded zucchini
- ⅓ teaspoon lemon juice, at room temperature
- 4 teaspoons olive oil
- 4 teaspoons sugar
- 1⅓ teaspoons table salt
- 1 cup whole-wheat flour
- 2 cups white bread flour
- 1 cup quick oats
- 2¼ teaspoons bread machine yeast

Directions:

1.   Choose the size of loaf you would like to make and measure your ingredients.

2.   Add the ingredients to the bread pan in the order listed above.

3.   Place the pan in the bread machine and close the lid.

4.   Turn on the bread maker. Select the White/Basic setting, then the loaf size, and finally the crust color. Start the cycle.

5.   When the cycle is finished and the bread is baked, carefully remove the pan from the machine. Use a potholder as the handle will be very hot. Let rest for a few minutes.

6.   Remove the bread from the pan and allow to cool on a wire rack for at least 10 minutes before slicing.

CAKE RECIPES/QUICK BREAD/SWEET ROLLS

Cocoa Banana Bread

Ingredients:

- 8 slices (1 pound)
- 2 bananas, mashed
- 1 1/2 eggs, at room temperature
- 1/2 cup packed light brown sugar
- 3/8 cup unsalted butter, melted
- 3/8 cup sour cream, at room temperature
- 1/6 cup sugar
- 1 teaspoon pure vanilla extract
- 2/3 cup all-purpose flour
- 1/3 cup quick oats
- 1 1/2 tablespoons unsweetened cocoa powder
- 2/3 teaspoon baking soda
- 12 slices (1 ½ pounds)
- 3 bananas, mashed
- 2 eggs, at room temperature
- ¾ cup packed light brown sugar
- ½ cup unsalted butter, melted
- ½ cup sour cream, at room temperature
- ¼ cup sugar
- 1½ teaspoons pure vanilla extract
- 1 cup all-purpose flour
- ½ cup quick oats
- 2 tablespoons unsweetened cocoa powder
- 1 teaspoon baking soda
- 16 slices (2 pounds)
- 4 bananas, mashed
- 3 eggs, at room temperature
- 1 cup packed light brown sugar
- ¾ cup unsalted butter, melted
- ¾ cup sour cream, at room temperature
- ⅓ cup sugar
- 2 teaspoons pure vanilla extract
- 1⅓ cups all-purpose flour
- ⅔ cup quick oats
- 3 tablespoons unsweetened cocoa powder
- 1⅓ teaspoons baking soda

Directions:

1. Choose the size of loaf you would like to make and measure your ingredients.
2. Add the ingredients to the bread pan in the order listed above.
3. Place the pan in the bread machine and close the lid.
4. Turn on the bread maker. Select the Quick/Rapid setting, then the loaf size, and finally the crust color. Start the cycle.
5. When the cycle is finished and the bread is baked, carefully remove the pan from the machine. Use a potholder as the handle will be very hot. Let rest for a few minutes.
6. Remove the bread from the pan and allow to cool on a wire rack for at least 10 minutes before slicing.

Sweet Flaxseed Bread

Ingredients:

- 8 slices (1 pound)
- ¾ cup milk, at room temperature
- 1 tablespoon melted butter
- 1 tablespoon honey
- ¾ teaspoon salt
- 2 tablespoons flaxseeds
- 2 cups white bread flour
- ¾ teaspoon bread machine yeast
- 12 slices (1 ½ pounds)
- 1 1/8 cups milk, at room temperature
- 1 1/2 tablespoons melted butter
- 1 1/2 tablespoons honey
- 1 1/8 teaspoons salt
- 3 tablespoons flaxseeds
- 3 cups white bread flour
- 1 1/8 teaspoons bread machine yeast
- 16 slices (2 pounds)
- 1 1/2 cups milk, at room temperature
- 2 tablespoons melted butter
- 2 tablespoons honey
- 1 1/2 teaspoons salt
- 4 tablespoons flaxseeds
- 4 cups white bread flour
- 1 1/2 teaspoons bread machine yeast

Directions:

1. Choose the size of loaf you would like to make and measure your ingredients.
2. Add the ingredients to the bread pan in the order listed above.
3. Place the pan in the bread machine and close the lid.
4. Turn on the bread maker. Select the White/Basic setting, then the loaf size, and finally the crust color. Start the cycle.
5. When the cycle is finished and the bread is baked, carefully remove the pan from the machine. Use a potholder as the handle will be very hot. Let rest for a few minutes.
6. Remove the bread from the pan and allow to cool on a wire rack for at least 10 minutes before slicing.

Sweet Almond Anise Bread

Ingredients:

- 8 slices (1 pound)
- ¾ cup lukewarm water
- ¼ cup butter
- ¼ cup sugar
- ½ teaspoon salt
- 3 cups bread flour
- 1 teaspoon anise seed
- 2 teaspoons active dry yeast
- ½ cup almonds, chopped
- 12 slices (1 ½ pounds)
- 1 1/8 cups lukewarm water
- 3/8 cup butter
- 3/8 cup sugar
- 3/4 teaspoon salt
- 4 1/2 cups bread flour
- 1 1/2 teaspoons anise seed
- 3 teaspoons active dry yeast
- 3/4 cup almonds, chopped
- 16 slices (2 pounds)
- 1 1/2 cups lukewarm water
- 1/2 cup butter
- 1/2 cup sugar
- 1 teaspoon salt
- 6 cups bread flour
- 2 teaspoons anise seed

- 4 teaspoons active dry yeast
- 1 cup almonds, chopped

Directions:

1. Choose the size of loaf you would like to make and measure your ingredients.
2. Add the ingredients to the bread pan in the order listed above (except almonds) .
3. Place the pan in the bread machine and close the lid.
4. Turn on the bread maker. Select the White/Basic setting, then the loaf size, and finally the crust color. Start the cycle.
5. When the cycle is finished and the bread is baked, carefully remove the pan from the machine. Use a potholder as the handle will be very hot. Let rest for a few minutes.
6. Remove the bread from the pan and allow to cool on a wire rack for at least 10 minutes before slicing.

Buttermilk Pecan Bread

Ingredients:

- 8 slices (1 pound)
- 1/2 cup buttermilk, at room temperature
- 1/2 cup butter, at room temperature
- 2/3 tablespoon instant coffee granules
- 1 1/2 eggs, at room temperature
- 1/2 cup sugar
- 1 1/2cups all-purpose flour
- 1/3 tablespoon baking powder
- 1/3 teaspoon table salt
- 2/3 cup chopped pecans
- 12 slices (1 ½ pounds)
- ¾ cup buttermilk, at room temperature
- ¾ cup butter, at room temperature
- 1 tablespoon instant coffee granules
- 3 eggs, at room temperature
- ¾ cup sugar
- 2 cups all-purpose flour
- ½ tablespoon baking powder
- ½ teaspoon table salt
- 1 cup chopped pecans
- 16 slices (2 pounds)
- 1 cup buttermilk, at room temperature
- 1 cup butter, at room temperature

- 1⅓ tablespoons instant coffee granules
- 3 eggs, at room temperature
- 1 cup sugar
- 3 cups all-purpose flour
- ⅔ tablespoon baking powder
- ⅔ teaspoon table salt
- 1⅓ cups chopped pecans

Directions:

1. Choose the size of loaf you would like to make and measure your ingredients.
2. Add the ingredients to the bread pan in the order listed above.
3. Place the pan in the bread machine and close the lid.
4. Turn on the bread maker. Select the Quick/Rapid setting, then the loaf size, and finally the crust color. Start the cycle.
5. When the cycle is finished and the bread is baked, carefully remove the pan from the machine. Use a potholder as the handle will be very hot. Let rest for a few minutes.
6. Remove the bread from the pan and allow to cool on a wire rack for at least 10 minutes before slicing.

Milk Sweet Bread

Ingredients:
- 8 slices (1 pound)
- 2/3 cup lukewarm milk
- 1/2 egg, at room temperature
- 1 1/3 tablespoons butter, softened
- 1/3 cup sugar
- 2/3 teaspoon table salt
- 2 cups white bread flour
- 1 1/8 teaspoons bread machine yeast
- 12 slices (1 ½ pounds)
- 1 cup lukewarm milk
- 1 egg, at room temperature
- 2 tablespoons butter, softened
- ½ cup sugar
- 1 teaspoon table salt
- 3 cups white bread flour
- 2¼ teaspoons bread machine yeast
- 16 slices (2 pounds)
- 1⅓ cups lukewarm milk

- 1 egg, at room temperature
- 2⅔ tablespoons butter, softened
- ⅔ cup sugar
- 1⅓ teaspoons table salt
- 4 cups white bread flour
- 2¼ teaspoons bread machine yeast

Directions:

1. Choose the size of loaf you would like to make and measure your ingredients.
2. Add the ingredients to the bread pan in the order listed above.
3. Place the pan in the bread machine and close the lid.
4. Turn on the bread maker. Select the Sweet setting, then the loaf size, and finally the crust color. Start the cycle.
5. When the cycle is finished and the bread is baked, carefully remove the pan from the machine. Use a potholder as the handle will be very hot. Let rest for a few minutes.
6. Remove the bread from the pan and allow to cool on a wire rack for at least 10 minutes before slicing.

Honey Bread

Ingredients:
- 8 slices (1 pound)
- ¾ cups milk, at 80 degrees F
- 2 tablespoons honey
- 1 tablespoon butter, melted and cooled
- ¾ teaspoon salt
- ½ cup whole wheat flour
- ½ cup prepared granola crushed
- 1¼ cups white bread flour
- 1 teaspoon bread machine yeast
- 12 slices (1 ½ pounds)
- 1 1/8 cups milk, at 80 degrees F
- 3 tablespoons honey
- 1 1/2 tablespoons butter, melted and cooled
- 1 1/8 teaspoons salt
- 3/4 cup whole wheat flour
- 3/4 cup prepared granola crushed
- 1 7/8 cups white bread flour
- 1 1/2 teaspoons bread machine yeast
- 16 slices (2 pounds)

- 1 1/2 cups milk, at 80 degrees F
- 4 tablespoons honey
- 2 tablespoons butter, melted and cooled
- 1 1/2 teaspoons salt
- 1 cup whole wheat flour
- 1 cup prepared granola crushed
- 2 1/2cups white bread flour
- 2 teaspoons bread machine yeast

Directions:

1. Choose the size of loaf you would like to make and measure your ingredients.

2. Add the ingredients to the bread pan in the order listed above.

3. Place the pan in the bread machine and close the lid.

4. Turn on the bread maker. Select the White/Basic setting, then the loaf size, and finally the crust color. Start the cycle.

5. When the cycle is finished and the bread is baked, carefully remove the pan from the machine. Use a potholder as the handle will be very hot. Let rest for a few minutes.

6. Remove the bread from the pan and allow to cool on a wire rack for at least 10 minutes before slicing.

Cinnamon Pecan Coffee Cake

Ingredients:
- 8 slices (1 pound)
- 1 cup butter, unsalted
- 1 cup sugar
- 2 eggs
- 1 cup sour cream
- 1 teaspoon vanilla extract
- 2 cups all-purpose flour
- 1 teaspoon baking powder
- 1 teaspoon baking soda
- 1/2 teaspoon salt
- For the topping:
- 1/2 cup brown sugar
- 1/4 cup sugar
- 1/2 teaspoon cinnamon
- 1/2 cup pecans, chopped
- 12 slices (1 ½ pounds)
- 1 1/2 cups butter, unsalted
- 1 1/2 cups sugar
- 3 eggs
- 1 1/2 cups sour cream
- 1 1/2 teaspoons vanilla extract
- 3 cups all-purpose flour
- 1 1/2 teaspoons baking powder
- 1 1/2 teaspoons baking soda
- 3/4 teaspoon salt
- For the topping:
- 1/2 cup brown sugar
- 1/4 cup sugar
- 1/2 teaspoon cinnamon
- 1/2 cup pecans, chopped
- 16 slices (2 pounds)
- 2 cups butter, unsalted
- 2 cups sugar
- 4 eggs
- 2 cups sour cream
- 2 teaspoons vanilla extract
- 4 cups all-purpose flour
- 2 teaspoons baking powder
- 2 teaspoons baking soda
- 1 teaspoon salt
- For the topping:
- 1/2 cup brown sugar
- 1/4 cup sugar
- 1/2 teaspoon cinnamon
- 1/2 cup pecans, chopped

Directions:

1. Choose the size of loaf you would like to make and measure your ingredients.

2. Add the ingredients to the bread pan in the order listed above.

3. Place the pan in the bread machine and close the lid.

4. Turn on the bread maker. Select the Cake setting, then the loaf size, and finally the crust color. Start the cycle.

5. When kneading cycle is done, after about 20 minutes, sprinkle 1/2 cup of topping on top of dough and continue baking.

6. During the last hour of baking time, sprinkle the remaining 1/2 cup of topping on the cake.

7. When the cycle is finished and the bread is baked, carefully remove the pan from the machine. Use a potholder as the handle will be very hot. Let rest for a few minutes.

8. Remove the bread from the pan and allow to cool on a wire rack for at least 10 minutes before slicing.

Cinnamon Rum Bread

Ingredients:

- 8 slices (1 pound)
- 9/16 cup lukewarm water
- 1/2 egg, at room temperature
- 1/8 cup butter, melted and cooled
- 1/8 cup sugar
- 2 teaspoons rum extract
- 5/6 teaspoon table salt
- 2 cups white bread flour
- 2/3 teaspoon ground cinnamon
- 1/8 teaspoon ground nutmeg
- 2/3 teaspoon bread machine yeast
- 12 slices (1 ½ pounds)
- ¾ cup lukewarm water
- 1 egg, at room temperature
- 3 tablespoons butter, melted and cooled
- 3 tablespoons sugar
- 1 tablespoon rum extract
- 1¼ teaspoons table salt
- 3 cups white bread flour
- 1 teaspoon ground cinnamon
- ¼ teaspoon ground nutmeg
- 1 teaspoon bread machine yeast
- 16 slices (2 pounds)
- 1⅛ cups lukewarm water
- 1 egg, at room temperature
- ¼ cup butter, melted and cooled
- ¼ cup sugar
- 4 teaspoons rum extract
- 1⅔ teaspoons table salt
- 4 cups white bread flour
- 1⅓ teaspoons ground cinnamon
- ¼ teaspoon ground nutmeg
- 1⅓ teaspoons bread machine yeast

Directions:

1. Choose the size of loaf you would like to make and measure your ingredients.

2. Add the ingredients to the bread pan in the order listed above.

3. Place the pan in the bread machine and close the lid.

4. Turn on the bread maker. Select the Sweet setting, then the loaf size, and finally the crust color. Start the cycle.

5. When the cycle is finished and the bread is baked, carefully remove the pan from the machine. Use a potholder as the handle will be very hot. Let rest for a few minutes.

6. Remove the bread from the pan and allow to cool on a wire rack for at least 10 minutes before slicing.

Cinnabun Coffee Cake

Ingredients:

- 8 slices (1 pound)
- For the dough:
- 7/12 cup milk
- 1 teaspoon vanilla extract
- 2/3 large egg yolk
- 1 1/3 tablespoons unsalted butter, cut into pieces
- 1 1/2 cups unbleached all-purpose flour
- 1/6 cup sugar
- 2/3 teaspoon salt
- 1 1/3 teaspoons SAF yeast or 1 2/3 teaspoons bread machine yeast
- For the oat crumb topping:
- 3/4 cup unbleached all-purpose flour
- 3/4 cup light brown sugar
- 1/2 cup rolled oats
- 1/2 cup chopped pecans
- 11/2 teaspoons ground cinnamon or apple pie spice
- 1/2 cup (1 stick) unsalted butter, at room temperature
- Confectioners' Sugar Icing
- 12 slices (1 ½ pounds)
- For the dough:
- 7/8 cup milk
- 11/2 teaspoons vanilla extract
- 1 large egg yolk
- 2 tablespoons unsalted butter, cut into pieces

- 21/4 cups unbleached all-purpose flour
- 1/4 cup sugar
- 1 teaspoon salt
- 2 teaspoons SAF yeast or 21/2 teaspoons bread machine yeast
- For the oat crumb topping:
- 3/4 cup unbleached all-purpose flour
- 3/4 cup light brown sugar
- 1/2 cup rolled oats
- 1/2 cup chopped pecans
- 11/2 teaspoons ground cinnamon or apple pie spice
- 1/2 cup (1 stick) unsalted butter, at room temperature
- Confectioners' Sugar Icing
- 16 slices (2 pounds)
- For the dough:
- 1 1/6 cups milk
- 2 teaspoons vanilla extract
- 1 1/3 large egg yolks
- 2 2/3 tablespoons unsalted butter, cut into pieces
- 3 cups unbleached all-purpose flour
- 1/3 cup sugar
- 1 1/3 teaspoons salt
- 2 2/3 teaspoons SAF yeast or 3 1/3 teaspoons bread machine yeast
- For the oat crumb topping:
- 3/4 cup unbleached all-purpose flour
- 3/4 cup light brown sugar
- 1/2 cup rolled oats
- 1/2 cup chopped pecans
- 11/2 teaspoons ground cinnamon or apple pie spice
- 1/2 cup (1 stick) unsalted butter, at room temperature
- Confectioners' Sugar Icing

Directions:

1. Choose the size of loaf you would like to make and measure your ingredients.
2. Add all the dough ingredients to the bread pan in the order listed above.
3. Place the pan in the bread machine and close the lid.
4. Turn on the bread maker. Select the Dough setting, then the loaf size, and finally the crust color. Start the cycle.

5. While the Dough cycle is running, prepare the topping. Combine the flour, sugar, oats, pecans, and cinnamon in a small bowl. Rub the butter in with your fingers to make clumped crumbs. You can also do this quickly in a food processor.
6. Grease a 13-by-9-inch metal or Pyrex baking dish.
7. When the cycle is finished and the bread is baked, with a large rubber spatula, scrape the batter into the pan. Using floured fingers, spread the batter evenly to fill the pan to the edges. Sprinkle with the topping. Cover loosely with plastic wrap and let rest at room temperature for 30 minutes.
8. Meanwhile, preheat the oven to 375°F (350°F if using a glass pan).
9. Bake for 20 to 25 minutes, or until the edges are golden brown and a cake tester inserted into the center comes out clean. Place the pan on a wire rack and prepare the icing. With a large spoon, drizzle the top in a back-and-forth pattern. Serve warm, out of the pan.

King Cake

Ingredients:
- 8 slices (1 pound)
- For the Dough:
- 2/3 egg, lightly beaten
- 1/6 cup filtered water
- 1/3 teaspoon salt
- 1 1/3 tablespoons unsalted butter, room temperature
- 2/3 cup sour cream
- 2 1/3 tablespoons sugar
- 2 1/3 cups all-purpose flour
- 1 2/3 teaspoons bread machine yeast
- For the Filling:
- 1 cup cream cheese, room temperature
- 1/2 cup confectioners' sugar
- 1/2 cup sugar
- 2 teaspoons ground cinnamon
- 5 tablespoons unsalted butter, melted
- For the Icing:
- 1/2 cup cream cheese, room temperature
- 1/4 cup unsalted butter, room temperature
- 2 1/2 cups confectioners' sugar
- 1 teaspoon pure vanilla extract
- Purple, green, and yellow cake glitter
- Flour, for surface

- 12 slices (1 ½ pounds)
- For the Dough:
- 1 egg, lightly beaten
- 1/4 cup filtered water
- 1/2 teaspoon salt
- 2 tablespoons unsalted butter, room temperature
- 1 cup sour cream
- 3 1/2 tablespoons sugar
- 3 1/2 cups all-purpose flour
- 2 1/2 teaspoons bread machine yeast
- For the Filling:
- 1 cup cream cheese, room temperature
- 1/2 cup confectioners' sugar
- 1/2 cup sugar
- 2 teaspoons ground cinnamon
- 5 tablespoons unsalted butter, melted
- For the Icing:
- 1/2 cup cream cheese, room temperature
- 1/4 cup unsalted butter, room temperature
- 2 1/2 cups confectioners' sugar
- 1 teaspoon pure vanilla extract
- Purple, green, and yellow cake glitter
- Flour, for surface
- 16 slices (2 pounds)
- 1 1/3 egg, lightly beaten
- 1/3 cup filtered water
- 2/3 teaspoon salt
- 2 2/3 tablespoons unsalted butter, room temperature
- 1 1/3 cup sour cream
- 4 2/3 tablespoons sugar
- 4 2/3 cups all-purpose flour
- 3 1/3 teaspoons bread machine yeast
- For the Filling:
- 1 cup cream cheese, room temperature
- 1/2 cup confectioners' sugar
- 1/2 cup sugar
- 2 teaspoons ground cinnamon
- 5 tablespoons unsalted butter, melted
- For the Icing:
- 1/2 cup cream cheese, room temperature
- 1/4 cup unsalted butter, room temperature
- 2 1/2 cups confectioners' sugar
- 1 teaspoon pure vanilla extract
- Purple, green, and yellow cake glitter
- Flour, for surface

Directions:

1. Choose the size of loaf you would like to make and measure your ingredients.

2. Add the dough ingredients to the bread pan in the order listed above.

3. Place the pan in the bread machine and close the lid.

4. Turn on the bread maker. Select the Dough setting, then the loaf size, and finally the crust color. Start the cycle.

5. Check the dough after five minutes of mixing and add 1 to 2 more tablespoons of water or flour if the dough is too dry or too wet.

6. In a large mixing bowl, beat the cream cheese and 1/2 cup confectioners' sugar until smooth; set aside. Mix 1/2 cup sugar, 2 teaspoons cinnamon, and 5 tablespoons melted butter until combined; set aside.

7. Line a large baking sheet with parchment paper and set aside.

8. Remove the dough and roll out into a 10-by-28-inch rectangle on a floured surface. Trim the edges as needed with scissors.

9. Spread the cream cheese mixture on the dough to within 1 inch of the edges.

10. Spread sugar-cinnamon mixture on the cream cheese to within 1 inch of the edges of the dough.

11. Starting at one of the long edges, roll the dough tightly into a log. Pinch the edges to seal the log and place the rolled dough onto the lined baking sheet, seam side down, and form the dough into a ring.

12. Moisten the ends of the dough with a little water and pinch the two ends together to seal. Place a large greased can in the center to maintain a nice circle in the center. Cover with a towel and let rise in a warm place until doubled in size, about 30 minutes.

13. Preheat oven to 350°F. Bake the cake until the top is golden brown, about 25 minutes.

14. Mix the ingredients for the icing until just smooth in a mixing bowl.

15. Remove the cake from the oven and allow to cool for 10 minutes on a wire rack.

16. While the cake is still warm, spoon the icing onto the cake and sprinkle with purple, green and yellow glitter.

Honey Pound Cake

Ingredients:

- 8 slices (1 pound)
- 1 cup butter, unsalted
- 1/4 cup honey
- 2 tablespoons whole milk
- 4 eggs, beaten
- 1 cup sugar
- 2 cups flour
- 12 slices (1 ½ pounds)
- 1 1/2 cups butter, unsalted
- 3/8 cup honey
- 3 tablespoons whole milk
- 6 eggs, beaten
- 1 1/2 cups sugar
- 3 cups flour
- 16 slices (2 pounds)
- 2 cups butter, unsalted
- 1/2 cup honey
- 4 tablespoons whole milk
- 8 eggs, beaten
- 2 cups sugar
- 4 cups flour

Directions:

1. Choose the size of loaf you would like to make and measure your ingredients.
2. Bring the butter to room temperature and cut into 1/2-inch cubes.
3. Add the ingredients to the bread pan in the order listed above.
4. Place the pan in the bread machine and close the lid.
5. Turn on the bread maker. Select the Sweet Bread setting, then the loaf size, and finally the crust color. Start the cycle.
6. When the cycle is finished and the bread is baked, carefully remove the pan from the machine. Use a potholder as the handle will be very hot. Let rest for a few minutes.
7. Remove the bread from the pan and allow to cool on a wire rack for at least 10 minutes before slicing.

Multi-grain Honey Bread

Ingredients:

- 8 slices (1 pound)
- 1 and 1/3 cups warm water
- 1 tablespoon active dry yeast
- 3 tablespoons dry milk powder
- 2 tablespoons honey
- 2 teaspoons salt
- 1 whole egg
- 1 cup whole wheat flour
- 2½ cups bread flour
- ¾ cups 7-grain cereal
- 12 slices (1 ½ pounds)
- 1 1/2 and 1/2 cups warm water
- 1 1/2 tablespoons active dry yeast
- 4 1/2 tablespoons dry milk powder
- 3 tablespoons honey
- 3 teaspoons salt
- 1 1/2 whole eggs
- 1 1/2 cups whole wheat flour
- 3 3/4 cups bread flour
- 1 1/2 cups 7-grain cereal
- 16 slices (2 pounds)
- 2 and 2/3 cups warm water
- 2 tablespoons active dry yeast
- 6 tablespoons dry milk powder
- 4 tablespoons honey
- 4 teaspoons salt
- 2 whole eggs
- 2 cups whole wheat flour
- 5 cups bread flour
- 1 1/2 cups 7-grain cereal

Directions:

1. Choose the size of loaf you would like to make and measure your ingredients.
2. Add the ingredients to the bread pan in the order listed above.
3. Place the pan in the bread machine and close the lid.
4. Turn on the bread maker. Select the White/Basic setting, then the loaf size, and finally the crust color. Start the cycle.
5. When the cycle is finished and the bread is baked, carefully remove the pan from the machine. Use a

potholder as the handle will be very hot. Let rest for a few minutes.

6. Remove the bread from the pan and allow to cool on a wire rack for at least 10 minutes before slicing.

Sweet Vanilla Bread

Ingredients:
- 8 slices (1 pound)
- 3/8 cup lukewarm milk
- 1/8 cup unsalted butter, melted
- 1/8 cup sugar
- 1/2 egg, at room temperature
- 1 teaspoon pure vanilla extract
- 1/4 teaspoon almond extract
- 1 2/3 cups white bread flour
- 1 teaspoon bread machine yeast
- 12 slices (1 ½ pounds)
- ½ cup + 1 tablespoon lukewarm milk
- 3 tablespoons unsalted butter, melted
- 3 tablespoons sugar
- 1 egg, at room temperature
- 1½ teaspoons pure vanilla extract
- ⅓ teaspoon almond extract
- 2½ cups white bread flour
- 1½ teaspoons bread machine yeast
- 16 slices (2 pounds)
- ¾ cup lukewarm milk
- ¼ cup unsalted butter, melted
- ¼ cup sugar
- 1 egg, at room temperature
- 2 teaspoons pure vanilla extract
- ½ teaspoon almond extract
- 3⅓ cups white bread flour
- 2 teaspoons bread machine yeast

Directions:
1. Choose the size of loaf you would like to make and measure your ingredients.
2. Add the ingredients to the bread pan in the order listed above.
3. Place the pan in the bread machine and close the lid.
4. Turn on the bread maker. Select the White/Basic setting, then the loaf size, and finally the crust color. Start the cycle.

5. When the cycle is finished and the bread is baked, carefully remove the pan from the machine. Use a potholder as the handle will be very hot. Let rest for a few minutes.

6. Remove the bread from the pan and allow to cool on a wire rack for at least 10 minutes before slicing.

Rainbow Swirl Cake

Ingredients:
- 8 slices (1 pound)
- 2/3 cup milk plus 2/3 egg yolk
- 2 cups unbleached all-purpose flour
- 1 2/3 tablespoons sugar
- 1 1/2 teaspoons active dry yeast
- 1 tablespoon unsalted butter, softened
- 1 1/3 teaspoons salt
- Red, yellow, green and blue food coloring
- Flour, for surface
- 12 slices (1 ½ pounds)
- 1 cup milk plus 1 egg yolk
- 3 cups unbleached all-purpose flour
- 2 1/2 tablespoons sugar
- 2 1/4 teaspoons active dry yeast
- 1 1/2 tablespoons unsalted butter, softened
- 2 teaspoons salt
- Red, yellow, green and blue food coloring
- Flour, for surface
- 16 slices (2 pounds)
- 1 1/3 cups milk plus 1 1/3 egg yolks
- 4 cups unbleached all-purpose flour
- 3 1/3 tablespoons sugar
- 3 teaspoons active dry yeast
- 2 tablespoons unsalted butter, softened
- 2 2/3 teaspoons salt
- Red, yellow, green and blue food coloring
- Flour, for surface

Directions:
1. Choose the size of loaf you would like to make and measure your ingredients.
2. Whisk milk and egg yolk together in a microwave safe bowl and microwave 30 seconds and add to the bread pan.

3. Whisk together flour, sugar and yeast in a large mixing bowl and add to the bread pan.

4. Add milk mixture, butter, salt, and stir to combine and add to the bread pan.

5. Place the pan in the bread machine and close the lid.

6. Turn on the bread maker. Select the Dough setting, then the loaf size, and finally the crust color. Start the cycle.

7. When kneading is finished, divide dough into 5 equal dough balls and place each one in a small bowl and cover with a tea towel.

8. Remove one piece from a bowl and place it on a plastic cutting board. Add several drops of food coloring and knead the food coloring into the dough with gloved hands, adding more food coloring until it is fully incorporated.

9. Shape dough into a ball and return to its bowl. Repeat with remaining pieces of dough, dying each a different color; be sure to wash your hands and your work surface between each color.

10. Cover each bowl with plastic wrap and let rise until doubled; about 2 hours.

11. Punch down each dough ball when risen.

12. Roll the red dough ball out on a lightly floured surface into an 8-by-4-inch rectangle. Roll out yellow piece of dough into an 8-by-4-inch rectangle and place directly on top of the red dough. Repeat with green, blue, and purple dough balls until you have a stack of 8-by-4-inch rectangles.

13. Roll up dough tightly from the short end into a loaf.

14. Place loaf in a lightly greased 9-by-5-inch loaf pan. Cover with a tea towel or plastic wrap and let rise until doubled, about 1 hour.

15. Preheat oven to 375°F and bake until browned on top and a thermometer inserted in the bottom center reads 190°F, about 30 minutes.

16. When the bread is baked, carefully remove the pan from the machine. Use a potholder as the handle will be very hot. Let rest for a few minutes.

17. Remove the bread from the pan and allow to cool on a wire rack for at least 10 minutes before slicing.

Chocolate Marble Cake

Ingredients:

- 8 slices (1 pound)
- 1 cup water
- 1 teaspoon vanilla extract
- 1 teaspoon salt
- 2 1/3 cups bread flour
- 1 teaspoon instant yeast
- 2/3 cup semi-sweet chocolate chips
- 12 slices (1 ½ pounds)
- 1 1/2 cups water
- 1 1/2 teaspoons vanilla extract
- 1 1/2 teaspoons salt
- 3 1/2 cups bread flour
- 1 1/2 teaspoons instant yeast
- 1 cup semi-sweet chocolate chips
- 16 slices (2 pounds)
- 2 cups water
- 2 teaspoons vanilla extract
- 2 teaspoons salt
- 4 2/3 cups bread flour
- 2 teaspoons instant yeast
- 1 1/3 cups semi-sweet chocolate chips

Directions:

1. Choose the size of loaf you would like to make and measure your ingredients.

2. Add the ingredients to the bread pan in the order listed above (except the chocolate chips).

3. Place the pan in the bread machine and close the lid.

4. Turn on the bread maker. Select the Sweet Bread setting, then the loaf size, and finally the crust color. Start the cycle.

5. Check the dough after 10 to 15 minutes of kneading.

6. Add the chocolate chips about 3 minutes before the end of the second kneading cycle.

7. When the cycle is finished and the bread is baked, carefully remove the pan from the machine. Use a potholder as the handle will be very hot. Let rest for a few minutes.

8. Remove the bread from the pan and allow to cool on a wire rack for at least 10 minutes before slicing.

Pumpkin Spice Cake

Ingredients:

- 8 slices (1 pound)
- 1 cup sugar
- 1 cup canned pumpkin
- 1/3 cup vegetable oil
- 1 teaspoon vanilla extract
- 2 eggs
- 1 1/2 cups all-purpose flour
- 2 teaspoons baking powder
- 1/4 teaspoon salt
- 1 teaspoon ground cinnamon
- 1/4 teaspoon ground nutmeg
- 1/8 teaspoon ground cloves
- Shortening, for greasing pan
- 12 slices (1 ½ pounds)
- 1 1/2 cups sugar
- 1 1/2 cups canned pumpkin
- 1/2 cup vegetable oil
- 1 1/2 teaspoons vanilla extract
- 3 eggs
- 2 1/4 cups all-purpose flour
- 4 teaspoons baking powder
- 1/2 teaspoon salt
- 2 teaspoons ground cinnamon
- 1/2 teaspoon ground nutmeg
- 1/4 teaspoon ground cloves
- Shortening, for greasing pan
- 16 slices (2 pounds)
- 2 cups sugar
- 2 cups canned pumpkin
- 2/3 cup vegetable oil
- 2 teaspoons vanilla extract
- 4 eggs
- 3 cups all-purpose flour
- 4 teaspoons baking powder
- 1/2 teaspoon salt
- 2 teaspoons ground cinnamon
- 1/2 teaspoon ground nutmeg
- 1/4 teaspoon ground cloves
- Shortening, for greasing pan

Directions:

1. Choose the size of loaf you would like to make and measure your ingredients.
2. Grease bread pan and kneading blade generously with shortening.
3. Add the ingredients to the bread pan in the order listed above.
4. Place the pan in the bread machine and close the lid.
5. Turn on the bread maker. Select the Rapid setting, then the loaf size, and finally the crust color. Start the cycle.
6. Open the lid three minutes into the cycle and carefully scrape down sides of pan with a rubber spatula; close lid to continue cycle.
7. When the cycle is finished and the bread is baked, carefully remove the pan from the machine. Use a potholder as the handle will be very hot. Let rest for a few minutes.
8. Remove the bread from the pan and allow to cool on a wire rack for at least 10 minutes before slicing.

Carrot Cake Bread

Ingredients:

- 8 slices (1 pound)
- Non-stick cooking spray
- 1/4 cup vegetable oil
- 2 large eggs, room temperature
- 1/2 teaspoon pure vanilla extract
- 1/2 cup sugar
- 1/4 cup light brown sugar
- 1/4 cup crushed pineapple with juice (from can or fresh)
- 1 1/4 cups unbleached, all-purpose flour
- 1 teaspoon baking powder
- 1/4 teaspoon baking soda
- 1/4 teaspoon salt
- 1 teaspoon ground cloves
- 3/4 teaspoon ground cinnamon
- 1 cup freshly grated carrots
- 1/3 cup chopped pecans
- 1/3 cup golden raisins
- 12 slices (1 ½ pounds)
- Non-stick cooking spray
- 3/8 cup vegetable oil

- 3 large eggs, room temperature
- 3/4 teaspoon pure vanilla extract
- 3/4 cup sugar
- 3/8 cup light brown sugar
- 3/8 cup crushed pineapple with juice (from can or fresh)
- 1 7/8 cups unbleached, all-purpose flour
- 1 1/2 teaspoons baking powder
- 3/8 teaspoon baking soda
- 3/8 teaspoon salt
- 1 1/2 teaspoons ground cloves
- 1 1/8 teaspoons ground cinnamon
- 1 1/2 cups freshly grated carrots
- 1/2 cup chopped pecans
- 1/2 cup golden raisins
- 16 slices (2 pounds)
- Non-stick cooking spray
- 1/2 cup vegetable oil
- 4 large eggs, room temperature
- 1 teaspoon pure vanilla extract
- 1 cup sugar
- 1/2 cup light brown sugar
- 1/2 cup crushed pineapple with juice (from can or fresh)
- 2 1/2 cups unbleached, all-purpose flour
- 2 teaspoons baking powder
- 1/2 teaspoon baking soda
- 1/2 teaspoon salt
- 2 teaspoons ground cloves
- 1 1/2 teaspoons ground cinnamon
- 2 cups freshly grated carrots
- 2/3 cup chopped pecans
- 2/3 cup golden raisins

Directions:

1. Choose the size of loaf you would like to make and measure your ingredients.

2. Coat the inside of the bread pan with non-stick cooking spray.

3. Add the ingredients to the bread pan in the order listed above.

4. Place the pan in the bread machine and close the lid.

5. Turn on the bread maker. Select the Express Bake setting, then the loaf size, and finally the crust color. Start the cycle.

6. While the batter is mixing, scrape the sides of the bread pan with a rubber spatula to fully incorporate ingredients.

7. When the cycle is finished and the bread is baked, carefully remove the pan from the machine. Use a potholder as the handle will be very hot. Let rest for a few minutes.

8. Remove the bread from the pan and allow to cool on a wire rack for at least 10 minutes before slicing.

Hazelnut Honey Bread

Ingredients:
- 8 slices (1 pound)
- ½ cup milk, at room temperature
- 2 teaspoons melted butter, cooled
- 2 teaspoons honey
- 2/3 teaspoons salt
- 1/3 cup cooked wild rice, cooled
- 1/3 cup whole wheat flour
- 2/3 teaspoons caraway seeds
- 1 cup + 1 tablespoon white bread flour
- 1 teaspoon bread machine yeast
- 1/3 cup hazelnuts, chopped
- 12 slices (1 ½ pounds)
- 3/4 cup milk, at room temperature
- 3 teaspoons melted butter, cooled
- 3 teaspoons honey
- 1 teaspoons salt
- 1/2 cup cooked wild rice, cooled
- 1/2 cup whole wheat flour
- 1 teaspoons caraway seeds
- 1 1/2 cups + 1 1 /2tablespoons white bread flour
- 1 1/2 teaspoons bread machine yeast
- 1/2 cup hazelnuts, chopped
- 16 slices (2 pounds)
- 1 cup milk, at room temperature
- 4 teaspoons melted butter, cooled
- 4 teaspoons honey
- 1 1/3 teaspoons salt
- 2/3 cup cooked wild rice, cooled

- 2/3 cup whole wheat flour
- 1 1/3 teaspoons caraway seeds
- 2 cups + 2 tablespoons white bread flour
- 2 teaspoons bread machine yeast
- 2/3 cup hazelnuts, chopped

Directions:

1. Choose the size of loaf you would like to make and measure your ingredients.

2. Add the ingredients to the bread pan in the order listed above.

3. Place the pan in the bread machine and close the lid.

4. Turn on the bread maker. Select the White/Basic setting, then the loaf size, and finally the crust color. Start the cycle.

5. When the cycle is finished and the bread is baked, carefully remove the pan from the machine. Use a potholder as the handle will be very hot. Let rest for a few minutes.

6. Remove the bread from the pan and allow to cool on a wire rack for at least 10 minutes before slicing.

Apple Raisin Nut Cake

Ingredients:

- 8 slices (1 pound)
- 2 large eggs, lightly beaten
- 1/4 cup milk
- 1/3 cup butter, melted
- 1 1/2 cups all-purpose flour
- 3 teaspoons baking powder
- 1/4 cup sugar
- 1/4 teaspoon salt
- 1 teaspoon cinnamon
- 1 teaspoon pure vanilla extract
- Add after the kneading process:
- 1 small apple, peeled and roughly chopped
- 1/4 cup raisins
- 1/4 cup walnuts, chopped
- 1 teaspoon all-purpose flour
- 12 slices (1 ½ pounds)
- 3 large eggs, lightly beaten
- 3/8 cup milk
- 1/2 cup butter, melted
- 2 1/4 cups all-purpose flour

- 4 1/2 teaspoons baking powder
- 3/8 cup sugar
- 3/8 teaspoon salt
- 1 1/2 teaspoons cinnamon
- 1 1/2 teaspoons pure vanilla extract
- Add after the kneading process:
- 1 1/2 small apples, peeled and roughly chopped
- 3/8 cup raisins
- 3/8 cup walnuts, chopped
- 1 1/2 teaspoons all-purpose flour
- 16 slices (2 pounds)
- 4 large eggs, lightly beaten
- 1/2 cup milk
- 2/3 cup butter, melted
- 3 cups all-purpose flour
- 6 teaspoons baking powder
- 1/2 cup sugar
- 1/2 teaspoon salt
- 2 teaspoons cinnamon
- 2 teaspoons pure vanilla extract
- Add after the kneading process:
- 2 small apples, peeled and roughly chopped
- 1/2 cup raisins
- 1/2 cup walnuts, chopped
- 2 teaspoons all-purpose flour

Directions:

1. Choose the size of loaf you would like to make and measure your ingredients.

2. Add the ingredients to the bread pan in the order listed above.

3. Place the pan in the bread machine and close the lid.

4. Turn on the bread maker. Select the Sweet setting, then the loaf size, and finally the crust color. Start the cycle.

5. Mix apples, raisins, walnuts, and flour together in a small mixing bowl. Add to dough after the kneading process.

6. When the cycle is finished and the bread is baked, carefully remove the pan from the machine. Use a potholder as the handle will be very hot. Let rest for a few minutes.

7. Remove the bread from the pan and allow to cool on a wire rack for at least 10 minutes before slicing.

Chocolate Chip Bread

Ingredients:

- 8 slices (1 pound)
- 2/3 cup sour cream
- 1 1/2 eggs, at room temperature
- 2/3 cup sugar
- 3/8 cup unsalted butter, melted
- 1/6 cup plain Greek yogurt
- 1 1/8 cups all-purpose flour
- 1/3 cup unsweetened cocoa powder
- 1/3 teaspoon baking powder
- 1/3 teaspoon table salt
- 2/3 cup milk chocolate chips
- 12 slices (1 ½ pounds)
- 1 cup sour cream
- 2 eggs, at room temperature
- 1 cup sugar
- ½ cup unsalted butter, melted
- ¼ cup plain Greek yogurt
- 1¾ cups all-purpose flour
- ½ cup unsweetened cocoa powder
- ½ teaspoon baking powder
- ½ teaspoon table salt
- 1 cup milk chocolate chips
- 16 slices (2 pounds)
- 1⅓ cups sour cream
- 3 eggs, at room temperature
- 1⅓ cups sugar
- ¾ cup unsalted butter, melted
- ⅓ cup plain Greek yogurt
- 2¼ cups all-purpose flour
- ⅔ cup unsweetened cocoa powder
- ⅔ teaspoon baking powder
- ⅔ teaspoon table salt
- 1⅓ cups milk chocolate chips

Directions:

1. Choose the size of loaf you would like to make and measure your ingredients.

2. Add the ingredients to the bread pan in the order listed above.

3. Place the pan in the bread machine and close the lid.

4. Turn on the bread maker. Select the Quick/Rapid setting, then the loaf size, and finally the crust color. Start the cycle.

5. When the cycle is finished and the bread is baked, carefully remove the pan from the machine. Use a potholder as the handle will be very hot. Let rest for a few minutes.

6. Remove the bread from the pan and allow to cool on a wire rack for at least 10 minutes before slicing.

White And Dark Chocolate Tea Cake

Ingredients:

- 8 slices (1 pound)
- 1 cup plain yogurt
- 1/4 cup buttermilk
- 2 large eggs
- 1/4 cup vegetable oil
- 2 teaspoons vanilla extract
- 2/3 cup light brown sugar
- 21/2 cups unbleached all-purpose flour
- 1/3 cup unsweetened Dutch-process cocoa powder
- 1/2 teaspoon baking powder
- 11/2 teaspoons baking soda
- 1/2 teaspoon instant espresso powder
- 1/4 teaspoon salt
- 1 cup white chocolate chips or chunks broken off a bar of white chocolate
- 12 slices (1 ½ pounds)
- 1 1/2 cups plain yogurt
- 3/8 cup buttermilk
- 3 large eggs
- 3/8 cup vegetable oil
- 3 teaspoons vanilla extract
- 1 cup light brown sugar
- 3 3/4 cups unbleached all-purpose flour
- 1/2 cup unsweetened Dutch-process cocoa powder
- 3/4 teaspoon baking powder
- 2 1/4 teaspoons baking soda
- 3/4 teaspoon instant espresso powder
- 3/8 teaspoon salt
- 1 1/2 cups white chocolate chips or chunks broken off a bar of white chocolate
- 16 slices (2 pounds)

- 2 cups plain yogurt
- 1/2 cup buttermilk
- 4 large eggs
- 1/2 cup vegetable oil
- 4 teaspoons vanilla extract
- 1 1/3 cups light brown sugar
- 5 cups unbleached all-purpose flour
- 2/3 cup unsweetened Dutch-process cocoa powder
- 1 teaspoon baking powder
- 3 teaspoons baking soda
- 1 teaspoon instant espresso powder
- 1/2 teaspoon salt
- 2 cups white chocolate chips or chunks broken off a bar of white chocolate

Directions:

1. Choose the size of loaf you would like to make and measure your ingredients.

2. Add the ingredients to the bread pan in the order listed above.

3. Place the pan in the bread machine and close the lid.

4. Turn on the bread maker. Select the Quick Bread/Cake setting, then the loaf size, and finally the crust color. Start the cycle.

5. When the cycle is finished and the bread is baked, carefully remove the pan from the machine. Use a potholder as the handle will be very hot. Let rest for a few minutes.

6. Remove the bread from the pan and allow to cool on a wire rack for at least 10 minutes before slicing.

Lemon Cake

Ingredients:

- 8 slices (1 pound)
- 3 large eggs, beaten
- 1/3 cup 2% milk
- 1/2 cup butter, melted
- 2 cups all-purpose flour
- 3 teaspoons baking powder
- 1 1/3 cup sugar
- 1 teaspoon vanilla extract
- 2 lemons, zested
- For the glaze:
- 1 cup powdered sugar
- 2 tablespoons lemon juice, freshly squeezed
- 12 slices (1 ½ pounds)
- 4 1/2 large eggs, beaten
- 1/2 cup 2% milk
- 3/4 cup butter, melted
- 3 cups all-purpose flour
- 4 1/2 teaspoons baking powder
- 2 cups sugar
- 1 1/2 teaspoons vanilla extract
- 3 lemons, zested
- For the glaze:
- 1 1/2 cups powdered sugar
- 3 tablespoons lemon juice, freshly squeezed
- 16 slices (2 pounds)
- 6 large eggs, beaten
- 2/3 cup 2% milk
- 1 cup butter, melted
- 4 cups all-purpose flour
- 6 teaspoons baking powder
- 2 2/3 cups sugar
- 2 teaspoons vanilla extract
- 4 lemons, zested
- For the glaze:
- 2 cups powdered sugar
- 4 tablespoons lemon juice, freshly squeezed

Directions:

1. Choose the size of loaf you would like to make and measure your ingredients.

2. Prepare the glaze by whisking the powdered sugar and lemon juice together in a small mixing bowl and set aside.

3. Add the ingredients to the bread pan in the order listed above.

4. Place the pan in the bread machine and close the lid.

5. Turn on the bread maker. Select the Sweet Bread setting, then the loaf size, and finally the crust color. Start the cycle.

6. When the cycle is finished and the bread is baked, carefully remove the pan from the machine. Use a potholder as the handle will be very hot. Let rest for a few minutes.

7. Remove the bread from the pan and allow to cool on a wire rack for at least 10 minutes before slicing.

Choco Banana Oatmeal Bread

Ingredients:

- 8 slices (1 pound)
- 3 bananas, mashed
- 2 whole eggs, at room temperature
- ¾ cup packed light brown sugar
- 1/2 cup butter
- ½ cup sour cream
- ¼ cup sugar
- 1½ teaspoons vanilla extract
- 1 cup all-purpose flour
- ½ cup quick oats
- 2 tablespoons unsweetened cocoa powder
- 1 teaspoon baking soda
- 12 slices (1 ½ pounds)
- 4 1/2 bananas, mashed
- 3 whole eggs, at room temperature
- 1 1/8 cups packed light brown sugar
- 3/4 cup butter
- 3/4 cup sour cream
- 3/8 cup sugar
- 2 1/4 teaspoons vanilla extract
- 1 1/2 cups all-purpose flour
- 3/4 cup quick oats
- 3 tablespoons unsweetened cocoa powder
- 1 1/2 teaspoons baking soda
- 16 slices (2 pounds)
- 6 bananas, mashed
- 4 whole eggs, at room temperature
- 1 1/2 cups packed light brown sugar
- 1 cup butter
- 1 cup sour cream
- 1/2 cup sugar
- 3 teaspoons vanilla extract
- 2 cups all-purpose flour
- 1 cup quick oats
- 4 tablespoons unsweetened cocoa powder
- 2 teaspoons baking soda

Directions:

1. Choose the size of loaf you would like to make and measure your ingredients.

2. Add the banana, eggs, brown sugar, butter, sour cream, vanilla and sugar to the bread pan in the order listed above.

3. Place the pan in the bread machine and close the lid.

4. Turn on the bread maker. Select the Quick/Rapid setting, then the loaf size, and finally the crust color. Start the cycle.

5. Mix the dry ingredients in a bowl and add the dry ingredients to the bread machine once the machine beeps.

6. When the cycle is finished and the bread is baked, carefully remove the pan from the machine. Use a potholder as the handle will be very hot. Let rest for a few minutes.

7. Remove the bread from the pan and allow to cool on a wire rack for at least 10 minutes before slicing.

Sweet Pineapple Bread

Ingredients:

- 8 slices (1 pound)
- 1/4 cup unsalted butter, melted
- 1 egg, at room temperature
- 3/8 cup coconut milk, at room temperature
- 3/8 cup pineapple juice, at room temperature
- 2/3 cup sugar
- 1 teaspoon coconut extract
- 1 1/2 cups all-purpose flour
- 1/2 cup shredded sweetened coconut
- 2/3 teaspoon baking powder
- 3/8 teaspoon table salt
- 12 slices (1 ½ pounds)
- 6 tablespoons unsalted butter, melted
- 2 eggs, at room temperature
- ½ cup coconut milk, at room temperature
- ½ cup pineapple juice, at room temperature
- 1 cup sugar
- 1½ teaspoons coconut extract
- 2 cups all-purpose flour
- ¾ cup shredded sweetened coconut
- 1 teaspoon baking powder
- ½ teaspoon table salt
- 16 slices (2 pounds)
- ½ cup unsalted butter, melted

- 2 eggs, at room temperature
- ¾ cup coconut milk, at room temperature
- ¾ cup pineapple juice, at room temperature
- 1⅓ cups sugar
- 2 teaspoons coconut extract
- 3 cups all-purpose flour
- 1 cup shredded sweetened coconut
- 1⅓ teaspoons baking powder
- ¾ teaspoon table salt

Directions:

1. Choose the size of loaf you would like to make and measure your ingredients.

2. Add the ingredients to the bread pan in the order listed above.

3. Place the pan in the bread machine and close the lid.

4. Turn on the bread maker. Select the Quick/Rapid setting, then the loaf size, and finally the crust color. Start the cycle.

5. When the cycle is finished and the bread is baked, carefully remove the pan from the machine. Use a potholder as the handle will be very hot. Let rest for a few minutes.

6. Remove the bread from the pan and allow to cool on a wire rack for at least 10 minutes before slicing.

Sweet Sour Maple Bread

Ingredients:

- 8 slices (1 pound)
- 6 tablespoons water at 80 degrees F
- 6 tablespoons sour cream
- 1½ tablespoons butter, at room temperature
- ¾ tablespoons maple syrup
- ½ teaspoon salt
- 1¾ cups white bread flour
- 1 1/8 teaspoons bread machine yeast
- 12 slices (1 ½ pounds)
- 9 tablespoons water at 80 degrees F
- 9 tablespoons sour cream
- 2 1/4 tablespoons butter, at room temperature
- 1 1/8 tablespoons maple syrup
- 3/4 teaspoon salt
- 2 5/8 cups white bread flour
- 1 3/4 teaspoons bread machine yeast
- 16 slices (2 pounds)
- 12 tablespoons water at 80 degrees F
- 12 tablespoons sour cream
- 3 tablespoons butter, at room temperature
- 1 1/2 tablespoons maple syrup
- 1 teaspoon salt
- 3 1/2 cups white bread flour
- 2 1/4 teaspoons bread machine yeast

Directions:

1. Choose the size of loaf you would like to make and measure your ingredients.

2. Add the ingredients to the bread pan in the order listed above.

3. Place the pan in the bread machine and close the lid.

4. Turn on the bread maker. Select the White/Basic setting, then the loaf size, and finally the crust color. Start the cycle.

5. When the cycle is finished and the bread is baked, carefully remove the pan from the machine. Use a potholder as the handle will be very hot. Let rest for a few minutes.

6. Remove the bread from the pan and allow to cool on a wire rack for at least 10 minutes before slicing.

HOLIDAY BREAD RECIPES

Holiday Eggnog Bread

Ingredients:

- 8 slices (1 pound)
- 3/4 cup eggnog, at room temperature
- 3/4 tablespoon unsalted butter, melted
- 1 tablespoon sugar
- 5/8 teaspoon table salt
- 1/4 teaspoon ground cinnamon
- 1/4 teaspoon ground nutmeg
- 2 cups white bread flour
- 7/8 teaspoon bread machine yeast
- 12 slices (1 ½ pounds)
- 1⅛ cups eggnog, at room temperature
- 1⅛ tablespoons unsalted butter, melted
- 1½ tablespoons sugar
- 1 teaspoon table salt
- ⅓ teaspoon ground cinnamon
- ⅓ teaspoon ground nutmeg
- 3 cups white bread flour
- 1⅓ teaspoons bread machine yeast
- 16 slices (2 pounds)
- 1½ cups eggnog, at room temperature
- 1½ tablespoons unsalted butter, melted
- 2 tablespoons sugar
- 1¼ teaspoons table salt
- ½ teaspoon ground cinnamon
- ½ teaspoon ground nutmeg
- 4 cups white bread flour
- 1¾ teaspoons bread machine yeast

Directions:

1. Choose the size of loaf you would like to make and measure your ingredients.

2. Add the ingredients to the bread pan in the order listed above.

3. Place the pan in the bread machine and close the lid.

4. Turn on the bread maker. Select the White/Basic setting, then the loaf size, and finally the crust color. Start the cycle.

5. When the cycle is finished and the bread is baked, carefully remove the pan from the machine. Use a potholder as the handle will be very hot. Let rest for a few minutes.

6. Remove the bread from the pan and allow to cool on a wire rack for at least 10 minutes before slicing.

Christmas Eggnog Bread

Ingredients:

- 8 slices (1 pound)
- 1 cup eggnog
- ½ cup milk
- 4 cups bread flour
- ½ cup dried cranberries
- 1¼ teaspoons salt
- 2 tablespoons sugar
- 1 tablespoon butter
- 1 teaspoon cinnamon
- 1¾ teaspoons bread machine yeast
- 12 slices (1 ½ pounds)
- 1 1/2 cups eggnog
- 3/4 cup milk
- 6 cups bread flour
- 3/4 cup dried cranberries
- 1 7/8 teaspoons salt
- 3 tablespoons sugar
- 1 1/2 tablespoons butter
- 1 1/2 teaspoons cinnamon
- 2 5/8 teaspoons bread machine yeast
- 16 slices (2 pounds)
- 2 cups eggnog
- 1 cup milk
- 8 cups bread flour
- 1 cup dried cranberries
- 2 1/2 teaspoons salt
- 4 tablespoons sugar
- 2 tablespoons butter
- 2 teaspoons cinnamon
- 3 1/2 teaspoons bread machine yeast

Directions:

1. Choose the size of loaf you would like to make and measure your ingredients.

2. Add the ingredients to the bread pan in the order listed above.

3. Place the pan in the bread machine and close the lid.

4. Turn on the bread maker. Select the White/Basic setting, then the loaf size, and finally the crust color. Start the cycle.

5. When the cycle is finished and the bread is baked, carefully remove the pan from the machine. Use a potholder as the handle will be very hot. Let rest for a few minutes.

6. Remove the bread from the pan and allow to cool on a wire rack for at least 10 minutes before slicing.

Welsh Bara Brith

Ingredients:
- 8 slices (1 pound)
- 11/4 cups boiling water
- 2 Earl Grey tea bags (can be decaffeinated)
- One 8-ounce bag mixed dried fruit, chopped (about 1 cup)
- 1 large egg
- 1/2 cup milk
- 1 tablespoon unsalted butter, melted or room temperature
- 3 tablespoons orange marmalade, ginger marmalade, or apricot preserves (you can use a sugar-free fruit spread)
- 1 cup light brown sugar
- 23/4 cups unbleached all-purpose flour
- 1 cup dark or golden raisins
- 1/4 cup chopped candied orange peel (shown here) or currants
- 23/4 teaspoons baking powder
- 2 teaspoons apple pie spice
- 3/4 teaspoon salt
- 12 slices (1 ½ pounds)
- 1 7/8 cups boiling water
- 3 Earl Grey tea bags (can be decaffeinated)
- One 12-ounce bag mixed dried fruit, chopped (about 1 cup)
- 1 1/2 large eggs
- 3/4 cup milk
- 1 1/2 tablespoons unsalted butter, melted or room temperature
- 4 1/2 tablespoons orange marmalade, ginger marmalade, or apricot preserves (you can use a sugar-free fruit spread)
- 1 1/2 cups light brown sugar
- 4 1/8 cups unbleached all-purpose flour
- 1 1/2 cups dark or golden raisins
- 3/8 cup chopped candied orange peel (shown here) or currants
- 4 1/8 teaspoons baking powder
- 3 teaspoons apple pie spice
- 1 1/8 teaspoons salt
- 16 slices (2 pounds)
- 2 1/2 cups boiling water
- 4 Earl Grey tea bags (can be decaffeinated)
- One 16-ounce bag mixed dried fruit, chopped (about 2 cups)
- 2 large eggs
- 1 cup milk
- 2 tablespoons unsalted butter, melted or room temperature
- 6 tablespoons orange marmalade, ginger marmalade, or apricot preserves (you can use a sugar-free fruit spread)
- 2 cups light brown sugar
- 5 1/2 cups unbleached all-purpose flour
- 2 cups dark or golden raisins
- 1/2 cup chopped candied orange peel (shown here) or currants
- 5 1/2 teaspoons baking powder
- 4 teaspoons apple pie spice
- 1 1/2 teaspoons salt

Directions:
1. Choose the size of loaf you would like to make and measure your ingredients.

2. Pour the boiling water into a 4-cup glass measuring cup. Add the tea bags and let steep for 10 minutes; remove and squeeze the tea bags dry. Add the dried fruit and stir well. Let stand at room temperature for 1 to 4 hours to plump the fruit and come to room temperature.

3. Add the ingredients to the bread pan in the order listed above.

4. Place the pan in the bread machine and close the lid.

5. Turn on the bread maker. Select the Quick Bread/Cake setting, then the loaf size, and finally the crust color. Start the cycle.

6. When the machine beeps at the end of the cycle, press Stop/Reset and program for the Bake Only cycle for an additional 20 minutes to finish baking.

7. When the cycle is finished and the bread is baked, carefully remove the pan from the machine. Use a potholder as the handle will be very hot. Let rest for a few minutes.

8. Remove the bread from the pan and allow to cool on a wire rack for at least 10 minutes before slicing.

Beer Pizza Dough

Ingredients:
- 8 slices (1 pound)
- 2/3 cup beer, at room temperature
- 1/8 cup olive oil
- 2/3 tablespoon sugar
- 2/3 teaspoon table salt
- 2 cups white bread flour or all-purpose flour
- 1 teaspoon bread machine yeast
- 12 slices (1 ½ pounds)
- 1 cup beer, at room temperature
- 3 tablespoons olive oil
- 1 tablespoon sugar
- 1 teaspoon table salt
- 3 cups white bread flour or all-purpose flour
- 1½ teaspoons bread machine yeast
- 16 slices (2 pounds)
- 1⅓ cups beer, at room temperature
- ¼ cup olive oil
- 1⅓ tablespoons sugar
- 1⅓ teaspoons table salt
- 4 cups white bread flour or all-purpose flour
- 2 teaspoons bread machine yeast

Directions:
1. Choose the size of dough you would like to make and measure your ingredients.

2. Add the ingredients to the bread pan in the order listed above.

3. Place the pan in the bread machine and close the lid.

4. Turn on the bread maker. Select the Dough setting and then the dough size. Start the machine.

5. When the cycle is finished, carefully remove the dough from the pan.

6. Place the dough on a lightly floured surface and roll to make a pizza crust of your desired thickness. Set aside for 10–15 minutes.

7. Top with your favorite pizza sauce, toppings, cheese, etc.

8. Bake in an oven at 400°F or 204°C for 15–20 minutes or until the edges turn lightly golden.

Orange Gingerbread With Orange Whipped Cream

Ingredients:
- 8 slices (1 pound)
- For the gingerbread:
- 4 tablespoons unsalted butter, melted
- 1/2 cup light molasses
- 2 large eggs
- Grated zest of 1 orange
- 1/2 cup light brown sugar
- 3/4 cup buttermilk
- 2 teaspoons baking soda dissolved in 1/4 cup hot water
- 21/2 cups unbleached all-purpose flour
- 1/2 teaspoon baking powder
- 2 teaspoons ground ginger
- 11/2 teaspoons apple pie spice or 1/2 teaspoon ground cinnamon, 1/2 teaspoon allspice, and 1/2 teaspoon cloves
- 3/4 teaspoon salt
- 2 tablespoons chopped candied ginger, optional
- For the orange whipped cream:
- 1 cup heavy cream
- 2 tablespoons confectioners' sugar
- 2 tablespoons Grand Marnier orange liqueur or thawed orange juice concentrate
- 1/2 teaspoon vanilla extract
- 12 slices (1 ½ pounds)
- For the gingerbread:
- 6 tablespoons unsalted butter, melted
- 3/4 cup light molasses

- 3 large eggs
- Grated zest of 1 1/2 oranges
- 3/4 cup light brown sugar
- 1 1/8 cups buttermilk
- 3 teaspoons baking soda dissolved in 3/8 cup hot water
- 3 3/4 cups unbleached all-purpose flour
- 3/4 teaspoon baking powder
- 3 teaspoons ground ginger
- 2 1/4 teaspoons apple pie spice or 3/4 teaspoon ground cinnamon, 3/4 teaspoon allspice, and 3/4 teaspoon cloves
- 1 1/8 teaspoons salt
- 3 tablespoons chopped candied ginger, optional
- For the orange whipped cream:
- 1 cup heavy cream
- 2 tablespoons confectioners' sugar
- 2 tablespoons Grand Marnier orange liqueur or thawed orange juice concentrate
- 1/2 teaspoon vanilla extract
- 16 slices (2 pounds)
- For the gingerbread:
- 8 tablespoons unsalted butter, melted
- 1 cup light molasses
- 4 large eggs
- Grated zest of 2 oranges
- 1 cup light brown sugar
- 1 1/2 cups buttermilk
- 4 teaspoons baking soda dissolved in 1/2 cup hot water
- 5 cups unbleached all-purpose flour
- 1 teaspoon baking powder
- 4 teaspoons ground ginger
- 3 teaspoons apple pie spice or 1 teaspoon ground cinnamon, 1 teaspoon allspice, and 1 teaspoon cloves
- 1 1/2 teaspoons salt
- 4 tablespoons chopped candied ginger, optional
- For the orange whipped cream:
- 1 cup heavy cream
- 2 tablespoons confectioners' sugar
- 2 tablespoons Grand Marnier orange liqueur or thawed orange juice concentrate
- 1/2 teaspoon vanilla extract

Directions:

1. Choose the size of loaf you would like to make and measure your ingredients.

2. To prepare the orange whipped cream, combine all the ingredients in a chilled bowl. Beat with an electric mixer until soft peaks are formed. Cover and chill until needed.

3. To make the gingerbread, add the gingerbread ingredients to the bread pan in the order listed above.

4. Place the pan in the bread machine and close the lid.

5. Turn on the bread maker. Select the Quick Bread/Cake setting, then the loaf size, and finally the crust color. Start the cycle.

6. When the machine beeps at the end of the cycle, check the loaf for doneness. If the indentation remains, press Stop/Reset and program for the Bake Only cycle; check at intervals until the loaf is done.

7. When the cycle is finished and the bread is baked, carefully remove the pan from the machine. Use a potholder as the handle will be very hot. Let rest for a few minutes.

8. Remove the bread from the pan and allow to cool on a wire rack for at least 10 minutes before slicing.

Amaretto Bread

Ingredients:

- 8 slices (1 pound)
- 1/2 cup (2 ounces) whole almonds
- 2/3 cup commercial eggnog
- 1/6 cup amaretto liqueur
- 1 large egg yolk
- 1 1/2 tablespoons unsalted butter, cut into pieces, or almond oil
- 2 cups bread flour
- 1 tablespoon sugar
- 2/3 tablespoon gluten
- 3/4 teaspoon salt
- 1/2 tablespoon SAF yeast or 1/2 tablespoon plus 1/4 teaspoon bread machine yeast
- 1/8 cup Almond Confectioners' Sugar, for dusting (opposite)
- 12 slices (1½ pounds)
- 3/4 cup (3 ounces) whole almonds

- 1 cup plus 1 tablespoon commercial eggnog
- 1/4 cup amaretto liqueur
- 2 large egg yolks
- 2 tablespoons unsalted butter, cut into pieces, or almond oil
- 3 cups bread flour
- 1 tablespoon sugar
- 1 tablespoon gluten
- 11/4 teaspoons salt
- 21/2 teaspoons SAF yeast or 1 tablespoon bread machine yeast
- 1/4 cup Almond Confectioners' Sugar, for dusting (opposite)
- 16 slices (2 pounds)
- 1 cup (4 ounces) whole almonds
- 11/3 cups commercial eggnog
- 1/3 cup amaretto liqueur
- 2 large egg yolks
- 3 tablespoons unsalted butter, cut into pieces, or almond oil
- 4 cups bread flour
- 2 tablespoons sugar
- 1 tablespoon plus 1 teaspoon gluten
- 11/2 teaspoons salt
- 1 tablespoon SAF yeast or 1 tablespoon plus 1/2 teaspoon bread machine yeast
- 1/4 cup Almond Confectioners' Sugar, for dusting (opposite)

Directions:

1. Preheat the oven to 350°F.
2. Coarsely chop the almonds and spread them evenly on a clean baking sheet. Bake until lightly toasted, about 5 to 7 minutes. Remove from the oven and let cool.
3. Choose the size of loaf you would like to make and measure your ingredients.
4. Add the ingredients to the bread pan in the order listed above.
5. Place the pan in the bread machine and close the lid.
6. Turn on the bread maker. Select the Basic setting, then the loaf size, and finally the crust color. Start the cycle.

7. When the machine beeps, or between Knead 1 and Knead 2, add the almonds. Touch and press the dough with your fingers. It should be soft and pliable.
8. When the cycle is finished and the bread is baked, carefully remove the pan from the machine. Use a potholder as the handle will be very hot. Let rest for a few minutes.
9. Remove the bread from the pan and allow to cool on a wire rack for at least 10 minutes, then dust with Almond Confectioners' Sugar before slicing.

Milk Honey Sourdough Bread

Ingredients:

- 8 slices (1 pound)
- 1/4 cup lukewarm milk
- 1 cup sourdough starter
- 1/8 cup olive oil
- 1 tablespoon honey
- 2/3 teaspoon salt
- 2 cups white bread flour
- 2/3 teaspoon bread machine yeast
- 12 slices (1 ½ pounds)
- ⅓ cup lukewarm milk
- 1½ cups sourdough starter
- 3 tablespoons olive oil
- 1½ tablespoons honey
- 1 teaspoon salt
- 3 cups white bread flour
- 1 teaspoon bread machine yeast
- 16 slices (2 pounds)
- ½ cup lukewarm milk
- 2 cups sourdough starter
- ¼ cup olive oil
- 2 tablespoons honey
- 1⅓ teaspoons salt
- 4 cups white bread flour
- 1⅓ teaspoons bread machine yeast

Directions:

1. Choose the size of loaf you would like to make and measure your ingredients.
2. Add the ingredients to the bread pan in the order listed above.
3. Place the pan in the bread machine and close the lid.

4. Turn on the bread maker. Select the White/Basic setting, then the loaf size, and finally the crust color. Start the cycle.

5. When the cycle is finished and the bread is baked, carefully remove the pan from the machine. Use a potholder as the handle will be very hot. Let rest for a few minutes.

6. Remove the bread from the pan and allow to cool on a wire rack for at least 10 minutes before slicing.

Anise Christmas Bread

Ingredients:
- 8 slices (1 pound)
- 9/16 cup water
- 1/2 large egg plus 1/2 egg yolk
- 1 1/2 tablespoons unsalted butter, cut into pieces
- 1/2 teaspoon anise extract
- 1 3/4 cups bread flour
- 1/8 cup sugar
- 1 1/2 tablespoons dry buttermilk powder
- 2/3 tablespoon gluten
- 3/4 teaspoon salt
- 1 1/4 teaspoons SAF yeast or 1/2 tablespoon bread machine yeast
- 1/2 cup whole glacéed cherries or chopped glacéed apricots (shown here)
- 12 slices (1½ pounds)
- 7/8 cup water
- 1 large egg
- 2 tablespoons unsalted butter, cut into pieces
- 3/4 teaspoon anise extract
- 21/2 cups bread flour
- 3 tablespoons sugar
- 2 tablespoons dry buttermilk powder
- 1 tablespoon gluten
- 11/4 teaspoons salt
- 21/4 teaspoons SAF yeast or 23/4 teaspoons bread machine yeast
- 3/4 cup whole glacéed cherries or chopped glacéed apricots (shown here)
- 16 slices (2 pounds)
- 11/8 cups water
- 1 large egg plus 1 egg yolk

- 3 tablespoons unsalted butter, cut into pieces
- 1 teaspoon anise extract
- 31/2 cups bread flour
- 1/4 cup sugar
- 3 tablespoons dry buttermilk powder
- 1 tablespoon plus 1 teaspoon gluten
- 1 1/2 teaspoons salt
- 2 1/2 teaspoons SAF yeast or 1 tablespoon bread machine yeast
- 1 cup whole glacéed cherries or chopped glacéed apricots (shown here)

Directions:
1. Choose the size of loaf you would like to make and measure your ingredients.

2. Add the ingredients to the bread pan in the order listed above (except the cherries or apricots).

3. Place the pan in the bread machine and close the lid.

4. Turn on the bread maker. Select the Sweet Bread/Fruit and Nut cycle setting, then the loaf size, and finally the crust color. Start the cycle.

5. When the machine beeps, or between Knead 1 and Knead 2, add the fruit.

6. When the cycle is finished and the bread is baked, carefully remove the pan from the machine. Use a potholder as the handle will be very hot. Let rest for a few minutes.

7. Remove the bread from the pan and allow to cool on a wire rack for at least 10 minutes before slicing.

Holiday Chocolate Bread

Ingredients:
- 8 slices (1 pound)
- 1/2 cup + 1 1/2 tablespoons lukewarm milk
- 1/2 egg, at room temperature
- 1 tablespoon unsalted butter, melted
- 3/4 teaspoon pure vanilla extract
- 1 1/3 tablespoons sugar
- 1/2 teaspoon table salt
- 2 cups white bread flour
- 2/3 teaspoon bread machine yeast
- 1/3 cup white chocolate chips
- 1/4 cup dried cranberries
- 12 slices (1 ½ pounds)

- ⅞ cup lukewarm milk
- 1 egg, at room temperature
- 1½ tablespoons unsalted butter, melted
- 1 teaspoon pure vanilla extract
- 2 tablespoons sugar
- ¾ teaspoon table salt
- 3 cups white bread flour
- 1 teaspoon bread machine yeast
- ½ cup white chocolate chips
- ⅓ cup dried cranberries
- 16 slices (2 pounds)
- 1 cup + 3 tablespoons lukewarm milk
- 1 egg, at room temperature
- 2 tablespoons unsalted butter, melted
- 1½ teaspoons pure vanilla extract
- 2⅔ tablespoons sugar
- 1 teaspoon table salt
- 4 cups white bread flour
- 1⅓ teaspoons bread machine yeast
- ⅔ cup white chocolate chips
- ½ cup dried cranberries

Directions:

1. Choose the size of loaf you would like to make and measure your ingredients.

2. Add all of the ingredients except for the chocolate chips and cranberries to the bread pan in the order listed above.

3. Place the pan in the bread machine and close the lid.

4. Turn on the bread maker. Select the White/Basic or Fruit/Nut (if your machine has this setting) setting, then the loaf size, and finally the crust color. Start the cycle.

5. When the machine signals to add ingredients, add the chocolate chips and cranberries. (Some machines have a fruit/nut hopper where you can add the chocolate chips and cranberries when you start the machine. The machine will automatically add them to the dough during the baking process.)

6. When the cycle is finished and the bread is baked, carefully remove the pan from the machine. Use a potholder as the handle will be very hot. Let rest for a few minutes.

7. Remove the bread from the pan and allow to cool on a wire rack for at least 10 minutes before slicing.

Hungarian Spring Bread

Ingredients:

- 8 slices (1 pound)
- For the dough:
- 1/2 cup sour cream, at room temperature
- 1/4 cup buttermilk
- 2/3 large egg plus 2/3 egg yolk
- 1 teaspoon vanilla extract
- 1/3 teaspoon almond extract
- 2 tablespoons unsalted butter or margarine, cut into pieces and softened
- 2 cups bread flour
- 1/6 cup sugar
- 1 teaspoon salt
- 1 2/3 teaspoons SAF yeast or 2/3 tablespoon bread machine yeast
- 1/4 cup golden raisins
- 1/4 cup diced lemon confit (shown here) or candied lemon peel
- 1/6 cup pecan pieces
- 2/3 tablespoon unbleached all-purpose flour
- For the lemon icing:
- 3/4 cup sifted confectioners' sugar
- 1 teaspoon grated lemon zest
- 1 teaspoon fresh lemon juice or syrup from the lemon confit
- 1 to 11/2 tablespoons warm milk
- 1 teaspoon soft butter
- 12 slices (1 ½ pounds)
- For the dough:
- 3/4 cup sour cream, at room temperature
- 1/3 cup buttermilk
- 1 large egg plus 1 egg yolk
- 11/2 teaspoons vanilla extract
- 1/2 teaspoon almond extract
- 3 tablespoons unsalted butter or margarine, cut into pieces and softened
- 3 cups bread flour
- 1/4 cup sugar
- 11/2 teaspoons salt
- 21/2 teaspoons SAF yeast or 1 tablespoon bread machine yeast
- 1/3 cup golden raisins

- 1/3 cup diced lemon confit (shown here) or candied lemon peel
- 1/4 cup pecan pieces
- 1 tablespoon unbleached all-purpose flour
- For the lemon icing:
- 3/4 cup sifted confectioners' sugar
- 1 teaspoon grated lemon zest
- 1 teaspoon fresh lemon juice or syrup from the lemon confit
- 1 to 11/2 tablespoons warm milk
- 1 teaspoon soft butter
- 16 slices (2 pounds)
- For the dough:
- 1 cup sour cream, at room temperature
- 1/2 cup buttermilk
- 1 1/3 large eggs plus 1 1/3 egg yolks
- 2 teaspoons vanilla extract
- 2/3 teaspoon almond extract
- 4 tablespoons unsalted butter or margarine, cut into pieces and softened
- 4 cups bread flour
- 1/3 cup sugar
- 2 teaspoons salt
- 3 1/3 teaspoons SAF yeast or 1 1/3 tablespoons bread machine yeast
- 1/2 cup golden raisins
- 1/2 cup diced lemon confit (shown here) or candied lemon peel
- 1/3 cup pecan pieces
- 1 1/3 tablespoons unbleached all-purpose flour
- For the lemon icing:
- 3/4 cup sifted confectioners' sugar
- 1 teaspoon grated lemon zest
- 1 teaspoon fresh lemon juice or syrup from the lemon confit
- 1 to 11/2 tablespoons warm milk
- 1 teaspoon soft butter

Directions:

1. Choose the size of loaf you would like to make and measure your ingredients.
2. To make the dough, add the dough ingredients to the bread pan in the order listed above (except the raisins, lemon peel, and pecans).
3. Place the pan in the bread machine and close the lid.
4. Turn on the bread maker. Select the Sweet Bread setting, then the loaf size, and finally the crust color. Start the cycle. (This recipe is not suitable for use with the Delay Timer.)
5. Sprinkle the fruit and nuts with the tablespoon of flour.
6. When the machine beeps, or between Knead 1 and Knead 2, add the raisins, lemon peel, and nuts. The dough ball will look dry at first and take about 7 minutes to smooth out.
7. To make the icing, combine the icing ingredients in a small bowl and whisk until smooth. Adjust the consistency by adding more milk, a few drops at a time.
8. When the cycle is finished and the bread is baked, carefully remove the pan from the machine. Use a potholder as the handle will be very hot. Let rest for a few minutes.
9. Remove the bread from the pan and allow to cool on a wire rack for at least 10 minutes before slicing. Using an oversized spoon, drizzle the icing over the top of the loaf in a back and forth motion. As the glaze cools, it will set.

Dry Fruit Cinnamon Bread

Ingredients:
- 8 slices (1 pound)
- 5/6 cup lukewarm milk
- 1/6 cup unsalted butter, melted
- 1/3 teaspoon pure vanilla extract
- 1/8 teaspoon pure almond extract
- 1/6 cup light brown sugar
- 2/3 teaspoon table salt
- 1 teaspoon ground cinnamon
- 2 cups white bread flour
- 5/6 teaspoon bread machine yeast
- 1/3 cup dried mixed fruit
- 1/3 cup golden raisins, chopped
- 12 slices (1 ½ pounds)
- 1¼ cups lukewarm milk
- ¼ cup unsalted butter, melted
- ½ teaspoon pure vanilla extract
- ¼ teaspoon pure almond extract

- 3 tablespoons light brown sugar
- 1 teaspoon table salt
- 2 teaspoons ground cinnamon
- 3 cups white bread flour
- 1 teaspoon bread machine yeast
- ½ cup dried mixed fruit
- ½ cup golden raisins, chopped
- 16 slices (2 pounds)
- 1⅔ cups lukewarm milk
- ⅓ cup unsalted butter, melted
- ⅔ teaspoon pure vanilla extract
- ¼ teaspoon pure almond extract
- ⅓ cup light brown sugar
- 1⅓ teaspoons table salt
- 2 teaspoons ground cinnamon
- 4 cups white bread flour
- 1⅓ teaspoons bread machine yeast
- ⅔ cup dried mixed fruit
- ⅔ cup golden raisins, chopped

Directions:

1. Choose the size of loaf you would like to make and measure your ingredients.

2. Add all of the ingredients except for the mixed fruit and raisins to the bread pan in the order listed above.

3. Place the pan in the bread machine and close the lid.

4. Turn on the bread maker. Select the White/Basic or Fruit/Nut (if your machine has this setting) setting, then the loaf size, and finally the crust color. Start the cycle.

5. When the machine signals to add ingredients, add the mixed fruit and raisins. (Some machines have a fruit/nut hopper where you can add the mixed fruit and raisins when you start the machine. The machine will automatically add them to the dough during the baking process.)

6. When the cycle is finished and the bread is baked, carefully remove the pan from the machine. Use a potholder as the handle will be very hot. Let rest for a few minutes.

7. Remove the bread from the pan and allow to cool on a wire rack for at least 10 minutes before slicing.

Classic Sourdough Bread

Ingredients:

- 8 slices (1 pound)
- 1 1/3 tablespoons lukewarm water
- 1 1/3 cups sourdough starter
- 1 1/3 tablespoons unsalted butter, melted
- 1 1/3 teaspoons sugar
- 1 teaspoon salt
- 1 2/3 cups white bread flour
- 1 teaspoon bread machine yeast
- Sourdough Starter
- 1 cup lukewarm water
- 1 cup all-purpose flour
- 1 1/4 teaspoons bread machine yeast
- 12 slices (1 ½ pounds)
- 2 tablespoons lukewarm water
- 2 cups sourdough starter
- 2 tablespoons unsalted butter, melted
- 2 teaspoons sugar
- 1½ teaspoons salt
- 2½ cups white bread flour
- 1½ teaspoons bread machine yeast
- Sourdough Starter
- 1 1/2 cup lukewarm water
- 1 1/2 cup all-purpose flour
- 1 7/8 teaspoons bread machine yeast
- 16 slices (2 pounds)
- 2⅔ tablespoons lukewarm water
- 2⅔ cups sourdough starter
- 2⅔ tablespoons unsalted butter, melted
- 2⅔ teaspoons sugar
- 2 teaspoons salt
- 3⅓ cups white bread flour
- 2 teaspoons bread machine yeast
- Sourdough Starter
- 2 cups lukewarm water
- 2 cups all-purpose flour
- 2½ teaspoons bread machine yeast

Directions:

1. Starter:

2. Add the water, flour, and yeast to a medium-size non-metallic bowl. Mix well until no lumps are visible.

3. Cover the bowl loosely and leave it in a warm area of your kitchen for 5–8 days. Do not place in a fridge or under direct sunlight.

4. Stir the mixture several times every day. Always put the cover back on the bowl afterward.

5. The starter is ready to use when it appears bubbly and has a sour smell.

6. Sourdough Bread:

7. Choose the size of loaf you would like to make and measure your ingredients.

8. Add the ingredients to the bread pan in the order listed above.

9. Place the pan in the bread machine and close the lid.

10. Turn on the bread maker. Select the White/Basic setting, then the loaf size, and finally the crust color. Start the cycle.

11. When the cycle is finished and the bread is baked, carefully remove the pan from the machine. Use a potholder as the handle will be very hot. Let rest for a few minutes.

12. Remove the bread from the pan and allow to cool on a wire rack for at least 10 minutes before slicing.

Basil Pizza Dough

Ingredients:
- 8 slices (1 pound)
- 5/8 cup lukewarm water
- 1/8 cup olive oil
- 5/8 teaspoon table salt
- 1 teaspoon sugar
- 1 teaspoon basil, dried
- 2 cups white bread flour or all-purpose flour
- 1 teaspoon bread machine yeast
- 12 slices (1 ½ pounds)
- 1 cup lukewarm water
- 3 tablespoons olive oil
- 1 teaspoon table salt
- 1½ teaspoons sugar
- 1½ teaspoons basil, dried
- 3 cups white bread flour or all-purpose flour
- 1½ teaspoons bread machine yeast
- 16 slices (2 pounds)
- 1¼ cups lukewarm water
- ¼ cup olive oil
- 1¼ teaspoons table salt
- 2 teaspoons sugar

- 2 teaspoons basil, dried
- 4 cups white bread flour or all-purpose flour
- 2 teaspoons bread machine yeast

Directions:

1. Choose the size of dough you would like to make and measure your ingredients.

2. Add the ingredients to the bread pan in the order listed above.

3. Place the pan in the bread machine and close the lid.

4. Turn on the bread maker. Select the Dough setting and then the dough size. Start the machine.

5. When the cycle is finished, carefully remove the dough from the pan.

6. Place the dough on a lightly floured surface and roll to make a pizza crust of your desired thickness. Set aside for 10–15 minutes.

7. Top with your favorite pizza sauce, toppings, cheese, etc.

8. Bake in an oven at 400°F or 204°C for 15–20 minutes or until the edges turn lightly golden.

Easter Bread

Ingredients:
- 8 slices (1 pound)
- 1/2 cup lukewarm milk
- 1 egg, at room temperature
- 11/3 tablespoons unsalted butter, melted
- 1/6 cup sugar
- 1/2 teaspoon table salt
- 11/6 teaspoons lemon zest
- 2 cups white bread flour
- 11/8 teaspoons bread machine yeast
- 12 slices (1 ½ pounds)
- ¾ cup lukewarm milk
- 2 eggs, at room temperature
- 2 tablespoons unsalted butter, melted
- ¼ cup sugar
- 1 teaspoon table salt
- 2 teaspoons lemon zest
- 3 cups white bread flour
- 2 teaspoons bread machine yeast
- 16 slices (2 pounds)
- 1 cup lukewarm milk

- 2 eggs, at room temperature
- 2⅔ tablespoons unsalted butter, melted
- ⅓ cup sugar
- 1 teaspoon table salt
- 2⅓ teaspoons lemon zest
- 4 cups white bread flour
- 2¼ teaspoons bread machine yeast

Directions:

1. Choose the size of loaf you would like to make and measure your ingredients.

2. Add the ingredients to the bread pan in the order listed above.

3. Place the pan in the bread machine and close the lid.

4. Turn on the bread maker. Select the White/Basic setting, then the loaf size, and finally the crust color. Start the cycle.

5. When the cycle is finished and the bread is baked, carefully remove the pan from the machine. Use a potholder as the handle will be very hot. Let rest for a few minutes.

6. Remove the bread from the pan and allow to cool on a wire rack for at least 10 minutes before slicing.

Grandma's Favorite Gingerbread

Ingredients:

- 8 slices (1 pound)
- 2/3 cup buttermilk at 80 degrees F
- 1 egg, at room temperature
- 2 2/3 tablespoons dark molasses
- 2 teaspoons melted butter, cooled
- 2 tablespoons honey
- 1 teaspoon salt
- 1 teaspoon ground ginger
- 2/3 teaspoon ground cinnamon
- 1/3 teaspoon ground nutmeg
- 1/8 teaspoon ground cloves
- 2 1/3 cups white bread flour
- 1 1/3 teaspoons bread machine yeast
- 12 slices (1 ½ pounds)
- 1 cup buttermilk at 80 degrees F
- 1 1/2 eggs, at room temperature
- 4 tablespoons dark molasses
- 3 teaspoons melted butter, cooled

- 3 tablespoons honey
- 1 1/2 teaspoons salt
- 1 1/2teaspoons ground ginger
- 1 teaspoon ground cinnamon
- 1/2 teaspoon ground nutmeg
- 3/16 teaspoon ground cloves
- 3 1/2 cups white bread flour
- 2 teaspoons bread machine yeast
- 16 slices (2 pounds)
- 1 1/3 cups buttermilk at 80 degrees F
- 2 eggs, at room temperature
- 5 1/3 tablespoons dark molasses
- 4 teaspoons melted butter, cooled
- 4 tablespoons honey
- 2 teaspoons salt
- 2 teaspoons ground ginger
- 1 1/3 teaspoons ground cinnamon
- 2/3 teaspoon ground nutmeg
- 1/4 teaspoon ground cloves
- 4 2/3 cups white bread flour
- 2 2/3 teaspoons bread machine yeast

Directions:

1. Choose the size of loaf you would like to make and measure your ingredients.

2. Add the ingredients to the bread pan in the order listed above.

3. Place the pan in the bread machine and close the lid.

4. Turn on the bread maker. Select the Sweet Bread setting, then the loaf size, and finally the crust color. Start the cycle.

5. When the cycle is finished and the bread is baked, carefully remove the pan from the machine. Use a potholder as the handle will be very hot. Let rest for a few minutes.

6. Remove the bread from the pan and allow to cool on a wire rack for at least 10 minutes before slicing.

Portuguese Sweet Bread

Ingredients:

- 8 slices (1 pound)
- 3/8 cup evaporated milk
- 1/6 cup plus 1/2 tablespoon water
- 1 large egg

- 2 tablespoons butter, melted
- 1/4 teaspoon lemon extract
- 1/2 tablespoon plus 1/2 teaspoon vanilla extract or vanilla powder
- 1 7/8 cups bread flour
- 1/4 cup light brown sugar
- 3/4 tablespoon instant potato flakes
- 1/2 tablespoon gluten
- 1 teaspoon salt
- 1 1/2 teaspoons SAF yeast or 1/2 tablespoon plus 1/4 teaspoon bread machine yeast
- 12 slices (1½ pounds)
- 2/3 cup evaporated milk
- 1/4 cup plus 1 tablespoon water
- 2 large eggs
- 3 tablespoons butter, melted
- 1/2 teaspoon lemon extract
- 1 tablespoon vanilla extract or vanilla powder
- 3 cups bread flour
- 1/3 cup light brown sugar
- 1 tablespoon instant potato flakes
- 2 teaspoons gluten
- 11/2 teaspoons salt
- 21/2 teaspoons SAF yeast or 1 tablespoon bread machine yeast
- 16 slices (2 pounds)
- 3/4 cup evaporated milk
- 1/3 cup plus 1 tablespoon water
- 2 large eggs
- 4 tablespoons butter, melted
- 1/2 teaspoon lemon extract
- 1 tablespoon plus 1 teaspoon vanilla extract or vanilla powder
- 33/4 cups bread flour
- 1/2 cup light brown sugar
- 11/2 tablespoons instant potato flakes
- 1 tablespoon gluten
- 2 teaspoons salt
- 3 teaspoons SAF yeast or 1 tablespoon plus 1/2 teaspoon bread machine yeast

Directions:

1. Choose the size of loaf you would like to make and measure your ingredients.

2. Add the ingredients to the bread pan in the order listed above.

3. Place the pan in the bread machine and close the lid.

4. Turn on the bread maker. Select the Basic/Sweet Bread setting, then the loaf size, and finally the crust color. Start the cycle. (This recipe is not suitable for use with the Delay Timer.)

5. When the cycle is finished and the bread is baked, carefully remove the pan from the machine. Use a potholder as the handle will be very hot. Let rest for a few minutes.

6. Remove the bread from the pan and allow to cool on a wire rack for at least 10 minutes before slicing.

Challah Bread

Ingredients:
- 8 slices (1 pound)
- 1/2 cup + 3/8 teaspoon water, lukewarm between 80 and 90°F
- 1 1/4 tablespoons unsalted butter, melted
- 1 small egg, beaten
- 1 1/4 tablespoons sugar
- 7/8 teaspoon salt
- 2 1/4 cups white bread flour
- 1 teaspoon bread machine yeast or rapid rise yeast
- For oven baking:
- 1 egg yolk
- 2 tablespoons cold water
- 1 tablespoon poppy seed (optional)
- 12 slices (1 ½ pounds)
- ¾ cup +1 tablespoon water, lukewarm between 80 and 90°F
- 2 tablespoons unsalted butter, melted
- 1 egg, beaten
- 2 tablespoons sugar
- 1 ½ teaspoons salt
- 3 ¼ cups white bread flour
- 1 ½ teaspoons bread machine yeast or rapid rise yeast
- For oven baking:
- 1 egg yolk
- 2 tablespoons cold water
- 1 tablespoon poppy seed (optional)

- 16 slices (2 pounds)
- 1 cup +¾ teaspoon water, lukewarm between 80 and 90⁰F
- 2 ½ tablespoons unsalted butter, melted
- 2 small eggs, beaten
- 2 ½ tablespoons sugar
- 1 ¾ teaspoons salt
- 4 ½ cups white bread flour
- 2 teaspoons bread machine yeast or rapid rise yeast
- For oven baking:
- 1 egg yolk
- 2 tablespoons cold water
- 1 tablespoon poppy seed (optional)

Directions:

1. Choose the size of loaf you would like to make and measure your ingredients.
2. Add the ingredients to the bread pan in the order listed above.
3. Place the pan in the bread machine and close the lid.
4. Turn on the bread maker. Select the Dough setting, then the loaf size, and finally the crust color. Start the cycle.
5. Lightly flour a working surface and prepare a large baking sheet by greasing it with cooking spray or vegetable oil or line with parchment paper or a silicone mat.
6. Preheat the oven to 375°F and place the oven rack in the middle position.
7. After the dough cycle is done, carefully remove the dough from the pan and place it on the working surface. Divide dough in three even parts.
8. Roll each part into 13-inch-long cables for the 1 ½ pound Challah bread or 17-inch for the 2-pound loaf. Arrange the dough cables side by side and start braiding from its middle part.
9. In order to make a seal, pinch ends and tuck the ends under the braid.
10. Arrange the loaf onto the baking sheet; cover the sheet with a clean kitchen towel. Let rise for 45-60 minutes or more until it doubles in size.
11. In a mixing bowl, mix the egg yolk and cold water to make an egg wash. Gently brush the egg wash over the loaf. Sprinkle top with the poppy seed, if desired.
12. Bake for about 25-30 minutes or until loaf turns golden brown and is fully cooked.

Easter Rye Bread With Fruit

Ingredients:

- 8 slices (1 pound)
- 1/2 cup water
- 1 1/2 tablespoons brandy
- 1/2 large egg
- 1/8 cup vegetable oil
- 11/2 cups bread flour
- 1/2 cup light or medium rye flour
- 1/3 cup chopped almonds
- 1/8 cup dark brown sugar
- 2/3 tablespoon gluten
- 1 teaspoon crushed cardamom seeds
- Grated zest of 1/2 lemon
- Grated zest of 1/2 orange
- 3/4 teaspoon salt
- 1/2 tablespoon SAF yeast or 1/2 tablespoon plus 1/4 teaspoon bread machine yeast
- 5/8 cup golden raisins
- 12 slices (1½ pounds)
- 3/4 cup water
- 3 tablespoons brandy
- 1 large egg
- 3 tablespoons vegetable oil
- 21/4 cups bread flour
- 3/4 cup light or medium rye flour
- 1/2 cup chopped almonds
- 3 tablespoons dark brown sugar
- 1 tablespoon gluten
- 11/2 teaspoons crushed cardamom seeds
- Grated zest of 1 lemon
- Grated zest of 1 orange
- 11/4 teaspoons salt
- 21/2 teaspoons SAF yeast or 1 tablespoon bread machine yeast
- 1 cup golden raisins
- 16 slices (2 pounds)
- 1 cup water
- 3 tablespoons brandy
- 1 large egg

- 1/4 cup vegetable oil
- 3 cups bread flour
- 1 cup light or medium rye flour
- 2/3 cup chopped almonds
- 1/4 cup dark brown sugar
- 1 tablespoon plus 1 teaspoon gluten
- 2 teaspoons crushed cardamom seeds
- Grated zest of 1 lemon
- Grated zest of 1 orange
- 11/2 teaspoons salt
- 1 tablespoon SAF yeast or 1 tablespoon plus 1/2 teaspoon bread machine yeast
- 11/4 cups golden raisins

Directions:

1. Choose the size of loaf you would like to make and measure your ingredients.

2. Add the ingredients to the bread pan in the order listed above (except the raisins).

3. Place the pan in the bread machine and close the lid.

4. Turn on the bread maker. Select the Sweet Bread or Fruit and Nut setting, then the loaf size, and finally the crust color. Start the cycle. (This recipe is not suitable for use with the Delay Timer.)

5. When the machine beeps, or between Knead 1 and Knead 2, add the raisins.

6. When the cycle is finished and the bread is baked, carefully remove the pan from the machine. Use a potholder as the handle will be very hot. Let rest for a few minutes.

7. Remove the bread from the pan and allow to cool on a wire rack for at least 10 minutes before slicing.

Holiday Raisin Bread With Candied Peels

Ingredients:

- 8 slices (1 pound)
- 2/3 cup milk
- 1 1/2 tablespoons honey
- 2 cups bread flour
- 2/3 tablespoon gluten
- 1 teaspoon salt
- 1 1/4 teaspoons SAF yeast or 1/2 tablespoon bread machine yeast
- 1/4 cup rum raisins (shown here)
- 1/6 cup chopped candied grapefruit peel or candied lemon peel (opposite)
- 1/4 cup chopped candied orange peel (opposite)
- 12 slices (1½ pounds)
- 11/8 cups milk
- 2 tablespoons honey
- 3 cups bread flour
- 1 tablespoon gluten
- 11/2 teaspoons salt
- 2 teaspoons SAF yeast or 21/2 teaspoons bread machine yeast
- 1/3 cup rum raisins (shown here)
- 1/4 cup chopped candied grapefruit peel or candied lemon peel (opposite)
- 1/3 cup chopped candied orange peel (opposite)
- 16 slices (2 pounds)
- 11/3 cups milk
- 3 tablespoons honey
- 4 cups bread flour
- 1 tablespoon plus 1 teaspoon gluten
- 2 teaspoons salt
- 21/2 teaspoons SAF yeast or 1 tablespoon bread machine yeast
- 1/2 cup rum raisins (shown here)
- 1/3 cup chopped candied grapefruit peel or candied lemon peel (opposite)
- 1/2 cup chopped candied orange peel (opposite)

Directions:

1. Choose the size of loaf you would like to make and measure your ingredients.

2. Add the ingredients to the bread pan in the order listed above (except the raisins and candied peels).

3. Place the pan in the bread machine and close the lid.

4. Turn on the bread maker. Select the Sweet Bread/Fruit and Nut setting, then the loaf size, and finally the crust color. Start the cycle. (This recipe is not suitable for use with the Delay Timer.)

5. When the machine beeps, or between Knead 1 and Knead 2, add the raisins and candied peels.

6. When the cycle is finished and the bread is baked, carefully remove the pan from the machine. Use a

potholder as the handle will be very hot. Let rest for a few minutes.

7. Remove the bread from the pan and allow to cool on a wire rack for at least 10 minutes before slicing.

Champagne-soaked Baba

Ingredients:
- 8 slices (1 pound)
- For the dough:
- 1/4 cup water
- 1 1/2 large eggs
- 1/4 cup (1/2 stick) unsalted butter, melted
- 1 1/2 cups bread flour
- 1 tablespoons sugar
- 3/8 teaspoon grated lemon zest
- 3/8 teaspoon salt
- 7/8 teaspoons SAF yeast or 1 1/8 teaspoons bread machine yeast
- For the soaking syrup:
- 3/8 cup sugar
- 3/8 cup water
- 1/4 cup sweet champagne or Asti Spumante
- For apricot glaze:
- 1/6 cup apricot jam
- 12 slices (1½ pounds)
- For the dough:
- 1/3 cup water
- 3 large eggs
- 6 tablespoons unsalted butter, melted
- 2 cups bread flour
- 11/2 tablespoons sugar
- 1/2 teaspoon grated lemon zest
- 1/2 teaspoon salt
- 11/4 teaspoons SAF yeast or 13/4 teaspoons bread machine yeast
- For the soaking syrup:
- 3/4 cup sugar
- 3/4 cup water
- 1/2 cup sweet champagne or Asti Spumante
- For apricot glaze:
- 1/3 cup apricot jam
- 16 slices (2 pounds)
- For the dough:
- 1/2 cup water
- 3 large eggs

- 1/2 cup (1 stick) unsalted butter, melted
- 3 cups bread flour
- 2 tablespoons sugar
- 3/4 teaspoon grated lemon zest
- 3/4 teaspoon salt
- 13/4 teaspoons SAF yeast or 21/4 teaspoons bread machine yeast
- For the soaking syrup:
- 3/4 cup sugar
- 3/4 cup water
- 1/2 cup sweet champagne or Asti Spumante
- For apricot glaze:
- 1/3 cup apricot jam

Directions:
1. Choose the size of loaf you would like to make and measure your ingredients.
2. Add all the dough ingredients to the bread pan in the order listed above.
3. Place the pan in the bread machine and close the lid.
4. Turn on the bread maker. Select the Sweet Bread setting, then the loaf size, and finally the crust color. Start the cycle. (This recipe is not suitable for use with the Delay Timer.)
5. Meanwhile make the soaking syrup. Combine the sugar and water in a small pan and heat until sugar is dissolved, about 5 minutes. Cool until warm. Add the champagne; set aside.
6. When the baking cycle is finished and the bread is baked, carefully remove the pan from the machine. Use a potholder as the handle will be very hot. Let rest for a few minutes.
7. Pierce the top of the baba in a few places with a bamboo skewer. Turn out of the pan onto a deep plate. Slowly pour the champagne soaking syrup all over the cake and let it stand to absorb the puddle that collects at the base. Cover with plastic wrap.
8. To prepare the apricot glaze, place the jam in a small saucepan and boil for 2 minutes to liquify. Drain off any extra soaking syrup from the plate. Brush the cake all over with hot glaze to seal in moisture. Cool and transfer to a clean serving plate before serving, turning the baba on its side to cut into round slices. Store the baba in the refrigerator.

Coffee Caraway Seed Bread

Ingredients:

- 8 slices (1 pound)
- 1/2 cup lukewarm water
- 1/4 cup brewed coffee, lukewarm
- 1 tablespoon balsamic vinegar
- 1 tablespoon olive oil
- 1 tablespoon dark molasses
- 1/2 tablespoon light brown sugar
- 1/2 teaspoon table salt
- 1 teaspoon caraway seeds
- 1/8 cup unsweetened cocoa powder
- 1/2 cup dark rye flour
- 1 1/4 cups white bread flour
- 1 teaspoon bread machine yeast
- 12 slices (1 ½ pounds)
- ¾ cup lukewarm water
- ⅓ cup brewed coffee, lukewarm
- 1½ tablespoons balsamic vinegar
- 1½ tablespoons olive oil
- 1½ tablespoons dark molasses
- ¾ tablespoon light brown sugar
- ¾ teaspoon table salt
- 1½ teaspoons caraway seeds
- 3 tablespoons unsweetened cocoa powder
- ¾ cup dark rye flour
- 1¾ cups white bread flour
- 1½ teaspoons bread machine yeast
- 16 slices (2 pounds)
- 1 cup lukewarm water
- ½ cup brewed coffee, lukewarm
- 2 tablespoons balsamic vinegar
- 2 tablespoons olive oil
- 2 tablespoons dark molasses
- 1 tablespoon light brown sugar
- 1 teaspoon table salt
- 2 teaspoons caraway seeds
- ¼ cup unsweetened cocoa powder
- 1 cup dark rye flour
- 2½ cups white bread flour
- 2 teaspoons bread machine yeast

Directions:

1. Choose the size of loaf you would like to make and measure your ingredients.
2. Add the ingredients to the bread pan in the order listed above.
3. Place the pan in the bread machine and close the lid.
4. Turn on the bread maker. Select the Whole Wheat/Wholegrain setting, then the loaf size, and finally the crust color. Start the cycle.
5. When the cycle is finished and the bread is baked, carefully remove the pan from the machine. Use a potholder as the handle will be very hot. Let rest for a few minutes.
6. Remove the bread from the pan and allow to cool down on a wire rack for at least 10 minutes or more before slicing.

St. Patrick's Rum Bread

Ingredients:

- 8 slices (1 pound)
- 1 whole egg
- 1 tablespoon rum extract
- 3 tablespoons bread flour
- 3 tablespoons packed brown sugar
- 1¼ teaspoons salt
- ½ teaspoon ground cinnamon
- ¼ teaspoon ground nutmeg
- ¼ teaspoon ground cardamom
- 1 teaspoon bread machine yeast
- Topping
- 1 egg yolk, beaten
- 1½ teaspoon pecans, chopped
- 1½ teaspoon brown sugar
- 12 slices (1 ½ pounds)
- 1 1/2 whole eggs
- 1 1/2tablespoons rum extract
- 4 1/2 tablespoons bread flour
- 4 1/2 tablespoons packed brown sugar
- 1 7/8 teaspoons salt
- 3/4 teaspoon ground cinnamon
- 3/8 teaspoon ground nutmeg
- 3/8 teaspoon ground cardamom
- 1 1/2 teaspoons bread machine yeast
- 16 slices (2 pounds)

- 2 whole eggs
- 2 tablespoons rum extract
- 6 tablespoons bread flour
- 6 tablespoons packed brown sugar
- 2 1/2 teaspoons salt
- 1 teaspoon ground cinnamon
- 1/2 teaspoon ground nutmeg
- 1/2 teaspoon ground cardamom
- 2 teaspoons bread machine yeast

Directions:

1. Choose the size of loaf you would like to make and measure your ingredients.

2. Break an egg into 1 cup and add water to fill out a measuring cup.

3. Add egg mixture to the machine.

4. Add the ingredients to the bread pan in the order listed above.

5. Place the pan in the bread machine and close the lid.

6. Turn on the bread maker. Select the White/Basic setting, then the loaf size, and finally the crust color. Start the cycle.

7. When just 40 minutes of the cycle remains, make the topping mixture and brush the top of the bread.

8. When the cycle is finished and the bread is baked, carefully remove the pan from the machine. Use a potholder as the handle will be very hot. Let rest for a few minutes.

9. Remove the bread from the pan and allow to cool on a wire rack for at least 10 minutes before slicing.

Cinnamon Beer Bread

Ingredients:

- 8 slices (1 pound)
- 1 cup beer, at room temperature
- 1/2 cup unsalted butter, melted
- 1/6 cup honey
- 2 cups all-purpose flour
- 2/3 teaspoon table salt
- 1/6 teaspoon ground cinnamon
- 2/3 tablespoon baking powder
- 12 slices (1 ½ pounds)
- 1½ cups beer, at room temperature
- ⅓ cup unsalted butter, melted

- ¼ cup honey
- 3 cups all-purpose flour
- 1 teaspoon table salt
- ¼ teaspoon ground cinnamon
- 1 tablespoon baking powder
- 16 slices (2 pounds)
- 2 cups beer, at room temperature
- 1 cup unsalted butter, melted
- ⅓ cup honey
- 4 cups all-purpose flour
- 1⅓ teaspoons table salt
- ⅓ teaspoon ground cinnamon
- 1⅓ tablespoons baking powder

Directions:

1. Choose the size of loaf you would like to make and measure your ingredients.

2. Add the ingredients to the bread pan in the order listed above.

3. Place the pan in the bread machine and close the lid.

4. Turn on the bread maker. Select the Quick/Rapid setting, then the loaf size, and finally the crust color. Start the cycle.

5. When the cycle is finished and the bread is baked, carefully remove the pan from the machine. Use a potholder as the handle will be very hot. Let rest for a few minutes.

6. Remove the bread from the pan and allow to cool on a wire rack for at least 10 minutes before slicing.

White Chocolate Cranberry Party Loaf

Ingredients:

- 8 slices (1 pound)
- ½ cup milk, at room temperature
- 1 egg, at room temperature
- 2/3 teaspoons pure vanilla extract
- 4 teaspoons sugar
- ½ teaspoon salt
- 2 cups white bread flour
- ¾ teaspoon instant yeast
- ½ cup white chocolate chips
- ½ cup cranberries
- 12 slices (1 ½ pounds)
- 3/4 cup milk, at room temperature

- 1 1/2 eggs, at room temperature
- 1 teaspoon pure vanilla extract
- 6 teaspoons sugar
- 3/4 teaspoon salt
- 3 cups white bread flour
- 1 1/8 teaspoons instant yeast
- 3/4 cup white chocolate chips
- 3/4 cup cranberries
- 16 slices (2 pounds)
- 1 cup milk, at room temperature
- 2 eggs, at room temperature
- 1 1/3 teaspoons pure vanilla extract
- 8 teaspoons sugar
- 1 teaspoon salt
- 4 cups white bread flour
- 1 1/2 teaspoons instant yeast
- 1 cup white chocolate chips
- 1 cup cranberries

Directions:

1. Choose the size of loaf you would like to make and measure your ingredients.

2. Add the ingredients to the bread pan in the order listed above (except chocolate chips and cranberries).

3. Place the pan in the bread machine and close the lid.

4. Turn on the bread maker. Select the White/Basic setting, then the loaf size, and finally the crust color. Start the cycle.

5. Add chocolate chips and cranberries once the machine beeps.

6. When the cycle is finished and the bread is baked, carefully remove the pan from the machine. Use a potholder as the handle will be very hot. Let rest for a few minutes.

7. Remove the bread from the pan and allow to cool on a wire rack for at least 10 minutes before slicing.

Portuguese Holiday Bread

Ingredients:

- 8 slices (1 pound)
- 2/3 cup milk at 80 degrees F
- 1 whole egg, at room temperature
- 4 teaspoons butter, soft
- 1/3 cup sugar
- 2 cups white bread flour
- 1½ teaspoons bread machine yeast
- 12 slices (1 ½ pounds)
- 1 cup milk at 80 degrees F
- 1 1/2 whole eggs, at room temperature
- 6 teaspoons butter, soft
- 1/2 cup sugar
- 3 cups white bread flour
- 2 1/4 teaspoons bread machine yeast
- 16 slices (2 pounds)
- 1 1/3 cups milk at 80 degrees F
- 2 whole eggs, at room temperature
- 8 teaspoons butter, soft
- 2/3 cup sugar
- 4 cups white bread flour
- 3 teaspoons bread machine yeast

Directions:

1. Choose the size of loaf you would like to make and measure your ingredients.

2. Add the ingredients to the bread pan in the order listed above.

3. Place the pan in the bread machine and close the lid.

4. Turn on the bread maker. Select the Sweet Bread setting, then the loaf size, and finally the crust color. Start the cycle.

5. When the cycle is finished and the bread is baked, carefully remove the pan from the machine. Use a potholder as the handle will be very hot. Let rest for a few minutes.

6. Remove the bread from the pan and allow to cool on a wire rack for at least 10 minutes before slicing.

SOURDOUGH BREAD RECIPES

Classic Sourdough Rye

Ingredients:

* 8 slices (1 pound)
* For the sponge:
* 1/2 cup Next-Day Rye Sourdough Starter
* 3/4 cup water
* 3/4 cup light or medium rye flour
* 1/4 teaspoon SAF or bread machine yeast
* For the dough:
* 3/4 tablespoon unsalted butter, melted
* 11/2 cups bread flour
* 3/4 tablespoon sugar
* 1/2 tablespoon plus 1/2 teaspoon caraway seeds
* 1 teaspoon salt
* 5/8 teaspoon SAF yeast or 1 3/4 teaspoons bread machine yeast
* 12 slices (1 ½ pounds)
* For the sponge:
* 3/4 cup Next-Day Rye Sourdough Starter
* 11/8 cups water
* 11/8 cups light or medium rye flour
* 1/2 teaspoon SAF or bread machine yeast
* For the dough:
* 1 tablespoon unsalted butter, melted
* 21/4 cups bread flour
* 1 tablespoon sugar
* 1 tablespoon caraway seeds
* 11/2 teaspoons salt
* 1 teaspoon SAF yeast or 11/2 teaspoons bread machine yeast
* 16 slices (2 pounds)
* For the sponge:
* 1 cup Next-Day Rye Sourdough Starter
* 11/2 cups water
* 11/2 cups light or medium rye flour
* 1/2 teaspoon SAF or bread machine yeast
* For the dough:
* 11/2 tablespoons unsalted butter, melted
* 3 cups bread flour
* 11/2 tablespoons sugar

* 1 tablespoon plus 1 teaspoon caraway seeds
* 2 teaspoons salt
* 11/4 teaspoons SAF yeast or 13/4 teaspoons bread machine yeast

Directions:

1. Choose the size of loaf you would like to make and measure your ingredients.

2. To make the sponge, place the sponge ingredients in the bread pan. Program for the Dough cycle; press Start. When the machine beeps at the end of the cycle, press Stop and unplug the machine. Let the sponge starter sit in the machine for 8 hours, or as long as overnight.

3. Add all the dough ingredients to the bread pan in the order listed above (including the sponge).

4. Place the pan in the bread machine and close the lid.

5. Turn on the bread maker. Select the Basic or French Bread setting, then the loaf size, and finally the crust color. Start the cycle. (This recipe is not suitable for use with the Delay Timer.)

6. When the cycle is finished and the bread is baked, carefully remove the pan from the machine. Use a potholder as the handle will be very hot. Let rest for a few minutes.

7. Remove the bread from the pan and allow to cool on a wire rack for at least 10 minutes before slicing.

Sourdough Carrot Poppy Seed Bread

Ingredients:

* 8 slices (1 pound)
* 1/2 cup sourdough starter (shown here to here)
* 1/3 cup buttermilk
* 1 tablespoon olive or walnut oil
* 1 2/3 cups bread flour
* 1/3 cup whole wheat flour
* 3/4 cup shredded raw carrots
* 11/2 tablespoons minced dried apricots
* 5/8 tablespoon poppy seeds
* 5/8 tablespoon sugar
* 1 teaspoon salt
* 7/8 teaspoon SAF yeast or 1 1/8 teaspoons bread machine yeast

* 12 slices (1 ½ pounds)
* 3/4 cup sourdough starter (shown here to here)
* 1/2 cup buttermilk
* 11/2 tablespoons olive or walnut oil
* 21/2 cups bread flour
* 1/2 cup whole wheat flour
* 11/4 cups shredded raw carrots
* 2 tablespoons minced dried apricots
* 1 tablespoon poppy seeds
* 1 tablespoon sugar
* 11/2 teaspoons salt
* 11/4 teaspoons SAF yeast or 13/4 teaspoons bread machine yeast
* 16 slices (2 pounds)
* 1 cup sourdough starter (shown here to here)
* 2/3 cup buttermilk
* 2 tablespoons olive or walnut oil
* 31/3 cups bread flour
* 2/3 cup whole wheat flour
* 11/2 cups shredded raw carrots
* 3 tablespoons minced dried apricots
* 11/4 tablespoons poppy seeds
* 11/4 tablespoons sugar
* 2 teaspoons salt
* 13/4 teaspoons SAF yeast or 21/4 teaspoons bread machine yeast

Directions:

1.   Choose the size of loaf you would like to make and measure your ingredients.

2.   Add the ingredients to the bread pan in the order listed above.

3.   Place the pan in the bread machine and close the lid.

4.   Turn on the bread maker. Select the Basic setting, then the loaf size, and finally the crust color. Start the cycle.

5.   When the cycle is finished and the bread is baked, carefully remove the pan from the machine. Use a potholder as the handle will be very hot. Let rest for a few minutes.

6.   Remove the bread from the pan and allow to cool on a wire rack for at least 10 minutes before slicing.

Sourdough Raisin Bread

Ingredients:

* 8 slices (1 pound)
* 7/8 cup raisins
* 3/8 cup sourdough starter (shown here to here)
* 1/3 cup fat-free milk
* 1 large egg
* 1 1/2 tablespoons margarine, cut into pieces
* 2 cups bread flour
* 1 1/4 tablespoons sugar
* 1 teaspoon salt
* 5/8 teaspoon SAF yeast or 7/8 teaspoon bread machine yeast
* 12 slices (1 ½ pounds)
* 11/2 cups raisins
* 1/2 cup sourdough starter (shown here to here)
* 1/2 cup fat-free milk
* 2 large eggs
* 2 tablespoons margarine, cut into pieces
* 3 cups bread flour
* 2 tablespoons sugar
* 11/2 teaspoons salt
* 1 teaspoon SAF yeast or 11/2 teaspoons bread machine yeast
* 16 slices (2 pounds)
* 13/4 cup raisins
* 3/4 cups sourdough starter (shown here to here)
* 2/3 cup fat-free milk
* 2 large eggs
* 3 tablespoons margarine, cut into pieces
* 4 cups bread flour
* 21/2 tablespoons sugar
* 2 teaspoons salt
* 11/4 teaspoons SAF yeast or 13/4 teaspoons bread machine yeast

Directions:

1.   Choose the size of loaf you would like to make and measure your ingredients.

2.   Place the raisins in a bowl and cover with hot water. Let stand for 11/2 hours at room temperature to soften. Drain the raisins and pat as dry as possible, as any moisture will be incorporated into the dough.

3. Add the ingredients to the bread pan in the order listed above.

4. Place the pan in the bread machine and close the lid.

5. Turn on the bread maker. Select the Basic setting, then the loaf size, and finally the crust color. Start the cycle.

6. Add the raisins during the first 10 minutes of Knead 2. Gradually sprinkle in the raisins while the machine is kneading. If the dough looks too sticky after the raisins are incorporated, sprinkle another 1 to 2 tablespoons of flour around the paddle while the machine is running.

7. When the cycle is finished and the bread is baked, carefully remove the pan from the machine. Use a potholder as the handle will be very hot. Let rest for a few minutes.

8. Remove the bread from the pan and allow to cool on a wire rack for at least 10 minutes before slicing.

Orange Sourdough Bread With Cranberries, Pecans, And Golden Raisins

Ingredients:
- 8 slices (1 pound)
- 3/8 cup French Buttermilk Starter, or any white flour sourdough starter
- 1/2 cup orange juice
- 11/2 tablespoons butter, cut into pieces
- 2 1/8 cups bread flour
- 1/8 cup sugar
- 3/4 teaspoon salt
- 1 teaspoon SAF yeast or 11/4 teaspoons bread machine yeast
- 1/3 cup dried cranberries
- 1/4 cup golden raisins
- 1/4 cup chopped pecans
- 12 slices (1 ½ pounds)
- 1/2 cup French Buttermilk Starter, or any white flour sourdough starter
- 3/4 cup orange juice
- 2 tablespoons butter, cut into pieces
- 31/4 cups bread flour
- 3 tablespoons sugar
- 1 teaspoon salt
- 13/4 teaspoons SAF yeast or 21/4 teaspoons bread machine yeast
- 1/2 cup dried cranberries
- 1/3 cup golden raisins
- 1/3 cup chopped pecans
- 16 slices (2 pounds)
- 3/4 cup French Buttermilk Starter, or any white flour sourdough starter
- 1 cup orange juice
- 3 tablespoons butter, cut into pieces
- 41/4 cups bread flour
- 1/4 cup sugar
- 11/2 teaspoons salt
- 2 teaspoons SAF yeast or 21/2 teaspoons bread machine yeast
- 2/3 cup dried cranberries
- 1/2 cup golden raisins
- 1/2 cup chopped pecans

Directions:
1. Choose the size of loaf you would like to make and measure your ingredients.

2. Add the ingredients to the bread pan in the order listed above (except the fruit and nuts).

3. Place the pan in the bread machine and close the lid.

4. Turn on the bread maker. Select the Basic/Fruit and Nut setting, then the loaf size, and finally the crust color. Start the cycle. (This recipe is not suitable for use with the Delay Timer.)

5. When the machine beeps, or between Knead 1 and Knead 2, add the fruits and nuts.

6. When the cycle is finished and the bread is baked, carefully remove the pan from the machine. Use a potholder as the handle will be very hot. Let rest for a few minutes.

7. Remove the bread from the pan and allow to cool on a wire rack for at least 10 minutes before slicing.

Sourdough Bread With Fresh Pears And Walnuts

Ingredients:
- 8 slices (1 pound)
- 1/2 cup sourdough starter (shown here to here)
- 1/4 cup buttermilk

* 1 teaspoon vanilla extract
* 11 /2 tablespoons butter, cut into pieces
* 2 cups bread flour
* 1/4 cup rolled oats
* 2 tablespoons light brown sugar
* 1/4 cup walnuts
* 1/2 tablespoon apple pie spice
* 1 teaspoon salt
* 7/8 teaspoon SAF yeast or 11/8 teaspoons bread machine yeast
* 1 cup peeled, cored, and chopped fresh pear (about 1 large pear)
* 12 slices (1 ½ pounds)
* 3/4 cup sourdough starter (shown here to here)
* 1/3 cup buttermilk
* 11/2 teaspoons vanilla extract
* 2 tablespoons butter, cut into pieces
* 3 cups bread flour
* 1/3 cup rolled oats
* 3 tablespoons light brown sugar
* 1/3 cup walnuts
* 2 teaspoons apple pie spice
* 11/2 teaspoons salt
* 11/4 teaspoons SAF yeast or 13/4 teaspoons bread machine yeast
* 11/2 cups peeled, cored, and chopped fresh pear (1 to 2 large pears)
* 16 slices (2 pounds)
* 1 cup sourdough starter (shown here to here)
* 1/2 cup buttermilk
* 2 teaspoons vanilla extract
* 3 tablespoons butter, cut into pieces
* 4 cups bread flour
* 1/2 cup rolled oats
* 4 tablespoons light brown sugar
* 1/2 cup walnuts
* 1 tablespoon apple pie spice
* 2 teaspoons salt
* 13/4 teaspoons SAF yeast or 21/4 teaspoons bread machine yeast
* 2 cups peeled, cored, and chopped fresh pear (about 2 large pears)

Directions:

1. Choose the size of loaf you would like to make and measure your ingredients.
2. Add the ingredients to the bread pan in the order listed above (except the pears).
3. Place the pan in the bread machine and close the lid.
4. Turn on the bread maker. Select the Basic or Sweet Bread setting, then the loaf size, and finally the crust color. Start the cycle. (This recipe is not suitable for use with the Delay Timer.)
5. About 5 minutes into the kneading, sprinkle the pears into the dough, a few at a time, until all the pears are added.
6. When the cycle is finished and the bread is baked, carefully remove the pan from the machine. Use a potholder as the handle will be very hot. Let rest for a few minutes.
7. Remove the bread from the pan and allow to cool on a wire rack for at least 10 minutes before slicing.

Sourdough Banana Nut Bread

Ingredients:
* 8 slices (1 pound)
* 3/8 cup sourdough starter
* 1/4 cup buttermilk
* 1/3 cup sliced bananas
* 1/2 large egg
* 1 1/2 tablespoons nut oil
* 1 2/3 cups bread flour
* 1/3 cup whole wheat flour
* 1/3 cup chopped macadamia nuts or pecans
* 2 tablespoons chopped dried pineapple or dates
* 11 /2 tablespoons light brown sugar
* 3/4 teaspoon salt
* 11/8 teaspoons SAF yeast or 1 3/8 teaspoons bread machine yeast
* 12 slices (1 ½ pounds)
* 1/2 cup sourdough starter
* 1/4 cup buttermilk
* 1/2 cup sliced bananas
* 1 large egg
* 2 tablespoons nut oil
* 21/2 cups bread flour
* 1/2 cup whole wheat flour

- 1/2 cup chopped macadamia nuts or pecans
- 3 tablespoons chopped dried pineapple or dates
- 2 tablespoons light brown sugar
- 11/4 teaspoons salt
- 13/4 teaspoons SAF yeast or 21/4 teaspoons bread machine yeast
- 16 slices (2 pounds)
- 3/4 cups sourdough starter
- 1/2 cup buttermilk
- 2/3 cup sliced bananas
- 1 large egg
- 3 tablespoons nut oil
- 31/3 cups bread flour
- 2/3 cup whole wheat flour
- 2/3 cup chopped macadamia nuts or pecans
- 4 tablespoons chopped dried pineapple or dates
- 3 tablespoons light brown sugar
- 11/2 teaspoons salt
- 21/4 teaspoons SAF yeast or 23/4 teaspoons bread machine yeast

Directions:

1. Choose the size of loaf you would like to make and measure your ingredients.

2. Add the ingredients to the bread pan in the order listed above.

3. Place the pan in the bread machine and close the lid.

4. Turn on the bread maker. Select the Basic setting, then the loaf size, and finally the crust color. Start the cycle.

5. When the cycle is finished and the bread is baked, carefully remove the pan from the machine. Use a potholder as the handle will be very hot. Let rest for a few minutes.

6. Remove the bread from the pan and allow to cool on a wire rack for at least 10 minutes before slicing.

Sourdough Pesto Bread

Ingredients:

- 8 slices (1 pound)
- 2/3 cup sourdough starter (shown here to here)
- 1/4 cup fat-free milk
- 1 1/2 tablespoons olive oil
- 1/8 cup pesto
- 2 cups bread flour
- 3/4 tablespoon sugar
- 7/8 teaspoon garlic powder
- 5/8 teaspoon dried marjoram
- 5/8 teaspoon dried basil
- 3/4 teaspoon salt
- 7/8 teaspoon SAF yeast or 1 1/8 teaspoons bread machine yeast
- 12 slices (1 ½ pounds)
- 1 cup sourdough starter (shown here to here)
- 1/3 cup fat-free milk
- 2 tablespoons olive oil
- 3 tablespoons pesto
- 3 cups bread flour
- 1 tablespoon sugar
- 11/2 teaspoons garlic powder
- 1 teaspoon dried marjoram
- 1 teaspoon dried basil
- 1 teaspoon salt
- 11/2 teaspoons SAF yeast or 2 teaspoons bread machine yeast
- 16 slices (2 pounds)
- 11/3 cups sourdough starter (shown here to here)
- 1/2 cup fat-free milk
- 3 tablespoons olive oil
- 1/4 cup pesto
- 4 cups bread flour
- 11/2 tablespoons sugar
- 13/4 teaspoons garlic powder
- 11/4 teaspoons dried marjoram
- 11/4 teaspoons dried basil
- 11/2 teaspoons salt
- 13/4 teaspoons SAF yeast or 21/4 teaspoons bread machine yeast

Directions:

1. Choose the size of loaf you would like to make and measure your ingredients.

2. Add the ingredients to the bread pan in the order listed above.

3. Place the pan in the bread machine and close the lid.

4. Turn on the bread maker. Select the Basic setting, then the loaf size, and finally the crust color. Start the

cycle. (This recipe is not suitable for use with the Delay Timer.)

5.   When the cycle is finished and the bread is baked, carefully remove the pan from the machine. Use a potholder as the handle will be very hot. Let rest for a few minutes.

6.   Remove the bread from the pan and allow to cool on a wire rack for at least 10 minutes before slicing.

Sourdough Cottage Cheese Bread With Fresh Herbs

Ingredients:
- 8 slices (1 pound)
- 1/2 cup sourdough starter (shown here to here)
- 1/2 cup cottage cheese
- 1 1/2 tablespoons olive oil
- 2 cups bread flour
- 1/8 cup chopped fresh watercress leaves, loosely packed
- 1/2 tablespoon chopped fresh chives
- 1/2 tablespoon chopped fresh basil
- 1/2 tablespoon chopped fresh dill
- 1 teaspoon chopped fresh marjoram
- 1/8 teaspoon dried lemon rind or 1/4 teaspoon fresh lemon zest
- 1 teaspoon salt
- 7/8 teaspoon SAF yeast or 1 1/8 teaspoons bread machine yeast
- 12 slices (1 ½ pounds)
- 3/4 cup sourdough starter (shown here to here)
- 3/4 cup cottage cheese
- 2 tablespoons olive oil
- 3 cups bread flour
- 1/4 cup chopped fresh watercress leaves, loosely packed
- 1 tablespoon chopped fresh chives
- 1 tablespoon chopped fresh basil
- 1 tablespoon chopped fresh dill
- 2 teaspoons chopped fresh marjoram
- 1/4 teaspoon dried lemon rind or 1/2 teaspoon fresh lemon zest
- 11/2 teaspoons salt
- 11/2 teaspoons SAF yeast or 2 teaspoons bread machine yeast
- 16 slices (2 pounds)
- 1 cup sourdough starter (shown here to here)
- 1 cup cottage cheese
- 3 tablespoons olive oil
- 4 cups bread flour
- 1/4 cup chopped fresh watercress leaves, loosely packed
- 1 tablespoon chopped fresh chives
- 1 tablespoon chopped fresh basil
- 1 tablespoon chopped fresh dill
- 2 teaspoons chopped fresh marjoram
- 1/4 teaspoon dried lemon rind or 1/2 teaspoon fresh lemon zest
- 2 teaspoons salt
- 13/4 teaspoons SAF yeast or 21/4 teaspoons bread machine yeast

Directions:
1.   Choose the size of loaf you would like to make and measure your ingredients.
2.   Add the ingredients to the bread pan in the order listed above.
3.   Place the pan in the bread machine and close the lid.
4.   Turn on the bread maker. Select the Basic setting, then the loaf size, and finally the crust color. Start the cycle.
5.   When the cycle is finished and the bread is baked, carefully remove the pan from the machine. Use a potholder as the handle will be very hot. Let rest for a few minutes.
6.   Remove the bread from the pan and allow to cool on a wire rack for at least 10 minutes before slicing.

White Sourdough Bread

Ingredients:
- 8 slices (1 pound)
- 1/2 cup sourdough starter (shown here to here)
- 3/8 cup fat-free milk
- 1 1/2 tablespoons unsalted butter, melted
- 1 tablespoon honey
- 2 cups bread flour
- 1 teaspoon salt

- 7/8 teaspoon SAF yeast or 11/8 teaspoons bread machine yeast
- 12 slices (1 ½ pounds)
- 3/4 cup sourdough starter (shown here to here)
- 1/2 cup fat-free milk
- 2 tablespoons unsalted butter, melted
- 11/2 tablespoons honey
- 3 cups bread flour
- 11/2 teaspoons salt
- 11/2 teaspoons SAF yeast or 2 teaspoons bread machine yeast
- 16 slices (2 pounds)
- 1 cup sourdough starter (shown here to here)
- 3/4 cup fat-free milk
- 3 tablespoons unsalted butter, melted
- 2 tablespoons honey
- 4 cups bread flour
- 2 teaspoons salt
- 13/4 teaspoons SAF yeast or 21/4 teaspoons bread machine yeast

Directions:

1. Choose the size of loaf you would like to make and measure your ingredients.

2. Add the ingredients to the bread pan in the order listed above.

3. Place the pan in the bread machine and close the lid.

4. Turn on the bread maker. Select the Basic setting, then the loaf size, and finally the crust color. Start the cycle.

5. When the cycle is finished and the bread is baked, carefully remove the pan from the machine. Use a potholder as the handle will be very hot. Let rest for a few minutes.

6. Remove the bread from the pan and allow to cool on a wire rack for at least 10 minutes before slicing.

Sourdough Tomato Bread With Feta

Ingredients:

- 8 slices (1 pound)
- 1/2 cup sourdough starter (shown here to here)
- 3/8 cup chopped canned tomatoes with some liquid
- 1 1/2 tablespoons olive oil
- 2 cups bread flour
- 3/8 cup crumbled feta cheese
- 3/8 teaspoon salt
- 7/8 teaspoon SAF yeast or 1 1/8 teaspoons bread machine yeast
- 12 slices (1 ½ pounds)
- 3/4 cup sourdough starter (shown here to here)
- 3/4 cup chopped canned tomatoes with some liquid
- 2 tablespoons olive oil
- 3 cups bread flour
- 2/3 cup crumbled feta cheese
- 1/2 teaspoon salt
- 11/4 teaspoons SAF yeast or 1 3/4 teaspoons bread machine yeast
- 16 slices (2 pounds)
- 1 cup sourdough starter (shown here to here)
- 3/4 cup chopped canned tomatoes with some liquid
- 3 tablespoons olive oil
- 4 cups bread flour
- 3/4 cup crumbled feta cheese
- 3/4 teaspoon salt
- 13/4 teaspoons SAF yeast or 21/4 teaspoons bread machine yeast

Directions:

1. Choose the size of loaf you would like to make and measure your ingredients.

2. Add the ingredients to the bread pan in the order listed above.

3. Place the pan in the bread machine and close the lid.

4. Turn on the bread maker. Select the Basic setting, then the loaf size, and finally the crust color. Start the cycle.

5. When the cycle is finished and the bread is baked, carefully remove the pan from the machine. Use a potholder as the handle will be very hot. Let rest for a few minutes.

6. Remove the bread from the pan and allow to cool on a wire rack for at least 10 minutes before slicing.

Sourdough Cornmeal Bread

Ingredients:

- 8 slices (1 pound)
- 3/4 cup white flour sourdough starter (shown here to here)

- 7/16 cup plus 1/2 tablespoon fat-free milk
- 11/2 tablespoons olive oil or lard
- 2 tablespoons honey or molasses
- 13/4 cups bread flour
- 3/8 cup yellow cornmeal
- 1 teaspoon salt
- 1 teaspoon SAF yeast or 11/4 teaspoons bread machine yeast
- 12 slices (1 ½ pounds)
- 11/4 cups white flour sourdough starter (shown here to here)
- 1/2 cup plus 2 tablespoons fat-free milk
- 2 tablespoons olive oil or lard
- 3 tablespoons honey or molasses
- 21/2 cups bread flour
- 2/3 cup yellow cornmeal
- 11/2 teaspoons salt
- 11/2 teaspoons SAF yeast or 2 teaspoons bread machine yeast
- 16 slices (2 pounds)
- 11/2 cups white flour sourdough starter (shown here to here)
- 7/8 cup plus 1 tablespoon fat-free milk
- 3 tablespoons olive oil or lard
- 4 tablespoons honey or molasses
- 31/2 cups bread flour
- 3/4 cup yellow cornmeal
- 2 teaspoons salt
- 2 teaspoons SAF yeast or 21/2 teaspoons bread machine yeast

Directions:

1. Choose the size of loaf you would like to make and measure your ingredients.

2. Add the ingredients to the bread pan in the order listed above.

3. Place the pan in the bread machine and close the lid.

4. Turn on the bread maker. Select the Basic setting, then the loaf size, and finally the crust color. Start the cycle.

5. When the cycle is finished and the bread is baked, carefully remove the pan from the machine. Use a potholder as the handle will be very hot. Let rest for a few minutes.

6. Remove the bread from the pan and allow to cool on a wire rack for at least 10 minutes before slicing.

Sourdough Sunflower Seed Honey Bread

Ingredients:

- 8 slices (1 pound)
- 2/3 cup sourdough starter
- 1/3 cup fat-free milk
- 1/6 cup margarine, cut into pieces
- 3/4 cup bread flour
- 11/4 cups whole wheat flour
- 1/6 cup dark brown sugar
- 1/4 cup raw sunflower seeds
- 1 1/2 tablespoons chopped walnuts
- 1 teaspoon salt
- 7/8 teaspoon SAF yeast or 11/8 teaspoons bread machine yeast
- 12 slices (1 ½ pounds)
- 1 cup sourdough starter
- 1/2 cup fat-free milk
- 1/4 cup margarine, cut into pieces
- 1 cup bread flour
- 2 cups whole wheat flour
- 1/4 cup dark brown sugar
- 1/3 cup raw sunflower seeds
- 2 tablespoons chopped walnuts
- 11/2 teaspoons salt
- 11/2 teaspoons SAF yeast or 2 teaspoons bread machine yeast
- 16 slices (2 pounds)
- 11/3 cups sourdough starter
- 2/3 cup fat-free milk
- 1/3 cup margarine, cut into pieces
- 11/2 cups bread flour
- 21/2 cups whole wheat flour
- 1/3 cup dark brown sugar
- 1/2 cup raw sunflower seeds
- 3 tablespoons chopped walnuts
- 2 teaspoons salt
- 13/4 teaspoons SAF yeast or 21/4 teaspoons bread machine yeast

Directions:

1. Choose the size of loaf you would like to make and measure your ingredients.

2. Add the ingredients to the bread pan in the order listed above.

3. Place the pan in the bread machine and close the lid.

4. Turn on the bread maker. Select the Whole Wheat setting, then the loaf size, and finally the crust color. Start the cycle.

5. When the cycle is finished and the bread is baked, carefully remove the pan from the machine. Use a potholder as the handle will be very hot. Let rest for a few minutes.

6. Remove the bread from the pan and allow to cool on a wire rack for at least 10 minutes before slicing.

Sourdough Buckwheat Bread

Ingredients:
- 8 slices (1 pound)
- 5/8 cup white flour sourdough starter (shown here to here)
- 1/4 cup buttermilk
- 1/2 large egg
- Grated zest of 1/2 orange
- 1 1/2 tablespoons unsalted butter, melted
- 11/3 cups bread flour
- 1/3 cup whole wheat flour
- 1/3 cup buckwheat flour
- 1 3/4 tablespoons light brown sugar
- 1 teaspoon salt
- 7/8 teaspoon SAF yeast or 11/8 teaspoons bread machine yeast
- 12 slices (1 ½ pounds)
- 1 cup white flour sourdough starter (shown here to here)
- 1/4 cup buttermilk
- 1 large egg
- Grated zest of 1 orange
- 2 tablespoons unsalted butter, melted
- 2 cups bread flour
- 1/2 cup whole wheat flour
- 1/2 cup buckwheat flour
- 3 tablespoons light brown sugar
- 11/2 teaspoons salt

- 11/2 teaspoons SAF yeast or 2 teaspoons bread machine yeast
- 16 slices (2 pounds)
- 11/4 cups white flour sourdough starter (shown here to here)
- 1/2 cup buttermilk
- 1 large egg
- Grated zest of 1 orange
- 3 tablespoons unsalted butter, melted
- 22/3 cups bread flour
- 2/3 cup whole wheat flour
- 2/3 cup buckwheat flour
- 31/2 tablespoons light brown sugar
- 2 teaspoons salt
- 13/4 teaspoons SAF yeast or 21/4 teaspoons bread machine yeast

Directions:

1. Choose the size of loaf you would like to make and measure your ingredients.

2. Add the ingredients to the bread pan in the order listed above.

3. Place the pan in the bread machine and close the lid.

4. Turn on the bread maker. Select the Basic setting, then the loaf size, and finally the crust color. Start the cycle.

5. When the cycle is finished and the bread is baked, carefully remove the pan from the machine. Use a potholder as the handle will be very hot. Let rest for a few minutes.

6. Remove the bread from the pan and allow to cool on a wire rack for at least 10 minutes before slicing.

Sourdough Whole Wheat Bread

Ingredients:
- 8 slices (1 pound)
- 2/3 cup any sourdough starter (shown here to here)
- 1/4 cup fat-free milk
- 13/4 tablespoons canola oil
- 1/6 cup molasses
- 11/4 cups bread flour
- 3/4 cup whole wheat flour
- 1 teaspoon salt

- 7/8 teaspoon SAF yeast or 11/8 teaspoons bread machine yeast
- 12 slices (1 ½ pounds)
- 1 cup any sourdough starter (shown here to here)
- 1/3 cup fat-free milk
- 3 tablespoons canola oil
- 1/4 cup molasses
- 13/4 cups bread flour
- 11/4 cups whole wheat flour
- 11/2 teaspoons salt
- 11/4 teaspoons SAF yeast or 13/4 teaspoons bread machine yeast
- 16 slices (2 pounds)
- 11/3 cups any sourdough starter (shown here to here)
- 1/2 cup fat-free milk
- 31/2 tablespoons canola oil
- 1/3 cup molasses
- 21/2 cups bread flour
- 11/2 cups whole wheat flour
- 2 teaspoons salt
- 13/4 teaspoons SAF yeast or 21/4 teaspoons bread machine yeast

Directions:

1. Choose the size of loaf you would like to make and measure your ingredients.

2. Add the ingredients to the bread pan in the order listed above.

3. Place the pan in the bread machine and close the lid.

4. Turn on the bread maker. Select the Whole Wheat setting, then the loaf size, and finally the crust color. Start the cycle.

5. Check the consistency of the dough during Knead 2 and add a little more milk or flour as needed.

6. When the cycle is finished and the bread is baked, carefully remove the pan from the machine. Use a potholder as the handle will be very hot. Let rest for a few minutes.

7. Remove the bread from the pan and allow to cool on a wire rack for at least 10 minutes before slicing.

GLUTEN-FREE RECIPES

Gluten-free Cinnamon Raisin Bread

Ingredients:
- 8 slices (1 pound)
- 3/4 cup almond milk
- 2 tablespoons flax meal
- 6 tablespoons warm water
- 1 1/2 teaspoons apple cider vinegar
- 2 tablespoons butter
- 1 1/2 tablespoons honey
- 1 2/3 cups brown rice flour
- 1/4 cup corn starch
- 2 tablespoons potato starch
- 1 1/2 teaspoons xanthan gum
- 1 tablespoon cinnamon
- 1/2 teaspoon salt
- 1 teaspoon active dry yeast
- 1/2 cup raisins
- 12 slices (1 ½ pounds)
- 1 1/8 cups almond milk
- 3 tablespoons flax meal
- 9 tablespoons warm water
- 2 1/4 teaspoons apple cider vinegar
- 3 tablespoons butter
- 2 1/4 tablespoons honey
- 2 1/2 cups brown rice flour
- 3/8 cup corn starch
- 3 tablespoons potato starch
- 2 1/4 teaspoons xanthan gum
- 1 1/2 tablespoons cinnamon
- 3/4 teaspoon salt
- 1 1/2 teaspoons active dry yeast
- 3/4 cup raisins
- 16 slices (2 pounds)
- 1 1/2 cups almond milk
- 4 tablespoons flax meal
- 12 tablespoons warm water
- 3 teaspoons apple cider vinegar
- 4 tablespoons butter
- 3 tablespoons honey
- 3 1/3 cups brown rice flour
- 1/2 cup corn starch
- 4 tablespoons potato starch
- 3 teaspoons xanthan gum
- 2 tablespoons cinnamon
- 1 teaspoon salt
- 2 teaspoons active dry yeast
- 1 cup raisins

Directions:
1. Choose the size of loaf you would like to make and measure your ingredients.
2. Mix together flax and water and let stand for 5 minutes.
3. Combine dry ingredients in a separate bowl, except for yeast.
4. Add wet ingredients to the bread pan.
5. Add the dry mixture on top and make a well in the middle of the dry mixture.
6. Add the yeast to the well.
7. Place the pan in the bread machine and close the lid.
8. Turn on the bread maker. Select the Gluten Free setting, then the loaf size, and finally the crust color. Start the cycle.
9. After first kneading and rise cycle, add raisins.
10. When the cycle is finished and the bread is baked, carefully remove the pan from the machine. Use a potholder as the handle will be very hot. Let rest for a few minutes.
11. Remove the bread from the pan and allow to cool on a wire rack for at least 10 minutes before slicing.

Mix Seed Bread

Ingredients:
- 8 slices (1 pound)
- 1 1/8 cups lukewarm milk
- 1/4cup + 1 /2tablespoon cooking oil
- 3/4 teaspoons vinegar
- 1 1/2eggs, slightly beaten
- 3/4 tablespoons sugar
- 3/4 teaspoons table salt
- 1 3/4 cups gluten-free flour(s) of your choice
- 1 1/2 tablespoons poppy seeds

* 1 1/2 tablespoons pumpkin seeds
* 1 1/2 tablespoons sunflower seeds
* 1 1/2 teaspoons bread machine yeast
* 12 slices (1½ pounds)
* 2 cups lukewarm milk
* 6 tablespoons cooking oil
* 1 teaspoon vinegar
* 2 eggs, slightly beaten
* 1 tablespoon sugar
* 1 teaspoon table salt
* 2⅔ cups gluten-free flour(s) of your choice
* 2 tablespoons poppy seeds
* 2 tablespoons pumpkin seeds
* 2 tablespoons sunflower seeds
* 2 teaspoons bread machine yeast
* 16 slices (2 pounds)
* 2¼ cups lukewarm milk
* ½ cup + 1 tablespoon cooking oil
* 1½ teaspoons vinegar
* 3 eggs, slightly beaten
* 1½ tablespoons sugar
* 1½ teaspoons table salt
* 3½ cups gluten-free flour(s) of your choice
* 3 tablespoons poppy seeds
* 3 tablespoons pumpkin seeds
* 3 tablespoons sunflower seeds
* 3 teaspoons bread machine yeast

Directions:

1. Choose the size of loaf you would like to make and measure your ingredients.

2. Add the ingredients to the bread pan in the order listed above.

3. Place the pan in the bread machine and close the lid.

4. Turn on the bread maker. Select the White/Basic or Gluten-Free (if your machine has this setting) setting, then the loaf size, and finally the crust color. Start the cycle.

5. When the cycle is finished and the bread is baked, carefully remove the pan from the machine. Use a potholder as the handle will be very hot. Let rest for a few minutes.

6. Remove the bread from the pan and allow to cool on a wire rack for at least 10 minutes before slicing.

Gluten-free Pull-apart Rolls

Ingredients:

* 8 slices (1 pound)
* 1 cup warm water
* 2 tablespoons butter, unsalted
* 1 egg, room temperature
* 1 teaspoon apple cider vinegar
* 2 3/4 cups gluten-free almond-blend flour
* 1 1/2 teaspoons xanthan gum
* 1/4 cup sugar
* 1 teaspoon salt
* 2 teaspoons active dry yeast
* 12 slices (1 ½ pounds)
* 1 1/2 cups warm water
* 3 tablespoons butter, unsalted
* 1 1/2 eggs, room temperature
* 1 1/2 teaspoons apple cider vinegar
* 4 1/8 cups gluten-free almond-blend flour
* 2 1/4 teaspoons xanthan gum
* 3/8 cup sugar
* 1 1/2 teaspoons salt
* 3 teaspoons active dry yeast
* 16 slices (2 pounds)
* 2 cups warm water
* 4 tablespoons butter, unsalted
* 2 eggs, room temperature
* 2 teaspoons apple cider vinegar
* 5 1/2 cups gluten-free almond-blend flour
* 3 teaspoons xanthan gum
* 1/2 cup sugar
* 2 teaspoons salt
* 4 teaspoons active dry yeast

Directions:

1. Choose the size of loaf you would like to make and measure your ingredients.

2. Add wet ingredients to the bread pan.

3. Mix dry ingredients except for yeast, and put in the bread pan.

4. Make a well in the center of the dry ingredients and add the yeast.

5. Place the pan in the bread machine and close the lid.

6. Turn on the bread maker. Select the Dough setting, then the loaf size, and finally the crust color. Start the cycle.

7. Spray an 8-inch round cake pan with non-stick cooking spray.

8. When Dough cycle is complete, roll dough out into 9 balls, place in cake pan, and baste each with warm water.

9. Cover with a towel and let rise in a warm place for 1 hour.

10. Preheat oven to 400°F.

11. Bake for 26 to 28 minutes; until golden brown.

12. Brush with butter and serve.

Gluten-free Oat & Honey Bread

Ingredients:

- 8 slices (1 pound)
- 1 1/4 cups warm water
- 3 tablespoons honey
- 2 eggs
- 3 tablespoons butter, melted
- 1 1/4 cups gluten-free oats
- 1 1/4 cups brown rice flour
- 1/2 cup potato starch
- 2 teaspoons xanthan gum
- 1 1/2 teaspoons sugar
- 3/4 teaspoon salt
- 1 1/2 tablespoons active dry yeast
- 12 slices (1 ½ pounds)
- 1 7/8 cups warm water
- 4 1/2 tablespoons honey
- 3 eggs
- 4 1/2 tablespoons butter, melted
- 1 7/8 cups gluten-free oats
- 1 7/8 cups brown rice flour
- 3/4 cup potato starch
- 3 teaspoons xanthan gum
- 2 1/4 teaspoons sugar
- 1 1/8 teaspoons salt
- 2 1/4 tablespoons active dry yeast
- 16 slices (2 pounds)
- 2 1/2 cups warm water
- 6 tablespoons honey
- 4 eggs
- 6 tablespoons butter, melted
- 2 1/2 cups gluten-free oats
- 2 1/2 cups brown rice flour
- 1 cup potato starch
- 4 teaspoons xanthan gum
- 3 teaspoons sugar
- 1 1/2 teaspoons salt
- 3 tablespoons active dry yeast

Directions:

1. Choose the size of loaf you would like to make and measure your ingredients.

2. Add the ingredients to the bread pan in the order listed above (except yeast).

3. Place the pan in the bread machine and close the lid.

4. Turn on the bread maker. Select the Gluten-Free setting, then the loaf size, and finally the crust color. Start the cycle.

5. When the cycle is finished and the bread is baked, carefully remove the pan from the machine. Use a potholder as the handle will be very hot. Let rest for a few minutes.

6. Remove the bread from the pan and allow to cool on a wire rack for at least 10 minutes before slicing.

Cheese Potato Bread

Ingredients:

- 8 slices (1 pound)
- 5/8 cups lukewarm water
- 1 1/2 tablespoons vegetable oil
- 1 1/2 large eggs, beaten
- 1/4 cup dry skim milk powder
- 1/8 cup sugar
- 1/2 teaspoon apple cider vinegar
- 3/4 teaspoon table salt
- 1/4 cup cornstarch
- 3/8 cup cottage cheese
- 1/8 cup snipped chives
- 1/4 cup instant potato buds
- 1/4 cup potato starch
- 1/4 cup tapioca flour
- 1 cups white rice flour
- 1 1/8 teaspoon bread machine yeast

- 12 slices (1½ pounds)
- 1 cup lukewarm water
- 2¼ tablespoons vegetable oil
- 2 large eggs, beaten
- ⅓ cup dry skim milk powder
- 3 tablespoons sugar
- ¾ teaspoon apple cider vinegar
- 1⅛ teaspoons table salt
- ⅓ cup cornstarch
- ½ cup cottage cheese
- 3 tablespoons snipped chives
- ⅓ cup instant potato buds
- ⅓ cup potato starch
- ⅓ cup tapioca flour
- 1½ cups white rice flour
- 1½ teaspoons bread machine yeast
- 16 slices (2 pounds)
- 1¼ cups lukewarm water
- 3 tablespoons vegetable oil
- 3 large eggs, beaten
- ½ cup dry skim milk powder
- ¼ cup sugar
- 1 teaspoon apple cider vinegar
- 1½ teaspoons table salt
- ½ cup cornstarch
- ¾ cup cottage cheese
- ¼ cup snipped chives
- ½ cup instant potato buds
- ½ cup potato starch
- ½ cup tapioca flour
- 2 cups white rice flour
- 2¼ teaspoons bread machine yeast

Directions:

1. Choose the size of loaf you would like to make and measure your ingredients.

2. Add the ingredients to the bread pan in the order listed above.

3. Place the pan in the bread machine and close the lid.

4. Turn on the bread maker. Select the White/Basic or Gluten-Free (if your machine has this setting) setting, then the loaf size, and finally the crust color. Start the cycle.

5. When the cycle is finished and the bread is baked, carefully remove the pan from the machine. Use a potholder as the handle will be very hot. Let rest for a few minutes.

6. Remove the bread from the pan and allow to cool on a wire rack for at least 10 minutes before slicing.

Italian Herb Bread

Ingredients:

- 8 slices (1 pound)
- 1 2/3 cups lukewarm water
- 1 1/2 eggs, beaten
- 1/6 cup vegetable oil
- 1 teaspoons table salt
- 1/8 cup sugar
- 5/8 cups white bean flour
- 5/8 tablespoons mixed Italian herbs, dried
- 5/8 cups white rice flour
- 5/8 cups potato starch
- 1/3 cup tapioca flour
- 2/3 tablespoons xanthan gum
- 1 1/3–1 1/2 teaspoons bread machine yeast
- 12 slices (1½ pounds)
- 1½ cups lukewarm water
- 3 eggs, beaten
- ¼ cup vegetable oil
- 1½ teaspoons table salt
- 3 tablespoons sugar
- 1 cup white bean flour
- 1 tablespoon mixed Italian herbs, dried
- 1 cup white rice flour
- 1 cup potato starch
- ⅓ cup tapioca flour
- 1 tablespoon xanthan gum
- 2¼ teaspoons bread machine yeast
- 16 slices (2 pounds)
- 3⅓ cups lukewarm water
- 3 eggs, beaten
- ⅓ cup vegetable oil
- 2 teaspoons table salt
- ¼ cup sugar
- 1¼ cups white bean flour
- 1¼ tablespoons mixed Italian herbs, dried

- 1¼ cups white rice flour
- 1¼ cups potato starch
- ⅔ cup tapioca flour
- 1⅓ tablespoons xanthan gum
- 2⅔–3 teaspoons bread machine yeast

Directions:

1. Choose the size of loaf you would like to make and measure your ingredients.

2. Add the ingredients to the bread pan in the order listed above.

3. Place the pan in the bread machine and close the lid.

4. Turn on the bread maker. Select the White/Basic or Gluten-Free (if your machine has this setting) setting, then the loaf size, and finally the crust color. Start the cycle.

5. When the cycle is finished and the bread is baked, carefully remove the pan from the machine. Use a potholder as the handle will be very hot. Let rest for a few minutes.

6. Remove the bread from the pan and allow to cool on a wire rack for at least 10 minutes before slicing.

Instant Cocoa Bread

Ingredients:

- 8 slices (1 pound)
- 3/4 cup lukewarm water
- 1 1/2 large eggs, beaten
- 1 1/2 tablespoons molasses
- 1 tablespoon canola oil
- 1/2 teaspoon apple cider vinegar
- 1 1/2 tablespoons light brown sugar
- 3/4 teaspoons table salt
- 1 cup white rice flour
- 1/3 cup potato starch
- 1/6 cup tapioca flour
- 1 1/4 teaspoons xanthan gum
- 1 teaspoon cocoa powder
- 1 teaspoon instant coffee granules
- 1 1/2 teaspoons bread machine yeast
- 12 slices (1½ pounds)
- 1⅛ cups lukewarm water
- 2 large eggs, beaten
- 2¼ tablespoons molasses
- 1½ tablespoons canola oil
- ¾ teaspoon apple cider vinegar
- 2¼ tablespoons light brown sugar
- 1⅛ teaspoons table salt
- 1½ cups white rice flour
- ½ cup potato starch
- ¼ cup tapioca flour
- 1½ teaspoons xanthan gum
- 1½ teaspoons cocoa powder
- 1½ teaspoons instant coffee granules
- 2 teaspoons bread machine yeast
- 16 slices (2 pounds)
- 1½ cups lukewarm water
- 3 large eggs, beaten
- 3 tablespoons molasses
- 2 tablespoons canola oil
- 1 teaspoon apple cider vinegar
- 3 tablespoons light brown sugar
- 1½ teaspoons table salt
- 2 cups white rice flour
- ⅔ cup potato starch
- ⅓ cup tapioca flour
- 2½ teaspoons xanthan gum
- 2 teaspoons cocoa powder
- 2 teaspoons instant coffee granules
- 3 teaspoons bread machine yeast

Directions:

1. Choose the size of loaf you would like to make and measure your ingredients.

2. Add the ingredients to the bread pan in the order listed above.

3. Place the pan in the bread machine and close the lid.

4. Turn on the bread maker. Select the White/Basic or Gluten-Free (if your machine has this setting) setting, then the loaf size, and finally the crust color. Start the cycle.

5. When the cycle is finished and the bread is baked, carefully remove the pan from the machine. Use a potholder as the handle will be very hot. Let rest for a few minutes.

6. Remove the bread from the pan and allow to cool on a wire rack for at least 10 minutes before slicing.

Pecan Cranberry Bread

Ingredients:

- 8 slices (1 pound)
- 3/4 cups lukewarm water
- 1/8 cup canola oil
- 1/2 tablespoon orange zest
- 1/2 teaspoon apple cider vinegar
- 1 1/2 eggs, slightly beaten
- 1 1/2 tablespoons sugar
- 1/2 teaspoon table salt
- 1 cup white rice flour
- 1/3 cup nonfat dry milk powder
- 1/4 cup tapioca flour
- 1/4 cup potato starch
- 1/6 cup corn starch
- 1/2 tablespoon xanthan gum
- 1 teaspoon bread machine yeast
- 1/3 cup dried cranberries
- 1/3 cup pecan pieces
- 12 slices (1½ pounds)
- 1⅛ cups lukewarm water
- 3 tablespoons canola oil
- ¾ tablespoon orange zest
- ¾ teaspoon apple cider vinegar
- 2 eggs, slightly beaten
- 2¼ tablespoons sugar
- ¾ teaspoon table salt
- 1½ cups white rice flour
- ½ cup nonfat dry milk powder
- ⅓ cup tapioca flour
- ⅓ cup potato starch
- ¼ cup corn starch
- ¾ tablespoon xanthan gum
- 1½ teaspoons bread machine yeast
- ½ cup dried cranberries
- ½ cup pecan pieces
- 16 slices (2 pounds)
- 1½ cups lukewarm water
- ¼ cup canola oil
- 1 tablespoon orange zest
- 1 teaspoon apple cider vinegar
- 3 eggs, slightly beaten
- 3 tablespoons sugar
- 1 teaspoon table salt
- 2 cup white rice flour
- ⅔ cup nonfat dry milk powder
- ½ cup tapioca flour
- ½ cup potato starch
- ⅓ cup corn starch
- 1 tablespoon xanthan gum
- 2 teaspoons bread machine yeast
- ⅔ cup dried cranberries
- ⅔ cup pecan pieces

Directions:

1. Choose the size of loaf you would like to make and measure your ingredients.
2. Add all of the ingredients except for the pecans and cranberries to the bread pan in the order listed above.
3. Place the pan in the bread machine and close the lid.
4. Turn on the bread maker. Select the Gluten Free or Fruit/Nut (if your machine has this setting) setting, then the loaf size, and finally the crust color. Start the cycle. (If you don't have either of the above settings, use Basic/White.)
5. When the machine signals to add ingredients, add the pecans and cranberries. (Some machines have a fruit/nut hopper where you can add the pecans and cranberries when you start the machine. The machine will automatically add them to the dough during the baking process.)
6. When the cycle is finished and the bread is baked, carefully remove the pan from the machine. Use a potholder as the handle will be very hot. Let rest for a few minutes.
7. Remove the bread from the pan and allow to cool on a wire rack for at least 10 minutes before slicing.

Grain-free Chia Bread

Ingredients:

- 8 slices (1 pound)
- 1 cup warm water
- 3 large organic eggs, room temperature
- 1/4 cup olive oil
- 1 tablespoon apple cider vinegar
- 1 cup gluten-free chia seeds, ground to flour
- 1 cup almond meal flour

- 1/2 cup potato starch
- 1/4 cup coconut flour
- 3/4 cup millet flour
- 1 tablespoon xanthan gum
- 1 1/2 teaspoons salt
- 2 tablespoons sugar
- 3 tablespoons nonfat dry milk
- 6 teaspoons instant yeas
- 12 slices (1 ½ pounds)
- 1 1/2 cups warm water
- 4 1/2 large organic eggs, room temperature
- 3/8 cup olive oil
- 1 1/2 tablespoons apple cider vinegar
- 1 1/2 cups gluten-free chia seeds, ground to flour
- 1 1/2 cups almond meal flour
- 3/4 cup potato starch
- 3/8 cup coconut flour
- 1 1/8 cups millet flour
- 1 1/2 tablespoons xanthan gum
- 2 1/4 teaspoons salt
- 3 tablespoons sugar
- 4 1/2 tablespoons nonfat dry milk
- 9 teaspoons instant yeas
- 16 slices (2 pounds)
- 2 cups warm water
- 6 large organic eggs, room temperature
- 1/2 cup olive oil
- 2 tablespoons apple cider vinegar
- 2 cups gluten-free chia seeds, ground to flour
- 2 cups almond meal flour
- 1 cup potato starch
- 1/2 cup coconut flour
- 1 1/2 cups millet flour
- 2 tablespoons xanthan gum
- 3 teaspoons salt
- 4 tablespoons sugar
- 6 tablespoons nonfat dry milk
- 12 teaspoons instant yeas

Directions:

1. Choose the size of loaf you would like to make and measure your ingredients.

2. Whisk wet ingredients together and add to the bread pan.

3. Whisk dry ingredients, except yeast, together and add on top of wet ingredients.

4. Make a well in the dry ingredients and add yeast.

5. Place the pan in the bread machine and close the lid.

6. Turn on the bread maker. Select the Whole Wheat setting, then the loaf size, and finally the crust color. Start the cycle.

7. When the cycle is finished and the bread is baked, carefully remove the pan from the machine. Use a potholder as the handle will be very hot. Let rest for a few minutes.

8. Remove the bread from the pan and allow to cool on a wire rack for at least 10 minutes before slicing.

Gluten-free Sourdough Bread

Ingredients:

- 8 slices (1 pound)
- 1 cup water
- 3 eggs
- 3/4 cup ricotta cheese
- 1/4 cup honey
- 1/4 cup vegetable oil
- 1 teaspoon cider vinegar
- 3/4 cup gluten-free sourdough starter
- 2 cups white rice flour
- 2/3 cup potato starch
- 1/3 cup tapioca flour
- 1/2 cup dry milk powder
- 3 1/2 teaspoons xanthan gum
- 1 1/2 teaspoons salt
- 12 slices (1 ½ pounds)
- 1 1/2 cups water
- 4 1/2 eggs
- 1 1/8 cups ricotta cheese
- 3/8 cup honey
- 3/8 cup vegetable oil
- 1 1/2 teaspoons cider vinegar
- 1 1/8 cups gluten-free sourdough starter
- 3 cups white rice flour
- 1 cup potato starch
- 1/2 cup tapioca flour
- 3/4 cup dry milk powder
- 5 1/4 teaspoons xanthan gum

- 2 1/4 teaspoons salt
- 16 slices (2 pounds)
- 2 cups water
- 6 eggs
- 1 1/2 cups ricotta cheese
- 1/2 cup honey
- 1/2 cup vegetable oil
- 2 teaspoons cider vinegar
- 1 1/2 cups gluten-free sourdough starter
- 4 cups white rice flour
- 1 1/3 cups potato starch
- 2/3 cup tapioca flour
- 1 cup dry milk powder
- 7 teaspoons xanthan gum
- 3 teaspoons salt

Directions:

1. Choose the size of loaf you would like to make and measure your ingredients.

2. Combine wet ingredients and pour into bread pan.

3. Mix together dry ingredients in a large mixing bowl, and add on top of the wet ingredients.

4. Place the pan in the bread machine and close the lid.

5. Turn on the bread maker. Select the Gluten-Free setting, then the loaf size, and finally the crust color. Start the cycle.

6. When the cycle is finished and the bread is baked, carefully remove the pan from the machine. Use a potholder as the handle will be very hot. Let rest for a few minutes.

7. Remove the bread from the pan and allow to cool on a wire rack for at least 10 minutes before slicing.

Garlic Parsley Bread

Ingredients:

- 8 slices (1 pound)
- 3/4 cups almond or coconut milk
- 1/8 cup flax meal
- 6 tablespoons warm water
- 2 tablespoon butter
- 1 1/2 tablespoons maple syrup
- 1 1/2 teaspoon apple cider vinegar
- 1/8 cup parsley, loosely chopped
- 5–6 cloves garlic, minced
- 1/2 teaspoon table salt
- 1 5/8 cups brown rice flour
- 1/4 cup corn starch
- 1/8 cup potato starch
- 1 1/2 teaspoons xanthan gum
- 1 tablespoons garlic powder
- 1 tablespoons onion powder
- 1 teaspoons bread machine yeast
- 12 slices (1½ pounds)
- 1¼ cups almond or coconut milk
- 3 tablespoons flax meal
- ½ cup + 1 tablespoon warm water
- 3 tablespoons butter
- 2¼ tablespoons maple syrup
- 2¼ teaspoons apple cider vinegar
- 3 tablespoons parsley, loosely chopped
- 8–9 cloves garlic, minced
- ¾ teaspoon table salt
- 6 tablespoons + 2 teaspoons brown rice flour
- ⅓ cup corn starch
- 3 tablespoons potato starch
- 2 teaspoons xanthan gum
- 1¼ tablespoons garlic powder
- 1½ tablespoons onion powder
- 1½ teaspoons bread machine yeast
- 16 slices (2 pounds)
- 1½ cups almond or coconut milk
- ¼ cup flax meal
- 12 tablespoons warm water
- 4 tablespoon butter
- 3 tablespoons maple syrup
- 3 teaspoon apple cider vinegar
- ¼ cup parsley, loosely chopped
- 10–12 cloves garlic, minced
- 1 teaspoon table salt
- 3¼ cups brown rice flour
- ½ cup corn starch
- ¼ cup potato starch
- 3 teaspoons xanthan gum
- 2 tablespoons garlic powder
- 2 tablespoons onion powder
- 2 teaspoons bread machine yeast

Directions:

1.   Combine the water and flax meal in a bowl; set aside for 5–10 minutes to mix well.

2.   Choose the size of loaf you would like to make and measure your ingredients.

3.   Add the ingredients to the bread pan in the order listed above, including the flax meal.

4.   Place the pan in the bread machine and close the lid.

5.   Turn on the bread maker. Select the White/Basic or Gluten-Free (if your machine has this setting) setting, then the loaf size, and finally the crust color. Start the cycle.

6.   When the cycle is finished and the bread is baked, carefully remove the pan from the machine. Use a potholder as the handle will be very hot. Let rest for a few minutes.

7.   Remove the bread from the pan and allow to cool on a wire rack for at least 10 minutes before slicing.

Walnut Banana Bread

Ingredients:
- 8 slices (1 pound)
- 1/4 cup lukewarm water
- 1 1/2 tablespoons canola oil
- 1/2 teaspoon apple cider vinegar
- 1 egg, beaten
- 1 small banana, mashed
- 1/2 teaspoon table salt
- 3/8 cup brown rice flour
- 3/8 cup white rice flour
- 3/8 cup amaranth flour
- 1/4 cup corn starch
- 1/2 tablespoon xanthan gum
- 1/2 teaspoon cinnamon
- 1/4 teaspoon nutmeg
- 1 teaspoon bread machine yeast
- 1/2 cup walnuts, chopped
- 12 slices (1½ pounds)
- ⅓ cup lukewarm water
- 2 tablespoons canola oil
- ¾ teaspoon apple cider vinegar
- 2 eggs, beaten
- 1½ small bananas, mashed
- ¾ teaspoon table salt
- ½ cup brown rice flour
- ½ cup white rice flour
- ½ cup amaranth flour
- ⅓ cup corn starch
- ¾ tablespoon xanthan gum
- ¾ teaspoon cinnamon
- ⅓ teaspoon nutmeg
- 1½ teaspoons bread machine yeast
- ¾ cup walnuts, chopped
- 16 slices (2 pounds)
- ½ cup lukewarm water
- 3 tablespoons canola oil
- 1 teaspoon apple cider vinegar
- 2 eggs, beaten
- 2 small banana, mashed
- 1 teaspoon table salt
- ¾ cup brown rice flour
- ¾ cup white rice flour
- ¾ cup amaranth flour
- ½ cup corn starch
- 1 tablespoon xanthan gum
- 1 teaspoon cinnamon
- ½ teaspoon nutmeg
- 2 teaspoons bread machine yeast
- 1 cup walnuts, chopped

Directions:

1.   Choose the size of loaf you would like to make and measure your ingredients.

2.   Add the ingredients to the bread pan in the order listed above.

3.   Place the pan in the bread machine and close the lid.

4.   Turn on the bread maker. Select the Quick/Rapid setting, then the loaf size, and finally the crust color. Start the cycle.

5.   When the cycle is finished and the bread is baked, carefully remove the pan from the machine. Use a potholder as the handle will be very hot. Let rest for a few minutes.

6.   Remove the bread from the pan and allow to cool on a wire rack for at least 10 minutes before slicing.

Pecan Apple Spice Bread

Ingredients:

- 8 slices (1 pound)
- 1/4 cup lukewarm water
- 1 1/2 tablespoons canola oil
- 1/2 teaspoon apple cider vinegar
- 1 1/2 tablespoons light brown sugar, packed
- 1/2 cup Granny Smith apples, grated
- 3/2 eggs, room temperature, slightly beaten
- 3/8 cup brown rice flour
- 3/8 cup tapioca flour
- 3/8 cup millet flour
- 1/4 cup corn starch
- 1 tablespoon apple pie spice
- 1/2 tablespoon xanthan gum
- 1/2 teaspoon table salt
- 1 teaspoon bread machine yeast
- 1/4 cup pecans, chopped
- 12 slices (1½ pounds)
- ⅓ cup lukewarm water
- 2¼ tablespoons canola oil
- ¾ teaspoon apple cider vinegar
- 2¼ tablespoons light brown sugar, packed
- ¾ cup Granny Smith apples, grated
- 2 eggs, room temperature, slightly beaten
- ½ cup brown rice flour
- ½ cup tapioca flour
- ½ cup millet flour
- ⅓ cup corn starch
- 1½ tablespoons apple pie spice
- ¾ tablespoon xanthan gum
- ¾ teaspoon table salt
- 1¼ teaspoons bread machine yeast
- ⅓ cup pecans, chopped
- 16 slices (2 pounds)
- ½ cup lukewarm water
- 3 tablespoons canola oil
- 1 teaspoon apple cider vinegar
- 3 tablespoons light brown sugar, packed
- 1 cup Granny Smith apples, grated
- 3 eggs, room temperature, slightly beaten
- ¾ cup brown rice flour
- ¾ cup tapioca flour
- ¾ cup millet flour
- ½ cup corn starch
- 2 tablespoons apple pie spice
- 1 tablespoon xanthan gum
- 1 teaspoon table salt
- 2 teaspoons bread machine yeast
- ½ cup pecans, chopped

Directions:

1. Choose the size of loaf you would like to make and measure your ingredients.

2. Add all of the ingredients except for the pecans to the bread pan in the order listed above.

3. Place the pan in the bread machine and close the lid.

4. Turn on the bread maker. Select the White/Basic or Gluten-Free (if your machine has this setting) setting, then the loaf size, and finally the crust color. Start the cycle.

5. When the machine signals to add ingredients, add the chopped pecans.

6. When the cycle is finished and the bread is baked, carefully remove the pan from the machine. Use a potholder as the handle will be very hot. Let rest for a few minutes.

7. Remove the bread from the pan and allow to cool on a wire rack for at least 10 minutes before slicing.

Classic White Bread

Ingredients:

- 8 slices (1 pound)
- 3/4 cup lukewarm water
- 1/8 cup canola oil
- ½ teaspoon apple cider vinegar
- 1 1/2 eggs, room temperature, slightly beaten
- 1 cup white rice flour
- 1/4 cup tapioca flour
- ⅓ cup nonfat dry milk powder
- 1/4 cup potato starch
- 1/6 cup cornstarch
- 1 1/2 tablespoons sugar
- ½ tablespoon xanthan gum
- ½ teaspoon table salt
- 1 teaspoon bread machine yeast
- 12 slices (1½ pounds)

- 1 1/8 cup lukewarm water
- 3 tablespoons canola oil
- ¾ teaspoon apple cider vinegar
- 2 eggs, room temperature, slightly beaten
- 1½ cups white rice flour
- ⅔ cup tapioca flour
- ½ cup nonfat dry milk powder
- ½ cup potato starch
- ⅓ cup cornstarch
- 2 tablespoons sugar
- ⅔ tablespoon xanthan gum
- ⅔ teaspoon table salt
- 1¼ teaspoons bread machine yeast
- 16 slices (2 pounds)
- 1½ cups lukewarm water
- ¼ cup canola oil
- 1 teaspoon apple cider vinegar
- 3 eggs, room temperature, slightly beaten
- 2 cups white rice flour
- ½ cup tapioca flour
- ⅔ cup nonfat dry milk powder
- ½ cup potato starch
- ⅓ cup cornstarch
- 3 tablespoons sugar
- 1 tablespoon xanthan gum
- 1 teaspoon table salt
- 2 teaspoons bread machine yeast

Directions:

1. Choose the size of loaf you would like to make and measure your ingredients.

2. Add the ingredients to the bread pan in the order listed above.

3. Place the pan in the bread machine and close the lid.

4. Turn on the bread maker. Select the White/Basic or Gluten-Free (if your machine has this setting) setting, then the loaf size, and finally the crust color. Start the cycle.

5. When the cycle is finished and the bread is baked, carefully remove the pan from the machine. Use a potholder as the handle will be very hot. Let rest for a few minutes.

6. Remove the bread from the pan and allow to cool on a wire rack for at least 10 minutes before slicing.

Sorghum Bread Recipe

Ingredients:

- 8 slices (1 pound)
- 1 1/2 cups sorghum flour
- 1 cup tapioca starch
- 1/2 cup brown or white sweet rice flour
- 1 teaspoon xanthan gum
- 1 teaspoon guar gum
- 1/2 teaspoon salt
- 3 tablespoons sugar
- 2 1/4 teaspoons instant yeast
- 3 eggs (room temperature, lightly beaten)
- 1/4 cup oil
- 1 1/2 teaspoons vinegar
- 3/4-1 cup milk (105 - 115°F)
- 12 slices (1 ½ pounds)
- 2 1/4 cups sorghum flour
- 1 1/2 cups tapioca starch
- 3/4 cup brown or white sweet rice flour
- 1 1/2 teaspoons xanthan gum
- 1 1/2 teaspoons guar gum
- 3/4 teaspoon salt
- 4 1/2 tablespoons sugar
- 3 3/8 teaspoons instant yeast
- 4 1/2 eggs (room temperature, lightly beaten)
- 3/8 cup oil
- 2 1/4 teaspoons vinegar
- 1 1/8-1 1/2 cups milk (105 - 115°F)
- 16 slices (2 pounds)
- 3 cups sorghum flour
- 2 cups tapioca starch
- 1 cup brown or white sweet rice flour
- 2 teaspoons xanthan gum
- 2 teaspoons guar gum
- 1 teaspoon salt
- 6 tablespoons sugar
- 4 1/2 teaspoons instant yeast
- 6 eggs (room temperature, lightly beaten)
- 1/2 cup oil
- 3 teaspoons vinegar
- 1 1/2 - 2 cups milk (105 - 115°F)

Directions:

1. Choose the size of loaf you would like to make and measure your ingredients.
2. Combine the dry ingredients in a mixing bowl, except for yeast.
3. Add the wet ingredients to the bread pan, then add the dry ingredients on top.
4. Make a well in the center of the dry ingredients and add the yeast. Place the pan in the bread machine and close the lid.
5. Turn on the bread maker. Select the Basic setting, then the loaf size, and finally the crust color. Start the cycle.
6. When the cycle is finished and the bread is baked, carefully remove the pan from the machine. Use a potholder as the handle will be very hot. Let rest for a few minutes.
7. Remove the bread from the pan and allow to cool on a wire rack for at least 10 minutes before slicing.

Easy Gluten-free, Dairy-free Bread

Ingredients:

- 8 slices (1 pound)
- 1 cup warm water
- 1 1/3 teaspoons active dry yeast
- 1 1/3 teaspoons sugar
- 1 1/3 eggs, room temperature
- 2/3 egg white, room temperature
- 1 tablespoon apple cider vinegar
- 3 tablespoons olive oil
- 2 2/9 cups multi-purpose gluten-free flour
- 12 slices (1 ½ pounds)
- 1 1/2 cups warm water
- 2 teaspoons active dry yeast
- 2 teaspoons sugar
- 2 eggs, room temperature
- 1 egg white, room temperature
- 1 1/2 tablespoons apple cider vinegar
- 4 1/2 tablespoons olive oil
- 3 1/3 cups multi-purpose gluten-free flour
- 16 slices (2 pounds)
- 2 cups warm water
- 2 2/3 teaspoons active dry yeast
- 2 2/3 teaspoons sugar

- 2 2/3 eggs, room temperature
- 1 1/3 egg whites, room temperature
- 2 tablespoons apple cider vinegar
- 6 tablespoons olive oil
- 4 4/9 cups multi-purpose gluten-free flour

Directions:

1. Choose the size of loaf you would like to make and measure your ingredients.
2. Add the yeast and sugar to the warm water and stir to mix in a large mixing bowl; set aside until foamy, about 8 to 10 minutes.
3. Whisk the 2 eggs and 1 egg white together in a separate mixing bowl and add to baking pan of bread maker.
4. Add apple cider vinegar and oil to bread pan.
5. Add foamy yeast/water mixture to bread pan.
6. Add the multi-purpose gluten-free flour on top.
7. Place the pan in the bread machine and close the lid.
8. Turn on the bread maker. Select the Gluten-Free setting, then the loaf size, and finally the crust color. Start the cycle.
9. When the cycle is finished and the bread is baked, carefully remove the pan from the machine. Use a potholder as the handle will be very hot. Let rest for a few minutes.
10. Remove the bread from the pan and allow to cool on a wire rack for at least 10 minutes before slicing.

Gluten-free Pumpkin Pie Bread

Ingredients:

- 8 slices (1 pound)
- 1/4 cup olive oil
- 2 large eggs, beaten
- 1 tablespoon bourbon vanilla extract
- 1 cup canned pumpkin
- 4 tablespoons honey
- 1/4 teaspoon lemon juice
- 1/2 cup buckwheat flour
- 1/4 cup millet flour
- 1/4 cup sorghum flour
- 1/2 cup tapioca starch
- 1 cup light brown sugar
- 2 teaspoons baking powder

- 1 teaspoon baking soda
- 1/2 teaspoon sea salt
- 1 teaspoon xanthan gum
- 1 teaspoon ground cinnamon
- 1 teaspoon allspice
- 1-2 tablespoons peach juice
- 12 slices (1 ½ pounds)
- 3/8 cup olive oil
- 3 large eggs, beaten
- 1 1/2 tablespoons bourbon vanilla extract
- 1 1/2 cups canned pumpkin
- 6 tablespoons honey
- 3/8 teaspoon lemon juice
- 3/4 cup buckwheat flour
- 3/8 cup millet flour
- 3/8 cup sorghum flour
- 3/4 cup tapioca starch
- 1 1/2 cups light brown sugar
- 3 teaspoons baking powder
- 1 1/2 teaspoons baking soda
- 3/4 teaspoon sea salt
- 1 1/2 teaspoons xanthan gum
- 1 1/2 teaspoons ground cinnamon
- 1 1/2 teaspoons allspice
- 1 1/2-3 tablespoons peach juice
- 16 slices (2 pounds)
- 1/2 cup olive oil
- 4 large eggs, beaten
- 2 tablespoons bourbon vanilla extract
- 2 cups canned pumpkin
- 8 tablespoons honey
- 1/2 teaspoon lemon juice
- 1 cup buckwheat flour
- 1/2 cup millet flour
- 1/2 cup sorghum flour
- 1 cup tapioca starch
- 2 cups light brown sugar
- 4 teaspoons baking powder
- 2 teaspoons baking soda
- 1 teaspoon sea salt
- 2 teaspoons xanthan gum
- 2 teaspoons ground cinnamon
- 2 teaspoons allspice
- 2-4 tablespoons peach juice

Directions:

1. Choose the size of loaf you would like to make and measure your ingredients.
2. Mix dry ingredients together in a bowl and put aside.
3. Add wet ingredients to pan, except peach juice.
4. Add mixed dry ingredients to bread pan.
5. Place the pan in the bread machine and close the lid.
6. Turn on the bread maker. Select the Sweet bread setting, then the loaf size, and finally the crust color. Start the cycle.
7. As it begins to mix the ingredients, use a soft silicone spatula to scrape down the sides.
8. If the batter is stiff, add one tablespoon at a time of peach juice until the batter becomes slightly thinner than muffin batter.
9. When the cycle is finished and the bread is baked, carefully remove the pan from the machine. Use a potholder as the handle will be very hot. Let rest for a few minutes.
10. Remove the bread from the pan and allow to cool on a wire rack for at least 10 minutes before slicing.

Gluten-free Simple Sandwich Bread

Ingredients:

- 8 slices (1 pound)
- 1 1/2 cups sorghum flour
- 1 cup tapioca starch or potato starch (not potato flour!)
- 1/2 cup gluten-free millet flour or gluten-free oat flour
- 2 teaspoons xanthan gum
- 1 1/4 teaspoons fine sea salt
- 2 1/2 teaspoons gluten-free yeast for bread machines
- 1 1/4 cups warm water
- 3 tablespoons extra virgin olive oil
- 1 tablespoon honey or raw agave nectar
- 1/2 teaspoon mild rice vinegar or lemon juice
- 2 organic free-range eggs, beaten
- 12 slices (1 ½ pounds)
- 2 1/4 cups sorghum flour
- 1 1/2 cups tapioca starch or potato starch (not potato flour!)

- 3/4 cup gluten-free millet flour or gluten-free oat flour
- 3 teaspoons xanthan gum
- 1 7/8 teaspoons fine sea salt
- 3 3/4 teaspoons gluten-free yeast for bread machines
- 1 7/8 cups warm water
- 4 1/2 tablespoons extra virgin olive oil
- 1 1/2 tablespoons honey or raw agave nectar
- 3/4 teaspoon mild rice vinegar or lemon juice
- 3 organic free-range eggs, beaten
- 16 slices (2 pounds)
- 3 cups sorghum flour
- 2 cups tapioca starch or potato starch (not potato flour!)
- 1 cup gluten-free millet flour or gluten-free oat flour
- 4 teaspoons xanthan gum
- 2 1/2 teaspoons fine sea salt
- 5 teaspoons gluten-free yeast for bread machines
- 2 1/2 cups warm water
- 6 tablespoons extra virgin olive oil
- 2 tablespoons honey or raw agave nectar
- 1 teaspoon mild rice vinegar or lemon juice
- 4 organic free-range eggs, beaten

Directions:

1. Choose the size of loaf you would like to make and measure your ingredients.

2. Whisk together the dry ingredients except the yeast and set aside.

3. Add the liquid ingredients to the bread pan first, then gently pour the mixed dry ingredients on top of the liquid.

4. Make a well in the center of the dry ingredients and add the yeast.

5. Place the pan in the bread machine and close the lid.

6. Turn on the bread maker. Select the Rapid setting, then the loaf size, and finally the crust color. Start the cycle.

7. When the cycle is finished and the bread is baked, carefully remove the pan from the machine. Use a potholder as the handle will be very hot. Let rest for a few minutes.

8. Remove the bread from the pan and allow to cool on a wire rack for at least 10 minutes before slicing.

Gluten-free Brown Bread

Ingredients:

- 8 slices (1 pound)
- 2 large eggs, lightly beaten
- 1 3/4 cups warm water
- 3 tablespoons canola oil
- 1 cup brown rice flour
- 3/4 cup oat flour
- 1/4 cup tapioca starch
- 1 1/4 cups potato starch
- 1 1/2 teaspoons salt
- 2 tablespoons brown sugar
- 2 tablespoons gluten-free flaxseed meal
- 1/2 cup nonfat dry milk powder
- 2 1/2 teaspoons xanthan gum
- 3 tablespoons psyllium, whole husks
- 2 1/2 teaspoons gluten-free yeast for bread machines
- 12 slices (1 ½ pounds)
- 3 large eggs, lightly beaten
- 2 5/8 cups warm water
- 4 1/2 tablespoons canola oil
- 1 1/2 cups brown rice flour
- 1 1/8 cups oat flour
- 3/8 cup tapioca starch
- 1 7/8 cups potato starch
- 2 1/4 teaspoons salt
- 3 tablespoons brown sugar
- 3 tablespoons gluten-free flaxseed meal
- 3/4 cup nonfat dry milk powder
- 3 3/4 teaspoons xanthan gum
- 4 1/2 tablespoons psyllium, whole husks
- 3 3/4 teaspoons gluten-free yeast for bread machines
- 16 slices (2 pounds)
- 4 large eggs, lightly beaten
- 3 1/2 cups warm water
- 6 tablespoons canola oil
- 2 cups brown rice flour
- 1 1/2 cups oat flour
- 1/2 cup tapioca starch
- 2 1/2 cups potato starch
- 3 teaspoons salt
- 4 tablespoons brown sugar
- 4 tablespoons gluten-free flaxseed meal

- 1 cup nonfat dry milk powder
- 5 teaspoons xanthan gum
- 6 tablespoons psyllium, whole husks
- 5 teaspoons gluten-free yeast for bread machines

Directions:

1. Choose the size of loaf you would like to make and measure your ingredients.

2. Add all the wet ingredients to the bread pan in the order listed above and stir until combined.

3. Whisk all of the dry ingredients except the yeast together in a large mixing bowl.

4. Add the dry ingredients on top of the wet ingredients.

5. Make a well in the center of the dry ingredients and add the yeast.

6. Place the pan in the bread machine and close the lid.

7. Turn on the bread maker. Select the Gluten-Free setting, then the loaf size, and finally the crust color. Start the cycle.

8. When the cycle is finished and the bread is baked, carefully remove the pan from the machine. Use a potholder as the handle will be very hot. Let rest for a few minutes.

9. Remove the bread from the pan and allow to cool on a wire rack for at least 10 minutes before slicing.

Basic Honey Bread

Ingredients:

- 8 slices (1 pound)
- 1 cup warm milk
- 1/6 cup unsalted butter, melted
- 1 egg, beaten
- 5/8 teaspoon apple cider vinegar
- 1/3 cup honey
- 5/8 teaspoon table salt
- 2 cups gluten-free flour(s) of your choice
- 1 teaspoon xanthan gum
- 1 teaspoon bread machine yeast
- 12 slices (1½ pounds)
- 1½ cups warm milk
- ¼ cup unsalted butter, melted
- 2 eggs, beaten
- 1 teaspoon apple cider vinegar

- ½ cup honey
- 1 teaspoon table salt
- 3 cups gluten-free flour(s) of your choice
- 1½ teaspoons xanthan gum
- 1¾ teaspoons bread machine yeast
- 16 slices (2 pounds)
- 2 cups warm milk
- ⅓ cup unsalted butter, melted
- 2 eggs, beaten
- 1¼ teaspoons apple cider vinegar
- ⅔ cup honey
- 1¼ teaspoons table salt
- 4 cups gluten-free flour(s) of your choice
- 2 teaspoons xanthan gum
- 2 teaspoons bread machine yeast

Directions:

1. Choose the size of loaf you would like to make and measure your ingredients.

2. Add the ingredients to the bread pan in the order listed above.

3. Place the pan in the bread machine and close the lid.

4. Turn on the bread maker. Select the White/Basic or Gluten-Free (if your machine has this setting) setting, then the loaf size, and finally the crust color. Start the cycle.

5. When the cycle is finished and the bread is baked, carefully remove the pan from the machine. Use a potholder as the handle will be very hot. Let rest for a few minutes.

6. Remove the bread from the pan and allow to cool on a wire rack for at least 10 minutes before slicing.

Gluten-free Whole Grain Bread

Ingredients:

- 8 slices (1 pound)
- 2/3 cup sorghum flour
- 1/2 cup buckwheat flour
- 1/2 cup millet flour
- 3/4 cup potato starch
- 2 1/4 teaspoons xanthan gum
- 1 1/4 teaspoons salt
- 3/4 cup skim milk
- 1/2 cup water

- 1 tablespoon instant yeast
- 5 teaspoons agave nectar, separated
- 1 large egg, lightly beaten
- 4 tablespoons extra virgin olive oil
- 1/2 teaspoon cider vinegar
- 1 tablespoon poppy seeds
- 12 slices (1 ½ pounds)
- 1 cup sorghum flour
- 3/4 cup buckwheat flour
- 3/4 cup millet flour
- 1 1/8 cups potato starch
- 3 3/8 teaspoons xanthan gum
- 1 7/8 teaspoons salt
- 1 1/8 cups skim milk
- 3/4 cup water
- 1 1/2 tablespoons instant yeast
- 7 1/2 teaspoons agave nectar, separated
- 1 1/2 large eggs, lightly beaten
- 6 tablespoons extra virgin olive oil
- 3/4 teaspoon cider vinegar
- 1 1/2 tablespoons poppy seeds
- 16 slices (2 pounds)
- 1 1/3 cups sorghum flour
- 1 cup buckwheat flour
- 1 cup millet flour
- 1 1/2 cups potato starch
- 4 1/2 teaspoons xanthan gum
- 2 1/2 teaspoons salt
- 1 1/2 cups skim milk
- 1 cup water
- 2 tablespoons instant yeast
- 10 teaspoons agave nectar, separated
- 2 large eggs, lightly beaten
- 8 tablespoons extra virgin olive oil
- 1 teaspoon cider vinegar
- 2 tablespoons poppy seeds

Directions:

1. Choose the size of loaf you would like to make and measure your ingredients.

2. Whisk sorghum, buckwheat, millet, potato starch, xanthan gum, and sea salt in a bowl and set aside.

3. Combine milk and water in a glass measuring cup. Heat to between 110°F and 120°F. Add 2 teaspoons of agave nectar and yeast and stir to combine. Cover and set aside for a few minutes.

4. Combine the egg, olive oil, remaining agave, and vinegar in another mixing bowl. Add yeast and milk mixture. Pour wet ingredients into the bottom of bread pan.

5. Add all the dry ingredients to the bread pan in the order listed above.

6. Place the pan in the bread machine and close the lid.

7. Turn on the bread maker. Select the Gluten-Free setting, then the loaf size, and finally the crust color. Start the cycle.

8. After second kneading cycle, sprinkle with poppy seeds.

9. When the cycle is finished and the bread is baked, carefully remove the pan from the machine. Use a potholder as the handle will be very hot. Let rest for a few minutes.

10. Remove the bread from the pan and allow to cool on a wire rack for at least 10 minutes before slicing.

Gluten-free Crusty Boule Bread

Ingredients:

- 8 slices (1 pound)
- 2 1/6 cups gluten-free flour mix
- 2/3 tablespoon active dry yeast
- 1 teaspoon kosher salt
- 2/3 tablespoon guar gum
- 8/9 cup warm water
- 1 1/3 large eggs, room temperature
- 1 1/3 tablespoons, plus 2 teaspoons olive oil
- 2/3 tablespoon honey
- 12 slices (1 ½ pounds)
- 3 1/4 cups gluten-free flour mix
- 1 tablespoon active dry yeast
- 1 1/2 teaspoons kosher salt
- 1 tablespoon guar gum
- 1 1/3 cups warm water
- 2 large eggs, room temperature
- 2 tablespoons, plus 2 teaspoons olive oil
- 1 tablespoon honey
- 16 slices (2 pounds)
- 4 1/3 cups gluten-free flour mix

- 1 1/3 tablespoons active dry yeast
- 2 teaspoons kosher salt
- 1 1/3 tablespoons guar gum
- 1 7/9 cups warm water
- 2 2/3 large eggs, room temperature
- 2 2/3 tablespoons, plus 2 teaspoons olive oil
- 1 1/3 tablespoons honey

Directions:

1. Choose the size of loaf you would like to make and measure your ingredients.
2. Combine all of the dry ingredients, except the yeast, in a large mixing bowl and set aside.
3. Whisk together the water, eggs, oil, and honey in a separate mixing bowl.
4. Pour the wet ingredients into the bread pan.
5. Add the dry ingredients on top of the wet ingredients.
6. Make a well in the center of the dry ingredients and add the yeast.
7. Place the pan in the bread machine and close the lid.
8. Turn on the bread maker. Select the Gluten-Free setting, then the loaf size, and finally the crust color. Start the cycle.
9. When the cycle is finished and the bread is baked, carefully remove the pan from the machine. Use a potholder as the handle will be very hot. Let rest for a few minutes.
10. Remove the bread from the pan and allow to cool on a wire rack for at least 10 minutes before slicing.
11. Hollow out and fill with soup or dip to use as a boule, or slice for serving.

Gluten-free Pizza Crust

Ingredients:

- 8 slices (1 pound)
- 2 large eggs, room temperature
- 1/3 cup olive oil
- 2/3 cup milk
- 1/3 cup water
- 1 1/3 cups rice flour
- 2/3 cup cornstarch, and extra for dusting
- 1/3 cup potato starch
- 1/3 cup sugar
- 1 1/3 tablespoons yeast
- 2 teaspoons xanthan gum
- 2/3 teaspoon salt
- 12 slices (1 ½ pounds)
- 3 large eggs, room temperature
- 1/2 cup olive oil
- 1 cup milk
- 1/2 cup water
- 2 cups rice flour
- 1 cup cornstarch, and extra for dusting
- 1/2 cup potato starch
- 1/2 cup sugar
- 2 tablespoons yeast
- 3 teaspoons xanthan gum
- 1 teaspoon salt
- 16 slices (2 pounds)
- 4 large eggs, room temperature
- 2/3 cup olive oil
- 1 1/3 cups milk
- 2/3 cup water
- 2 2/3 cups rice flour
- 1 1/3 cups cornstarch, and extra for dusting
- 2/3 cup potato starch
- 2/3 cup sugar
- 2 2/3 tablespoons yeast
- 4 teaspoons xanthan gum
- 1 1/3 teaspoons salt

Directions:

1. Choose the size of loaf you would like to make and measure your ingredients.
2. Combine the wet ingredients in a separate bowl and pour into the bread pan.
3. Combine the dry ingredients (except yeast) and add to the bread pan.
4. Make a well in the center of the dry ingredients and add the yeast.Place the pan in the bread machine and close the lid.
5. Turn on the bread maker. Select the Dough setting, then the loaf size, and finally the crust color. Start the cycle.
6. When the cycle is finished and the bread is baked, carefully remove the pan from the machine. Use a

potholder as the handle will be very hot. Let rest for a few minutes.

7. Press it out on a surface lightly sprinkled with corn starch and create a pizza shape.

8. Remove the bread from the pan and allow to cool on a wire rack for at least 10 minutes before slicing.

Gluten-free Potato Bread

Ingredients:
- 8 slices (1 pound)
- 1/2 medium russet potato, baked, or mashed leftovers
- 1 packet gluten-free quick yeast
- 1 1/2 tablespoons honey
- 3/8 cup warm almond milk
- 1 egg, 1 egg white
- 1 5/6 cups almond flour
- 1 1/2 cups tapioca flour
- 1/2 teaspoon sea salt
- 1/2 teaspoon dried chives
- 1/2 tablespoon apple cider vinegar
- 1/8 cup olive oil
- 12 slices (1 ½ pounds)
- 3/4 medium russet potato, baked, or mashed leftovers
- 1 1/2 packets gluten-free quick yeast
- 2 1/4 tablespoons honey
- 9/16 cup warm almond milk
- 1 1/2 eggs, 1 1/2 eggs white
- 2 3/4 cups almond flour
- 2 1/4 cups tapioca flour
- 3/4 teaspoon sea salt
- 3/4 teaspoon dried chives
- 3/4 tablespoon apple cider vinegar
- 3/16 cup olive oil
- 16 slices (2 pounds)
- 1 medium russet potato, baked, or mashed leftovers
- 2 packets gluten-free quick yeast
- 3 tablespoons honey
- 3/4 cup warm almond milk
- 2 eggs, 1 egg white
- 3 2/3 cups almond flour
- 3/4 cup tapioca flour

- 1 teaspoon sea salt
- 1 teaspoon dried chives
- 1 tablespoon apple cider vinegar
- 1/4 cup olive oil

Directions:
1. Choose the size of loaf you would like to make and measure your ingredients.
2. Combine all of the dry ingredients, except the yeast, in a large mixing bowl and set aside.
3. Whisk together the milk, eggs, oil, apple cider, and honey in a separate mixing bowl.
4. Pour the wet ingredients into the bread pan.
5. Add the dry ingredients on top of the wet ingredients.
6. Create a well in the dry ingredients and add the yeast.
7. Place the pan in the bread machine and close the lid.
8. Turn on the bread maker. Select the Gluten-Free setting, then the loaf size, and finally the crust color. Start the cycle.
9. When the cycle is finished and the bread is baked, carefully remove the pan from the machine. Use a potholder as the handle will be very hot. Let rest for a few minutes.
10. Remove the bread from the pan and allow to cool on a wire rack for at least 10 minutes before slicing.

Onion Buttermilk Bread

Ingredients:
- 8 slices (1 pound)
- 5/8 cup lukewarm water
- 1/8 cup unsalted butter, melted
- 1/2 teaspoon apple cider vinegar
- 1/8 cup dry buttermilk powder
- 1 1/2 large eggs, beaten
- 1/8 cup sugar
- 3/4 teaspoon table salt
- 1/4 cup potato flour
- 1/4 cup tapioca flour
- 1 cup white rice flour
- 1/2 tablespoon dill, chopped
- 1/8 cup green onion, chopped
- 1 3/4 teaspoons xanthan gum

- 1 1/2 teaspoons bread machine yeast
- 12 slices (1½ pounds)
- 1 cup lukewarm water
- 3 tablespoons unsalted butter, melted
- ¾ teaspoon apple cider vinegar
- 3 tablespoons dry buttermilk powder
- 3 medium eggs, beaten
- 3 tablespoons sugar
- 1 teaspoon table salt
- ⅓ cup potato flour
- ⅓ cup tapioca flour
- 1½ cups white rice flour
- ¾ tablespoon dill, chopped
- 3 tablespoons green onion, chopped
- 2⅔ teaspoons xanthan gum
- 1½ teaspoons bread machine yeast
- 16 slices (2 pounds)
- 1¼ cups lukewarm water
- ¼ cup unsalted butter, melted
- 1 teaspoon apple cider vinegar
- ¼ cup dry buttermilk powder
- 3 large eggs, beaten
- ¼ cup sugar
- 1½ teaspoons table salt

- ½ cup potato flour
- ½ cup tapioca flour
- 2 cup white rice flour
- 1 tablespoon dill, chopped
- ¼ cup green onion, chopped
- 3½ teaspoons xanthan gum
- 2¼ teaspoons bread machine yeast

Directions:

1. Choose the size of loaf you would like to make and measure your ingredients.

2. Add the ingredients to the bread pan in the order listed above.

3. Place the pan in the bread machine and close the lid.

4. Turn on the bread maker. Select the White/Basic or Gluten-Free (if your machine has this setting) setting, then the loaf size, and finally the crust color. Start the cycle.

5. When the cycle is finished and the bread is baked, carefully remove the pan from the machine. Use a potholder as the handle will be very hot. Let rest for a few minutes.

6. Remove the bread from the pan and allow to cool on a wire rack for at least 10 minutes before slicing.

EVERYDAY/WHITE/BASIC BREAD RECIPES

Peasant Bread

Ingredients:
- 8 slices (1 pound)
- 2 tablespoons full rounded yeast
- 2 cups white bread flour
- 1 1/2 tablespoons sugar
- 1 tablespoon salt
- 7/8 cup water
- For the topping:
- Olive oil
- Poppy seeds
- 12 slices (1 ½ pounds)
- 3 tablespoons full rounded yeast
- 3 cups white bread flour
- 2 1/4 tablespoons sugar
- 1 1/2 tablespoons salt
- 1 1/4 cups water
- For the topping:
- Olive oil
- Poppy seeds
- 16 slices (2 pounds)
- 4 tablespoons full rounded yeast
- 4 cups white bread flour
- 3 tablespoons sugar
- 2 tablespoons salt
- 1 3/4 cups water
- For the topping:
- Olive oil
- Poppy seeds

Directions:
1. Choose the size of loaf you would like to make and measure your ingredients.
2. Add water first, then add the dry ingredients to the bread machine, reserving yeast.
3. Make a well in the center of the dry ingredients and add the yeast.
4. Place the pan in the bread machine and close the lid.
5. Turn on the bread maker. Select the French setting, then the loaf size, and finally the crust color. Start the cycle.
6. When bread is finished, coat the top of loaf with a little olive oil and lightly sprinkle with poppy seeds.
7. When the cycle is finished and the bread is baked, carefully remove the pan from the machine. Use a potholder as the handle will be very hot. Let rest for a few minutes.
8. Remove the bread from the pan and allow to cool on a wire rack for at least 10 minutes before slicing.
9. Add water first, then add the dry ingredients to the bread machine, reserving yeast.
10. Make a well in the center of the dry ingredients and add the yeast.
11. Choose French cycle, light crust color, and push Start.

Slider Buns

Ingredients:
- 8 slices (1 pound)
- 5/6 cup milk
- 2/3 egg
- 1 1/3 tablespoons butter
- 1/2 teaspoon salt
- 1/6 cup white sugar
- 2 1/2 cups all-purpose flour
- 2/3 package active dry yeast
- Flour, for surface
- 12 slices (1 ½ pounds)
- 1 1/4 cups milk
- 1 egg
- 2 tablespoons butter
- 3/4 teaspoon salt
- 1/4 cup white sugar
- 3 3/4 cups all-purpose flour
- 1 package active dry yeast
- Flour, for surface
- 16 slices (2 pounds)
- 1 2/3 cups milk
- 1 1/3 eggs
- 2 2/3 tablespoons butter
- 1 teaspoon salt
- 1/3 cup white sugar

- 5 cups all-purpose flour
- 1 1/3 packages active dry yeast
- Flour, for surface

Directions:

1. Choose the size of loaf you would like to make and measure your ingredients.

2. Add the ingredients to the bread pan in the order listed above.

3. Place the pan in the bread machine and close the lid.

4. Turn on the bread maker. Select the Dough setting, then the loaf size, and finally the crust color. Start the cycle.

5. When the cycle is finished and the bread is baked, c roll dough out on a floured surface to about a 1-inch thickness.

6. Cut out 18 buns with a biscuit cutter or small glass and place them on a greased baking sheet.

7. Let buns rise about one hour or until they have doubled in size.

8. Bake at 350°F for 10 minutes.

9. Brush the tops of baked buns with melted butter and serve.

Prosciutto Parmesan Breadsticks

Ingredients:

- 8 slices (1 pound)
- 2/3 cup warm water
- 1/2 tablespoon butter
- 3/4 tablespoon sugar
- 3/4 teaspoon salt
- 2 cups bread flour
- 1 teaspoon yeast
- For the topping:
- 1/2 pound prosciutto, sliced very thin
- 1/2 cup of grated parmesan cheese
- 1 egg yolk
- 1 tablespoon of water
- 12 slices (1 ½ pounds)
- 1 cup warm water
- 3/4 tablespoon butter
- 1 1/8 tablespoons sugar
- 1 1/8 teaspoons salt
- 3 cups bread flour

- 1 1/2 teaspoons yeast
- For the topping:
- 1/2 pound prosciutto, sliced very thin
- 1/2 cup of grated parmesan cheese
- 1 egg yolk
- 1 tablespoon of water
- 16 slices (2 pounds)
- 1 1/3 cups warm water
- 1 tablespoon butter
- 1 1/2 tablespoons sugar
- 1 1/2 teaspoons salt
- 4 cups bread flour
- 2 teaspoons yeast
- For the topping:
- 1/2 pound prosciutto, sliced very thin
- 1/2 cup of grated parmesan cheese
- 1 egg yolk
- 1 tablespoon of water

Directions:

1. Choose the size of loaf you would like to make and measure your ingredients.

2. Add the ingredients to the bread pan in the order listed above (except yeast).

3. Make a well in the center of the dry ingredients and add the yeast.

4. Place the pan in the bread machine and close the lid.

5. Turn on the bread maker. Select the Dough setting, then the loaf size, and finally the crust color. Start the cycle.

6. When the cycle is finished and the bread is baked, drop the dough onto a lightly-floured surface.

7. Roll the dough out flat to about 1/4-inch thick, or about half a centimeter. Cover with plastic wrap and let rise for 20 to 30 minutes.

8. Sprinkle dough evenly with parmesan and carefully lay the prosciutto slices on the surface of the dough to cover as much of it as possible.

9. Preheat an oven to 400°F.

10. Cut the dough into 12 long strips, about one inch wide. Twist each end in opposite directions, twisting the toppings into the bread stick.

11. Place the breadsticks onto a lightly greased baking sheet.

12. Whisk the egg yolk and water together in a small mixing bowl and lightly baste each breadstick.

13. Bake for 8 to 10 minutes or until golden brown.

14. Remove from oven and serve warm.

Everything Bagel Loaf

Ingredients:

- 8 slices (1 pound)
- 2/3 cup plus 2 tablespoons water
- 1 1/3 tablespoons vegetable oil
- 1 teaspoon salt
- 1 1/3 tablespoons sugar
- 2 1/6 cups white bread flour
- 2 tablespoons Everything Bagel seasoning
- 1 1/3 teaspoons active dry yeast
- 12 slices (1 ½ pounds)
- 1 cup plus 3 tablespoons water
- 2 tablespoons vegetable oil
- 1 1/2 teaspoons salt
- 2 tablespoons sugar
- 3 1/4 cups white bread flour
- 3 tablespoons Everything Bagel seasoning
- 2 teaspoons active dry yeast
- 16 slices (2 pounds)
- 1 1/3 cups plus 4 tablespoons water
- 2 2/3 tablespoons vegetable oil
- 2 teaspoons salt
- 2 2/3 tablespoons sugar
- 4 1/3 cups white bread flour
- 4 tablespoons Everything Bagel seasoning
- 2 2/3 teaspoons active dry yeast

Directions:

1. Choose the size of loaf you would like to make and measure your ingredients.

2. Add the ingredients to the bread pan in the order listed above (except yeast).

3. Make a well in the flour and pour the yeast into it.

4. Place the pan in the bread machine and close the lid.

5. Turn on the bread maker. Select the Basic setting, then the loaf size, and finally the crust color. Start the cycle.

6. When the cycle is finished and the bread is baked, carefully remove the pan from the machine. Use a potholder as the handle will be very hot. Let rest for a few minutes.

7. Remove the bread from the pan and allow to cool on a wire rack for at least 10 minutes before slicing.

Milk Bread

Ingredients:

- 8 slices (1 pound)
- 2/3 cup whole milk
- 1 tablespoon unsalted butter or margarine, cut into pieces
- 2 cups bread flour
- 1 tablespoon sugar
- 1/2 tablespoon plus 1/2 teaspoon gluten
- 1 teaspoon salt
- 1 1/4 teaspoons SAF yeast or 1/2 tablespoon bread machine yeast
- 12 slices (1 ½ pounds)
- 11/8 cups whole milk
- 1 tablespoon unsalted butter or margarine, cut into pieces
- 3 cups bread flour
- 1 tablespoon sugar
- 1 tablespoon gluten
- 11/2 teaspoons salt
- 2 teaspoons SAF yeast or 21/2 teaspoons bread machine yeast
- 16 slices (2 pounds)
- 11/3 cups whole milk
- 2 tablespoons unsalted butter or margarine, cut into pieces
- 4 cups bread flour
- 2 tablespoons sugar
- 1 tablespoon plus 1 teaspoon gluten
- 2 teaspoons salt
- 21/2 teaspoons SAF yeast or 1 tablespoon bread machine yeast

Directions:

1. Choose the size of loaf you would like to make and measure your ingredients.

2. Add the ingredients to the bread pan in the order listed above.

3. Place the pan in the bread machine and close the lid.

4.   Turn on the bread maker. Select the Basic setting, then the loaf size, and finally the crust color. Start the cycle.

5.   When the cycle is finished and the bread is baked, carefully remove the pan from the machine. Use a potholder as the handle will be very hot. Let rest for a few minutes.

6.   Remove the bread from the pan and allow to cool on a wire rack for at least 10 minutes before slicing.

Pizza Dough

Ingredients:
- 8 slices (1 pound)
- 5/6 cup water
- 2 cups bread flour
- 2/3 teaspoon milk powder
- 2/3 tablespoon sugar
- 2/3 teaspoon salt
- 2/3 tablespoon yeast
- 12 slices (1 ½ pounds)
- 1 1/4 cups water
- 3 cups bread flour
- 1 teaspoon milk powder
- 1 tablespoon sugar
- 1 teaspoon salt
- 1 tablespoon yeast
- 16 slices (2 pounds)
- 1 2/3 cups water
- 4 cups bread flour
- 1 1/3 teaspoons milk powder
- 1 1/3 tablespoons sugar
- 1 1/3 teaspoons salt
- 1 1/3 tablespoons yeast

Directions:
1.   Choose the size of loaf you would like to make and measure your ingredients.
2.   Add the ingredients to the bread pan in the order listed above.
3.   Place the pan in the bread machine and close the lid.
4.   Turn on the bread maker. Select the Dough setting, then the loaf size, and finally the crust color. Start the cycle.

5.   When the cycle is finished and the bread is baked, prepare dough by rolling it out in a pizza pan about to a 1-inch thickness.

6.   Top with your favorite sauce, then cheese, then other toppings like pepperoni or veggies.

7.   Bake at 425°F for 15 to 20 minutes or until crust is golden on the edges. Remove the bread from the pan and allow to cool on a wire rack for at least 10 minutes before slicing.

Brioche

Ingredients:
- 8 slices (1 pound)
- 1/4 cup milk
- 2 eggs
- 4 tablespoons butter
- 1 1/2 tablespoons vanilla sugar
- 1/4 teaspoon salt
- 2 cups flour
- 1 1/2 teaspoon yeast
- 1 egg white, for finishing
- 12 slices (1 ½ pounds)
- 3/8 cup milk
- 3 eggs
- 6 tablespoons butter
- 2 1/4 tablespoons vanilla sugar
- 3/8 teaspoon salt
- 3 cups flour
- 2 1/4 teaspoons yeast
- 1 1/2 egg whites, for finishing
- 16 slices (2 pounds)
- 1/2 cup milk
- 4 eggs
- 8 tablespoons butter
- 3 tablespoons vanilla sugar
- 1/2 teaspoon salt
- 4 cups flour
- 3 teaspoons yeast
- 2 egg whites, for finishing

Directions:
1.   Choose the size of loaf you would like to make and measure your ingredients.

2. Add the ingredients to the bread pan in the order listed above (except yeast, egg white for finishing).

3. Make a well inside the flour and then add the yeast into the well.

4. Place the pan in the bread machine and close the lid.

5. Turn on the bread maker. Select the Dough setting, then the loaf size, and finally the crust color. Start the cycle.

6. When the cycle is finished and the bread is baked, remove dough, place dough on floured surface and divide into 12 equal size rolls.

7. Pinch walnut-sized ball of dough off each roll, making a smaller ball; make indent on top of roll and wet with milk; attach small ball to top making the traditional brioche shape.

8. Let rise for 30 minutes until almost double in size.

9. Preheat oven to 375°F.

10. Beat egg white, brush tops of brioche rolls, and bake at 375°F for 10 to 12 minutes, or until golden on top. Cool on rach before serving.

French Bread

Ingredients:
- 8 slices (1 pound)
- 1 large egg whites
- 5/8 cup water
- 2 cups bread flour
- 1/2 tablespoon plus 1 teaspoons gluten
- 1/2 tablespoon sugar
- 5/8 teaspoon salt
- 1 1/8 teaspoons SAF yeast or 1 3/8 teaspoons bread machine yeast
- 12 slices (1 ½ pounds)
- 2 large egg whites
- 1 cup water
- 3 cups bread flour
- 1 tablespoon gluten
- 2 teaspoons sugar
- 13/4 teaspoons salt
- 2 teaspoons SAF yeast or 21/2 teaspoons bread machine yeast
- 16 slices (2 pounds)
- 2 large egg whites

- 11/4 cups water
- 4 cups bread flour
- 1 tablespoon plus 2 teaspoons gluten
- 1 tablespoon sugar
- 21/2 teaspoons salt
- 21/4 teaspoons SAF yeast or 23/4 teaspoons bread machine yeast

Directions:

1. Choose the size of loaf you would like to make and measure your ingredients.

2. Using an electric mixer, beat the egg whites until almost stiff and soft peaks are formed.

3. Add the ingredients to the bread pan in the order listed above. Adding the egg whites in with the water.

4. Place the pan in the bread machine and close the lid.

5. Turn on the bread maker. Select the Basic/French setting, then the loaf size, and finally the crust color. Start the cycle. (This recipe is not suitable for use with the Delay Timer if using fresh eggs.)

6. When the cycle is finished and the bread is baked, carefully remove the pan from the machine. Use a potholder as the handle will be very hot. Let rest for a few minutes.

7. Remove the bread from the pan and allow to cool on a wire rack for at least 10 minutes before slicing.

Rye Bread

Ingredients:
- 8 slices (1 pound)
- 2/3 cup water
- 1 teaspoon salt
- 1 1/3 tablespoons sugar
- 2/3 tablespoon butter
- 1 1/3 teaspoons caraway seed
- 1 1/3 cups bread flour
- 2/3 cup rye flour
- 1 teaspoon quick active yeast
- 12 slices (1 ½ pounds)
- 1 cup water
- 1 1/2 teaspoons salt
- 2 tablespoons sugar
- 1 tablespoon butter
- 2 teaspoons caraway seed

- 2 cups bread flour
- 1 cup rye flour
- 1 1/2 teaspoons quick active yeast
- 16 slices (2 pounds)
- 1 1/3 cups water
- 2 teaspoons salt
- 2 2/3 tablespoons sugar
- 1 1/3 tablespoons butter
- 2 2/3 teaspoons caraway seed
- 2 2/3 cups bread flour
- 1 1/3 cups rye flour
- 2 teaspoons quick active yeast

Directions:

1. Choose the size of loaf you would like to make and measure your ingredients.

2. Add the ingredients to the bread pan in the order listed above.

3. Make a well in the center of the dry ingredients and add the yeast.

4. Place the pan in the bread machine and close the lid.

5. Turn on the bread maker. Select the Basic setting, then the loaf size, and finally the crust color. Start the cycle.

6. When the cycle is finished and the bread is baked, carefully remove the pan from the machine. Use a potholder as the handle will be very hot. Let rest for a few minutes.

7. Remove the bread from the pan and allow to cool on a wire rack for at least 10 minutes before slicing.

French Sandwich Pain Au Lait

Ingredients:
- 8 slices (1 pound)
- 5/6 cup water
- 3 tablespoons unsalted butter, cut into pieces
- 1 7/8 cups bread flour
- 1/8 cup barley flour
- 1/4 cup nonfat dry milk
- 1/2 tablespoon plus 1/2 teaspoon gluten
- 3/4 teaspoon sugar
- 1 teaspoon salt
- 1 1/8 teaspoons SAF yeast or 1 3/8 teaspoons bread machine yeast

- 12 slices (1 ½ pounds)
- 11/4 cups water
- 5 tablespoons unsalted butter, cut into pieces
- 27/8 cups bread flour
- 1/8 cup barley flour
- 1/3 cup nonfat dry milk
- 1 tablespoon gluten
- 1 teaspoon sugar
- 11/2 teaspoons salt
- 2 teaspoons SAF yeast or 21/2 teaspoons bread machine yeast
- 16 slices (2 pounds)
- 12/3 cups water
- 6 tablespoons unsalted butter, cut into pieces
- 33/4 cups bread flour
- 1/4 cup barley flour
- 1/2 cup nonfat dry milk
- 1 tablespoon plus 1 teaspoon gluten
- 11/2 teaspoons sugar
- 2 teaspoons salt
- 21/4 teaspoons SAF yeast or 23/4 teaspoons bread machine yeast

Directions:

1. Choose the size of loaf you would like to make and measure your ingredients.

2. Add the ingredients to the bread pan in the order listed above.

3. Place the pan in the bread machine and close the lid.

4. Turn on the bread maker. Select the Basic setting, then the loaf size, and finally the crust color. Start the cycle.

5. When the cycle is finished and the bread is baked, carefully remove the pan from the machine. Use a potholder as the handle will be very hot. Let rest for a few minutes.

6. Remove the bread from the pan and allow to cool on a wire rack for at least 10 minutes before slicing.

Cracked Wheat Bread

Ingredients:
- 8 slices (1 pound)
- 1 1/4 cup plus 1 tablespoon water
- 2 tablespoons vegetable oil

- 3 cups bread flour
- 3/4 cup cracked wheat
- 1 1/2 teaspoons salt
- 2 tablespoons sugar
- 2 1/4 teaspoons active dry yeast
- 12 slices (1 ½ pounds)
- 1 7/8 cups plus 1 1/2 tablespoons water
- 3 tablespoons vegetable oil
- 4 1/2 cups bread flour
- 1 1/8 cups cracked wheat
- 2 1/4 teaspoons salt
- 3 tablespoons sugar
- 3 3/8 teaspoons active dry yeast
- 16 slices (2 pounds)
- 2 1/2 cups plus 2 tablespoons water
- 4 tablespoons vegetable oil
- 6 cups bread flour
- 1 1/2 cups cracked wheat
- 3 teaspoons salt
- 4 tablespoons sugar
- 4 1/2 teaspoons active dry yeast

Directions:

1. Choose the size of loaf you would like to make and measure your ingredients.

2. Bring water to a boil.

3. Place cracked wheat in small mixing bowl, pour water over it and stir.

4. Cool to 80°F.

5. Add cracked wheat mixture to bread pan, followed by all ingredients (except yeast) in the order above listed.

6. Make a well in the center of the dry ingredients and add the yeast.

7. Place the pan in the bread machine and close the lid.

8. Turn on the bread maker. Select the Basic setting, then the loaf size, and finally the crust color. Start the cycle.

9. When the cycle is finished and the bread is baked, carefully remove the pan from the machine. Use a potholder as the handle will be very hot. Let rest for a few minutes.

10. Remove the bread from the pan and allow to cool on a wire rack for at least 10 minutes before slicing.

Sour Cream Bread

Ingredients:

- 8 slices (1 pound)
- 3/8 cup plus 1/2 tablespoon water
- 5/8 cup sour cream
- 2 1/6 cups bread flour
- 3/4 tablespoon light brown sugar
- 1/2 tablespoon gluten
- 3/4 teaspoon salt
- 1/2 tablespoon SAF yeast or 1/2 tablespoon plus 1/4 teaspoon bread machine yeast
- 12 slices (1 ½ pounds)
- 1/2 cup plus 1 tablespoon water
- 1 cup sour cream
- 31/2 cups bread flour
- 1 tablespoon light brown sugar
- 2 teaspoons gluten
- 11/4 teaspoons salt
- 2 teaspoons SAF yeast or 21/2 teaspoons bread machine yeast
- 16 slices (2 pounds)
- 3/4 cup plus 1 tablespoon water
- 1 1/4 cups sour cream
- 4 1/3 cups bread flour
- 11/2 tablespoons light brown sugar
- 1 tablespoon gluten
- 11/2 teaspoons salt
- 1 tablespoon SAF yeast or 1 tablespoon plus 1/2 teaspoon bread machine yeast

Directions:

1. Choose the size of loaf you would like to make and measure your ingredients.

2. Add the ingredients to the bread pan in the order listed above, with the water and sour cream put in first, and adding the dry ingredients in on top.

3. Place the pan in the bread machine and close the lid.

4. Turn on the bread maker. Select the Basic setting, then the loaf size, and finally the crust color. Start the cycle.

5. When the cycle is finished and the bread is baked, carefully remove the pan from the machine. Use a potholder as the handle will be very hot. Let rest for a few minutes.

6. Remove the bread from the pan and allow to cool on a wire rack for at least 10 minutes before slicing.

Sampler Oatmeal Loaf

Ingredients:

- 8 slices (1 pound)
- 3/4 cup buttermilk
- 1 tablespoon honey or maple syrup
- 2 teaspoons butter or margarine, softened
- 13/4 cups bread flour
- 1/2 cup rolled oats
- 2 teaspoons gluten
- 1 teaspoon salt
- 11/4 teaspoons SAF yeast or 11/2 teaspoons bread machine yeast
- 12 slices (1 ½ pounds)
- 1 1/8 cups buttermilk
- 1 1/2 tablespoons honey or maple syrup
- 3 teaspoons butter or margarine, softened
- 2 5/8 cups bread flour
- 3/4 cup rolled oats
- 3 teaspoons gluten
- 1 1/2 teaspoons salt
- 17/8 teaspoons SAF yeast or 2 1/4 teaspoons bread machine yeast
- 16 slices (2 pounds)
- 1 1/2 cups buttermilk
- 2 tablespoon honey or maple syrup
- 4 teaspoons butter or margarine, softened
- 3 1/2 cups bread flour
- 1 cup rolled oats
- 4 teaspoons gluten
- 2 teaspoon salt
- 2 1/2 teaspoons SAF yeast or 3 teaspoons bread machine yeast

Directions:

1. Choose the size of loaf you would like to make and measure your ingredients.

2. Add the ingredients to the bread pan in the order listed above (except the nuts).

3. Place the pan in the bread machine and close the lid.

4. Turn on the bread maker. Select the Basic/Sweet Bread setting, then the loaf size, and finally the crust color. Start the cycle. (This recipe is not suitable for use with the Delay Timer.)

5. When the machine beeps, or between Knead 1 and Knead 2, add the nuts.

6. When the cycle is finished and the bread is baked, carefully remove the pan from the machine. Use a potholder as the handle will be very hot. Let rest for a few minutes.

7. Remove the bread from the pan and allow to cool on a wire rack for at least 10 minutes before slicing.

House Bread

Ingredients:

- 8 slices (1 pound)
- 3/4 cup water
- 5/8 tablespoon olive oil
- 1 15/16 cups bread flour
- 3/4 tablespoon buckwheat flour
- 3/4 tablespoon dark rye flour
- 3/4 tablespoon toasted wheat germ
- 3/4 tablespoon powdered fructose
- 1/2 tablespoon plus 1 teaspoon gluten
- 1 teaspoon salt
- 1 1/8 teaspoons SAF yeast or 1 3/8 teaspoons bread machine yeast
- 12 slices (1 ½ pounds)
- 11/8 cups water
- 2 tablespoons olive oil
- 27/8 cups bread flour
- 1 tablespoon buckwheat flour
- 1 tablespoon dark rye flour
- 1 tablespoon toasted wheat germ
- 1 tablespoon powdered fructose
- 1 tablespoon gluten
- 11/2 teaspoons salt
- 2 teaspoons SAF yeast or 21/2 teaspoons bread machine yeast
- 16 slices (2 pounds)
- 1 1/2 cups water
- 2 1/2 tablespoons olive oil
- 3 7/8 cups bread flour
- 1 1/2 tablespoons buckwheat flour
- 1 1/2 tablespoons dark rye flour
- 1 1/2 tablespoons toasted wheat germ
- 1 1/2 tablespoons powdered fructose

- 1 tablespoon plus 1 teaspoon gluten
- 2 teaspoons salt
- 21/4 teaspoons SAF yeast or 23/4 teaspoons bread machine yeast

Directions:

1. Choose the size of loaf you would like to make and measure your ingredients.
2. Add the ingredients to the bread pan in the order listed above.
3. Place the pan in the bread machine and close the lid.
4. Turn on the bread maker. Select the Basic setting, then the loaf size, and finally the crust color. Start the cycle.
5. When the cycle is finished and the bread is baked, carefully remove the pan from the machine. Use a potholder as the handle will be very hot. Let rest for a few minutes.
6. Remove the bread from the pan and allow to cool on a wire rack for at least 10 minutes before slicing.

Onion Loaf

Ingredients:

- 8 slices (1 pound)
- 2/3 tablespoon butter
- 1 1/3 medium onions, sliced
- 2/3 cup water
- 2/3 tablespoon olive or vegetable oil
- 2 cups bread flour
- 1 1/3 tablespoons sugar
- 2/3 teaspoon salt
- 5/6 teaspoon bread machine or quick active dry yeast
- 12 slices (1 ½ pounds)
- 1 tablespoon butter
- 2 medium onions, sliced
- 1 cup water
- 1 tablespoon olive or vegetable oil
- 3 cups bread flour
- 2 tablespoons sugar
- 1 teaspoon salt
- 1 1/4 teaspoons bread machine or quick active dry yeast
- 16 slices (2 pounds)
- 1 1/3 tablespoons butter

- 2 2/3 medium onions, sliced
- 1 1/3 cups water
- 1 1/3 tablespoons olive or vegetable oil
- 4 cups bread flour
- 2 2/3 tablespoons sugar
- 1 1/3 teaspoons salt
- 1 2/3 teaspoons bread machine or quick active dry yeast

Directions:

1. Choose the size of loaf you would like to make and measure your ingredients.
2. Preheat a large skillet to medium-low heat and add butter to melt. Add onions and cook for 10 to 15 minutes, stirring often, until onions are brown and caramelized; remove from heat.
3. Add the ingredients to the bread pan in the order listed above (except onions).
4. Place the pan in the bread machine and close the lid.
5. Turn on the bread maker. Select the Basic setting, then the loaf size, and finally the crust color. Start the cycle.
6. Add 1/2 cup of the onions 5 to 10 minutes before the last kneading cycle ends.
7. When the cycle is finished and the bread is baked, carefully remove the pan from the machine. Use a potholder as the handle will be very hot. Let rest for a few minutes.
8. Remove the bread from the pan and allow to cool on a wire rack for at least 10 minutes before slicing.

Maple Buttermilk Bread

Ingredients:

- 8 slices (1 pound)
- 11/16 cup water
- 1 tablespoon unsalted butter, melted
- 1/8 cup plus 1/2 tablespoon maple syrup
- 2 cups bread flour
- 1/4 cup dry buttermilk powder
- 1/2 tablespoon plus 1/2 teaspoon gluten
- 1 teaspoon salt
- 1 1/8 teaspoons SAF yeast or 1 3/8 teaspoons bread machine yeast
- 12 slices (1 ½ pounds)

- 1 cup plus 1 tablespoon water
- 11/2 tablespoons unsalted butter, melted
- 3 tablespoons maple syrup
- 3 cups bread flour
- 1/3 cup dry buttermilk powder
- 1 tablespoon gluten
- 11/2 teaspoons salt
- 13/4 teaspoons SAF yeast or 21/4 teaspoons bread machine yeast
- 16 slices (2 pounds)
- 13/8 cups water
- 2 tablespoons unsalted butter, melted
- 1/4 cup plus 1 tablespoon maple syrup
- 4 cups bread flour
- 1/2 cup dry buttermilk powder
- 1 tablespoon plus 1 teaspoon gluten
- 2 teaspoons salt
- 21/4 teaspoons SAF yeast or 23/4 teaspoons bread machine yeast

Directions:

1. Choose the size of loaf you would like to make and measure your ingredients.
2. Add the ingredients to the bread pan in the order listed above.
3. Place the pan in the bread machine and close the lid.
4. Turn on the bread maker. Select the Basic setting, then the loaf size, and finally the crust color. Start the cycle.
5. When the cycle is finished and the bread is baked, carefully remove the pan from the machine. Use a potholder as the handle will be very hot. Let rest for a few minutes.
6. Remove the bread from the pan and allow to cool on a wire rack for at least 10 minutes before slicing.

Coconut Milk White Bread

Ingredients:

- 8 slices (1 pound)
- 3/4 cup canned coconut milk
- 2 cups bread flour
- 1/2 tablespoon plus 1/2 teaspoon gluten
- 1 teaspoon salt
- 5/8 teaspoon SAF yeast or 1/2 tablespoon bread machine yeast
- 12 slices (1 ½ pounds)
- 11/8 cups canned coconut milk
- 3 cups bread flour
- 1 tablespoon gluten
- 11/2 teaspoons salt
- 13/4 teaspoons SAF yeast or 21/4 teaspoons bread machine yeast
- 16 slices (2 pounds)
- 11/2 cups canned coconut milk
- 4 cups bread flour
- 1 tablespoon plus 1 teaspoon gluten
- 2 teaspoons salt
- 21/2 teaspoons SAF yeast or 1 tablespoon bread machine yeast

Directions:

1. Choose the size of loaf you would like to make and measure your ingredients.
2. Add the ingredients to the bread pan in the order listed above.
3. Place the pan in the bread machine and close the lid.
4. Turn on the bread maker. Select the Basic setting, then the loaf size, and finally the crust color. Start the cycle.
5. When the cycle is finished and the bread is baked, carefully remove the pan from the machine. Use a potholder as the handle will be very hot. Let rest for a few minutes.
6. Remove the bread from the pan and allow to cool on a wire rack for at least 10 minutes before slicing.

Sampler Country White Loaf

Ingredients:

- 8 slices (1 pound)
- 3/4 cup fat-free milk
- 1 tablespoon canola oil
- 17/8 cups bread flour
- 2 tablespoons barley flour
- 2 tablespoons toasted wheat germ
- 1 tablespoon sugar
- 2 teaspoons gluten
- 1 teaspoon salt

- 11/8 teaspoons SAF yeast or 11/2 teaspoons bread machine yeast
- 12 slices (1 ½ pounds)
- 1 1/8 cups fat-free milk
- 1 1/2 tablespoons canola oil
- 2 13/16 cups bread flour
- 3 tablespoons barley flour
- 3 tablespoons toasted wheat germ
- 1 1/2 tablespoons sugar
- 3 teaspoons gluten
- 1 1/2 teaspoons salt
- 1 11/16 teaspoons SAF yeast or 3 teaspoons bread machine yeast
- 16 slices (2 pounds)
- 1 1/2 cup fat-free milk
- 2 tablespoon canola oil
- 3 3/4 cups bread flour
- 4 tablespoons barley flour
- 4 tablespoons toasted wheat germ
- 2 tablespoon sugar
- 4 teaspoons gluten
- 2 teaspoon salt
- 2 1/4 teaspoons SAF yeast or 3 teaspoons bread machine yeast

Directions:

1. Choose the size of loaf you would like to make and measure your ingredients.

2. Add the ingredients to the bread pan in the order listed above.

3. Place the pan in the bread machine and close the lid.

4. Turn on the bread maker. Select the Basic setting, then the loaf size, and finally the crust color. Start the cycle.

5. When the cycle is finished and the bread is baked, carefully remove the pan from the machine. Use a potholder as the handle will be very hot. Let rest for a few minutes.

6. Remove the bread from the pan and allow to cool on a wire rack for at least 10 minutes before slicing.

Wine And Cheese Bread

Ingredients:
- 8 slices (1 pound)

- 3/4 cup white wine
- 1/2 cup white cheddar or gruyere cheese, shredded
- 1 1/2 tablespoons butter
- 1/2 teaspoon salt
- 3/4 teaspoon sugar
- 2 1/4 cups bread flour
- 1 1/2 teaspoons active dry yeast
- 12 slices (1 ½ pounds)
- 1 1/8 cups white wine
- 3/4 cup white cheddar or gruyere cheese, shredded
- 2 1/4 tablespoons butter
- 3/4 teaspoon salt
- 1 1/8 teaspoons sugar
- 3 3/8 cups bread flour
- 2 1/4 teaspoons active dry yeast
- 16 slices (2 pounds)
- 1 1/2 cups white wine
- 1 cup white cheddar or gruyere cheese, shredded
- 3 tablespoons butter
- 1 teaspoon salt
- 1 1/2 teaspoon sugar
- 4 1/2 cups bread flour
- 3 teaspoons active dry yeast

Directions:

1. Choose the size of loaf you would like to make and measure your ingredients.

2. Add the ingredients to the bread pan in the order listed above (except yeast).

3. Make a well in the flour and pour the yeast into it.

4. Place the pan in the bread machine and close the lid.

5. Turn on the bread maker. Select the Basic setting, then the loaf size, and finally the crust color. Start the cycle.

6. When the cycle is finished and the bread is baked, carefully remove the pan from the machine. Use a potholder as the handle will be very hot. Let rest for a few minutes.

7. Remove the bread from the pan and allow to cool on a wire rack for at least 10 minutes before slicing.

Basic White Bread

Ingredients:

- 8 slices (1 pound)
- 2/3 cup warm water
- 1 1/3 tablespoons agave nectar
- 1/6 cup applesauce
- 2 cups bread flour
- 2/3 teaspoon salt
- 1 1/2 teaspoons rapid rise yeast
- 12 slices (1 ½ pounds)
- 1 cup warm water
- 2 tablespoons agave nectar
- 1/4 cup applesauce
- 3 cups bread flour
- 1 teaspoon salt
- 2 1/4 teaspoons rapid rise yeast
- 16 slices (2 pounds)
- 1 1/3 cups warm water
- 2 2/3 tablespoons agave nectar
- 1/3 cup applesauce
- 4 cups bread flour
- 1 1/3 teaspoons salt
- 3 teaspoons rapid rise yeast

Directions:

1. Choose the size of loaf you would like to make and measure your ingredients.

2. Add the ingredients to the bread pan in the order listed above (except yeast).

3. Make a well in the center of the dry ingredients and add the yeast.

4. Place the pan in the bread machine and close the lid.

5. Turn on the bread maker. Select the Basic setting, then the loaf size, and finally the crust color. Start the cycle.

6. When the cycle is finished and the bread is baked, carefully remove the pan from the machine. Use a potholder as the handle will be very hot. Let rest for a few minutes.

7. Remove the bread from the pan and allow to cool on a wire rack for at least 10 minutes before slicing.

Classic White Sandwich Bread

Ingredients:

- 8 slices (1 pound)
- 1/2 cup water, lukewarm between 80 and 90°F
- 1 tablespoon unsalted butter, melted
- 1/2 teaspoon table salt
- 1/8 cup sugar
- 1 egg whites or 1/2 egg, beaten
- 1 1/2 cups white bread flour
- 3/4 teaspoon bread machine yeast
- 12 slices (1 ½ pounds)
- 3/4 cup water, lukewarm between 80 and 90°F
- 1 1/2 tablespoons unsalted butter, melted
- 3/4 teaspoon table salt
- 1 ½ ounces sugar
- 2 egg whites or 1 egg, beaten
- 2 1/4 cups white bread flour
- 1 1/8 teaspoons bread machine yeast
- 16 slices (2 pounds)
- 1 cup water, lukewarm between 80 and 90°F
- 2 tablespoons unsalted butter, melted
- 1 teaspoon table salt
- 1/4 cup sugar
- 2 egg whites or 1 egg, beaten
- 3 cups white bread flour
- 1 1/2 teaspoons bread machine yeast

Directions:

1. Choose the size of loaf you would like to make and measure your ingredients.

2. Add the ingredients to the bread pan in the order listed above.

3. Place the pan in the bread machine and close the lid.

4. Turn on the bread maker. Select the White/Basic setting, then the loaf size, and finally the crust color. Start the cycle.

5. When the cycle is finished and the bread is baked, carefully remove the pan from the machine. Use a potholder as the handle will be very hot. Let rest for a few minutes.

6. Remove the bread from the pan and allow to cool on a wire rack for at least 10 minutes before slicing.

Sampler Honey Whole Wheat Loaf

Ingredients:

- 8 slices (1 pound)
- 3/4 cup fat-free milk
- 2 tablespoons honey
- 1 tablespoon butter, softened
- 13/4 cups whole wheat flour
- 1/4 cup bread flour
- 1 tablespoon gluten
- 1 teaspoon salt
- 11/4 teaspoons SAF yeast or 11/2 teaspoons bread machine yeast
- 12 slices (1 ½ pounds)
- 1 1/8 cups fat-free milk
- 3 tablespoons honey
- 1 1/2 tablespoons butter, softened
- 2 5/8 cups whole wheat flour
- 3/8 cup bread flour
- 1 1/2 tablespoons gluten
- 1 1/2 teaspoon salt
- 1 7/8 teaspoons SAF yeast or 2 1/4 teaspoons bread machine yeast
- 16 slices (2 pounds)
- 1 1/2 cups fat-free milk
- 4 tablespoons honey
- 2 tablespoons butter, softened
- 3 1/2 cups whole wheat flour
- 1/2 cup bread flour
- 2 tablespoons gluten
- 2 teaspoons salt
- 2 1/2 teaspoons SAF yeast or 3 teaspoons bread machine yeast

Directions:

1. Choose the size of loaf you would like to make and measure your ingredients.

2. Add the ingredients to the bread pan in the order listed above.

3. Place the pan in the bread machine and close the lid.

4. Turn on the bread maker. Select the Basic setting, then the loaf size, and finally the crust color. Start the cycle.

5. When the cycle is finished and the bread is baked, carefully remove the pan from the machine. Use a potholder as the handle will be very hot. Let rest for a few minutes.

6. Remove the bread from the pan and allow to cool on a wire rack for at least 10 minutes before slicing.

Cheesy Sausage Loaf

Ingredients:

- 8 slices (1 pound)
- 2/3 cup warm water
- 2 2/3 teaspoons butter, softened
- 5/6 teaspoon salt
- 2/3 teaspoon sugar
- 2 cups bread flour
- 1 1/2 teaspoons active dry yeast
- 2/3 pound pork sausage roll, cooked and drained
- 1 cup Italian cheese, shredded
- 1/6 teaspoon garlic powder
- Pinch of black pepper
- 2/3 egg, lightly beaten
- Flour, for surface
- 12 slices (1 ½ pounds)
- 1 cup warm water
- 4 teaspoons butter, softened
- 1 1/4 teaspoons salt
- 1 teaspoon sugar
- 3 cups bread flour
- 2 1/4 teaspoons active dry yeast
- 1 pound pork sausage roll, cooked and drained
- 1 1/2 cups Italian cheese, shredded
- 1/4 teaspoon garlic powder
- Pinch of black pepper
- 1 egg, lightly beaten
- Flour, for surface
- 16 slices (2 pounds)
- 1 1/3 cups warm water
- 5 1/3 teaspoons butter, softened
- 1 2/3 teaspoons salt
- 1 1/3 teaspoons sugar
- 4 cups bread flour
- 3 teaspoons active dry yeast
- 1 1/3 pounds pork sausage roll, cooked and drained
- 2 cups Italian cheese, shredded
- 1/3 teaspoon garlic powder

- Pinch of black pepper
- 1 1/3 eggs, lightly beaten
- Flour, for surface

Directions:

1. Choose the size of loaf you would like to make and measure your ingredients.
2. Add the first five ingredients to the bread pan in the order listed above (except yeast).
3. Make a well in the flour and pour the yeast into it.
4. Place the pan in the bread machine and close the lid.
5. Turn on the bread maker. Select the Dough setting, then the loaf size, and finally the crust color. Start the cycle.
6. When the cycle is finished and the bread is baked, turn kneaded dough onto a lightly floured surface and roll into a 16-by-10-inch rectangle. Cover with plastic wrap and let rest for 10 minutes.
7. Combine sausage, cheese, garlic powder and pepper in a mixing bowl.
8. Spread sausage mixture evenly over the dough to within one 1/2 inch of edges. Start with a long side and roll up like a jelly roll, pinch seams to seal, and tuck ends under.
9. Place the loaf seam-side down on a greased baking sheet. Cover and let rise in a warm place for 30 minutes.
10. Preheat an oven to 350°F and bake 20 minutes.
11. Brush with egg and bake an additional 15 to 20 minutes until golden brown.
12. Remove to a cooling rack and serve warm.

Garlic Basil Knots

Ingredients:

- 8 slices (1 pound)
- 2/3 cup water
- 1 1/3 tablespoons butter, softened
- 2/3 egg, room temperature
- 2 1/6 cups all-purpose flour
- 1/6 cup sugar
- 2/3 teaspoon salt
- 2 teaspoons regular active dry yeast
- For the topping:
- 2 tablespoons butter, melted
- 2 cloves garlic, minced
- 3 fresh basil leaves, chopped fine
- Flour, for surface
- 12 slices (1 ½ pounds)
- 1 cup water
- 2 tablespoons butter, softened
- 1 egg, room temperature
- 3 1/4 cups all-purpose flour
- 1/4 cup sugar
- 1 teaspoon salt
- 3 teaspoons regular active dry yeast
- For the topping:
- 2 tablespoons butter, melted
- 2 cloves garlic, minced
- 3 fresh basil leaves, chopped fine
- Flour, for surface
- 16 slices (2 pounds)
- 1 1/3 cups water
- 2 2/3 tablespoons butter, softened
- 1 1/3 eggs, room temperature
- 4 1/3 cups all-purpose flour
- 1/3 cup sugar
- 1 1/3 teaspoons salt
- 4 teaspoons regular active dry yeast
- For the topping:
- 2 tablespoons butter, melted
- 2 cloves garlic, minced
- 3 fresh basil leaves, chopped fine
- Flour, for surface

Directions:

1. Choose the size of loaf you would like to make and measure your ingredients.
2. Add the ingredients to the bread pan in the order listed above.
3. Place the pan in the bread machine and close the lid.
4. Turn on the bread maker. Select the Dough setting, then the loaf size, and finally the crust color. Start the cycle.
5. Place parchment paper on a baking sheet and coat with cooking spray.
6. Flatten the dough onto a well-floured surface and cut into strips using a pizza cutter.
7. Tie each strip into a knot, making sure to keep them well-floured so they don't stick together. Place knots on

the baking sheet and cover with a cloth; set in a warm place to rise for 30 minutes.

8.   Preheat oven to 400°F and bake 9 to 12 minutes or until golden brown.

Potato Bread

Ingredients:
- 8 slices (1 pound)
- 1/2 cup water
- 4/9 cup instant mashed potatoes
- 2/3 egg
- 1 1/3 tablespoons butter, unsalted
- 1 1/3 tablespoons white sugar
- 1/6 cup dry milk powder
- 2/3 teaspoon salt
- 2 cups bread flour
- 1 teaspoon active dry yeast
- 12 slices (1 ½ pounds)
- 3/4 cup water
- 2/3 cup instant mashed potatoes
- 1 egg
- 2 tablespoons butter, unsalted
- 2 tablespoons white sugar
- 1/4 cup dry milk powder
- 1 teaspoon salt
- 3 cups bread flour
- 1 1/2 teaspoons active dry yeast
- 16 slices (2 pounds)
- 1 cup water
- 8/9 cup instant mashed potatoes
- 1 1/3 eggs
- 2 2/3 tablespoons butter, unsalted
- 2 2/3 tablespoons white sugar
- 1/3 cup dry milk powder
- 1 1/3 teaspoons salt
- 4 cups bread flour
- 2 teaspoons active dry yeast

Directions:

1.   Choose the size of loaf you would like to make and measure your ingredients.

2.   Add the ingredients to the bread pan in the order listed above (except yeast).

3.   Place the pan in the bread machine and close the lid.

4.   Turn on the bread maker. Select the Basic setting, then the loaf size, and finally the crust color. Start the cycle.

5.   When the cycle is finished and the bread is baked, carefully remove the pan from the machine. Use a potholder as the handle will be very hot. Let rest for a few minutes.

6.   Remove the bread from the pan and allow to cool on a wire rack for at least 10 minutes before slicing.

SPECIALITY FLOUR BREAD RECIPES

Gluten-free Buttermilk White Bread

Ingredients:

- 8 slices (1 pound)
- 2/3 cup buttermilk
- 1/3 cup water
- 2/3 teaspoon apple cider vinegar or rice vinegar
- 2 2/3 tablespoons butter or margarine, cut into pieces
- 2 2/3 large egg whites, beaten until foamy
- 2/3 cup white rice flour
- 2/3 cup brown rice flour
- 1/2 cup potato starch flour
- 1/6 cup tapioca flour
- 2 tablespoons light or dark brown sugar
- 2/3 tablespoon plus 1/3 teaspoon xanthan gum
- 1 teaspoon salt
- 2/3 tablespoon plus 2/3 teaspoon SAF yeast or 2/3 tablespoon plus 1/3 teaspoon machine yeast
- 12 slices (1 ½ pounds)
- 1 cup buttermilk
- 1/2 cup water
- 1 teaspoon apple cider vinegar or rice vinegar
- 4 tablespoons butter or margarine, cut into pieces
- 4 large egg whites, beaten until foamy
- 1 cup white rice flour
- 1 cup brown rice flour
- 3/4 cup potato starch flour
- 1/4 cup tapioca flour
- 3 tablespoons light or dark brown sugar
- 1 tablespoon plus 1/2 teaspoon xanthan gum
- 11/2 teaspoons salt
- 1 tablespoon plus 1 teaspoon SAF yeast or 1 tablespoon plus 1/2 teaspoon machine yeast
- 16 slices (2 pounds)
- 1 1/3 cups buttermilk
- 2/3 cup water
- 1 1/3 teaspoons apple cider vinegar or rice vinegar
- 5 1/3 tablespoons butter or margarine, cut into pieces
- 5 1/3 large egg whites, beaten until foamy
- 1 1/3 cups white rice flour
- 1 1/3 cups brown rice flour
- 1 cup potato starch flour
- 1/3 cup tapioca flour
- 4 tablespoons light or dark brown sugar
- 1 1/3 tablespoons plus 2/3 teaspoon xanthan gum
- 2 teaspoons salt
- 1 1/3 tablespoons plus 1 1/3 teaspoons SAF yeast or 1 1/3 tablespoons plus 2/3 teaspoon machine yeast

Directions:

1. Choose the size of loaf you would like to make and measure your ingredients.

2. Add the ingredients to the bread pan in the order listed above.

3. Place the pan in the bread machine and close the lid.

4. Turn on the bread maker. Select the Non-Gluten/Quick Yeast Bread setting, then the loaf size, and finally the crust color. Start the cycle.

5. When the cycle is finished and the bread is baked, carefully remove the pan from the machine. Use a potholder as the handle will be very hot. Let rest for a few minutes.

6. Remove the bread from the pan and allow to cool on a wire rack for at least 10 minutes before slicing.

Chickpea Flour Bread

Ingredients:

- 8 slices (1 pound)
- 3/4 cup evaporated milk or evaporated goat's milk
- 3/4 tablespoon olive oil
- 3/4 tablespoon honey
- 1 2/3 cups bread flour
- 1/3 cup chickpea flour
- 1 tablespoon gluten
- 1 teaspoon salt
- 1/6 teaspoon ground cinnamon
- 1/6 teaspoon crushed hot pepper flakes
- 1/2 tablespoon SAF yeast or 1/2 tablespoon plus 1/4 teaspoon bread machine yeast
- 12 slices (1½ pounds)
- 11/8 cups evaporated milk or evaporated goat's milk

- 1 tablespoon olive oil
- 1 tablespoon honey
- 21/2 cups bread flour
- 1/2 cup chickpea flour
- 1 tablespoon plus 2 teaspoons gluten
- 11/2 teaspoons salt
- 1/4 teaspoon ground cinnamon
- 1/4 teaspoon crushed hot pepper flakes
- 21/2 teaspoons SAF yeast or 1 tablespoon bread machine yeast
- 16 slices (2 pounds)
- 11/2 cups evaporated milk or evaporated goat's milk
- 11/2 tablespoons olive oil
- 11/2 tablespoons honey
- 31/3 cups bread flour
- 2/3 cup chickpea flour
- 2 tablespoons gluten
- 2 teaspoons salt
- 1/3 teaspoon ground cinnamon
- 1/3 teaspoon crushed hot pepper flakes
- 1 tablespoon SAF yeast or 1 tablespoon plus 1/2 teaspoon bread machine yeast

Directions:

1. Choose the size of loaf you would like to make and measure your ingredients.

2. Add the ingredients to the bread pan in the order listed above.

3. Place the pan in the bread machine and close the lid.

4. Turn on the bread maker. Select the Basic setting, then the loaf size, and finally the crust color. Start the cycle.

5. When the cycle is finished and the bread is baked, carefully remove the pan from the machine. Use a potholder as the handle will be very hot. Let rest for a few minutes.

6. Remove the bread from the pan and allow to cool on a wire rack for at least 10 minutes before slicing.

Brown Rice Flour Bread

Ingredients:

- 8 slices (1 pound)
- 5/6 cup water
- 1 1/2 tablespoons olive oil
- 1 1/2 tablespoons honey
- 7/8 cup whole wheat flour
- 5/8 cup bread flour
- 1/2 cup brown rice flour
- 1 tablespoon nonfat dry milk
- 1 tablespoon gluten
- 1 teaspoon salt
- 1/2 tablespoon plus 1/2 teaspoon SAF yeast or 1/2 tablespoon plus 3/4 teaspoon bread machine yeast
- 12 slices (1½ pounds)
- 11/4 cups water
- 2 tablespoons olive oil
- 2 tablespoons honey
- 11/4 cups whole wheat flour
- 1 cup bread flour
- 3/4 cup brown rice flour
- 11/2 tablespoons nonfat dry milk
- 11/2 tablespoons gluten
- 11/2 teaspoons salt
- 1 tablespoon SAF yeast or 1 tablespoon plus 1/2 teaspoon bread machine yeast
- 16 slices (2 pounds)
- 12/3 cups water
- 3 tablespoons olive oil
- 3 tablespoons honey
- 13/4 cups whole wheat flour
- 11/4 cups bread flour
- 1 cup brown rice flour
- 2 tablespoons nonfat dry milk
- 2 tablespoons gluten
- 2 teaspoons salt
- 1 tablespoon plus 1 teaspoon SAF yeast or 1 tablespoon plus 11/2 teaspoons bread machine yeast

Directions:

1. Choose the size of loaf you would like to make and measure your ingredients.

2. Add the ingredients to the bread pan in the order listed above.

3. Place the pan in the bread machine and close the lid.

4. Turn on the bread maker. Select the Whole Wheat setting, then the loaf size, and finally the crust color. Start the cycle.

5. When the cycle is finished and the bread is baked, carefully remove the pan from the machine. Use a potholder as the handle will be very hot. Let rest for a few minutes.

6. Remove the bread from the pan and allow to cool on a wire rack for at least 10 minutes before slicing.

Gluten-free Ricotta Potato Bread

Ingredients:
- 8 slices (1 pound)
- 11/3 cups water
- 3/4 cup ricotta cheese
- 1 teaspoon apple cider vinegar or rice vinegar
- 3 tablespoons vegetable or canola oil
- 3 large eggs, broken into a measuring cup to equal 3/4 cup (add water if needed)
- 21/4 cups white rice flour
- 1/2 cup instant potato flakes
- 1/3 cup potato starch flour
- 1/3 cup tapioca flour
- 1/2 cup dry buttermilk powder or nonfat dry milk
- 3 tablespoons sugar or powdered fructose
- 2 teaspoons xanthan gum
- 11/2 teaspoons salt
- 3/4 teaspoon baking soda
- 21/4 teaspoons SAF yeast or 23/4 teaspoons bread machine yeast
- 12 slices (1 ½ pounds)
- 2 cups water
- 1 1/8 cups ricotta cheese
- 1 1/2 teaspoons apple cider vinegar or rice vinegar
- 4 1/2 tablespoons vegetable or canola oil
- 4 1/2 large eggs, broken into a measuring cup to equal 3/4 cup (add water if needed)
- 3 3/8 cups white rice flour
- 3/4 cup instant potato flakes
- 1/2 cup potato starch flour
- 1/2 cup tapioca flour
- 3/4 cup dry buttermilk powder or nonfat dry milk
- 4 1/2 tablespoons sugar or powdered fructose
- 3 teaspoons xanthan gum
- 2 1/4 teaspoons salt
- 1 1/8 teaspoons baking soda
- 3 3/8 teaspoons SAF yeast or 4 teaspoons bread machine yeast
- 16 slices (2 pounds)
- 2 2/3 cups water
- 1 1/2 cups ricotta cheese
- 2 teaspoons apple cider vinegar or rice vinegar
- 6 tablespoons vegetable or canola oil
- 6 large eggs, broken into a measuring cup to equal 1 1/2 cups (add water if needed)
- 4 1/2 cups white rice flour
- 1 cup instant potato flakes
- 2/3 cup potato starch flour
- 2/3 cup tapioca flour
- 1 cup dry buttermilk powder or nonfat dry milk
- 6 tablespoons sugar or powdered fructose
- 4 teaspoons xanthan gum
- 3 teaspoons salt
- 1 1/2 teaspoons baking soda
- 4 1/2 teaspoons SAF yeast or 5 1/2 teaspoons bread machine yeast

Directions:
1. Choose the size of loaf you would like to make and measure your ingredients.
2. Add the ingredients to the bread pan in the order listed above.
3. Place the pan in the bread machine and close the lid.
4. Turn on the bread maker. Select the Non-Gluten/Quick Yeast Bread setting, then the loaf size, and finally the crust color. Start the cycle.
5. When the cycle is finished and the bread is baked, carefully remove the pan from the machine. Use a potholder as the handle will be very hot. Let rest for a few minutes.
6. Remove the bread from the pan and allow to cool on a wire rack for at least 10 minutes before slicing.

Buckwheat-millet Bread

Ingredients:
- 8 slices (1 pound)
- 3/4 cup water
- 1 tablespoon unsalted butter, cut into pieces
- 1 1/2 tablespoons dark honey
- 1 3/4 cups bread flour

- 1/4 cup light buckwheat flour
- 1/4 cup whole millet
- 2/3 tablespoon gluten
- 1 teaspoon salt
- 1 1/4 teaspoons SAF yeast or 1/2 tablespoon bread machine yeast
- 12 slices (1½ pounds)
- 11/8 cups water
- 1 tablespoon unsalted butter, cut into pieces
- 2 tablespoons dark honey
- 22/3 cups bread flour
- 1/3 cup light buckwheat flour
- 1/3 cup whole millet
- 1 tablespoon gluten
- 11/2 teaspoons salt
- 2 teaspoons SAF yeast or 21/2 teaspoons bread machine yeast
- 16 slices (2 pounds)
- 11/2 cups water
- 2 tablespoons unsalted butter, cut into pieces
- 3 tablespoons dark honey
- 31/2 cups bread flour
- 1/2 cup light buckwheat flour
- 1/2 cup whole millet
- 1 tablespoon plus 1 teaspoon gluten
- 2 teaspoons salt
- 21/2 teaspoons SAF yeast or 1 tablespoon bread machine yeast

Directions:

1. Choose the size of loaf you would like to make and measure your ingredients.

2. Add the ingredients to the bread pan in the order listed above.

3. Place the pan in the bread machine and close the lid.

4. Turn on the bread maker. Select the Basic setting, then the loaf size, and finally the crust color. Start the cycle.

5. When the cycle is finished and the bread is baked, carefully remove the pan from the machine. Use a potholder as the handle will be very hot. Let rest for a few minutes.

6. Remove the bread from the pan and allow to cool on a wire rack for at least 10 minutes before slicing.

Cornmeal And Hominy Bread

Ingredients:

- 8 slices (1 pound)
- 1/3 cup milk
- 1/3 cup water
- 1 1/2 tablespoons olive oil
- 2 cups bread flour
- 1/3 cup yellow cornmeal
- 1 1/2 tablespoons sugar
- 1 tablespoon gluten
- 1 teaspoon salt
- 1 1/4 teaspoons SAF yeast or 1/2 tablespoon bread machine yeast
- 3/4 cup canned hominy, rinsed
- 12 slices (1½ pounds)
- 1/2 cup milk
- 1/2 cup water
- 2 tablespoons olive oil
- 3 cups bread flour
- 1/2 cup yellow cornmeal
- 2 tablespoons sugar
- 11/2 tablespoons gluten
- 11/2 teaspoons salt
- 2 teaspoons SAF yeast or 21/2 teaspoons bread machine yeast
- 1 cup canned hominy, rinsed
- 16 slices (2 pounds)
- 2/3 cup milk
- 2/3 cup water
- 3 tablespoons olive oil
- 4 cups bread flour
- 2/3 cup yellow cornmeal
- 3 tablespoons sugar
- 2 tablespoons gluten
- 2 teaspoons salt
- 21/2 teaspoons SAF yeast or 1 tablespoon bread machine yeast
- 11/2 cups canned hominy, rinsed

Directions:

1. Choose the size of loaf you would like to make and measure your ingredients.

2. Add the ingredients to the bread pan in the order listed above (except the hominy).

3. Place the pan in the bread machine and close the lid.

4. Turn on the bread maker. Select the Basic/Fruit and Nut setting, then the loaf size, and finally the crust color. Start the cycle.

5. When the machine beeps, or between Knead 1 and Knead 2, add the hominy.

6. When the cycle is finished and the bread is baked, carefully remove the pan from the machine. Use a potholder as the handle will be very hot. Let rest for a few minutes.

7. Remove the bread from the pan and allow to cool on a wire rack for at least 10 minutes before slicing.

Chestnut Flour Bread

Ingredients:
- 8 slices (1 pound)
- 9/16 cup fat-free milk
- 1/2 large egg
- 2 tablespoons butter or margarine, cut into pieces
- 1 5/8 cups bread flour
- 3/8 cup chestnut flour
- 1 1/2 tablespoons dark brown sugar
- 1 1/2 tablespoons minced pecans
- 2/3 tablespoon gluten
- 1 teaspoon salt
- 1 1/4 teaspoons SAF yeast or 1/2 tablespoon bread machine yeast
- 12 slices (1½ pounds)
- 7/8 cup fat-free milk
- 1 large egg
- 3 tablespoons butter or margarine, cut into pieces
- 21/2 cups bread flour
- 1/2 cup chestnut flour
- 2 tablespoons dark brown sugar
- 2 tablespoons minced pecans
- 1 tablespoon gluten
- 11/2 teaspoons salt
- 2 teaspoons SAF yeast or 21/2 teaspoons bread machine yeast
- 16 slices (2 pounds)
- 11/8 cups fat-free milk
- 1 large egg
- 4 tablespoons butter or margarine, cut into pieces

- 31/4 cups bread flour
- 3/4 cup chestnut flour
- 3 tablespoons dark brown sugar
- 3 tablespoons minced pecans
- 1 tablespoon plus 1 teaspoon gluten
- 2 teaspoons salt
- 21/2 teaspoons SAF yeast or 1 tablespoon bread machine yeast

Directions:
1. Choose the size of loaf you would like to make and measure your ingredients.

2. Add the ingredients to the bread pan in the order listed above.

3. Place the pan in the bread machine and close the lid.

4. Turn on the bread maker. Select the Basic setting, then the loaf size, and finally the crust color. Start the cycle.

5. When the cycle is finished and the bread is baked, carefully remove the pan from the machine. Use a potholder as the handle will be very hot. Let rest for a few minutes.

6. Remove the bread from the pan and allow to cool on a wire rack for at least 10 minutes before slicing.

Quinoa Bread

Ingredients:
- 8 slices (1 pound)
- 1/3 cup water
- 1/3 cup buttermilk
- 3/8 cup firm-packed cooked quinoa (see cooking information here)
- 1 1/2 tablespoons sesame oil
- 1 1/2 tablespoons honey
- 2 cups bread flour
- 2/3 tablespoon gluten
- 1 teaspoon salt
- 1 1/4 teaspoons SAF yeast or 1/2 tablespoon bread machine yeast
- 12 slices (1½ pounds)
- 1/2 cup water
- 1/2 cup buttermilk
- 1/2 cup firm-packed cooked quinoa (see cooking information here)

- 2 tablespoons sesame oil
- 2 tablespoons honey
- 3 cups bread flour
- 1 tablespoon gluten
- 11/2 teaspoons salt
- 2 teaspoons SAF yeast or 21/2 teaspoons bread machine yeast
- 16 slices (2 pounds)
- 2/3 cup water
- 2/3 cup buttermilk
- 3/4 cup firm-packed cooked quinoa (see cooking information here)
- 3 tablespoons sesame oil
- 3 tablespoons honey
- 4 cups bread flour
- 1 tablespoon plus 1 teaspoon gluten
- 2 teaspoons salt
- 21/2 teaspoons SAF yeast or 1 tablespoon bread machine yeast

Directions:

1. Choose the size of loaf you would like to make and measure your ingredients.
2. Add the ingredients to the bread pan in the order listed above.
3. Place the pan in the bread machine and close the lid.
4. Turn on the bread maker. Select the Basic setting, then the loaf size, and finally the crust color. Start the cycle.
5. When the cycle is finished and the bread is baked, carefully remove the pan from the machine. Use a potholder as the handle will be very hot. Let rest for a few minutes.
6. Remove the bread from the pan and allow to cool on a wire rack for at least 10 minutes before slicing.

Gluten-free Mock Light Rye

Ingredients:

- 8 slices (1 pound)
- 5/6 cups water
- 2 tablespoons dark molasses
- 2/3 teaspoon apple cider or rice vinegar
- 1/6 cup vegetable or canola oil
- 2 large eggs, broken into a measuring cup to equal 1 1/8 cup (add water if needed)
- 1 1/2 cups white rice flour
- 2/3 cup brown rice flour
- 1/3 cup nonfat dry milk
- 1/6 cup dark brown sugar
- 2/3 tablespoon xanthan gum
- 2/3 tablespoon plus 2/3 teaspoon caraway seeds
- Grated zest of 2/3 large orange or 1 1/3 teaspoons dried orange peel
- 2 1/4 teaspoons salt
- 1 1/2 teaspoons SAF yeast or 1 5/6 teaspoons bread machine yeast
- 12 slices (1 ½ pounds)
- 11/4 cups water
- 3 tablespoons dark molasses
- 1 teaspoon apple cider or rice vinegar
- 1/4 cup vegetable or canola oil
- 3 large eggs, broken into a measuring cup to equal 3/4 cup (add water if needed)
- 21/4 cups white rice flour
- 7/8 cup brown rice flour
- 1/2 cup nonfat dry milk
- 1/4 cup dark brown sugar
- 1 tablespoon xanthan gum
- 1 tablespoon plus 1 teaspoon caraway seeds
- Grated zest of 1 large orange or 2 teaspoons dried orange peel
- 11/2 teaspoons salt
- 21/4 teaspoons SAF yeast or 23/4 teaspoons bread machine yeast
- 16 slices (2 pounds)
- 1 2/3 cups water
- 4 tablespoons dark molasses
- 1 1/3 teaspoons apple cider or rice vinegar
- 1/3 cup vegetable or canola oil
- 4 large eggs, broken into a measuring cup to equal 2 1/4 cup (add water if needed)
- 3 cups white rice flour
- 1 1/3 cups brown rice flour
- 2/3 cup nonfat dry milk
- 1/3 cup dark brown sugar
- 1 1/3 tablespoons xanthan gum
- 1 1/3 tablespoons plus 1 1/3 teaspoons caraway seeds

- Grated zest of 1 1/3 large oranges or 2 2/3 teaspoons dried orange peel
- 4 1/2 teaspoons salt
- 3 teaspoons SAF yeast or 3 2/3 teaspoons bread machine yeast

Directions:

1. Choose the size of loaf you would like to make and measure your ingredients.
2. Add the ingredients to the bread pan in the order listed above.
3. Place the pan in the bread machine and close the lid.
4. Turn on the bread maker. Select the Non-Gluten/Quick Yeast Bread setting, then the loaf size, and finally the crust color. Start the cycle.
5. When the cycle is finished and the bread is baked, carefully remove the pan from the machine. Use a potholder as the handle will be very hot. Let rest for a few minutes.
6. Remove the bread from the pan and allow to cool on a wire rack for at least 10 minutes before slicing.

Teff Honey Bread

Ingredients:

- 8 slices (1 pound)
- 3/4 cup water
- 1 1/2 tablespoons vegetable oil
- 1 1/2 tablespoons honey
- 1 5/8 cups bread flour
- 3/8 cup ivory or dark teff flour
- 2/3 tablespoon gluten
- 1 teaspoon salt
- 1/2 tablespoon SAF yeast or 1/2 tablespoon plus 1/4 teaspoon bread machine yeast
- 12 slices (1½ pounds)
- 11/8 cups water
- 2 tablespoons vegetable oil
- 2 tablespoons honey
- 21/4 cups bread flour
- 3/4 cup ivory or dark teff flour
- 1 tablespoon plus 1 teaspoon gluten
- 11/2 teaspoons salt
- 21/2 teaspoons SAF yeast or 1 tablespoon bread machine yeast

- 16 slices (2 pounds)
- 11/2 cups water
- 3 tablespoons vegetable oil
- 3 tablespoons honey
- 31/4 cups bread flour
- 3/4 cup ivory or dark teff flour
- 1 tablespoon plus 2 teaspoons gluten
- 2 teaspoons salt
- 1 tablespoon SAF yeast or 1 tablespoon plus 1/2 teaspoon bread machine yeast

Directions:

1. Choose the size of loaf you would like to make and measure your ingredients.
2. Add the ingredients to the bread pan in the order listed above.
3. Place the pan in the bread machine and close the lid.
4. Turn on the bread maker. Select the Basic setting, then the loaf size, and finally the crust color. Start the cycle.
5. When the cycle is finished and the bread is baked, carefully remove the pan from the machine. Use a potholder as the handle will be very hot. Let rest for a few minutes.
6. Remove the bread from the pan and allow to cool on a wire rack for at least 10 minutes before slicing.

Polenta-sunflower-millet Bread

Ingredients:

- 8 slices (1 pound)
- 3/4 cup water
- 1/8 cup honey
- 1 1/2 tablespoons sunflower seed oil
- 1 5/8 cups bread flour
- 3/8 cup whole wheat flour
- 1/6 cup polenta
- 1/8 cup whole raw millet
- 1/8 cup raw sunflower seeds
- 1 tablespoon gluten
- 1 teaspoon salt
- 1 1/4 teaspoons SAF yeast or 1/2 tablespoon bread machine yeast
- 12 slices (1½ pounds)
- 11/8 cups water

- 3 tablespoons honey
- 2 tablespoons sunflower seed oil
- 21/2 cups bread flour
- 1/2 cup whole wheat flour
- 1/4 cup polenta
- 3 tablespoons whole raw millet
- 3 tablespoons raw sunflower seeds
- 11/2 tablespoons gluten
- 11/2 teaspoons salt
- 13/4 teaspoons SAF yeast or 21/4 teaspoons bread machine yeast
- 16 slices (2 pounds)
- 11/2 cups water
- 1/4 cup honey
- 3 tablespoons sunflower seed oil
- 31/4 cups bread flour
- 3/4 cup whole wheat flour
- 1/3 cup polenta
- 1/4 cup whole raw millet
- 1/4 cup raw sunflower seeds
- 2 tablespoons gluten
- 2 teaspoons salt
- 21/2 teaspoons SAF yeast or 1 tablespoon bread machine yeast

Directions:

1. Choose the size of loaf you would like to make and measure your ingredients.

2. Add the ingredients to the bread pan in the order listed above.

3. Place the pan in the bread machine and close the lid.

4. Turn on the bread maker. Select the Basic/Whole Wheat setting, then the loaf size, and finally the crust color. Start the cycle.

5. When the cycle is finished and the bread is baked, carefully remove the pan from the machine. Use a potholder as the handle will be very hot. Let rest for a few minutes.

6. Remove the bread from the pan and allow to cool on a wire rack for at least 10 minutes before slicing.

Polenta-chestnut Bread

Ingredients:
- 8 slices (1 pound)

- 2/3 cup buttermilk
- 1/8 cup dark honey
- 1/8 cup olive oil
- 1 1/2 cups bread flour
- 3/8 cup chestnut flour
- 1/4 cup polenta
- 1 tablespoon gluten
- 1 teaspoon salt
- 1 3/8 teaspoons SAF yeast or 1/2 tablespoon plus 1/8 teaspoon bread machine yeast
- 12 slices (1½ pounds)
- 1 cup plus 1 tablespoon buttermilk
- 3 tablespoons dark honey
- 3 tablespoons olive oil
- 21/3 cups bread flour
- 1/2 cup chestnut flour
- 1/3 cup polenta
- 11/2 tablespoons gluten
- 11/2 teaspoons salt
- 21/4 teaspoons SAF yeast or 23/4 teaspoons bread machine yeast
- 16 slices (2 pounds)
- 11/3 cups buttermilk
- 1/4 cup dark honey
- 1/4 cup olive oil
- 3 cups bread flour
- 3/4 cup chestnut flour
- 1/2 cup polenta
- 2 tablespoons gluten
- 2 teaspoons salt
- 23/4 teaspoons SAF yeast or 1 tablespoon plus 1/4 teaspoon bread machine yeast

Directions:

1. Choose the size of loaf you would like to make and measure your ingredients.

2. Add the ingredients to the bread pan in the order listed above.

3. Place the pan in the bread machine and close the lid.

4. Turn on the bread maker. Select the Basic setting, then the loaf size, and finally the crust color. Start the cycle.

5. When the cycle is finished and the bread is baked, carefully remove the pan from the machine. Use a

potholder as the handle will be very hot. Let rest for a few minutes.

6. Remove the bread from the pan and allow to cool on a wire rack for at least 10 minutes before slicing.

Cornmeal Honey Bread

Ingredients:
- 8 slices (1 pound)
- 3/4 cup water
- 1 tablespoon unsalted butter cut into pieces
- 1/8 cup honey
- 1 3/4 cups bread flour
- 1/4 cup yellow cornmeal
- 1/4 cup dry buttermilk powder
- 1/2 tablespoon plus 1 teaspoons gluten
- 3/4 teaspoon salt
- 1 1/4 teaspoons SAF yeast or 1/2 tablespoon bread machine yeast
- 12 slices (1½ pounds)
- 11/8 cups water
- 11/2 tablespoons unsalted butter, cut into pieces
- 3 tablespoons honey
- 22/3 cups bread flour
- 1/3 cup yellow cornmeal
- 1/3 cup dry buttermilk powder
- 1 tablespoon plus 1 teaspoon gluten
- 1 teaspoon salt
- 13/4 teaspoons SAF yeast or 21/4 teaspoons bread machine yeast
- 16 slices (2 pounds)
- 11/2 cups water
- 2 tablespoons unsalted butter cut into pieces
- 1/4 cup honey
- 31/2 cups bread flour
- 1/2 cup yellow cornmeal
- 1/2 cup dry buttermilk powder
- 1 tablespoon plus 2 teaspoons gluten
- 11/2 teaspoons salt
- 21/2 teaspoons SAF yeast or 1 tablespoon bread machine yeast

Directions:
1. Choose the size of loaf you would like to make and measure your ingredients.

2. Add the ingredients to the bread pan in the order listed above.

3. Place the pan in the bread machine and close the lid.

4. Turn on the bread maker. Select the Basic setting, then the loaf size, and finally the crust color. Start the cycle.

5. When the cycle is finished and the bread is baked, carefully remove the pan from the machine. Use a potholder as the handle will be very hot. Let rest for a few minutes.

6. Remove the bread from the pan and allow to cool on a wire rack for at least 10 minutes before slicing.

Gluten-free Almond And Dried Fruit Holiday Bread

Ingredients:
- 8 slices (1 pound)
- For the dough:
- 11/2 cups water
- 2 teaspoons almond extract
- 1 teaspoon apple cider vinegar or rice vinegar
- 3 large eggs, broken into a measuring cup to equal 3/4 cup (add water if needed)
- 2 cups white rice flour
- 1/2 cup potato starch flour
- 1/2 cup tapioca flour or arrowroot
- 1/2 cup dry buttermilk powder or nonfat dry milk
- 1/3 cup sugar or 3 tablespoons powdered fructose
- 1 tablespoon xanthan gum
- 11/2 teaspoons ground cardamom
- 1/2 teaspoon ground mace or nutmeg
- Grated zest of 1 lemon or 1 teaspoon dried lemon peel
- 11/2 teaspoons salt
- 21/2 teaspoons SAF yeast or 1 tablespoon bread machine yeast
- 1/2 cup mixed dried fruit bits
- 2 tablespoons currants
- 1/3 cup toasted slivered almonds
- For the lemon glaze:
- 1 cup sifted confectioners' sugar
- 1 tablespoon melted butter or margarine
- 2 to 3 tablespoons fresh lemon juice, heated

- 12 slices (1 ½ pounds)
- For the dough:
- 2 1/4 cups water
- 3 teaspoons almond extract
- 1 1/2 teaspoons apple cider vinegar or rice vinegar
- 4 1/2 large eggs, broken into a measuring cup to equal 3/4 cup (add water if needed)
- 3 cups white rice flour
- 3/4 cup potato starch flour
- 3/4 cup tapioca flour or arrowroot
- 3/4 cup dry buttermilk powder or nonfat dry milk
- 1/2 cup sugar or 4 1/2 tablespoons powdered fructose
- 1 1/2 tablespoons xanthan gum
- 2 1/4 teaspoons ground cardamom
- 3/4 teaspoon ground mace or nutmeg
- Grated zest of 1 1/2 lemons or 1 1/2 teaspoons dried lemon peel
- 2 1/4 teaspoons salt
- 3 3/4 teaspoons SAF yeast or 1 1/2 tablespoons bread machine yeast
- 3/4 cup mixed dried fruit bits
- 3 tablespoons currants
- 1/2 cup toasted slivered almonds
- For the lemon glaze:
- 1 cup sifted confectioners' sugar
- 1 tablespoon melted butter or margarine
- 2 to 3 tablespoons fresh lemon juice, heated
- 16 slices (2 pounds)
- For the dough:
- 3 cups water
- 4 teaspoons almond extract
- 2 teaspoons apple cider vinegar or rice vinegar
- 6 large eggs, broken into a measuring cup to equal 3/4 cup (add water if needed)
- 4 cups white rice flour
- 1 cup potato starch flour
- 1 cup tapioca flour or arrowroot
- 1 cup dry buttermilk powder or nonfat dry milk
- 2/3 cup sugar or 6 tablespoons powdered fructose
- 2 tablespoons xanthan gum
- 3 teaspoons ground cardamom
- 1 teaspoon ground mace or nutmeg
- Grated zest of 2 lemons or 2 teaspoons dried lemon peel
- 3 teaspoons salt
- 5 teaspoons SAF yeast or 2 tablespoons bread machine yeast
- 1 cup mixed dried fruit bits
- 4 tablespoons currants
- 2/3 cup toasted slivered almonds
- For the lemon glaze:
- 1 cup sifted confectioners' sugar
- 1 tablespoon melted butter or margarine
- 2 to 3 tablespoons fresh lemon juice, heated

Directions:

1. Choose the size of loaf you would like to make and measure your ingredients.

2. Add the ingredients to the bread pan in the order listed above (except the raisins).

3. Place the pan in the bread machine and close the lid.

4. Turn on the bread maker. Select the Non-Gluten/Quick Yeast Bread setting, then the loaf size, and finally the crust color. Start the cycle.

5. Set a kitchen timer for 5 minutes. When the timer rings, open the lid and add the dried fruit and almonds.

6. When the cycle is finished and the bread is baked, carefully remove the pan from the machine. Use a potholder as the handle will be very hot. Let rest for a few minutes.

7. Remove the bread from the pan and allow to cool on a wire rack for at least 10 minutes before slicing.

8. To make the lemon glaze, combine the confectioners' sugar, butter, and lemon juice in a small bowl. Immediately pour over the top of the loaf, letting it dribble down the sides. Let cool to room temperature before slicing.

Wild Rice Bread

Ingredients:
- 8 slices (1 pound)
- 3/4 cup water
- 1/4 cup raw wild rice
- 1 1/2 tablespoons walnut oil
- 1/2 tablespoon light brown sugar
- 1 3/4 cups bread flour

- 1/4 cup pumpernickel rye flour
- 2/3 tablespoon gluten
- 1 teaspoon salt
- 1 1/8 teaspoons SAF yeast or 1 3/8 teaspoons bread machine yeast
- 12 slices (1½ pounds)
- 11/8 cups water
- 1/3 cup raw wild rice
- 21/2 tablespoons walnut oil
- 2 teaspoons light brown sugar
- 23/4 cups bread flour
- 1/3 cup pumpernickel rye flour
- 1 tablespoon plus 1 teaspoon gluten
- 11/2 teaspoons salt
- 2 teaspoons SAF yeast or 21/2 teaspoons bread machine yeast
- 16 slices (2 pounds)
- 11/2 cups water
- 1/2 cup raw wild rice
- 3 tablespoons walnut oil
- 1 tablespoon light brown sugar
- 31/2 cups bread flour
- 1/2 cup pumpernickel rye flour
- 1 tablespoon plus 2 teaspoons gluten
- 2 teaspoons salt
- 21/4 teaspoons SAF yeast or 23/4 teaspoons bread machine yeast

Directions:

1. Choose the size of loaf you would like to make and measure your ingredients.

2. Heat the water to a boil in a medium saucepan. Add the rice. Cover and simmer over low heat for 30 to 45 minutes, until the rice is tender. Strain the remaining cooking liquid into a 2-cup measure and add enough extra water to equal the original amount in the pan (11/8 cups for the 11/2-pound loaf or 11/2 cups for the 2-pound loaf). Set the liquid and rice aside separately to cool.

3. Add the ingredients to the bread pan in the order listed above (except the rice).

4. Place the pan in the bread machine and close the lid.

5. Turn on the bread maker. Select the Basic/Fruit and Nut setting, then the loaf size, and finally the crust color. Start the cycle. (This recipe is not suitable for use with the Delay Timer.)

6. When the machine beeps, or between Knead 1 and Knead 2, add the rice.

7. When the cycle is finished and the bread is baked, carefully remove the pan from the machine. Use a potholder as the handle will be very hot. Let rest for a few minutes.

8. Remove the bread from the pan and allow to cool on a wire rack for at least 10 minutes before slicing.

Low-gluten White Spelt Bread

Ingredients:

- 8 slices (1 pound)
- 2/3 cup water
- 1/6 cup apple juice concentrate, thawed
- 1 tablespoon canola oil or soft butter
- 4 1/2 cups white spelt flour
- 1/6 cup oat bran or cornmeal
- 2/3 tablespoon full-fat soy flour
- 5/6 teaspoon salt
- 1 2/3 teaspoons SAF yeast or 2/3 tablespoon bread machine yeast
- 12 slices (1 ½ pounds)
- 1 cup water
- 1/4 cup apple juice concentrate, thawed
- 11/2 tablespoons canola oil or soft butter
- 3 cups white spelt flour
- 1/4 cup oat bran or cornmeal
- 1 tablespoon full-fat soy flour
- 11/4 teaspoons salt
- 21/2 teaspoons SAF yeast or 1 tablespoon bread machine yeast
- 16 slices (2 pounds)
- 1 1/3 cups water
- 1/3 cup apple juice concentrate, thawed
- 2 tablespoons canola oil or soft butter
- 9 cups white spelt flour
- 1/3 cup oat bran or cornmeal
- 1 1/3 tablespoons full-fat soy flour
- 1 2/3 teaspoons salt
- 1 1 /9 teaspoons SAF yeast or 1 1/3 tablespoons bread machine yeast

Directions:

1. Choose the size of loaf you would like to make and measure your ingredients.

2. Add the ingredients to the bread pan in the order listed above.

3. Place the pan in the bread machine and close the lid.

4. Turn on the bread maker. Select the Basic setting, then the loaf size, and finally the crust color. Start the cycle.

5. Test the dough ball, and add 1 to 2 teaspoons spelt flour or water as needed, but leave the dough moist and slightly tacky.

6. When the cycle is finished and the bread is baked, carefully remove the pan from the machine. Use a potholder as the handle will be very hot. Let rest for a few minutes.

7. Remove the bread from the pan and allow to cool on a wire rack for at least 10 minutes before slicing.

Barley Bread

Ingredients:

*   8 slices (1 pound)
*   3/4 cup water
*   1 1/2 tablespoons light brown sugar
*   1 1/2 tablespoons vegetable oil
*   1 1/2 cups bread flour
*   1/3 cup barley flour
*   1/6 cup whole wheat flour
*   1/8 cup dry buttermilk powder
*   1 tablespoon gluten
*   3/4 teaspoon ground cinnamon
*   1 teaspoon salt
*   1 1/4 teaspoons SAF yeast or 1/2 tablespoon bread machine yeast
*   12 slices (1½ pounds)
*   1 cup plus 3 tablespoons water
*   2 tablespoons light brown sugar
*   2 tablespoons vegetable oil
*   21/4 cups bread flour
*   1/2 cup barley flour
*   1/4 cup whole wheat flour
*   3 tablespoons dry buttermilk powder
*   1 tablespoon plus 2 teaspoons gluten

*   1 teaspoon ground cinnamon
*   11/2 teaspoons salt
*   21/4 teaspoons SAF yeast or 23/4 teaspoons bread machine yeast
*   16 slices (2 pounds)
*   11/2 cups water
*   3 tablespoons light brown sugar
*   3 tablespoons vegetable oil
*   3 cups bread flour
*   2/3 cup barley flour
*   1/3 cup whole wheat flour
*   1/4 cup dry buttermilk powder
*   2 tablespoons gluten
*   11/2 teaspoons ground cinnamon
*   2 teaspoons salt
*   21/2 teaspoons SAF yeast or 1 tablespoon bread machine yeast

Directions:

1. Choose the size of loaf you would like to make and measure your ingredients.

2. Add the ingredients to the bread pan in the order listed above.

3. Place the pan in the bread machine and close the lid.

4. Turn on the bread maker. Select the Basic/Whole Wheat setting, then the loaf size, and finally the crust color. Start the cycle.

5. When the cycle is finished and the bread is baked, carefully remove the pan from the machine. Use a potholder as the handle will be very hot. Let rest for a few minutes.

6. Remove the bread from the pan and allow to cool on a wire rack for at least 10 minutes before slicing.

Cornell Bread

Ingredients:

*   8 slices (1 pound)
*   3/4 cup water
*   1 1/2 tablespoons canola oil
*   1 1/2 tablespoons honey
*   1 1/2 tablespoons dark brown sugar
*   1/2 large egg
*   1 cup whole wheat flour
*   3/4 cup bread flour

- 1/4 cup full-fat soy flour
- 1 tablespoon wheat germ
- 1/6 cup nonfat dry milk
- 1 tablespoon gluten
- 1 teaspoon salt
- 1/2 tablespoon SAF yeast or 1/2 tablespoon plus 1/4 teaspoon bread machine yeast
- 12 slices (1½ pounds)
- 11/8 cups water
- 2 tablespoons canola oil
- 2 tablespoons honey
- 2 tablespoons dark brown sugar
- 1 large egg
- 11/2 cups whole wheat flour
- 1 cup plus 2 tablespoons bread flour
- 1/3 cup full-fat soy flour
- 11/2 tablespoons wheat germ
- 1/4 cup nonfat dry milk
- 11/2 tablespoons gluten
- 11/2 teaspoons salt
- 21/2 teaspoons SAF yeast or 1 tablespoon bread machine yeast
- 16 slices (2 pounds)
- 11/2 cups water
- 3 tablespoons canola oil
- 3 tablespoons honey
- 3 tablespoons dark brown sugar
- 1 large egg
- 2 cups whole wheat flour
- 11/2 cups bread flour
- 1/2 cup full-fat soy flour
- 2 tablespoons wheat germ
- 1/3 cup nonfat dry milk
- 2 tablespoons gluten
- 2 teaspoons salt
- 1 tablespoon SAF yeast or 1 tablespoon plus 1/2 teaspoon bread machine yeast

Directions:

1. Choose the size of loaf you would like to make and measure your ingredients.

2. Add the ingredients to the bread pan in the order listed above.

3. Place the pan in the bread machine and close the lid.

4. Turn on the bread maker. Select the Whole Wheat setting, then the loaf size, and finally the crust color. Start the cycle.

5. When the cycle is finished and the bread is baked, carefully remove the pan from the machine. Use a potholder as the handle will be very hot. Let rest for a few minutes.

6. Remove the bread from the pan and allow to cool on a wire rack for at least 10 minutes before slicing.

Orange-buckwheat Bread

Ingredients:

- 8 slices (1 pound)
- 2/3 cup buttermilk
- 1/2 large egg
- 1 1/2 tablespoons unsalted butter, cut into pieces
- 1 1/2 cups bread flour
- 1/2 cup whole wheat flour
- 1/4 cup light buckwheat flour
- 1 1/2 tablespoons dark brown sugar
- Grated zest of 1/2 large orange
- 2/3 tablespoon gluten
- 1 teaspoon salt
- 1 1/4 teaspoons SAF yeast or 1/2 tablespoon bread machine yeast
- 12 slices (1½ pounds)
- 1 cup buttermilk
- 1 large egg
- 2 tablespoons unsalted butter, cut into pieces
- 2 cups bread flour
- 3/4 cup whole wheat flour
- 1/3 cup light buckwheat flour
- 2 tablespoons dark brown sugar
- Grated zest of 1 large orange
- 1 tablespoon gluten
- 11/2 teaspoons salt
- 21/4 teaspoons SAF yeast or 23/4 teaspoons bread machine yeast
- 16 slices (2 pounds)
- 11/3 cups buttermilk
- 1 large egg
- 3 tablespoons unsalted butter, cut into pieces
- 3 cups bread flour

- 1 cup whole wheat flour
- 1/2 cup light buckwheat flour
- 3 tablespoons dark brown sugar
- Grated zest of 1 large orange
- 1 tablespoon plus 1 teaspoon gluten
- 2 teaspoons salt
- 21/2 teaspoons SAF yeast or 1 tablespoon bread machine yeast

Directions:

1. Choose the size of loaf you would like to make and measure your ingredients.

2. Add the ingredients to the bread pan in the order listed above.

3. Place the pan in the bread machine and close the lid.

4. Turn on the bread maker. Select the Basic setting, then the loaf size, and finally the crust color. Start the cycle.

5. When the cycle is finished and the bread is baked, carefully remove the pan from the machine. Use a potholder as the handle will be very hot. Let rest for a few minutes.

6. Remove the bread from the pan and allow to cool on a wire rack for at least 10 minutes before slicing.

Gluten-free Chickpea-, Rice-, And Tapioca-flour Bread

Ingredients:

- 8 slices (1 pound)
- 5/6 cups water
- 2/3 teaspoon apple cider vinegar or rice vinegar
- 2 tablespoons maple syrup
- 2 tablespoons olive oil
- 2 large eggs, broken into a measuring cup to equal 1/2 cup (add water if needed)
- 2/3 cup chickpea flour
- 2/3 cup brown rice flour
- 1/3 cup cornstarch
- 1/3 cup tapioca flour
- 1/3 cup nonfat dry milk
- 1 1/3 tablespoons light brown sugar
- 2/3 tablespoon plus 2/3 teaspoon xanthan gum

- 1 teaspoon salt
- 1 1/2 teaspoons SAF yeast or 1 5/6 teaspoons bread machine yeast
- 12 slices (1 ½ pounds)
- 11/4 cups water
- 1 teaspoon apple cider vinegar or rice vinegar
- 3 tablespoons maple syrup
- 3 tablespoons olive oil
- 3 large eggs, broken into a measuring cup to equal 3/4 cup (add water if needed)
- 1 cup chickpea flour
- 1 cup brown rice flour
- 1/2 cup cornstarch
- 1/2 cup tapioca flour
- 1/2 cup nonfat dry milk
- 2 tablespoons light brown sugar
- 1 tablespoon plus 1 teaspoon xanthan gum
- 11/2 teaspoons salt
- 21/4 teaspoons SAF yeast or 23/4 teaspoons bread machine yeast
- 16 slices (2 pounds)
- 11/4 cups water
- 1 teaspoon apple cider vinegar or rice vinegar
- 3 tablespoons maple syrup
- 3 tablespoons olive oil
- 3 large eggs, broken into a measuring cup to equal 3/4 cup (add water if needed)
- 1 cup chickpea flour
- 1 cup brown rice flour
- 1/2 cup cornstarch
- 1/2 cup tapioca flour
- 1/2 cup nonfat dry milk
- 2 tablespoons light brown sugar
- 1 tablespoon plus 1 teaspoon xanthan gum
- 11/2 teaspoons salt
- 21/4 teaspoons SAF yeast or 23/4 teaspoons bread machine yeast

Directions:

1. Choose the size of loaf you would like to make and measure your ingredients.

2. Add the ingredients to the bread pan in the order listed above.

3. Place the pan in the bread machine and close the lid.

4. Turn on the bread maker. Select the Non-Gluten/Quick Yeast Bread setting, then the loaf size, and finally the crust color. Start the cycle.

5. When the cycle is finished and the bread is baked, carefully remove the pan from the machine. Use a potholder as the handle will be very hot. Let rest for a few minutes.

6. Remove the bread from the pan and allow to cool on a wire rack for at least 10 minutes before slicing.

MULTIGRAIN BREAD RECIPES

Bran Packed Healthy Bread

Ingredients:
- 8 slices (1 pound)
- ¾ cup milk at 80 degrees F
- 1½ tablespoons melted butter, cooled
- 2 tablespoons sugar
- 1 teaspoon salt
- ¼ cup wheat bran
- 1¾ cups white bread flour
- 1 teaspoon instant yeast
- 12 slices (1 ½ pounds)
- 1 1/8 cups milk at 80 degrees F
- 2 1/4 tablespoons melted butter, cooled
- 3 tablespoons sugar
- 1 1/2 teaspoons salt
- 3/8 cup wheat bran
- 2 5/8 cups white bread flour
- 1 1/2 teaspoons instant yeast
- 16 slices (2 pounds)
- 1 1/2 cups milk at 80 degrees F
- 3 tablespoons melted butter, cooled
- 4 tablespoons sugar
- 2 teaspoons salt
- 1/2 cup wheat bran
- 3 1/2 cups white bread flour
- 2 teaspoons instant yeast

Directions:

1. Choose the size of loaf you would like to make and measure your ingredients.

2. Add the ingredients to the bread pan in the order listed above.

3. Place the pan in the bread machine and close the lid.

4. Turn on the bread maker. Select the White/Basic setting, then the loaf size, and finally the crust color. Start the cycle.

5. When the cycle is finished and the bread is baked, carefully remove the pan from the machine. Use a potholder as the handle will be very hot. Let rest for a few minutes.

6. Remove the bread from the pan and allow to cool on a wire rack for at least 10 minutes before slicing.

Classic Whole Wheat Bread

Ingredients:
- 8 slices (1 pound)
- 1/2 cup lukewarm water
- 1/4 cup unsalted butter, melted
- 1 egg, at room temperature
- 1 teaspoon table salt
- 1/8 cup sugar
- 3/4 cup whole-wheat flour
- 1 1/4 cups white bread flour
- 1 1/8 teaspoons bread machine yeast
- 12 slices (1 ½ pounds)
- ¾ cup lukewarm water
- ⅓ cup unsalted butter, melted
- 2 eggs, at room temperature
- 1½ teaspoons table salt
- 3 tablespoons sugar
- 1 cup whole-wheat flour
- 2 cups white bread flour
- 1⅔ teaspoons bread machine yeast
- 16 slices (2 pounds)
- 1 cup lukewarm water
- ½ cup unsalted butter, melted
- 2 eggs, at room temperature
- 2 teaspoons table salt
- ¼ cup sugar
- 1½ cups whole-wheat flour
- 2½ cups white bread flour
- 2¼ teaspoons bread machine yeast

Directions:

1. Choose the size of loaf you would like to make and measure your ingredients.

2. Add the ingredients to the bread pan in the order listed above.

3. Place the pan in the bread machine and close the lid.

4. Turn on the bread maker. Select the Whole Wheat/ Wholegrain or White/Basic setting, wither one will work

well for this recipe. Then select the loaf size, and finally the crust color. Start the cycle.

5. When the cycle is finished and the bread is baked, carefully remove the pan from the machine. Use a potholder as the handle will be very hot. Let rest for a few minutes.

6. Remove the bread from the pan and allow to cool on a wire rack for at least 10 minutes before slicing.

Light Whole Wheat Bread

Ingredients:
- 8 slices (1 pound)
- 2/3 cup water
- 1/2 large egg
- 1 1/4 tablespoons vegetable or nut oil
- 1 5/8 cups bread flour
- 3/8 cup whole wheat flour
- 2 tablespoons dry buttermilk powder
- 1 1/4 tablespoons dark brown sugar
- 1/2 tablespoon plus 1/2 teaspoon gluten
- 1 teaspoon salt
- 1 1/4 teaspoons SAF yeast or 1/2 tablespoon bread machine yeast
- 12 slices (1 ½ pounds)
- 11/2-POUND LOAF
- 1 cup water
- 1 large egg
- 2 tablespoons vegetable or nut oil
- 21/2 cups bread flour
- 1/2 cup whole wheat flour
- 3 tablespoons dry buttermilk powder
- 2 tablespoons dark brown sugar
- 1 tablespoon gluten
- 11/2 teaspoons salt
- 2 teaspoons SAF yeast or 21/2 teaspoons bread machine yeast
- 16 slices (2 pounds)
- 11/3 cups water
- 1 large egg
- 21/2 tablespoons vegetable or nut oil
- 31/4 cups bread flour
- 3/4 cup whole wheat flour
- 4 tablespoons dry buttermilk powder

- 21/2 tablespoons dark brown sugar
- 1 tablespoon plus 1 teaspoon gluten
- 2 teaspoons salt
- 21/2 teaspoons SAF yeast or 1 tablespoon bread machine yeast

Directions:
1. Choose the size of loaf you would like to make and measure your ingredients.
2. Add the ingredients to the bread pan in the order listed above.
3. Place the pan in the bread machine and close the lid.
4. Turn on the bread maker. Select the Basic setting, then the loaf size, and finally the crust color. Start the cycle.
5. When the cycle is finished and the bread is baked, carefully remove the pan from the machine. Use a potholder as the handle will be very hot. Let rest for a few minutes.
6. Remove the bread from the pan and allow to cool on a wire rack for at least 10 minutes before slicing.

Old-fashioned Sesame-wheat Bread

Ingredients:
- 8 slices (1 pound)
- 3/8 cup water
- 3/8 cup milk
- 1 1/2 tablespoons butter, cut into pieces
- 1 1/2 cups bread flour
- 1/2 cup whole wheat flour
- 1 1/2 tablespoons light or dark brown sugar
- 1/2 tablespoon plus 1 teaspoon sesame seeds
- 1/2 tablespoon plus 1 teaspoon gluten
- 1 teaspoon salt
- 1 1/8 teaspoons SAF yeast or 1 3/8 teaspoons bread machine yeast
- 12 slices (1 ½ pounds)
- 3/4 cup water
- 3/8 cup milk
- 2 tablespoons butter, cut into pieces
- 21/4 cups bread flour
- 3/4 cup whole wheat flour
- 2 tablespoons light or dark brown sugar
- 1 tablespoon sesame seeds

- 1 tablespoon plus 1 teaspoon gluten
- 11/2 teaspoons salt
- 2 teaspoons SAF yeast or 21/2 teaspoons bread machine yeast
- 16 slices (2 pounds)
- 3/4 cup water
- 3/4 cup milk
- 3 tablespoons butter, cut into pieces
- 3 cups bread flour
- 1 cup whole wheat flour
- 3 tablespoons light or dark brown sugar
- 1 tablespoon plus 2 teaspoons sesame seeds
- 1 tablespoon plus 2 teaspoons gluten
- 2 teaspoons salt
- 21/4 teaspoons SAF yeast or 23/4 teaspoons bread machine yeast

Directions:

1. Choose the size of loaf you would like to make and measure your ingredients.
2. Add the ingredients to the bread pan in the order listed above.
3. Place the pan in the bread machine and close the lid.
4. Turn on the bread maker. Select the White/Basic setting, then the loaf size, and finally the crust color. Start the cycle.
5. When the cycle is finished and the bread is baked, carefully remove the pan from the machine. Use a potholder as the handle will be very hot. Let rest for a few minutes.
6. Remove the bread from the pan and allow to cool on a wire rack for at least 10 minutes before slicing.

Oat Quinoa Bread

Ingredients:

- 8 slices (1 pound)
- 2/3 cup lukewarm milk
- 3/8 cup cooked quinoa, cooled
- 2 1/2 tablespoons unsalted butter, melted
- 2 teaspoons sugar
- 2/3 teaspoon table salt
- 1 cup white bread flour
- 2 1/2 tablespoons quick oats
- 1/2 cup whole-wheat flour

- 1 teaspoon bread machine yeast
- 12 slices (1 ½ pounds)
- 1 cup lukewarm milk
- ⅔ cup cooked quinoa, cooled
- ¼ cup unsalted butter, melted
- 1 tablespoon sugar
- 1 teaspoon table salt
- 1½ cups white bread flour
- ¼ cup quick oats
- ¾ cup whole-wheat flour
- 1½ teaspoons bread machine yeast
- 16 slices (2 pounds)
- 1⅓ cups lukewarm milk
- ¾ cup cooked quinoa, cooled
- 5 tablespoons unsalted butter, melted
- 4 teaspoons sugar
- 1⅓ teaspoons table salt
- 2 cups white bread flour
- 5 tablespoons quick oats
- 1 cup whole-wheat flour
- 2 teaspoons bread machine yeast

Directions:

1. Choose the size of loaf you would like to make and measure your ingredients.
2. Add the ingredients to the bread pan in the order listed above.
3. Place the pan in the bread machine and close the lid.
4. Turn on the bread maker. Select the White/Basic setting, then the loaf size, and finally the crust color. Start the cycle.
5. When the cycle is finished and the bread is baked, carefully remove the pan from the machine. Use a potholder as the handle will be very hot. Let rest for a few minutes.
6. Remove the bread from the pan and allow to cool on a wire rack for at least 10 minutes before slicing.

Three-seed Whole Wheat Bread

Ingredients:

- 8 slices (1 pound)
- 5/6 cup water
- 1 1/2 tablespoons sunflower seed oil
- 1 cup bread flour

- 1 cup whole wheat flour
- 1/8 cup nonfat dry milk
- 1 1/2 tablespoons brown sugar
- 1/2 tablespoon plus 1/2 teaspoon gluten
- 3/4 teaspoon salt
- 1 1/4 teaspoon SAF yeast or 1/2 tablespoon bread machine yeast
- 1/4 cup raw sunflower seeds
- 1 1/4 tablespoon sesame seeds
- 1 1/4 teaspoon poppy seeds
- 12 slices (1 ½ pounds)
- 11/4 cups water
- 2 tablespoons sunflower seed oil
- 11/2 cups bread flour
- 11/2 cups whole wheat flour
- 3 tablespoons nonfat dry milk
- 2 tablespoons brown sugar
- 1 tablespoon gluten
- 1 teaspoon salt
- 2 teaspoons SAF yeast or 21/2 teaspoons bread machine yeast
- 1/3 cup raw sunflower seeds
- 2 tablespoons sesame seeds
- 2 teaspoons poppy seeds
- 16 slices (2 pounds)
- 12/3 cups water
- 3 tablespoons sunflower seed oil
- 2 cups bread flour
- 2 cups whole wheat flour
- 1/4 cup nonfat dry milk
- 3 tablespoons brown sugar
- 1 tablespoon plus 1 teaspoon gluten
- 11/2 teaspoons salt
- 21/2 teaspoons SAF yeast or 1 tablespoon bread machine yeast
- 1/2 cup raw sunflower seeds
- 21/2 tablespoons sesame seeds
- 21/2 teaspoons poppy seeds

Directions:

1. Choose the size of loaf you would like to make and measure your ingredients.
2. Add the ingredients to the bread pan in the order listed above (except the seeds).
3. Place the pan in the bread machine and close the lid.
4. Turn on the bread maker. Select the Basic/Whole Wheat setting, then the loaf size, and finally the crust color. Start the cycle. (This recipe is not suitable for use with the Delay Timer.)
5. When the machine beeps, or between Knead 1 and Knead 2, add all the seeds.
6. When the cycle is finished and the bread is baked, carefully remove the pan from the machine. Use a potholder as the handle will be very hot. Let rest for a few minutes.
7. Remove the bread from the pan and allow to cool on a wire rack for at least 10 minutes before slicing.

Sennebec Hill Bread

Ingredients:

- 8 slices (1 pound)
- 5/6 cup water
- 1/8 cup canola oil
- 1 1/2 tablespoons molasses
- 1 1/2 large egg yolks
- 1 1/8 cups bread flour
- 1/2 cup whole wheat flour
- 1/6 cup medium or dark rye flour
- 1 3/4 tablespoons rolled oats
- 1 3/4 tablespoons yellow cornmeal
- 1 3/4 tablespoons toasted wheat germ
- 1/6 cup nonfat dry milk
- 1 tablespoon gluten
- 1 teaspoon salt
- 12 slices (1½ pounds)
- 11/4 cups water
- 3 tablespoons canola oil
- 2 tablespoons molasses
- 2 large egg yolks
- 11/2 cups bread flour
- 3/4 cup whole wheat flour
- 1/2 cup medium or dark rye flour
- 3 tablespoons rolled oats
- 3 tablespoons yellow cornmeal
- 3 tablespoons toasted wheat germ
- 1/2 cup nonfat dry milk
- 11/2 tablespoons gluten

- 11/2 teaspoons salt
- 21/2 teaspoons SAF yeast or 1 tablespoon bread machine yeast
- 16 slices (2 pounds)
- 12/3 cups water
- 1/4 cup canola oil
- 3 tablespoons molasses
- 3 large egg yolks
- 21/4 cups bread flour
- 1 cup whole wheat flour
- 1/3 cup medium or dark rye flour
- 31/2 tablespoons rolled oats
- 31/2 tablespoons yellow cornmeal
- 31/2 tablespoons toasted wheat germ
- 1/3 cup nonfat dry milk
- 2 tablespoons gluten
- 2 teaspoons salt
- 1 tablespoon SAF yeast or 1 tablespoon plus 1/2 teaspoon bread machine yeast

Directions:

1. Choose the size of loaf you would like to make and measure your ingredients.

2. Add the ingredients to the bread pan in the order listed above.

3. Place the pan in the bread machine and close the lid.

4. Turn on the bread maker. Select the Whole Wheat setting, then the loaf size, and finally the crust color. Start the cycle.

5. When the cycle is finished and the bread is baked, carefully remove the pan from the machine. Use a potholder as the handle will be very hot. Let rest for a few minutes.

6. Remove the bread from the pan and allow to cool on a wire rack for at least 10 minutes before slicing.

Basic Seed Bread

Ingredients:
- 8 slices (1 pound)
- 3/4 cup lukewarm water
- 1 tablespoon unsalted butter, melted
- 1 tablespoon sugar
- 3/4 teaspoon table salt
- 1 5/8 cups white bread flour
- 3/8 cup ground chia seeds
- 2 tablespoons sesame seeds
- 1 teaspoon bread machine yeast
- 12 slices (1 ½ pounds)
- 1⅛ cups lukewarm water
- 1½ tablespoons unsalted butter, melted
- 1½ tablespoons sugar
- 1⅛ teaspoons table salt
- 2½ cups white bread flour
- ½ cup ground chia seeds
- 1½ tablespoons sesame seeds
- 1½ teaspoons bread machine yeast
- 16 slices (2 pounds)
- 1½ cups lukewarm water
- 2 tablespoons unsalted butter, melted
- 2 tablespoons sugar
- 1½ teaspoons table salt
- 3¼ cups white bread flour
- ¾ cup ground chia seeds
- 2 tablespoons sesame seeds
- 2 teaspoons bread machine yeast

Directions:

1. Choose the size of loaf you would like to make and measure your ingredients.

2. Add the ingredients to the bread pan in the order listed above.

3. Place the pan in the bread machine and close the lid.

4. Turn on the bread maker. Select the White/Basic setting, then the loaf size, and finally the crust color. Start the cycle.

5. When the cycle is finished and the bread is baked, carefully remove the pan from the machine. Use a potholder as the handle will be very hot. Let rest for a few minutes.

6. Remove the bread from the pan and allow to cool on a wire rack for at least 10 minutes before slicing.

Honey Wheat Berry Bread

Ingredients:
- 8 slices (1 pound)
- 3/8 cup wheat berries
- 1 1/2 tablespoons light or dark brown sugar
- 2/3 cup water

- 5/8 cup water
- 1/2 cup of the cooked and cooled wheat berries
- 1 1/2 tablespoons butter or margarine, cut into pieces
- 1/8 cup honey
- 1 cup bread flour
- 1 cup whole wheat flour
- 1 tablespoon gluten
- 1 teaspoon salt
- 1/2 tablespoon SAF yeast or 1/2 tablespoon plus 1/4 teaspoon bread machine yeast
- 12 slices (1½ pounds)
- 3/4 cup wheat berries
- 3 tablespoons light or dark brown sugar
- 11/3 cups water
- 1 cup water
- 2/3 cup of the cooked and cooled wheat berries
- 2 tablespoons butter or margarine, cut into pieces
- 3 tablespoons honey
- 11/2 cups bread flour
- 11/2 cups whole wheat flour
- 11/2 tablespoons gluten
- 11/2 teaspoons salt
- 21/2 teaspoons SAF yeast or 1 tablespoon bread machine yeast
- 16 slices (2 pounds)
- 3/4 cup wheat berries
- 3 tablespoons light or dark brown sugar
- 11/3 cups water
- 11/4 cups water
- 1 cup of the cooked and cooled wheat berries
- 3 tablespoons butter or margarine, cut into pieces
- 1/4 cup honey
- 2 cups bread flour
- 2 cups whole wheat flour
- 2 tablespoons gluten
- 2 teaspoons salt
- 1 tablespoon SAF yeast or 1 tablespoon plus 1/2 teaspoon bread machine yeast

Directions:

1. Choose the size of loaf you would like to make and measure your ingredients.

2. Combine the wheat berries, sugar, and 11/3 cups water in a saucepan. Bring to a boil. Reduce the heat to a simmer and partially cover. Simmer for 1 hour, until firm-chewy and slightly tender. Remove the mixture from the heat and let stand until room temperature, about 4 hours. You will have about 11/3 cups cooked wheat berries

3. Add the ingredients to the bread pan in the order listed above. (Store any extra cooked wheat berries in a covered container in the refrigerator up to 3 days or freeze them.)

4. Place the pan in the bread machine and close the lid.

5. Turn on the bread maker. Select the Basic setting, then the loaf size, and finally the crust color. Start the cycle.

6. When the cycle is finished and the bread is baked, carefully remove the pan from the machine. Use a potholder as the handle will be very hot. Let rest for a few minutes.

7. Remove the bread from the pan and allow to cool on a wire rack for at least 10 minutes before slicing.

Basic Bulgur Bread

Ingredients:
- 8 slices (1 pound)
- 1/4 cup lukewarm water
- 1/4 cup bulgur wheat
- 2/3 cup lukewarm milk
- 2/3 tablespoon unsalted butter, melted
- 2/3 tablespoon sugar
- 1/2 teaspoon table salt
- 2 cups bread flour
- 1 teaspoon bread machine yeast
- 12 slices (1 ½ pounds)
- ⅓ cup lukewarm water
- ⅓ cup bulgur wheat
- 1 cup lukewarm milk
- 1 tablespoon unsalted butter, melted
- 1 tablespoon sugar
- ¾ teaspoon table salt
- 3 cups bread flour
- 1½ teaspoons bread machine yeast
- 16 slices (2 pounds)

- ½ cup lukewarm water
- ½ cup bulgur wheat
- 1⅓ cups lukewarm milk
- 1⅓ tablespoons unsalted butter, melted
- 1⅓ tablespoons sugar
- 1 teaspoon table salt
- 4 cups bread flour
- 2 teaspoons bread machine yeast

Directions:

1. Choose the size of loaf you would like to make and measure your ingredients.

2. Add the water and bulgur wheat to the bread pan and set aside for 25–30 minutes for the bulgur wheat to soften.

3. Add the other ingredients to the bread pan in the order listed above.

4. Place the pan in the bread machine and close the lid.

5. Turn on the bread maker. Select the White/Basic setting, then the loaf size, and finally the crust color. Start the cycle.

6. When the cycle is finished and the bread is baked, carefully remove the pan from the machine. Use a potholder as the handle will be very hot. Let rest for a few minutes.

7. Remove the bread from the pan and allow to cool on a wire rack for at least 10 minutes before slicing.

Classic Corn Bread

Ingredients:
- 8 slices (1 pound)
- 2/3 cup lukewarm buttermilk
- 1/6 cup unsalted butter, melted
- 1 egg, at room temperature
- 1/6 cup sugar
- 3/4 teaspoon table salt
- 5/6 cup all-purpose flour
- 2/3 cup cornmeal
- 2/3 tablespoon baking powder
- 12 slices (1 ½ pounds)
- 1 cup lukewarm buttermilk
- ¼ cup unsalted butter, melted
- 2 eggs, at room temperature
- ¼ cup sugar

- 1 teaspoon table salt
- 1⅓ cups all-purpose flour
- 1 cup cornmeal
- 1 tablespoon baking powder
- 16 slices (2 pounds)
- 1⅓ cups lukewarm buttermilk
- ⅓ cup unsalted butter, melted
- 2 eggs, at room temperature
- ⅓ cup sugar
- 1½ teaspoons table salt
- 1⅔ cups all-purpose flour
- 1⅓ cups cornmeal
- 1⅓ tablespoon baking powder

Directions:

1. Choose the size of loaf you would like to make and measure your ingredients.

2. Add the ingredients to the bread pan in the order listed above.

3. Place the pan in the bread machine and close the lid.

4. Turn on the bread maker. Select the Quick/Rapid setting, then the loaf size, and finally the crust color. Start the cycle.

5. When the cycle is finished and the bread is baked, carefully remove the pan from the machine. Use a potholder as the handle will be very hot. Let rest for a few minutes.

6. Remove the bread from the pan and allow to cool on a wire rack for at least 10 minutes before slicing.

Dakota Bread

Ingredients:
- 8 slices (1 pound)
- 13/16 cup water
- 1 1/2 tablespoons canola oil
- 1 1/2 tablespoons honey
- 1 7/16 cups bread flour
- 1/2 cup whole wheat flour
- 1/6 cup raw bulgur cracked wheat
- 1/2 tablespoon gluten
- 1 teaspoon salt
- 1/6 cup raw sunflower seeds
- 1/6 cup raw pumpkin seeds, chopped
- 1 teaspoon sesame seeds

- 1 teaspoon poppy seeds
- 1 1/8 teaspoons SAF yeast or 1 3/8 teaspoons bread machine yeast
- 12 slices (1 ½ pounds)
- 11/4 cups water
- 2 tablespoons canola oil
- 2 tablespoons honey
- 21/4 cups bread flour
- 1/2 cup whole wheat flour
- 1/4 cup raw bulgur cracked wheat
- 2 teaspoons gluten
- 11/2 teaspoons salt
- 1/4 cup raw sunflower seeds
- 1/4 cup raw pumpkin seeds, chopped
- 2 teaspoons sesame seeds
- 11/2 teaspoons poppy seeds
- 2 teaspoons SAF yeast or 21/2 teaspoons bread machine yeast
- 16 slices (2 pounds)
- 15/8 cups water
- 3 tablespoons canola oil
- 3 tablespoons honey
- 27/8 cups bread flour
- 1 cup whole wheat flour
- 1/3 cup raw bulgur cracked wheat
- 1 tablespoon gluten
- 2 teaspoons salt
- 1/3 cup raw sunflower seeds
- 1/3 cup raw pumpkin seeds, chopped
- 2 teaspoons sesame seeds
- 2 teaspoons poppy seeds
- 21/4 teaspoons SAF yeast or 23/4 teaspoons bread machine yeast

Directions:

1. Choose the size of loaf you would like to make and measure your ingredients.

2. Add the ingredients to the bread pan in the order listed above.

3. Place the pan in the bread machine and close the lid.

4. Turn on the bread maker. Select the Basic setting, then the loaf size, and finally the crust color. Start the cycle.

5. When the cycle is finished and the bread is baked, carefully remove the pan from the machine. Use a potholder as the handle will be very hot. Let rest for a few minutes.

6. Remove the bread from the pan and allow to cool on a wire rack for at least 10 minutes before slicing.

White Whole Wheat Bread

Ingredients:

- 8 slices (1 pound)
- 13/16 cup water
- 1 1/2 tablespoons nut oil or olive oil
- 1/6 cup maple syrup
- 2 1/6 cups white whole wheat flour
- 3/4 tablespoon gluten
- 1 teaspoon salt
- 1 1/4 teaspoons SAF yeast or 1/2 tablespoon bread machine yeast
- 12 slices (1 ½ pounds)
- 11/4 cups water
- 2 tablespoons nut oil or olive oil
- 1/4 cup maple syrup
- 31/4 cups white whole wheat flour
- 1 tablespoon gluten
- 11/2 teaspoons salt
- 2 teaspoons SAF yeast or 21/2 teaspoons bread machine yeast
- 16 slices (2 pounds)
- 15/8 cups water
- 3 tablespoons nut oil or olive oil
- 1/3 cup maple syrup
- 41/3 cups white whole wheat flour
- 11/2 tablespoons gluten
- 2 teaspoons salt
- 21/2 teaspoons SAF yeast or 1 tablespoon bread machine yeast

Directions:

1. Choose the size of loaf you would like to make and measure your ingredients.

2. Add the ingredients to the bread pan in the order listed above.

3. Place the pan in the bread machine and close the lid.

4. Turn on the bread maker. Select the Whole Wheat setting, then the loaf size, and finally the crust color. Start the cycle.

5. When the cycle is finished and the bread is baked, carefully remove the pan from the machine. Use a potholder as the handle will be very hot. Let rest for a few minutes.

6. Remove the bread from the pan and allow to cool on a wire rack for at least 10 minutes before slicing.

Buttermilk Whole Wheat Bread

Ingredients:
- 8 slices (1 pound)
- 3/4 cup buttermilk
- 1 1/2 tablespoons canola oil
- 1 1/4 tablespoons maple syrup
- 1 cup whole wheat flour
- 1 cups bread flour
- 1/2 tablespoon plus 1 teaspoon gluten
- 1 teaspoon salt
- 1 1/8 teaspoons SAF yeast or 1 3/8 teaspoons bread machine yeast
- 12 slices (1 ½ pounds)
- 11/8 cups buttermilk
- 2 tablespoons canola oil
- 2 tablespoons maple syrup
- 11/2 cups whole wheat flour
- 11/2 cups bread flour
- 1 tablespoon plus 1 teaspoon gluten
- 11/2 teaspoons salt
- 2 teaspoons SAF yeast or 21/2 teaspoons bread machine yeast
- 16 slices (2 pounds)
- 11/2 cups buttermilk
- 3 tablespoons canola oil
- 21/2 tablespoons maple syrup
- 2 cups whole wheat flour
- 2 cups bread flour
- 1 tablespoon plus 2 teaspoons gluten
- 2 teaspoons salt
- 21/4 teaspoons SAF yeast or 23/4 teaspoons bread machine yeast

Directions:

1. Choose the size of loaf you would like to make and measure your ingredients.

2. Add the ingredients to the bread pan in the order listed above.

3. Place the pan in the bread machine and close the lid.

4. Turn on the bread maker. Select the Basic/Whole Wheat setting, then the loaf size, and finally the crust color. Start the cycle.

5. When the cycle is finished and the bread is baked, carefully remove the pan from the machine. Use a potholder as the handle will be very hot. Let rest for a few minutes.

6. Remove the bread from the pan and allow to cool on a wire rack for at least 10 minutes before slicing.

Oat Bran Nutmeg Bread

Ingredients:
- 8 slices (1 pound)
- 1/2 cup lukewarm water
- 1 1/2 tablespoons unsalted butter, melted
- 1/8 cup blackstrap molasses
- 1/4 teaspoon table salt
- 1 1/2 cups whole-wheat bread flour
- 1/8 teaspoon ground nutmeg
- 1/2 cup oat bran
- 1 1/8 teaspoons bread machine yeast
- 12 slices (1 ½ pounds)
- ¾ cup lukewarm water
- 2¼ tablespoons unsalted butter, melted
- 3 tablespoons blackstrap molasses
- ⅓ teaspoon table salt
- 2¼ cups whole-wheat bread flour
- ¼ teaspoon ground nutmeg
- ¾ cup oat bran
- 1⅔ teaspoons bread machine yeast
- 16 slices (2 pounds)
- 1 cup lukewarm water
- 3 tablespoons unsalted butter, melted
- ¼ cup blackstrap molasses
- ½ teaspoon table salt
- 3 cups whole-wheat bread flour
- ¼ teaspoon ground nutmeg
- 1 cup oat bran

- 2¼ teaspoons bread machine yeast

Directions:

1. Choose the size of loaf you would like to make and measure your ingredients.

2. Add the ingredients to the bread pan in the order listed above.

3. Place the pan in the bread machine and close the lid.

4. Turn on the bread maker. Select the Whole Wheat/Wholegrain setting, then the loaf size, and finally the crust color. Start the cycle.

5. When the cycle is finished and the bread is baked, carefully remove the pan from the machine. Use a potholder as the handle will be very hot. Let rest for a few minutes.

6. Remove the bread from the pan and allow to cool on a wire rack for at least 10 minutes before slicing.

Awesome Golden Corn Bread

Ingredients:

- 8 slices (1 pound)
- 1 cup buttermilk at 80 degrees F
- 2 whole eggs, at room temperature
- ¼ cup melted butter, cooled
- 1⅓ cups all-purpose flour
- 1 cup cornmeal
- ¼ cup sugar
- 1 tablespoon baking powder
- 1 teaspoon salt
- 12 slices (1 ½ pounds)
- 1 1/2 cups buttermilk at 80 degrees F
- 3 whole eggs, at room temperature
- 3/8 cup melted butter, cooled
- 2 cups all-purpose flour
- 1 1/2 cups cornmeal
- 3/8 cup sugar
- 1 1/2 tablespoons baking powder
- 1 1/2 teaspoons salt
- 16 slices (2 pounds)
- 2 cups buttermilk at 80 degrees F
- 4 whole eggs, at room temperature
- 1/2 cup melted butter, cooled
- 2 2/3 cups all-purpose flour
- 2 cups cornmeal

- 1/2 cup sugar
- 1/2 tablespoon baking powder
- 1/2 teaspoon salt

Directions:

1. Choose the size of loaf you would like to make and measure your ingredients.

2. Add buttermilk, butter, and eggs to the bread pan.

3. Place the pan in the bread machine and close the lid.

4. Turn on the bread maker. Select the Quick/Rapid setting, then the loaf size, and finally the crust color. Start the cycle.

5. While the wet ingredients are being mixed in the machine, take a small bowl and combine it in flour, cornmeal, sugar, baking powder, and salt.

6. After the first fast mix is done and the machine gives the signal, add dry ingredients.

7. When the cycle is finished and the bread is baked, carefully remove the pan from the machine. Use a potholder as the handle will be very hot. Let rest for a few minutes.

8. Remove the bread from the pan and allow to cool on a wire rack for at least 10 minutes before slicing.

Nine-grain Honey Bread

Ingredients:

- 8 slices (1 pound)
- 7/8 cup boiling water
- 1/3 cup 9-grain cereal
- 1/8 cup honey
- 2 tablespoons unsalted butter, cut into pieces
- 1 cup bread flour
- 2/3 cup whole wheat flour
- 1/3 cup dry buttermilk powder
- 1 tablespoon gluten
- 3/4 teaspoon salt
- 1/2 tablespoon SAF yeast or 1/2 tablespoon plus 1/4 teaspoon bread machine yeast
- 12 slices (1½ pounds)
- 11/4 cups boiling water
- 1/2 cup 9-grain cereal
- 3 tablespoons honey
- 3 tablespoons unsalted butter, cut into pieces
- 12/3 cups bread flour

- 1 cup whole wheat flour
- 1/3 cup dry buttermilk powder
- 11/2 tablespoons gluten
- 11/4 teaspoons salt
- 21/2 teaspoons SAF yeast or 1 tablespoon bread machine yeast
- 16 slices (2 pounds)
- 13/4 cups boiling water
- 2/3 cup 9-grain cereal
- 1/4 cup honey
- 4 tablespoons unsalted butter, cut into pieces
- 2 cups bread flour
- 11/3 cups whole wheat flour
- 2/3 cup dry buttermilk powder
- 2 tablespoons gluten
- 11/2 teaspoons salt
- 1 tablespoon SAF yeast or 1 tablespoon plus 1/2 teaspoon bread machine yeast

Directions:

1. Choose the size of loaf you would like to make and measure your ingredients.

2. Pour the boiling water over the cracked grain cereal in a bowl. Add the honey and butter. Let stand for 1 hour to soften the grains.

3. Add the ingredients to the bread pan in the order listed above. Adding the cereal and its soaking liquid as the liquid ingredients.

4. Place the pan in the bread machine and close the lid.

5. Turn on the bread maker. Select the Basic/Whole Wheat setting, then the loaf size, and finally the crust color. Start the cycle.

6. When the cycle is finished and the bread is baked, carefully remove the pan from the machine. Use a potholder as the handle will be very hot. Let rest for a few minutes.

7. Remove the bread from the pan and allow to cool on a wire rack for at least 10 minutes before slicing.

Tecate Ranch Whole Wheat Bread

Ingredients:

- 8 slices (1 pound)
- 7/8 cup water
- 1/8 cup canola oil

- 1 1/2 tablespoons honey
- 1 1/2 tablespoons molasses
- 2 1/4 cups whole wheat flour
- 1/4 cup wheat bran
- 1 3/4 tablespoons gluten
- 1/2 tablespoon plus 1/2 teaspoon poppy seeds
- 1 teaspoon salt
- 1/2 tablespoon plus 1/4 teaspoon SAF yeast or 1/2 tablespoon plus 1/2 teaspoon bread machine yeast
- 12 slices (1 ½ pounds)
- 11/3 cups water
- 3 tablespoons canola oil
- 2 tablespoons honey
- 2 tablespoons molasses
- 31/4 cups whole wheat flour
- 1/3 cup wheat bran
- 21/2 tablespoons gluten
- 1 tablespoon poppy seeds
- 11/2 teaspoons salt
- 1 tablespoon SAF yeast or 1 tablespoon plus 1/2 teaspoon bread machine yeast
- 16 slices (2 pounds)
- 13/4 cups water
- 1/4 cup canola oil
- 3 tablespoons honey
- 3 tablespoons molasses
- 41/2 cups whole wheat flour
- 1/2 cup wheat bran
- 31/2 tablespoons gluten
- 1 tablespoon plus 1 teaspoon poppy seeds
- 2 teaspoons salt
- 1 tablespoon plus 1/2 teaspoon SAF yeast or 1 tablespoon plus 1 teaspoon bread machine yeast

Directions:

1. Choose the size of loaf you would like to make and measure your ingredients.

2. Add the ingredients to the bread pan in the order listed above.

3. Place the pan in the bread machine and close the lid.

4. After 10 minutes, check the dough ball with your finger. It will be sticky. Add 1 to 2 tablespoons more flour. The dough will still be very sticky; Wait it to absorb the liquid during the rises. If you add too much

flour, the bread will be dense, rather than springy. If you don't add the extra flour as needed, the top can collapse.

5. Turn on the bread maker. Select the Whole Wheat setting, then the loaf size, and finally the crust color. Start the cycle.

6. When the cycle is finished and the bread is baked, carefully remove the pan from the machine. Use a potholder as the handle will be very hot. Let rest for a few minutes.

7. Remove the bread from the pan and allow to cool on a wire rack for at least 10 minutes before slicing.

Whole-grain Daily Bread

Ingredients:
- 8 slices (1 pound)
- 2/3 cup buttermilk
- 1/2 cup cooked whole grain of choice, firmly packed
- 1 1/2 tablespoons canola oil
- 1 1/2 tablespoons honey
- 1 2/3 cups bread flour
- 1/3 cup whole wheat flour
- 1/6 cup rolled oats
- 1/2 tablespoon plus 1/2 teaspoon gluten
- 1 teaspoon salt
- 1 1/4 teaspoons SAF yeast or 1/2 tablespoon bread machine yeast
- 12 slices (1½ pounds)
- 1 cup buttermilk
- 3/4 cup cooked whole grain of choice, firmly packed
- 2 tablespoons canola oil
- 2 tablespoons honey
- 21/2 cups bread flour
- 1/2 cup whole wheat flour
- 1/4 cup rolled oats
- 1 tablespoon gluten
- 11/2 teaspoons salt
- 2 teaspoons SAF yeast or 21/2 teaspoons bread machine yeast
- 16 slices (2 pounds)
- 11/3 cups buttermilk
- 1 cup cooked whole grain of choice, firmly packed
- 3 tablespoons canola oil
- 3 tablespoons honey

- 31/3 cups bread flour
- 2/3 cup whole wheat flour
- 1/3 cup rolled oats
- 1 tablespoon plus 1 teaspoon gluten
- 2 teaspoons salt
- 21/2 teaspoons SAF yeast or 1 tablespoon bread machine yeast

Directions:
1. Choose the size of loaf you would like to make and measure your ingredients.
2. Add the ingredients to the bread pan in the order listed above.
3. Place the pan in the bread machine and close the lid.
4. Turn on the bread maker. Select the Basic setting, then the loaf size, and finally the crust color. Start the cycle.
5. Reach in and touch the dough with your fingers, being careful to avoid the rotating blade. The dough ball will be quite soft. Add another tablespoon of flour if it is too sticky around the blade.
6. When the cycle is finished and the bread is baked, carefully remove the pan from the machine. Use a potholder as the handle will be very hot. Let rest for a few minutes.
7. Remove the bread from the pan and allow to cool on a wire rack for at least 10 minutes before slicing.

Multigrain Honey Bread

Ingredients:
- 8 slices (1 pound)
- 3/4 cup lukewarm water
- 1 tablespoon unsalted butter, melted
- 1/2 tablespoon honey
- 1/2 teaspoon table salt
- 3/4 cup multigrain flour
- 1 3/8 cups white bread flour
- 1 teaspoon bread machine yeast
- 12 slices (1 ½ pounds)
- 1⅛ cups lukewarm water
- 2 tablespoons unsalted butter, melted
- 1½ tablespoons honey
- 1½ teaspoons table salt
- 1⅛ cups multigrain flour

- 2 cups white bread flour
- 1½ teaspoons bread machine yeast
- 16 slices (2 pounds)
- 1½ cups lukewarm water
- 2 tablespoons unsalted butter, melted
- 1 tablespoon honey
- 1 teaspoon table salt
- 1½ cups multigrain flour
- 2¾ cups white bread flour
- 2 teaspoons bread machine yeast

Directions:

1. Choose the size of loaf you would like to make and measure your ingredients.

2. Add the ingredients to the bread pan in the order listed above.

3. Place the pan in the bread machine and close the lid.

4. Turn on the bread maker. Select the White/Basic setting, then the loaf size, and finally the crust color. Start the cycle.

5. When the cycle is finished and the bread is baked, carefully remove the pan from the machine. Use a potholder as the handle will be very hot. Let rest for a few minutes.

6. Remove the bread from the pan and allow to cool on a wire rack for at least 10 minutes before slicing.

Seven Grain Bread

Ingredients:
- 8 slices (1 pound)
- 1 1/3 cups warm water
- 1 tablespoon active dry yeast
- 3 tablespoons dry milk powder
- 2 tablespoons honey
- 2 teaspoons salt
- 1 whole egg
- 1 cup whole wheat flour
- 2½ cups bread flour
- ¾ cups 7-grain cereal
- 12 slices (1 ½ pounds)
- 2 cups warm water
- 1 1/2 tablespoons active dry yeast
- 4 1/2 tablespoons dry milk powder
- 3 tablespoons honey

- 3 teaspoons salt
- 1 1/2 whole eggs
- 1 1/2 cups whole wheat flour
- 3 3/4 cups bread flour
- 1 1/8 cups 7-grain cereal
- 16 slices (2 pounds)
- 2 2/3 cups warm water
- 2 tablespoons active dry yeast
- 6 tablespoons dry milk powder
- 4 tablespoons honey
- 4 teaspoons salt
- 2 whole eggs
- 2 cups whole wheat flour
- 5 cups bread flour
- 1 1/2 cups 7-grain cereal

Directions:

1. Choose the size of loaf you would like to make and measure your ingredients.

2. Add the ingredients to the bread pan in the order listed above.

3. Place the pan in the bread machine and close the lid.

4. Turn on the bread maker. Select the White/Basic setting, then the loaf size, and finally the crust color. Start the cycle.

5. When the cycle is finished and the bread is baked, carefully remove the pan from the machine. Use a potholder as the handle will be very hot. Let rest for a few minutes.

6. Remove the bread from the pan and allow to cool on a wire rack for at least 10 minutes before slicing.

Simple Dark Rye Loaf

Ingredients:
- 8 slices (1 pound)
- ⅔ cup water at 80 degrees F
- 1 tablespoon melted butter, cooled
- ¼ cup molasses
- ¼ teaspoon salt
- 1 tablespoon unsweetened cocoa powder
- ½ cup rye flour
- pinch of ground nutmeg
- 1¼ cups white bread flour
- 1⅛ teaspoons instant yeast

- 12 slices (1 ½ pounds)
- 1 cup water at 80 degrees F
- 1 1/2 tablespoons melted butter, cooled
- 3/8 cup molasses
- 3/8 teaspoon salt
- 1 1/2 tablespoons unsweetened cocoa powder
- 3/4 cup rye flour
- pinch of ground nutmeg
- 1 7/8 cups white bread flour
- 13/4 teaspoons instant yeast
- 16 slices (2 pounds)
- 1 1/3 cups water at 80 degrees F
- 2 tablespoons melted butter, cooled
- 1/2 cup molasses
- 1/2 teaspoon salt
- 2 tablespoons unsweetened cocoa powder
- 1 cup rye flour
- pinch of ground nutmeg
- 2 1/2 cups white bread flour
- 2 1/4 teaspoons instant yeast

Directions:

1. Choose the size of loaf you would like to make and measure your ingredients.

2. Add the ingredients to the bread pan in the order listed above.

3. Place the pan in the bread machine and close the lid.

4. Turn on the bread maker. Select the White/Basic setting, then the loaf size, and finally the crust color. Start the cycle.

5. When the cycle is finished and the bread is baked, carefully remove the pan from the machine. Use a potholder as the handle will be very hot. Let rest for a few minutes.

6. Remove the bread from the pan and allow to cool on a wire rack for at least 10 minutes before slicing.

Graham Indian Bread

Ingredients:

- 8 slices (1 pound)
- 2/3 cup buttermilk
- 1/6 cup water
- 1 1/2 tablespoons unsalted butter, cut into pieces
- 1 cup bread flour
- 5/8 cup graham flour
- 3/8 cup yellow cornmeal
- 1/8 cup sugar
- 1/2 tablespoon plus 1/2 teaspoon gluten
- 7/8 teaspoon salt
- 1 1/4 teaspoons SAF yeast or 1/2 tablespoon bread machine yeast
- 12 slices (1½ pounds)
- 1 cup buttermilk
- 1/4 cup water
- 2 tablespoons unsalted butter, cut into pieces
- 11/2 cups bread flour
- 1 cup graham flour
- 1/2 cup yellow cornmeal
- 3 tablespoons sugar
- 1 tablespoon gluten
- 11/4 teaspoons salt
- 2 teaspoons SAF yeast or 21/2 teaspoons bread machine yeast
- 16 slices (2 pounds)
- 11/3 cups buttermilk
- 1/3 cup water
- 3 tablespoons unsalted butter, cut into pieces
- 2 cups bread flour
- 11/4 cups graham flour
- 3/4 cup yellow cornmeal
- 1/4 cup sugar
- 1 tablespoon plus 1 teaspoon gluten
- 13/4 teaspoons salt
- 21/2 teaspoons SAF yeast or 1 tablespoon bread machine yeast

Directions:

1. Choose the size of loaf you would like to make and measure your ingredients.

2. Add the ingredients to the bread pan in the order listed above.

3. Place the pan in the bread machine and close the lid.

4. Turn on the bread maker. Select the Whole Wheat setting, then the loaf size, and finally the crust color. Start the cycle.

5. When the cycle is finished and the bread is baked, carefully remove the pan from the machine. Use a

potholder as the handle will be very hot. Let rest for a few minutes.

6. Remove the bread from the pan and allow to cool on a wire rack for at least 10 minutes before slicing.

Irish Potato Brown Bread

Ingredients:

- 8 slices (1 pound)
- 5/6 cup water
- 2 tablespoons butter, cut into pieces
- 1 1/2 tablespoons honey
- 1 1/4 cup whole wheat flour
- 3/4 cup bread flour
- 1/6 cup instant potato flakes
- 1 tablespoon gluten
- 1 teaspoon salt
- 1 1/4 teaspoon SAF yeast or 1/2 tablespoon bread machine yeast
- 12 slices (1 ½ pounds)
- 11/4 cups water
- 3 tablespoons butter, cut into pieces
- 2 tablespoons honey
- 2 cups whole wheat flour
- 1 cup bread flour
- 1/4 cup instant potato flakes
- 1 tablespoon plus 2 teaspoons gluten
- 11/2 teaspoons salt
- 2 teaspoons SAF yeast or 21/2 teaspoons bread machine yeast
- 16 slices (2 pounds)
- 12/3 cups water
- 4 tablespoons butter, cut into pieces
- 3 tablespoons honey
- 21/2 cups whole wheat flour
- 11/2 cups bread flour
- 1/3 cup instant potato flakes
- 2 tablespoons gluten
- 2 teaspoons salt
- 21/2 teaspoons SAF yeast or 1 tablespoon bread machine yeast

Directions:

1. Choose the size of loaf you would like to make and measure your ingredients.

2. Add the ingredients to the bread pan in the order listed above.

3. Place the pan in the bread machine and close the lid.

4. Turn on the bread maker. Select the Whole Wheat setting, then the loaf size, and finally the crust color. Start the cycle.

5. When the cycle is finished and the bread is baked, carefully remove the pan from the machine. Use a potholder as the handle will be very hot. Let rest for a few minutes.

6. Remove the bread from the pan and allow to cool on a wire rack for at least 10 minutes before slicing.

Scandinavian Light Rye

Ingredients:

- 8 slices (1 pound)
- 3/4 cup water
- 1 tablespoon canola oil
- 1 1/4 cups bread flour
- 3/4 cup medium rye flour
- 1 1/2 tablespoons brown sugar
- 1/2 tablespoon plus 1 teaspoon gluten
- 1 tablespoon caraway seeds
- 1 teaspoon salt
- 1/2 tablespoon SAF yeast or 1/2 tablespoon plus 1/4 teaspoon bread machine yeast
- 12 slices (1 ½ pounds)
- 11/8 cups water
- 11/2 tablespoons canola oil
- 17/8 cups bread flour
- 11/8 cups medium rye flour
- 2 tablespoons brown sugar
- 1 tablespoon plus 1 teaspoon gluten
- 11/2 tablespoons caraway seeds
- 11/2 teaspoons salt
- 21/2 teaspoons SAF yeast or 1 tablespoon bread machine yeast
- 16 slices (2 pounds)
- 11/2 cups water
- 2 tablespoons canola oil
- 21/2 cups bread flour
- 11/2 cups medium rye flour
- 3 tablespoons brown sugar

- 1 tablespoon plus 2 teaspoons gluten
- 2 tablespoons caraway seeds
- 2 teaspoons salt
- 1 tablespoon SAF yeast or 1 tablespoon plus 1/2 teaspoon bread machine yeast

Directions:

1. Choose the size of loaf you would like to make and measure your ingredients.
2. Add the ingredients to the bread pan in the order listed above.
3. Place the pan in the bread machine and close the lid.
4. Turn on the bread maker. Select the Basic setting, then the loaf size, and finally the crust color. Start the cycle.
5. When the cycle is finished and the bread is baked, carefully remove the pan from the machine. Use a potholder as the handle will be very hot. Let rest for a few minutes.
6. Remove the bread from the pan and allow to cool on a wire rack for at least 10 minutes before slicing.

British Hot Cross Buns

Ingredients:
- 8 slices (1 pound)
- 1/2 cup warm milk
- 2 tablespoons butter, unsalted
- 1/6 cup white sugar
- 1/3 teaspoon salt
- 2/3 egg
- 2/3 egg white
- 2 cups all-purpose flour
- 2/3 tablespoon active dry yeast
- 1/2 cup dried raisins
- 2/3 teaspoon ground cinnamon
- For Brushing:
- 1 egg yolk
- 2 tablespoons water
- For the Crosses:
- 2 tablespoons flour
- Cold water
- 1/2 tablespoon sugar
- 12 slices (1 ½ pounds)
- 3/4 cup warm milk
- 3 tablespoons butter, unsalted
- 1/4 cup white sugar
- 1/2 teaspoon salt
- 1 egg
- 1 egg white
- 3 cups all-purpose flour
- 1 tablespoon active dry yeast
- 3/4 cup dried raisins
- 1 teaspoon ground cinnamon
- For Brushing:
- 1 egg yolk
- 2 tablespoons water
- For the Crosses:
- 2 tablespoons flour
- Cold water
- 1/2 tablespoon sugar
- 16 slices (2 pounds)
- 1 cup warm milk
- 4 tablespoons butter, unsalted
- 1/3 cup white sugar
- 2/3 teaspoon salt
- 1 1/3 eggs
- 1 1/3 egg whites
- 4 cups all-purpose flour
- 1 1/3 tablespoons active dry yeast
- 1 cup dried raisins
- 1 1/3 teaspoons ground cinnamon
- For Brushing:
- 1 egg yolk
- 2 tablespoons water
- For the Crosses:
- 2 tablespoons flour
- Cold water
- 1/2 tablespoon sugar

Directions:
1. Choose the size of loaf you would like to make and measure your ingredients.
2. Add the first eight ingredients to the bread pan in the order listed above.
3. Place the pan in the bread machine and close the lid.
4. Turn on the bread maker. Select the Dough setting, then the loaf size, and finally the crust color. Start the cycle.
5. Add raisins and cinnamon 5 minutes before kneading cycle ends.
6. When the cycle is finished and the bread is baked, allow to rest in machine until doubled, about 30 minutes.
7. Punch down on a floured surface, cover, and let rest 10 minutes.
8. Shape into 12 balls and place in a greased 9-by-12-inch pan.
9. Cover and let rise in a warm place until doubled, about 35-40 minutes.
10. Mix egg yolk and 2 tablespoons water and baste each bun.
11. Mix the cross ingredients to form pastry.
12. Roll out pastry and cut into thin strips. Place across the buns to form crosses.
13. Bake at 375°F for 20 minutes.
14. Remove the bread from the pan and allow to cool on a wire rack for at least 10 minutes before slicing.

Italian Panettone

Ingredients:

- 8 slices (1 pound)
- 1/2 cup warm water
- 2 2/3 large egg yolks
- 1 1/3 teaspoons vanilla extract
- 1/3 cup sugar
- 2/3 teaspoon lemon zest
- 2/3 teaspoon orange zest
- 1/3 teaspoon salt
- 1/3 cup unsalted butter, softened and cut into pieces
- 2 1/6 cups unbleached flour
- 2/3 package bread machine yeast
- 1/3 cup golden raisins
- 1/3 cup raisins
- 1 egg white, slightly beaten
- 2 2/3 sugar cubes, crushed
- 12 slices (1 ½ pounds)
- 3/4 cup warm water
- 4 large egg yolks
- 2 teaspoons vanilla extract
- 1/2 cup sugar
- 1 teaspoon lemon zest
- 1 teaspoon orange zest
- 1/2 teaspoon salt
- 1/2 cup unsalted butter, softened and cut into pieces
- 3 1/4 cups unbleached flour
- 1 package bread machine yeast
- 1/2 cup golden raisins
- 1/2 cup raisins
- 1 egg white, slightly beaten
- 4 sugar cubes, crushed
- 16 slices (2 pounds)
- 1 cup warm water
- 5 1/3 large egg yolks
- 2 2/3 teaspoons vanilla extract
- 2/3 cup sugar
- 1 1/3 teaspoons lemon zest
- 1 1/3 teaspoons orange zest
- 2/3 teaspoon salt
- 2/3 cup unsalted butter, softened and cut into pieces
- 4 1/3 cups unbleached flour
- 1 1/3 packages bread machine yeast

- 2/3 cup golden raisins
- 2/3 cup raisins
- 2 egg whites, slightly beaten
- 5 1/3 sugar cubes, crushed

Directions:

1. Choose the size of loaf you would like to make and measure your ingredients.
2. Add the ingredients to the bread pan in the order listed above.
3. Lay pieces of butter around the outside of the pan on top of the flour.
4. Press a well into the flour and add the yeast.
5. Place the pan in the bread machine and close the lid.
6. Turn on the bread maker. Select the Dough setting, then the loaf size, and finally the crust color. Start the cycle.
7. At the second kneading cycle add golden raisins.
8. Let dough rise until doubled.
9. Prepare the pan/baking case: cut a circle of parchment paper to line the bottom of the 6-inch cake pan and spray with non-stick cooking spray.
10. Cut another piece of parchment to line the inside of the brown paper bag after you have cut the bottom out of the bag.
11. Fold the top edge down to form a cuff then spray the inside of the parchment with cooking spray. Place the paper case in the pan.
12. Punch the dough down and knead into a ball.
13. Add it to the paper-lined pan case and allow to rise until almost doubled.
14. Preheat the oven to 350°F.
15. Baste the top of the panettone dough with the beaten egg white and sprinkle with the crushed sugar cubes.
16. Bake for 30 minutes, then reduce heat to 325°F and bake another 30 minutes.
17. Remove from oven and allow to cool in pan for about 15 minutes, then cool on a rack until ready to serve.

Greek Easter Bread

Ingredients:

- 8 slices (1 pound)
- 1/3 cup fresh butter

- 1/2 cup milk
- 1/2 cup sugar
- 1/2 teaspoon mastic
- 1/4 teaspoon salt
- 1/2 package active dry yeast
- 1 1/2 eggs
- 2 1/2 cups strong yellow flour
- 1/2 egg, for brushing blended with 1 teaspoon water
- 12 slices (1 ½ pounds)
- 1/2 cup fresh butter
- 3/4 cup milk
- 3/4 cup sugar
- 3/4 teaspoon mastic
- 3/8 teaspoon salt
- 3/4 package active dry yeast
- 2 1/4 eggs
- 3 3/4 cups strong yellow flour
- 3/4 egg, for brushing blended with 1 1/2 teaspoons water
- 16 slices (2 pounds)
- 2/3 cup fresh butter
- 1 cup milk
- 1 cup sugar
- 1 teaspoon mastic
- 1/2 teaspoon salt
- 1 package active dry yeast
- 3 eggs
- 5 cups strong yellow flour
- 1 egg, for brushing blended with 2 teaspoons water

Directions:

1. Choose the size of loaf you would like to make and measure your ingredients.

2. Heat milk and butter until melted in a saucepan (do not boil). Add to the bread pan.

3. Add sugar and mastic to a food processor and blend. Add to the bread pan.

4. Add remaining ingredients to the bread pan.

5. Place the pan in the bread machine and close the lid.

6. Turn on the bread maker. Select the Dough setting, then the loaf size, and finally the crust color. Start the cycle.

7. When the cycle is finished and the bread is baked, leave the dough to rise for one hour.

8. Shape into 2 loaves, cover, and leave to rise for 50 more minutes.

9. Baste with egg wash.

10. Bake at 320°F for 30 to 40 minutes or until golden brown.

11. Remove the bread from the pan and allow to cool on a wire rack for at least 10 minutes before slicing.

Russian Rye Bread

Ingredients:

- 8 slices (1 pound)
- 1 1/4 cups warm water
- 1 3/4 cups rye flour
- 1 3/4 cups whole wheat flour
- 2 tablespoons malt (or beer kit mixture)
- 1 tablespoon molasses
- 2 tablespoons white vinegar
- 1 teaspoon salt
- 1/2 tablespoon coriander seeds
- 1/2 tablespoon caraway seeds
- 2 teaspoons active dry yeast
- 12 slices (1 ½ pounds)
- 1 7/8 cups warm water
- 2 5/8 cups rye flour
- 2 5/8 cups whole wheat flour
- 3 tablespoons malt (or beer kit mixture)
- 1 1/2 tablespoons molasses
- 3 tablespoons white vinegar
- 1 1/2 teaspoons salt
- 3/4 tablespoon coriander seeds
- 3/4 tablespoon caraway seeds
- 3 teaspoons active dry yeast
- 16 slices (2 pounds)
- 2 1/2 cups warm water
- 3 1/2 cups rye flour
- 3 1/2 cups whole wheat flour
- 4 tablespoons malt (or beer kit mixture)
- 2 tablespoons molasses
- 4 tablespoons white vinegar
- 2 teaspoons salt
- 1 tablespoon coriander seeds
- 1 tablespoon caraway seeds
- 2 teaspoons active dry yeast

Directions:

1. Choose the size of loaf you would like to make and measure your ingredients.

2. Mix dry ingredients together in a bowl, except for yeast.

3. Add wet ingredients to bread pan first; top with dry ingredients.

4. Make a well in the center of the dry ingredients and add the yeast.

5. Place the pan in the bread machine and close the lid.

6. Turn on the bread maker. Select the Basic setting, then the loaf size, and finally the crust color. Start the cycle.

7. When the cycle is finished and the bread is baked, carefully remove the pan from the machine. Use a potholder as the handle will be very hot. Let rest for a few minutes.

8. Remove the bread from the pan and allow to cool on a wire rack for at least 10 minutes before slicing.

Russian Black Bread

Ingredients:

- 8 slices (1 pound)
- 5/6 cup dark rye flour
- 1 2/3 cups unbleached flour
- 2/3 teaspoon instant coffee
- 1 1/3 tablespoons unsweetened cocoa powder
- 2/3 tablespoon whole caraway seeds
- 1/3 teaspoon dried minced onion
- 1/3 teaspoon fennel seeds
- 2/3 teaspoon sea salt
- 1 1/3 teaspoons active dry yeast
- 1 cup water, at room temperature
- 2/3 teaspoon sugar
- 1 tablespoon dark molasses
- 1 tablespoon apple cider vinegar
- 2 tablespoons vegetable oil
- 12 slices (1 ½ pounds)
- 1 1/4 cups dark rye flour
- 2 1/2 cups unbleached flour
- 1 teaspoon instant coffee
- 2 tablespoons unsweetened cocoa powder
- 1 tablespoon whole caraway seeds
- 1/2 teaspoon dried minced onion
- 1/2 teaspoon fennel seeds
- 1 teaspoon sea salt
- 2 teaspoons active dry yeast
- 1 1/3 cups water, at room temperature
- 1 teaspoon sugar
- 1 1/2 tablespoons dark molasses
- 1 1/2 tablespoons apple cider vinegar
- 3 tablespoons vegetable oil
- 16 slices (2 pounds)
- 1 2/3 cups dark rye flour
- 3 1/3 cups unbleached flour
- 1 1/3 teaspoons instant coffee
- 2 2/3 tablespoons unsweetened cocoa powder
- 1 1/3 tablespoons whole caraway seeds
- 2/3 teaspoon dried minced onion
- 2/3 teaspoon fennel seeds
- 1 1/3 teaspoons sea salt
- 2 2/3 teaspoons active dry yeast
- 2 cups water, at room temperature
- 1 1/3 teaspoons sugar
- 2 tablespoons dark molasses
- 2 tablespoons apple cider vinegar
- 4 tablespoons vegetable oil

Directions:

1. Choose the size of loaf you would like to make and measure your ingredients.

2. Mix dry ingredients together in a bowl, except for yeast.

3. Add wet ingredients to bread pan first; top with dry ingredients.

4. Make a well in the center of the dry ingredients and add the yeast.

5. Place the pan in the bread machine and close the lid.

6. Turn on the bread maker. Select the Basic setting, then the loaf size, and finally the crust color. Start the cycle.

7. When the cycle is finished and the bread is baked, carefully remove the pan from the machine. Use a potholder as the handle will be very hot. Let rest for a few minutes.

8. Remove the bread from the pan and allow to cool on a wire rack for at least 10 minutes before slicing.

Fiji Sweet Potato Bread

Ingredients:

- 8 slices (1 pound)
- 5/6 cup sweet potato, mashed
- 6 2/3 tablespoons canned coconut milk
- 2/3 teaspoon ginger, fresh grated
- 2/3 tablespoon lemon zest
- 1 1/3tablespoons honey
- 1 1/3 tablespoons olive oil
- 2 cups bread flour
- 2/3 teaspoon salt
- 1 1/2 teaspoons rapid rise yeast
- 12 slices (1 ½ pounds)
- 1 1/4 cups sweet potato, mashed
- 10 tablespoons canned coconut milk
- 1 teaspoon ginger, fresh grated
- 1 tablespoon lemon zest
- 2 tablespoons honey
- 2 tablespoons olive oil
- 3 cups bread flour
- 1 teaspoon salt
- 2 1/4 teaspoons rapid rise yeast
- 16 slices (2 pounds)
- 1 2/3 cups sweet potato, mashed
- 13 1/3 tablespoons canned coconut milk
- 1 1/3 teaspoons ginger, fresh grated
- 1 1/3 tablespoons lemon zest
- 2 2/3tablespoons honey
- 2 2/3 tablespoons olive oil
- 4 cups bread flour
- 1 1/3 teaspoons salt
- 3 teaspoons rapid rise yeast

Directions:

1. Choose the size of loaf you would like to make and measure your ingredients.

2. Add the ingredients to the bread pan in the order listed above (except yeast).

3. Make a well in the center of the dry ingredients and add the yeast.

4. Place the pan in the bread machine and close the lid.

5. Turn on the bread maker. Select the Basic setting, then the loaf size, and finally the crust color. Start the cycle.

6. When the cycle is finished and the bread is baked, carefully remove the pan from the machine. Use a potholder as the handle will be very hot. Let rest for a few minutes.

7. Remove the bread from the pan and allow to cool on a wire rack for at least 10 minutes before slicing.

Za'atar Bread

Ingredients:

- 8 slices (1 pound)
- 1/4 cup za'atar seasoning
- 1 1/3 tablespoons onion powder
- 2/3 cup warm water
- 1 1/3 tablespoons agave nectar
- 1/6 cup applesauce
- 2 cups bread flour
- 2/3 teaspoon salt
- 1 1/2 teaspoons rapid rise yeast
- 12 slices (1 ½ pounds)
- 1/3 cup za'atar seasoning
- 2 tablespoons onion powder
- 1 cup warm water
- 2 tablespoons agave nectar
- 1/4 cup applesauce
- 3 cups bread flour
- 1 teaspoon salt
- 2 1/4 teaspoons rapid rise yeast
- 16 slices (2 pounds)
- 1/2 cup za'atar seasoning
- 2 2/3 tablespoons onion powder
- 1 1/3 cups warm water
- 2 2/3 tablespoons agave nectar
- 1/3 cup applesauce
- 4 cups bread flour
- 1 1/3 teaspoons salt
- 3 teaspoons rapid rise yeast

Directions:

1. Choose the size of loaf you would like to make and measure your ingredients.

2. Add the ingredients to the bread pan in the order listed above (except yeast).

3. Make a well in the center of the dry ingredients and add the yeast.

4. Place the pan in the bread machine and close the lid.

5. Turn on the bread maker. Select the Basic setting, then the loaf size, and finally the crust color. Start the cycle.

6. When the cycle is finished and the bread is baked, carefully remove the pan from the machine. Use a potholder as the handle will be very hot. Let rest for a few minutes.

7. Remove the bread from the pan and allow to cool on a wire rack for at least 10 minutes before slicing.

Portuguese Corn Bread

Ingredients:
- 8 slices (1 pound)
- 1 cup yellow cornmeal
- 1 1/4 cups cold water, divided
- 1 1/2 teaspoons active dry yeast
- 1 1/2 cups bread flour
- 2 teaspoons sugar
- 3/4 teaspoon salt
- 1 tablespoon olive oil
- 12 slices (1 ½ pounds)
- 1 1/2 cup yellow cornmeal
- 1 7/8 cups cold water, divided
- 2 1/4 teaspoons active dry yeast
- 2 1/4 cups bread flour
- 3 teaspoons sugar
- 1 1/8 teaspoons salt
- 1 1/2 tablespoons olive oil
- 16 slices (2 pounds)
- 2 cups yellow cornmeal
- 2 1/2 cups cold water, divided
- 3 teaspoons active dry yeast
- 3 cups bread flour
- 4 teaspoons sugar
- 1 1/2 teaspoons salt
- 2 tablespoons olive oil

Directions:
1. Choose the size of loaf you would like to make and measure your ingredients.

2. Stir cornmeal into 3/4 cup of the cold water until lumps disappear.

3. Add cornmeal mixture and the remaining ingredients to the bread pan in the order listed above (except yeast).

4. Make a well in the center of the dry ingredients and add the yeast.

5. Place the pan in the bread machine and close the lid.

6. Turn on the bread maker. Select the Sweet Bread setting, then the loaf size, and finally the crust color. Start the cycle.

7. When the cycle is finished and the bread is baked, carefully remove the pan from the machine. Use a potholder as the handle will be very hot. Let rest for a few minutes.

8. Remove the bread from the pan and allow to cool on a wire rack for at least 10 minutes before slicing.

Hawaiian Bread

Ingredients:
- 8 slices (1 pound)
- 1/2 cup pineapple juice
- 2/3 egg
- 1 1/3 tablespoons olive oil
- 1 1/3 tablespoons whole milk
- 3 3/4 tablespoons sugar
- 1/2 teaspoon salt
- 2 cups bread flour
- 1 teaspoon active dry yeast
- 12 slices (1 ½ pounds)
- 3/4 cup pineapple juice
- 1 egg
- 2 tablespoons olive oil
- 2 tablespoons whole milk
- 2 1/2 tablespoons sugar
- 3/4 teaspoon salt
- 3 cups bread flour
- 1 1/2 teaspoons active dry yeast
- 16 slices (2 pounds)
- 1 cup pineapple juice
- 1 1/3 eggs
- 2 2/3 tablespoons olive oil
- 2 2/3 tablespoons whole milk
- 7 1/2 tablespoons sugar
- 1 teaspoon salt

- 4 cups bread flour
- 2 teaspoons active dry yeast

Directions:

1. Choose the size of loaf you would like to make and measure your ingredients.
2. Add the ingredients to the bread pan in the order listed above (except yeast).
3. Make a well in the center of the dry ingredients and add the yeast.
4. Place the pan in the bread machine and close the lid.
5. Turn on the bread maker. Select the Basic setting, then the loaf size, and finally the crust color. Start the cycle.
6. When the cycle is finished and the bread is baked, carefully remove the pan from the machine. Use a potholder as the handle will be very hot. Let rest for a few minutes.
7. Remove the bread from the pan and allow to cool on a wire rack for at least 10 minutes before slicing.

Mexican Sweet Bread

Ingredients:

- 8 slices (1 pound)
- 2/3 cup whole milk
- 1/6 cup butter
- 2/3 egg
- 1/6 cup sugar
- 2/3 teaspoon salt
- 2 cups bread flour
- 1 teaspoon yeast
- 12 slices (1 ½ pounds)
- 1 cup whole milk
- 1/4 cup butter
- 1 egg
- 1/4 cup sugar
- 1 teaspoon salt
- 3 cups bread flour
- 1 1/2 teaspoons yeast
- 16 slices (2 pounds)
- 1 1/3 cups whole milk
- 1/3 cup butter
- 1 1/3 eggs
- 1/3 cup sugar

- 1 1/3 teaspoons salt
- 4 cups bread flour
- 2 teaspoons yeast

Directions:

1. Choose the size of loaf you would like to make and measure your ingredients.
2. Add the ingredients to the bread pan in the order listed above (except yeast).
3. Make a well in the center of the dry ingredients and add the yeast.
4. Place the pan in the bread machine and close the lid.
5. Turn on the bread maker. Select the Sweet Bread setting, then the loaf size, and finally the crust color. Start the cycle.
6. When the cycle is finished and the bread is baked, carefully remove the pan from the machine. Use a potholder as the handle will be very hot. Let rest for a few minutes.
7. Remove the bread from the pan and allow to cool on a wire rack for at least 10 minutes before slicing.

Amish Wheat Bread

Ingredients:

- 8 slices (1 pound)
- 1 1/8 cups warm water
- 1 package active dry yeast
- 2 3/4 cups wheat flour
- 1/2 teaspoon salt
- 1/3 cup sugar
- 1/4 cup canola oil
- 1 large egg
- 12 slices (1 ½ pounds)
- 1 3/4 cups warm water
- 1 1/2 packages active dry yeast
- 4 cups wheat flour
- 3/4 teaspoon salt
- 1/2 cup sugar
- 3/8 cup canola oil
- 1 1/2 large eggs
- 16 slices (2 pounds)
- 2 1/4 cups warm water
- 2 packages active dry yeast
- 5 1/2 cups wheat flour

- 1 teaspoon salt
- 2/3 cup sugar
- 1/2 cup canola oil
- 2 large eggs

Directions:

1. Choose the size of loaf you would like to make and measure your ingredients.

2. Add warm water, sugar and yeast to bread maker pan; let sit for 8 minutes or until it foams.

3. Add the remaining ingredients to the bread pan in the order listed above.

4. Place the pan in the bread machine and close the lid.

5. Turn on the bread maker. Select the Basic setting, then the loaf size, and finally the crust color. Start the cycle.

6. When the cycle is finished and the bread is baked, carefully remove the pan from the machine. Use a potholder as the handle will be very hot. Let rest for a few minutes.

7. Remove the bread from the pan and allow to cool on a wire rack for at least 10 minutes before slicing.

Challah

Ingredients:

- 8 slices (1 pound)
- 1/2 cup warm water
- 1 package active dry yeast
- 1 tablespoon sugar
- 3 tablespoons butter, softened
- 1/2 teaspoon kosher salt
- 2 to 2 1/2 cups kosher all-purpose flour
- 2 eggs
- 1 egg yolk
- 1 teaspoon water
- 12 slices (1 ½ pounds)
- 3/4 cup warm water
- 1 1/2 packages active dry yeast
- 1 1/2 tablespoons sugar
- 4 1/2 tablespoons butter, softened
- 3/4 teaspoon kosher salt
- 3 to 3 3/4 cups kosher all-purpose flour
- 3 eggs
- 1 1/2 egg yolks

- 1 1/2 teaspoons water
- 16 slices (2 pounds)
- 1 cup warm water
- 2 packages active dry yeast
- 2 tablespoons sugar
- 6 tablespoons butter, softened
- 1 teaspoon kosher salt
- 4 to 5 cups kosher all-purpose flour
- 4 eggs
- 2 egg yolks
- 2 teaspoons water

Directions:

1. Choose the size of loaf you would like to make and measure your ingredients.

2. Add the first six ingredients to the bread pan in the order listed above.

3. Place the pan in the bread machine and close the lid.

4. Turn on the bread maker. Select the Dough setting, then the loaf size, and finally the crust color. Start the cycle.

5. When the cycle is finished and the bread is baked, transfer dough to a large mixing bowl sprayed with non-stick cooking spray. Spray dough with non-stick cooking spray and cover. Let rise in a warm place until doubled in size; about 45 minutes.

6. Punch dough down. Remove dough to lightly floured surface; pat dough and shape into a 10-by-6-inch rectangle.

7. Divide into 3 equal strips with a pizza cutter. Braid strips and place into a 9-by-5-inch loaf pan sprayed with non-stick cooking spray. Cover and let rise in warm place for about 30 to 45 minutes.

8. Beat egg yolk with 1 teaspoon water and baste loaf.

9. Bake at 375°F for 25 to 30 minutes, or until golden.

10. Remove the bread from the pan and allow to cool on a wire rack for at least 10 minutes before slicing.

Bread Of The Dead (pan De Muertos)

Ingredients:

- 8 slices (1 pound)
- 1/3 cup water
- 4 1/2 tablespoons butter
- 4 1/2 eggs

- 3/8 cup sugar
- 3/4 teaspoon salt
- 1/3 teaspoon orange zest
- 1/8 teaspoon star anise
- 2 1/3 cups bread flour
- 1 1/2 teaspoons bread machine yeast
- 12 slices (1 ½ pounds)
- 1/2 cup water
- 6 3/4 tablespoons butter
- 6 3/4 eggs
- 1/2 cup sugar
- 1 1/8 teaspoons salt
- 1/2 teaspoon orange zest
- 1/5 teaspoon star anise
- 3 1/2 cups bread flour
- 2 1/4 teaspoons bread machine yeast
- 16 slices (2 pounds)
- 2/3 cup water
- 9 tablespoons butter
- 9 eggs
- 3/4 cup sugar
- 1 1/2 teaspoons salt
- 2/3 teaspoon orange zest
- 1/4 teaspoon star anise
- 4 2/3 cups bread flour
- 3 teaspoons bread machine yeast

Directions:

1. Choose the size of loaf you would like to make and measure your ingredients.
2. Whisk together the dry ingredients and set aside.
3. Add the liquid ingredients to the bread pan first, then gently pour the mixed dry ingredients on top of the liquid.
4. Place the pan in the bread machine and close the lid.
5. Turn on the bread maker. Select the Sweet setting, then the loaf size, and finally the crust color. Start the cycle.
6. When the cycle is finished and the bread is baked, carefully remove the pan from the machine. Use a potholder as the handle will be very hot. Let rest for a few minutes.
7. Remove the bread from the pan and allow to cool on a wire rack for at least 10 minutes before slicing.

Italian Bread

Ingredients:

- 8 slices (1 pound)
- 2 cups unbleached flour
- 1/2 tablespoon light brown sugar
- 2/3 cups warm water
- 3/4 teaspoons salt
- 3/4 teaspoons olive oil
- 1/2 package active dry yeast
- 1/2 egg
- 1/2 tablespoon water
- 1 tablespoon cornmeal
- 12 slices (1 ½ pounds)
- 3 cups unbleached flour
- 3/4 tablespoon light brown sugar
- 1 cup warm water
- 1 1/8 teaspoons salt
- 1 1/8 teaspoons olive oil
- 3/4 package active dry yeast
- 3/4 egg
- 3/4 tablespoon water
- 1 1/2 tablespoons cornmeal
- 16 slices (2 pounds)
- 4 cups unbleached flour
- 1 tablespoon light brown sugar
- 1 1/3 cups warm water
- 1 1/2 teaspoons salt
- 1 1/2 teaspoons olive oil
- 1 package active dry yeast
- 1 egg
- 1 tablespoon water
- 2 tablespoons cornmeal

Directions:

1. Choose the size of loaf you would like to make and measure your ingredients.
2. Add the ingredients to the bread pan in the order listed above.
3. Place the pan in the bread machine and close the lid.
4. Turn on the bread maker. Select the Dough setting, then the loaf size, and finally the crust color. Start the cycle.

5. When the cycle is finished and the bread is baked, punch down the dough and turn it out onto a lightly floured surface.

6. Form into two loaves and place them seam-side down on a cutting board.

7. Generously sprinkle with cornmeal and cover the loaves with a damp cloth.

8. Let rise until doubled in volume, about 40 minutes.

9. Beat egg and 1 tablespoon of water in a small mixing bowl.

10. Baste loaves with egg wash.

11. Cut down the center of loaves with a sharp knife.

12. Bake in 475°F preheated oven for 30 to 35 minutes, or until loaves sound hollow when tapped on the bottom.

13. Remove the bread from the pan and allow to cool on a wire rack for at least 10 minutes before slicing.

COUNTRY BREAD RECIPES

Pain De Paris

Ingredients:

- 8 slices (1 pound)
- For the pâte fermentée:
- 1/4 cup water
- 5/8 cup bread flour
- 1/8 teaspoon sea salt
- 1/4 teaspoon SAF or 1/2 teaspoon bread machine yeast
- For the dough:
- 2/3 cup water
- 1 1/2 cups bread flour
- 11/4 teaspoons gluten with vitamin C
- 5/8 teaspoon SAF yeast or 7/8 teaspoon bread machine yeast
- 3/8 cup pâte fermentée
- 3/4 teaspoon sea salt
- 12 slices (1 ½ pounds)
- For the pâte fermentée:
- 1/2 cup water
- 11/4 cups bread flour
- Pinch of sea salt
- 1/2 teaspoon SAF or 1 teaspoon bread machine yeast
- For the dough:
- 1 cup minus 1 tablespoon water
- 2 cups bread flour
- 11/2 teaspoons gluten with vitamin C
- 3/4 teaspoon SAF yeast or 11/4 teaspoons bread machine yeast
- 1/2 cup pâte fermentée
- 1 teaspoon sea salt
- 16 slices (2 pounds)
- For the pâte fermentée:
- 1/2 cup water
- 11/4 cups bread flour
- 1/4 teaspoon sea salt
- 1/2 teaspoon SAF or 1 teaspoon bread machine yeast
- For the dough:

- 11/3 cups water
- 3 cups bread flour
- 21/2 teaspoons gluten with vitamin C
- 11/4 teaspoons SAF yeast or 13/4 teaspoons bread machine yeast
- 3/4 cup pâte fermentée
- 11/2 teaspoons sea salt

Directions:

1. Choose the size of loaf you would like to make and measure your ingredients.

2. To make the pâte fermentée starter, place the starter ingredients in the bread pan. Program for the Dough cycle; press Start. Set a kitchen timer for 10 minutes. When the timer rings, press Pause and set the timer again for 10 minutes. Let the starter rest for 10 minutes (the autolyse). When the timer rings, press Start to continue and finish the Dough cycle. When the machine beeps at the end of the cycle, press Stop and unplug the machine. Gently deflate the spongy starter, and let it sit in the bread machine for 3 to 12 hours, deflating it about every 4 hours. (If you are making the starter ahead of time, remove it from the machine at this point and refrigerate it for up to 48 hours. Bring to room temperature before making the dough.)

3. Rinse out a plastic dry measure with cold water. With the measuring cup still wet, measure out the starter (the pâte fermentée) according to the chosen loaf size. If you have not already stored the pâte fermentée earlier, you can store the rest of the starter (enough for 2 to 3 batches of Pain de Paris) in the refrigerator for up to 48 hours.

4. Add the ingredients to the bread pan in the order listed above. (You don't have to wash out the bread pan from the starter.)

5. Place the pan in the bread machine and close the lid.

6. Turn on the bread maker. Select the French Bread setting, then the loaf size, and finally the crust color. Start the cycle.

7. After Knead 1, press Pause. Add the reserved pâte fermentée and the salt. Press Start to continue. The dough will be moist and smooth.

8. When the cycle is finished and the bread is baked, carefully remove the pan from the machine. Use a potholder as the handle will be very hot. Let rest for a few minutes.

9. Remove the bread from the pan and allow to cool on a wire rack for at least 10 minutes before slicing.

Pane Italiano

Ingredients:
- 8 slices (1 pound)
- 5/6 cup water
- 1 5/8 cups bread flour
- 7/16 cup semolina flour
- 3/4 tablespoon instant potato flakes
- 3/4 tablespoon sugar
- 1/2 tablespoon gluten
- 1 teaspoon salt
- 11/8 teaspoons SAF yeast or 1 3/8 teaspoons bread machine yeast
- 12 slices (1 ½ pounds)
- 11/3 cups water
- 21/2 cups bread flour
- 2/3 cup semolina flour
- 1 tablespoon instant potato flakes
- 1 tablespoon sugar
- 2 teaspoons gluten
- 11/2 teaspoons salt
- 2 teaspoons SAF yeast or 21/2 teaspoons bread machine yeast
- 16 slices (2 pounds)
- 12/3 cups water
- 31/4 cups bread flour
- 7/8 cup semolina flour
- 11/2 tablespoons instant potato flakes
- 11/2 tablespoons sugar
- 1 tablespoon gluten
- 2 teaspoons salt
- 21/4 teaspoons SAF yeast or 23/4 teaspoons bread machine yeast

Directions:
1. Choose the size of loaf you would like to make and measure your ingredients.

2. Add the ingredients to the bread pan in the order listed above.

3. Place the pan in the bread machine and close the lid.

4. Turn on the bread maker. Select the Basic/French Bread setting, then the loaf size, and finally the crust color. Start the cycle.

5. If using the Basic cycle, after Knead 2, press Stop, reset the machine, and start the cycle again, allowing the dough to be kneaded an extra time.

6. When the cycle is finished and the bread is baked, carefully remove the pan from the machine. Use a potholder as the handle will be very hot. Let rest for a few minutes.

7. Remove the bread from the pan and allow to cool on a wire rack for at least 10 minutes before slicing.

Pain De Maison Sur Poolish\

Ingredients:
- 8 slices (1 pound)
- For the poolish:
- 2/3cup water
- 5/6 cup organic bread flour
- 1/6 teaspoon SAF or bread machine yeast
- For the dough:
- 1/4 cup water
- 3/4 teaspoon SAF yeast or 1 teaspoon bread machine yeast
- 11/3 cups organic bread flour
- 3/4 tablespoon sugar
- 2/3 tablespoon gluten
- 1 teaspoon salt
- 12 slices (1 ½ pounds)
- For the poolish:
- 1 cup water
- 11/4 cups organic bread flour
- 1/4 teaspoon SAF or bread machine yeast
- For the dough:
- 1/3 cup water
- 11/2 teaspoons SAF yeast or 2 teaspoons bread machine yeast
- 2 cups organic bread flour
- 1 tablespoon sugar
- 1 tablespoon gluten

- 11/2 teaspoons salt
- 16 slices (2 pounds)
- For the poolish:
- 11/3 cups water
- 12/3 cups organic bread flour
- 1/3 teaspoon SAF or bread machine yeast
- For the dough:
- 1/2 cup water
- 11/2 teaspoons SAF yeast or 2 teaspoons bread machine yeast
- 22/3 cups organic bread flour
- 11/2 tablespoons sugar
- 1 tablespoon plus 1 teaspoon gluten
- 2 teaspoons salt

Directions:

1. Choose the size of loaf you would like to make and measure your ingredients.

2. To make the poolish starter, place the water, flour, and yeast in the bread pan. Program for the Dough cycle, and set a kitchen timer for 10 minutes. When the timer rings, press Stop and unplug the machine. Let the starter sit in the machine for about 6 hours.

3. Add all the ingredients to the bread pan in the order listed above (including the poolish).

4. Place the pan in the bread machine and close the lid.

5. Turn on the bread maker. Select the French Bread setting, then the loaf size, and finally the crust color. Start the cycle. (This recipe is not suitable for use with the Delay Timer.)

6. When the cycle is finished, check the bread. If the crust is still pale and loaf is not done, reset for Bake Only for 12 minutes longer.

7. When the bread is baked, carefully remove the pan from the machine. Use a potholder as the handle will be very hot. Let rest for a few minutes.

8. Remove the bread from the pan and allow to cool on a wire rack for at least 10 minutes before slicing.

Chuck Williams's Country French

Ingredients:
- 8 slices (1 pound)
- 5/6 cup water
- 11/2 cups bread flour

- 1/2 cup whole wheat flour
- 1/2 tablespoon gluten
- 1 teaspoon salt
- 11/8 teaspoons SAF yeast or13/8 teaspoons bread machine yeast
- 12 slices (1 ½ pounds)
- 11/4 cups water
- 21/4 cups bread flour
- 3/4 cup whole wheat flour
- 2 teaspoons gluten
- 11/2 teaspoons salt
- 13/4 teaspoons SAF yeast or 21/4 teaspoons bread machine yeast
- 16 slices (2 pounds)
- 12/3 cups water
- 3 cups bread flour
- 1 cup whole wheat flour
- 1 tablespoon gluten
- 2 teaspoons salt
- 21/4 teaspoons SAF yeast or 23/4 teaspoons bread machine yeast

Directions:

1. Choose the size of loaf you would like to make and measure your ingredients.

2. Add the ingredients to the bread pan in the order listed above.

3. Place the pan in the bread machine and close the lid.

4. Turn on the bread maker. Select the Basic/French Bread setting, then the loaf size, and finally the crust color. Start the cycle.

5. When the cycle is finished and the bread is baked, carefully remove the pan from the machine. Use a potholder as the handle will be very hot. Let rest for a few minutes.

6. Remove the bread from the pan and allow to cool on a wire rack for at least 10 minutes before slicing.

Pain Ordinaire Au Beurre

Ingredients:
- 8 slices (1 pound)
- 5/6 cup water
- 3/4 tablespoon unsalted butter, cut into pieces
- 2 cups unbleached all-purpose flour

- 1/2 tablespoon gluten
- 1 teaspoon fine sea salt
- 11/8 teaspoons SAF yeast or 1 3/8 teaspoons bread machine yeast
- 12 slices (1 ½ pounds)
- 11/4 cups water
- 1 tablespoon unsalted butter, cut into pieces
- 3 cups unbleached all-purpose flour
- 2 teaspoons gluten
- 11/2 teaspoons fine sea salt
- 2 teaspoons SAF yeast or 21/2 teaspoons bread machine yeast
- 16 slices (2 pounds)
- 12/3 cups water
- 11/2 tablespoons unsalted butter, cut into pieces
- 4 cups unbleached all-purpose flour
- 1 tablespoon gluten
- 2 teaspoons fine sea salt
- 21/4 teaspoons SAF yeast or 23/4 teaspoons bread machine yeast

Directions:

1. Choose the size of loaf you would like to make and measure your ingredients.

2. Add the ingredients to the bread pan in the order listed above.

3. Place the pan in the bread machine and close the lid.

4. Turn on the bread maker. Select the Basic/French Bread setting, then the loaf size, and finally the crust color. Start the cycle.

5. When the cycle is finished and the bread is baked, carefully remove the pan from the machine. Use a potholder as the handle will be very hot. Let rest for a few minutes.

6. Remove the bread from the pan and allow to cool on a wire rack for at least 10 minutes before slicing.

Semolina Country Bread

Ingredients:

- 8 slices (1 pound)
- 7/8 cup water
- 1 1/2 tablespoons olive oil
- 1 1/8 cups bread flour
- 7/8 cup semolina flour
- 1 tablespoon sesame seeds
- 1/2 tablespoon plus 1/2 teaspoon gluten
- 1 teaspoon salt
- 11/8 teaspoons SAF yeast or 13/8 teaspoons bread machine yeast
- 12 slices (1 ½ pounds)
- 11/3 cups water
- 2 tablespoons olive oil
- 13/4 cups bread flour
- 11/4 cups semolina flour
- 1 tablespoon plus 1 teaspoon sesame seeds
- 1 tablespoon gluten
- 11/2 teaspoons salt
- 2 teaspoons SAF yeast or 21/2 teaspoons bread machine yeast
- 16 slices (2 pounds)
- 13/4 cups water
- 3 tablespoons olive oil
- 21/4 cups bread flour
- 13/4 cups semolina flour
- 2 tablespoons sesame seeds
- 1 tablespoon plus 1 teaspoon gluten
- 2 teaspoons salt
- 21/4 teaspoons SAF yeast or 23/4 teaspoons bread machine yeast

Directions:

1. Choose the size of loaf you would like to make and measure your ingredients.

2. Add the ingredients to the bread pan in the order listed above.

3. Place the pan in the bread machine and close the lid.

4. Turn on the bread maker. Select the Basic/French Bread setting, then the loaf size, and finally the crust color. Start the cycle.

5. When the cycle is finished and the bread is baked, carefully remove the pan from the machine. Use a potholder as the handle will be very hot. Let rest for a few minutes.

6. Remove the bread from the pan and allow to cool on a wire rack for at least 10 minutes before slicing.

Pane Toscana

Ingredients:

- 8 slices (1 pound)
- 7/8 cup water
- 1 3/4 cups bread flour
- 1/4 cup whole wheat flour
- 1/2 tablespoon plus 1/2 teaspoon gluten
- 11/8 teaspoons SAF yeast or 1 3/8 teaspoons bread machine yeast
- Pinch of sugar
- Pinch of salt
- 12 slices (1 ½ pounds)
- 11/3 cups water
- 22/3 cups bread flour
- 1/3 cup whole wheat flour
- 1 tablespoon gluten
- 13/4 teaspoons SAF yeast or 21/4 teaspoons bread machine yeast
- Pinch of sugar
- Pinch of salt
- 16 slices (2 pounds)
- 13/4 cups water
- 31/2 cups bread flour
- 1/2 cup whole wheat flour
- 1 tablespoon plus 1 teaspoon gluten
- 21/4 teaspoons SAF yeast or 23/4 teaspoons bread machine yeast
- Pinch of sugar
- Pinch of salt

Directions:

1. Choose the size of loaf you would like to make and measure your ingredients.

2. To make the sponge, place the water, 1 cup of the bread flour, the whole wheat flour, the gluten, and the yeast in the pan according to the order in the manufacturer's instructions. Program for the Dough cycle, and set a kitchen timer for 10 minutes. When the timer rings, press Stop and unplug the machine. Let the sponge rest in the machine for 1 hour.

3. To make the dough, add the remaining 12/3 cups bread flour (for the 11/2-pound loaf) or 21/2 cups (for the 2-pound loaf), the sugar, and salt to the sponge in the bread pan.

4. Place the pan in the bread machine and close the lid.

5. Turn on the bread maker. Select the French Bread setting, then the loaf size, and finally the crust color. Start the cycle.

6. When the cycle is finished and the bread is baked, carefully remove the pan from the machine. Use a potholder as the handle will be very hot. Let rest for a few minutes.

7. Remove the bread from the pan and allow to cool on a wire rack for at least 10 minutes before slicing.

Olive Oil Bread

Ingredients:

- 8 slices (1 pound)
- For the biga starter:
- 1/2 cup water
- 1 cup bread flour
- 1/4 teaspoon SAF yeast or bread machine yeast
- For the dough:
- 1/4 cup water
- 1/8 cup olive oil
- 1 cup bread flour
- 1/2 tablespoon sugar
- 1 teaspoon gluten
- 1 teaspoon salt
- 3/4 teaspoon SAF yeast or 1 teaspoon bread machine yeast
- 12 slices (1 ½ pounds)
- For the biga starter:
- 3/4 cup water
- 11/2 cups bread flour
- 1/2 teaspoon SAF yeast or bread machine yeast
- For the dough:
- 1/4 cup water
- 3 tablespoons olive oil
- 11/2 cups bread flour
- 2 teaspoons sugar
- 1 teaspoon gluten
- 11/2 teaspoons salt
- 11/4 teaspoons SAF yeast or 13/4 teaspoons bread machine yeast
- 16 slices (2 pounds)
- For the biga starter:

- 1 cup water
- 2 cups bread flour
- 1/2 teaspoon SAF yeast or bread machine yeast
- For the dough:
- 1/2 cup water
- 1/4 cup olive oil
- 2 cups bread flour
- 1 tablespoon sugar
- 2 teaspoons gluten
- 2 teaspoons salt
- 11/2 teaspoons SAF yeast or 2 teaspoons bread machine yeast

Directions:

1. Choose the size of loaf you would like to make and measure your ingredients.

2. To make the biga starter, place starter ingredients in the bread pan. Program for the Dough cycle and set a timer for 10 minutes. When the timer rings, press Stop and unplug the machine. Let the starter sit in the machine for 12 to 18 hours.

3. To make the dough, with a rubber spatula, break up the starter into 6 or 8 pieces and leave in the machine.

4. Add all the dough ingredients to the bread pan in the order listed above.

5. Place the pan in the bread machine and close the lid.

6. Turn on the bread maker. Select the French Bread setting, then the loaf size, and finally the crust color. Start the cycle.

7. When the cycle is finished and the bread is baked, carefully remove the pan from the machine. Use a potholder as the handle will be very hot. Let rest for a few minutes.

8. Remove the bread from the pan and allow to cool on a wire rack for at least 10 minutes before slicing.

RECIPE INDEX

A

Almond Milk Bread 63
Amaretto Bread 110
Amish Wheat Bread 206
Anise Christmas Bread 112
Anise Honey Bread 46
Apple Pie Bread 47
Apple Raisin Nut Cake 102
Applesauce Bread 29
Awesome Golden Corn Bread 193
Awesome Rosemary Bread 45

B

Banana Split Loaf 36
Barley Bread 180
Basic Bulgur Bread 189
Basic Honey Bread 149
Basic Pecan Bread 65
Basic Seed Bread 188
Basic White Bread 165
Basil Cheese Bread 42
Basil Pizza Dough 116
Basil Tomato Bread 77
Beer Bread With Cheddar 19
Beer Pizza Dough 109
Beetroot Bread 86
Black Olive Bread 37
Bourbon Nut Bread 70
Bran Packed Healthy Bread 184
Brazilian Nuts & Nutmeg Loaf 60
Bread Of The Dead (pan De Muertos) 207
Brioche 157
British Hot Cross Buns 200
Brown Rice Flour Bread 170
Brown Sugar Date Nut Swirl Bread 66
Buckwheat-millet Bread 171
Buttermilk Bread With Lavender 51
Buttermilk Cheese Bread 21
Buttermilk Pecan Bread 91
Buttermilk Whole Wheat Bread 192

C

California Nut Bread 62
Cappuccino Orange Bread 39
Caramel Apple Pecan Loaf 71
Caraway Potato Bread 76
Cardamom Honey Bread 51
Cardamom Tea Bread 54
Carrot Bread 86
Carrot Bread With Crystallized Ginger 74
Carrot Cake Bread 100
Challah 207
Challah Bread 118
Champagne-soaked Baba 121
Cheddar Bacon Bread 14
Cheddar Olive Bread 16
Cheese Potato Bread 137
Cheesy Basil Bread 50
Cheesy Broccoli & Cauliflower Bread 84
Cheesy Sausage Loaf 166
Cherry–wheat Berry Bread 30
Chestnut Flour Bread 173
Chicken Stuffing Bread 80
Chickpea Flour Bread 169
Choco Banana Oatmeal Bread 105
Chocolate Challah 24
Chocolate Cherry Bread 23
Chocolate Chip Bread 103
Chocolate Marble Cake 99
Christmas Eggnog Bread 107
Chuck Williams's Country French 212
Cinnabun Coffee Cake 94
Cinnamon Apple Bread 33
Cinnamon Beer Bread 123
Cinnamon Figs Bread 27
Cinnamon Pecan Coffee Cake 93
Cinnamon Pull-apart Bread 53
Cinnamon Rum Bread 94
Cinnamon Swirl Bread 17
Cinnamon-flavored Raisin Bread 52
Classic Corn Bread 190
Classic Sourdough Bread 115
Classic Sourdough Rye 125

Classic White Bread 144
Classic White Sandwich Bread 165
Classic Whole Wheat Bread 184
Cocoa Banana Bread 90
Cocoa Date Bread 31
Coconut Milk White Bread 163
Coffee Caraway Seed Bread 122
Corn, Poppy Seeds & Sour Cream Bread 63
Cornbread 83
Cornell Bread 180
Cornmeal And Hominy Bread 172
Cornmeal Honey Bread 177
Cornmeal Stuffing Bread 85
Cracked Wheat Bread 159
Cranberry Honey Bread 39
Cranberry Orange Pecan Bread 37
Cranberry Walnut Wheat Bread 30
Crescia Al Formaggio 21
Crunchy Wheat Herbed Bread 45

D

Dakota Bread 190
Delicious Flax Honey Bread 72
Delicious Honey Lavender Bread 50
Dried Apricot Whole Wheat Bread 15
Dried Cranberry Tea Bread 40
Dry Fruit Cinnamon Bread 114
Dutch Sugar Loaf 19

E

Easter Bread 116
Easter Rye Bread With Fruit 119
Easy Gluten-free, Dairy-free Bread 146
Egg Bread 18
Energizing Anise Lemon Bread 42
Everything Bagel Loaf 156

F

Feta And Spinach Bread 16
Fig And Walnut Bread 62
Fiji Sweet Potato Bread 204
French Bread 158
French Sandwich Pain Au Lait 159
Fresh Herb Bread 53
Fresh Herb Stuffing Bread With Fennel Seed And Pepper 77

G

Garlic Basil Knots 167
Garlic Parsley Bread 142
Gluten-free Almond And Dried Fruit Holiday Bread 177
Gluten-free Brown Bread 148
Gluten-free Buttermilk White Bread 169
Gluten-free Chickpea-, Rice-, And Tapioca-flour Bread 182
Gluten-free Cinnamon Raisin Bread 135
Gluten-free Crusty Boule Bread 150
Gluten-free Mock Light Rye 174
Gluten-free Oat & Honey Bread 137
Gluten-free Pizza Crust 151
Gluten-free Potato Bread 152
Gluten-free Pull-apart Rolls 136
Gluten-free Pumpkin Pie Bread 146
Gluten-free Ricotta Potato Bread 171
Gluten-free Simple Sandwich Bread 147
Gluten-free Sourdough Bread 141
Gluten-free Whole Grain Bread 149
Graham Indian Bread 197
Grain-free Chia Bread 140
Grandma's Favorite Gingerbread 117
Granola Bread 13
Greek Currant Bread 25
Greek Easter Bread 201
Green Onion Bread 79

H

Hawaiian Bread 205
Hazelnut Honey Bread 101
Herb Bread 49
Herb Garlic Cream Cheese Bread 48
Herb Light Rye Bread 61
Holiday Chocolate Bread 112
Holiday Eggnog Bread 107
Holiday Raisin Bread With Candied Peels 120
Honey Banana Bread 35
Honey Bread 92
Honey Potato Flakes Bread 83
Honey Pound Cake 97
Honey Wheat Berry Bread 188
Hot Paprika Onion Bread 88

House Bread 161
Hungarian Spring Bread 113

I

Inspiring Cinnamon Bread 46
Instant Cocoa Bread 139
Irish Potato Brown Bread 198
Italian Bread 208
Italian Herb Bread 138
Italian Onion Bread 82
Italian Panettone 201

K

King Cake 95

L

Lemon Cake 104
Lemon Flavored Poppy Loaf 44
Light Whole Wheat Bread 185
Lovely Aromatic Lavender Bread 47
Low-gluten White Spelt Bread 179

M

Maple Buttermilk Bread 162
Mesmerizing Walnut Bread 58
Mexican Sweet Bread 206
Milk Bread 156
Milk Honey Sourdough Bread 111
Milk Sweet Bread 92
Mix Seed Bread 135
Mix Seed Raisin Bread 67
Monterey Jack Loaf 14
Multigrain Honey Bread 195
Multi-grain Honey Bread 97

N

Nine-grain Honey Bread 193

O

Oat Bran Nutmeg Bread 192
Oat Quinoa Bread 186
Old-fashioned Sesame-wheat Bread 185
Olive Oil Bread 214
Olive Oil–pine Nut Bread 59
Onion Buttermilk Bread 152
Onion Chive Bread 82
Onion Loaf 162

Orange Almond Bread 58
Orange Bread 33
Orange Gingerbread With Orange Whipped Cream 109
Orange Sourdough Bread With Cranberries, Pecans, And Golden Raisins 127
Orange Walnut Candied Loaf 59
Orange-buckwheat Bread 181
Orange-cumin Bread 70

P

Pain Aux Trois Parfums 20
Pain D'ail 76
Pain De Maison Sur Poolish\ 211
Pain De Paris 210
Pain Ordinaire Au Beurre 212
Pane Italiano 211
Pane Toscana 214
Parmesan Nut Bread 13
Parsley Garlic Bread 43
Peasant Bread 154
Pecan Apple Spice Bread 144
Pecan Cranberry Bread 140
Pecan Raisin Bread 69
Pineapple Carrot Bread 28
Pistachio Cherry Bread 67
Pistachio Horseradish Apple Bread 65
Pizza Dough 157
Polenta-chestnut Bread 176
Polenta-sunflower-millet Bread 175
Polish Poppy Seed Bread 62
Portuguese Corn Bread 205
Portuguese Holiday Bread 124
Portuguese Sweet Bread 117
Potato Bread 168
Potato Bread With Caraway Seeds 64
Potato Honey Bread 81
Prosciutto Parmesan Breadsticks 155
Prosciutto Stuffing Bread 85
Prune Bread 32
Pumpkin Coconut Almond Bread 75
Pumpkin Spice Cake 100

Q

Quinoa Bread 173

R

Rainbow Swirl Cake 98
Raisin Bread 32
Raisin Candied Fruit Bread 38
Ricotta & Chive Loaf 48
Ricotta And Fresh Chive Bread 18
Romano Oregano Bread 52
Russian Black Bread 203
Russian Rye Bread 202
Rye Bread 158

S
Sampler Country White Loaf 163
Sampler Honey Whole Wheat Loaf 166
Sampler Oatmeal Loaf 161
Sauerkraut Rye Bread 81
Scandinavian Light Rye 198
Semolina Country Bread 213
Sennebec Hill Bread 187
Seven Grain Bread 196
Simple Dark Rye Loaf 196
Slider Buns 154
Sorghum Bread Recipe 145
Sour Cream Bread 160
Sour Cream Semolina Bread With Herb Swirl 56
Sourdough Banana Nut Bread 128
Sourdough Bread With Fresh Pears And Walnuts 127
Sourdough Buckwheat Bread 133
Sourdough Carrot Poppy Seed Bread 125
Sourdough Cornmeal Bread 131
Sourdough Cottage Cheese Bread With Fresh Herbs 130
Sourdough Pesto Bread 129
Sourdough Raisin Bread 126
Sourdough Sunflower Seed Honey Bread 132
Sourdough Tomato Bread With Feta 131
Sourdough Whole Wheat Bread 133
Spice Peach Bread 34
Spice Pumpkin Bread 55
Spicy Hot Red Pepper Bread 74

Spicy Pear Bread 22
St. Patrick's Rum Bread 122
Strawberry Oat Bread 36
Succulent Cranberry Cinnamon Bread 35
Sunflower Oatmeal Bread 72
Super Spice Bread 27
Sweet Almond Anise Bread 91
Sweet Flaxseed Bread 90
Sweet Pineapple Bread 105
Sweet Potato Bread 79
Sweet Sour Maple Bread 106
Sweet Vanilla Bread 98

T
Tecate Ranch Whole Wheat Bread 194
Teff Honey Bread 175
Three-seed Whole Wheat Bread 186
Toasted Coconut Bread 28
Toasted Walnut Bread 68
Tomato Bread 38

W
Walnut Banana Bread 143
Welsh Bara Brith 108
White And Dark Chocolate Tea Cake 103
White Chocolate Cranberry Party Loaf 123
White Sourdough Bread 130
White Whole Wheat Bread 191
Whole Wheat Basil Bread 43
Whole-grain Daily Bread 195
Wild Rice Bread 178
Wild Rice Cranberry Delight 41
Wine And Cheese Bread 164

Z
Za'atar Bread 204
Zucchini Bread 78
Zucchini Lemon Bread 88
Zucchini Spice Bread 87
Zuni Indian Bread 73